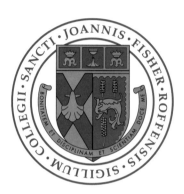

WE CHANGED
THE WORLD

Memoirs of a CNN Global Satellite Pioneer

WE CHANGED
THE WORLD

Memoirs of a CNN Global Satellite Pioneer

SIDNEY PIKE

First Edition 2005

Published in the United States by
Paragon House
1925 Oakcrest Avenue, Suite 7
St. Paul, MN 55113

Special thanks to CNN and its graphics department for providing archived photos.
Thanks also to Max Holland, author of "Deconstructing Monopoly" in *The CEO Goes to
Washington,* for permission to use his research on PanAmSat.

Library of Congress Cataloging-in-Publication Data

Pike, Sid, 1927-
We changed the world : memoirs of a CNN global satellite pioneer / Sidney Pike.--
1st ed.
    p. cm.
Includes bibliographical references and index.
ISBN 1-55778-855-3 (hardcover : alk. paper) 1. Pike, Sid, 1927- 2.
Television producers and directors--United States--Biography. 3. Cable News Network. I.
    Title.
PN1992.4.P48A3 2005
791.4502'32'092--dc22

                2005014673

The paper used in this publication meets the minimum requirements of American National
Standard for Information Sciences—Permanence of Paper for Printed Library Materials, AN-
SIZ39.48-1984.

Manufactured in the United States of America

10 9 8 7 6 5 4 3 2 1

For current information about all releases from Paragon House,
visit the web site at http://www.paragonhouse.com

To my wife, Lillian, and Susan, Steven, and Andrea and their families for their sacrifices in my visits to the global family of nations on an ongoing basis instead of to their own, so that I could contribute to advancing communication and understanding between people worldwide.

One of the primary reasons that some 11,000 satellite TV channels are broadcasting to billions around the world is Sid Pike's dogged determination to make CNN a global news channel, now in more countries than any business on earth.

—Dr. Joseph Pelton, Director of Telecommunications, George Washington University

I had been invited as a guest to represent CNN, which is watched even in these little villages. At the conclusion of the ceremony of dances and other incantations, from a distance a towering Zulu dance participant in full costume and regalia with shield and headdress, and who appeared to me to be about 13 feet tall, began walking in my direction. He was clearly walking towards me with something very intent on his mind to do. I stuck out my hand, somewhat as if I were at the Junior Chamber of Commerce in Topeka, and introduced myself. In an impeccable British accent, the tribesman dancer asked me to give his "very best to Sidney Pike," leaving me stunned. I assured him I would indeed do that. He tipped his shield and walked away.

—Ed Turner, CNN Executive Vice President, News Gathering, describing a conversation occuring in 1993 in the Upper Transvaal at the Saba Game Ranch in South Africa, near the border with Zimbabwe, at a celebration by the Zulu tribe living in the area

From a letter dated October 3, 1989 from Rene Anselmo, Chairman and founder of PanAmSat.

That you, Sid, have managed to interconnect the whole world for CNN is no small feat. Knowing what you have had to go through, it is more like a miracle. Someday, what we are pioneering will be commonplace, and it's going to be one hell of a lot better world for it.

Contents

Foreword

The development of Cable News Network (CNN) as a 24-hour cable news channel in 1980 revolutionized television news that began in 1948 with a 15-minute format. But the start of a CNN satellite signal that covered North and Central America was aimed primarily at domestic U.S. viewers. The signal was watched in Canada on cable and Central America by Spanish speaking viewers who spoke English. The rest of the world was unable to see CNN until 1984 when Sid Pike was given the assignment of developing CNN for television worldwide.

Sid's plan was not only to offer CNN by satellite to cable viewers outside the United States, but to television stations in countries that did not yet have cable, which was most of the world. One other satellite at that time carried CNN's 24-hour signal. That was the Sevens Network of Australia that monitored it and chose selected stories for its news. In exchange they gave CNN some of their coverage of Australia. Sid decided to use their signal for other Pacific Rim countries as the satellite signal covered most of the Western Pacific region.

Sid's business career began in 1950 in local television. After joining Turner, Sid used his knowledge of television station news to offer CNN as an augment to local news, to cover global breaking news instantly, or to carry the 24-hour signal in the late-night hours to fill the broadcast schedule.

The demand for CNN on both broadcast television and cable took off. Preparations for adding other global satellites began. That was not only how satellite 24-hour news coverage originated, but also how its success led to other sports and entertainment channels to follow its pioneering path of non-stop television programming. Sid Pike not only tells a lot about himself—his strengths and weaknesses—but also about facing formidable tasks and using one's creative imagination to circumvent obstacles to reach a goal. Students and adults alike can learn something about taking on projects and facing challenges not yet in sight but that lie somewhere in the future plans of global entrepreneurs.

Sid Pike's efforts to develop CNN internationally makes him a genuine pioneer. His leadership enabled CNN and many other Turner (now Time-Warner) channels and services to become the remarkable success of today.

Along with Ted Turner, Sid overcame countless skeptics who said, "it just cannot be done." Well, he and Ted and that maverick band of original staffers Ted assembled "did it."

They transformed the information world. They opened countries to independent news that never had known freedom of information.

As one of those who followed in the ground-breaking path that Sid established, I am deeply grateful to him for his leadership, vision, determination, and courage. Working for Ted was not always easy, because he demanded so much of all those who worked with him. But Ted achieved so much of his greatness because of women and men like Sid Pike—those who made Ted's dreams come true.

Tom Johnson
Chief Executive Officer

CNN News Group (1990-2001)
Publisher, *Los Angeles Times* (1977-1990)

Introduction

Almost immediately after Saddam Hussein's regime was toppled in Iraq in 2003, satellite television dishes sprang up all over the city of Baghdad and were being sold in stores, outdoor markets, and on street corners.

One young Iraqi man said, "Iraqis want to see how the outside world lives, how it thinks." An Iraqi woman remarked, "Satellite TV is a great way to shape Iraqi minds. We don't know the truth about our own land. Iraqis can now learn about their past. I want every Iraqi to have satellite."

I am immensely heartened by these words, and take pride in knowing that I played an important role in bringing the satellite age to television, and that I helped open the door that allowed the repressed, isolated, and disadvantaged countries of the world to access the information and educational tools that had been denied them for centuries.

When I started traveling the world in order to bring CNN to every corner of the globe, it was solely with the intention of building the Turner empire. Yet when I discovered the power of satellites, a new purpose evolved: enlightening the world's populations and letting the fresh winds of freedom blow through the newly opened window that satellite television now provided.

Ultimately, CNN International changed global communications and political reality, particularly when used by leaders of countries within the CNN satellite footprint to monitor each other's governments. CNN International became, and remains today, the preeminent global news service. Because of satellite television, visual communication took a quantum leap in its ability to inform, entertain, and, above all, enlighten not millions, but billions, of people.

The road to this accomplishment was not an easy one—it was paved with obstacles, setbacks, every conceivable cultural, political and language barrier, belligerent personalities, and governments fearful of losing control. There were intransigent, dictatorial leaders of countries to deal with and an uncooperative powerful international consortium that would not allow the unlimited free downlinking of satellite signals in two-thirds of the world. There were dangers and difficulties of endless travel, constantly changing diets, and long lonely stretches away from family and friends.

But there were triumphs, too—when I played David to more than one Goliath, when walls of ignorance and prejudice crumbled in the face of indelible truth. All of this led to a ringside seat for the world: witnessing the collapse of communism in Russia and the fall of the Berlin Wall, watching a young man standing in front of a tank in Tian an Men Square, viewing CNN reporters under a bed in a Baghdad hotel reporting the first night attack by U.S. forces. These images would never have occured, never seemed so immediate and vivid, nor helped to change the course of history were it not for CNN and satellite television.

Indeed, CNN came to function as a major communications system *among* countries and citizens. Governments can monitor the world without cost to their taxpayers. Citizens can monitor governments—and *their* government—and compare conditions across the world. International advertising on CNN enhances global business activity and the worldwide distribution of goods and services. For good or for bad, CNN also promotes Western values and civilization and reinforces written and spoken English as the international language. Amid these changes I retain my hope that CNN—as a provider of unbiased *global* news, not national news—will promote democracy as the preferred form of government in regions of the world that have not yet enjoyed much choice in the matter.

When I consider these achievements, I am proud and satisfied.

One issue remains important—an issue journalists, broadcasters, citizens, and government leaders never confronted before the advent of satellite television: Can a free nation support a television news service dedicated to unbiased reporting of global scope, rather than neutral (or worse) national coverage? I think the answer must be a resounding "yes!"

Part of this issue involves the challenge CNN posed to national broadcast systems and to an international consortium of such broadcasters, the

International Telecommunications Satellite Consortium (Intelsat).

One of my proudest professional triumphs was to help break the back of this monolithic monopoly of communications satellites ("intelsats").

It's monopolistic practices hindered innovation and creativity and charged exorbitant downlinking rates—that is, the cost for receiving communication signals transmitted from orbiting satellites. Intelsat's practices, I believed, created major obstacles and deep flaws in the global telecommunications system. I waged a long-term war against the Intelsat behemoth. By helping to pioneer alternatives to Intelsat, I helped make satellites and satellite communications financially feasible.

I was determined to change the way things worked.

No one trod this path before. I had almost no help in my endeavors. Yet I knew that if I could "bring down" Intelsat, we could begin to take out of their darkness a global population festering in illiteracy, intolerance, and misplaced loyalty to dictators and fundamentalist religions. Skirmish by skirmish, battle by battle, satellite television won this war. This book offers the details. In part I write this book as a wartime memoir.

I also want to give an insider's view of a remarkable company and its visionary leader, Ted Turner, whom I worked alongside for 25 years. I also want to examine and depict the rise and fall of the television empire that Turner built. More specifically, I want to chronicle how Turner Broadcasting System (TBS) grew from a 39-person decrepit television station to a multi-channel global television entity, and to show how and why leading corporate executives, some 20 years later, lost their faith and trust in Ted. In many ways, this loss of faith destroyed the extraordinary vision that was Ted Turner's and Ted's alone.

This book is also about believing in something and making it happen, whether it is what Ted originally conceived or what I eventually carried out around the world. Throughout the world, news on television—that marvelous invention of my generation—was not much more than radio with a picture of the news reader. In economically developed countries, television brought more extensive visual information and entertainment, but the developing countries could only afford cheap and poorly produced programs. That is, until CNN, with its endless continuum of news, became available. I'm proud of that. I'm proud to champion "underdogs." My sales trick was deceptively simple: Out came The Map. I didn't talk about CNN without

The Map. When I placed it on an office table, all those in the room looked down on the world, and although they didn't realize it, it made them feel godlike. The Map also got their attention. I made my usual pitch, pointing out the benefits of CNN's three major services: hard news, breaking news, and feature program material. I pointed out the countries that had already made agreements with CNN. As they studied the Map, I studied their faces, anticipated their questions and concerns, and tailored myself and comments to my audience. A good salesman doesn't sell; rather he helps customers solve problems and meet needs.

This book is also about loyalty and honesty and a work ethic that men and women of my generation knew and understood and practiced. Such principles have become trivialized and degraded. They infrequently exist in today's corporate world. Perhaps for that reason alone, I'm grateful that I was part of the Turner enterprise from its inception. Through the years, Ted and I maintained a loyalty and trust of each other, and had a shared determination to work hard and to succeed, sometimes against insurmountable odds.

Despite the often ruthless corporate gamesmanship and the daunting problems in launching CNN globally via satellite, I wouldn't trade my place in the CNN grand design, or the opportunity to work with the most dynamic media entrepreneur in the history of commercial television, for anything in the world.

Prologue

January 2004

I had been living in Moscow since October 1992. I was leasing an apartment from Henry Yushkiavitshus, a government official in then-Soviet television who was a friend of Ted Turner, the American television mogul. I had been working for Ted since 1971 to build TBS. Now Ted wanted me to develop joint television broadcast ventures globally with the same success I had achieved in taking CNN to practically all the countries of the world.

Before I left for Russia, my youngest daughter, Andrea, and her husband asked me jokingly if I were a CIA agent, because by then I had been traveling all over the world for 10 years. I laughed and told them, "I'm bringing CNN around the world." They didn't believe me. Oh, they knew I had been working for Ted Turner for over two decades, but they thought I was doing more. I denied it. They smiled. "Will you promise to leave us an envelope with the true story?" they asked, laughing. During this dreary Moscow winter I especially missed my daughter and her daughter, Julia, with her bright, enthusiastic personality. I longed to hear Julia say, "I miss you, Papa."

Often, I thought of the satellite in more "spiritual" terms: God's way of holding up a reflective mirror to show His favored species how to survive. We are faring badly—screwing up the environment and over-populating ourselves so that we compete for dwindling resources. A man in Sri Lanka has tried to show us the way. The British scientist and author, Arthur C. Clarke, has written about satellites and the "global village" it creates—a subject I talked to him about in Sri Lanka several years earlier.

I have a deep, abiding faith in satellites and the enriching power of communication to foster understanding and build communites. To this faith I wed a sense of my own unique talents. I have *empathy* for the people I deal with. This is my real talent. I can imagine and identify with the feelings of others in situations different from my own. I also have imagination, stamina, and the perseverance to overcome one obstacle after another, and this is clear to others in everything I say and do. I was in the field, on planes, in airports, and away from my family for long periods to build a global community of understanding, *a global family.* I believe this is why I was able to communicate with people in developing countries and in the economic behemoths like Japan. This empathy and energy made me successful and make me grateful.

Efforts to develop CNN succeeded almost everywhere I traveled between 1984 and 1992. Since 1984, I had been flying from continent to continent, making arrangements to bring down the CNN 24-hour signal from a mechanical marvel called a satellite that rotated in exact synchronization with the earth, as if frozen in place 22,300 miles above our planetary home.

However, I was having no success in this joint venture with Moscow's Channel 6, known at TV-6. Its board of directors, headed by Edward Sagalayev, and our team of negotiators, could not agree. TV-6 wanted millions of dollars and our film library, but we wanted veto control because of its lack of experience in running a commercial television station. This bothered them. The talks went poorly. We lived in different worlds and had established no trust. Such trust made possible the other CNN agreements I had negotiated around the globe over the last 10 years.

I never felt as old as I did during these negotiations. I was 66 years old and in the most exciting period of my television career. I hadn't thought about retiring, although most of my contemporaries had long since left for some island paradise or for their reward in heaven, or wherever their beliefs directed them.

I often ponder what it is about us that is immortal. The only part of our existence that remains on earth (as far as we know) is what we have thought, which, even when not in physical form, can outlast us for thousands of years. Think of Darwin, Einstein, Christ, Moses and, yes, Arthur C. Clarke and his satellite dream.

I thought about this again as my driver, Sergei, waited for me in the car one bleak Sunday morning in January. The car wasn't an expensive Western European one like those belonging to many executives of wealthy corporations doing business in Russia. It was a standard Russian car, and each year's model was the same as the year before.

I asked Sergei to drive to the CNN News Bureau across the Moscow River. The bureau had a special satellite phone. During the week, if the negotiations permitted, Sergei would take me, and those who helped me, to the bureau to phone other Turner offices and our families.

Sergei also liked to go to the CNN Bureau, because quite often the cook there would give him hot soup or other tasty dishes. He could also poke around inside the oversized refrigerator. Sometimes, I would also have the hot soup so that I wouldn't have to cook that night. The kitchen was where one of the satellite phones was located. Unless it was late in the evening or on a weekend, when most of the desks were unoccupied, we made our calls from the kitchen phone.

The CNN Bureau was located on the upper floors of an apartment building. Two apartments had been rented, and the walls between them torn down so that offices, editing rooms, and videotape storage areas to construct.

Steve Hurst was the Bureau Chief during my stay in Moscow. I liked him and his wife, Claire Shipman, who was a CNN reporter. They both covered stories occurring in Moscow and throughout Russia. Steve was very sympathetic regarding the problems we were having completing an agreement with TV-6, and he let us use the satellite phone as often as we needed to call Atlanta, Los Angeles, New York, or London. We made sure we didn't come to this small, confining Bureau apartment just before the daily newscast to Atlanta.

CNN reporters used the satellite phones during the 1991 Gulf War in Iraq, giving CNN a decided advantage over other television network coverage. The expensive service cost $120,000 a year. One's voice is uplinked, in a way similar to a video feed, to the satellite and then downlinked to whatever part of the world the caller has dialed. The phone located in the Moscow Bureau was tied into the Atlanta phone system, and when I dialed my home, I only needed to press the same numbers I would have dialed if I had been sitting in my office in Atlanta. Our technology was advancing so fast that I was occasionally frightened to think about the possibilities.

At 11:00 A.M. that Sunday, it was too early in the United States (only 3:00 A.M.) to make phone calls home. Sometimes, in the early evening, Sergei would bring me to the bureau, and I'd speak to my wife, Lillian, who understands my intense personality, my commitment to a work ethic, and my need to strive constantly to achieve a goal. I gave up long ago trying to understand what makes me the way I am, but I do think many aspects of my personality were forged during the Great Depression when I was very young.

I'd also phone my three children—Andrea lived in Atlanta, Susan and Steven in Boston—and speak to the five grandchildren. Then I'd thumb through my black phone book, calling anyone I could think of. Some numbers had been in the book so long I barely remembered the people I was talking to, but I needed to hear familiar voices and fill my ears with the sounds of English.

Then we drove back to my dreary apartment on the third floor of a state-owned apartment building. These blocks of high-rise, concrete dwellings gave Moscow a regimented look that reminded me of the newsreels that showed row after row of Communist soldiers strutting shoulder to shoulder in Red Square on holidays. Although the building I lived in had housed Communist Party officials and their families, including Nikita Khrushchev, the volatile leader of the former Soviet Union, it had the same smell of musty concrete and dust as the other buildings. The front of the building might as well have been the back since there was nothing in the way of ornamentation, no attractive entrance or lobby. These buildings were like human anthills—gray, utilitarian, exactly alike. During the day, clusters of two-legged ants emerged, dressed in gray or black. They joined the crowds commuting in sooty, colorless Moscow, a dark and somber city that hid its beauty beneath the surface—in the subways, where ornate chandeliers and statues greeted passengers at every station, and in the ballet and symphony concert halls. In the huge public parks, even during the spring and summer, there were no bright colors because gray smog blocked the sun.

As I turned the key in the lock and entered my apartment, moving quickly to turn off the alarm, I remembered the few times I had done it incorrectly and the police had called. In fewer than 15 minutes two policemen arrived at my door and inspected my passport. One of the cops was always friendly, and the other very officious. Do policemen form "good cop-bad cop" pairs all over the world? I never saw the same two policemen twice.

I was burglarized once. Upon returning from a few weeks home in Atlanta, I noticed things were askew and the curtains were missing from my bedroom window. The window was wide open, and when I looked out, I saw that the curtains had been tied together so someone could climb down to the pavement below. From the third-floor apartment, the burglar had to jump the last 15 feet. Another window was open on a balcony that faced the front of the building, and I assumed that was how the thief came. The silverware and the ornate dishes in the dining room cabinet hadn't been touched. Everything was in place except the bookshelf in the room that had a television set and a couch. Some books were lying open on the large, square, heavy wooden coffee table. The books removed from the shelf were in English. And mostly poetry.

Evidently my "cat burglar" was a young man interested in reading poetry in English. He had to have been young to climb down his curtain rope and jump that distance to the ground. I was relieved that nothing seemed to have been stolen, and I was even pleased that my poetry-loving burglar had not been caught. I wished I could have met him. I would have happily lent him books, and we could have talked about them. He had obviously triggered the alarm when he opened the window, and the arrival of the police had forced him to run to the bedroom and use the curtains for his escape.

This Sunday in January, I made myself some lunch and prepared for an afternoon and evening of reading. That was my only activity when I was not working. I read and read some more, because I couldn't get CNN on the television set in my apartment. I also thought a lot. I thought about the strange path my life had taken, which led to working, at age 44, for Ted Turner—the man who liked to play near the edge of a precipice.

I began drafting this book in 1996 and was planning for my retirement from Turner Broadcasting System later that year. At that time, TBS and TimeWarner were seeking approval from the Federal Trade Commission for TimeWarner's desire to acquire TBS, and by so doing to create the largest media conglomerate in the world. There were many people in the United States government and in the communications industry who did not want to see that happen. But in October 1996, TimeWarner swallowed TBS, the energetic company whose rise to fame had been so mercurial.

But could it digest TBS's founder and leader, the bombastic and irreverent Robert Edward Turner III?

In 1984, when I sailed into uncharted waters to begin my 10-year odyssey to plant CNN globally, I had the complete support of Ted Turner. No one else could interfere with that direct line of command. Unfortunately, that direct line between Ted and me, one that helped build TBS and CNN International, had stretched and stretched until neither of us could reach the other. But before that happened, our relationship and trust, along with many risk-taking events, changed the course of the company and my life. And, yes, we changed the world.

CHAPTER ONE

The Road to Atlanta

Undertake something that is difficult; it will do you good.
Unless you try to do something beyond what you have
already mastered, you will never grow.

—Ronald Osborn

On January 7, 1968, I said goodbye to my wife, Lillian, and our three children in Boston and headed south for Atlanta in a light blue Chevrolet convertible. I was 40 years old and convinced that my career in television broadcasting had peaked, and I was traveling the downhill side. As I drove the 1200 miles from Boston, I pondered my future with a new employer— Pacific and Southern Broadcasting. I was hired as Station Manager of their newly acquired WQXI-TV, Channel 11, located in a city that hadn't attracted national attention since General Sherman burned it to the ground during the Civil War.

As I drove into the outskirts of Atlanta, I received a cold, harsh welcome. A heavy ice storm was shutting down the city. My driving experience in Boston made me confident as I slipped around the Atlanta drivers who panicked as soon as the ice hit the streets.

It was after eight o'clock as I drove up hill to the television station, but

1

I didn't realize how close the building was to the end of the road. I hit the brakes and skidded past the front steps and parking lot driveway. Fortunately, the car stopped at the top of the embankment. In that moment I asked myself: *What the hell am I doing in Atlanta?*

Since 1950, I had worked as a television producer/director—first at Boston's WBZ-TV owned by Westinghouse, a very conservative company. Like most television stations in those years, it relied on its powerful signal, as well as on the major networks, to deliver its audience. Occasionally, to satisfy license requirements or advertisers interested in the local market, it made an effort to produce local programs. My job was to produce the Red Sox and Braves baseball games, which I discovered was very routine, unimaginative work. What I really enjoyed was the development of original ideas and new programs. Sometimes my desire to be innovative had been a problem for my employers. But the new television audiences and the station's advertising clients demanded new ideas, so I was tolerated, although treated as "off-the-wall" by the conservative management. (The major exception to this conservatism in my 48-year career was Ted Turner.) For example, because of the heavy community activity in Boston, WBZ decided to make each producer responsible for a different public service project every month. Mine was "Law and Order," and like my colleagues, I was required to suggest programming and public service announcements on that subject during a specific month. At a meeting in the conference room with station management, I presented my plans for special programs and station breaks, and just as I finished, the door burst open and five burly, state police officers announced, "This station's management is under arrest!" Each manager was handcuffed and marched through the building in front of the astonished employees to the waiting patrol cars. The bewildered executives stared at each other as if to say, "Is this a joke or is it for real?"

At the police station, each "prisoner" was booked, fingerprinted, photographed, and placed in a cell. I wanted them to taste, if only for a moment, their loss of freedom, so that they might imagine what it would be like to live in a totalitarian country. From the personal reports I got later, I succeeded, although some of the "arrested" managers did not appreciate my idea.

* * * * *

My "positive-aggressive" creative behavior actually began on August 6, 1927, after my mother tried everything possible, short of abortion, to prevent my birth. That alone is surely evidence of my fierce determination. My mother often told me about this, although always saying how wrong she had been and how proud she was of me. My two brothers, both now deceased, one eight years younger than I, the other 12 years younger, and our father, who owned a kosher butcher shop (we were Orthodox Jews—I became a Reformed Jew later in life) rounded out our family.

My first job, at age 10, was selling newspapers at a traffic light in what was then a Jewish ghetto in Dorchester, Massachusetts. I promoted myself two years later to soda jerk in a local drugstore. This job was most notable because it's where I met Lillian, who was 11 at the time. I thought she was cute, and so I gave her extra chocolate sprinkles on her ice cream cones. Amazingly, considering my competitiveness and the long hours I have always worked, the 10 years of international travel, and the months away at a time, this caring mother and supportive wife has stood by me. We are still married after 56 years (2005).

At age 12, I learned an important lesson about perseverance and commitment to one's goals. This was a lesson that could have benefited many talented people with whom I worked, and who failed to understand the ramifications of their decision to quit because of real or perceived mistreatment by their employer. I had joined a uniformed bicycle club and found myself quite often in a leadership role. When we were selected to participate in a city parade, the adult supervisor did not choose me to lead our event. So I quit. I didn't want to quit. I thought at the time that it was the right thing to do. I had been slighted.

But I wanted to be in the parade, and so I returned with my tail between my legs, but I never forgot my humiliation. From that time on, I never let my emotions dictate an action that would be harmful to the career path I had chosen. Over the years, even when I had many "reasons" to quit a job, I learned to set aside my hurt feelings and think only of my goals.

By 1944, the year I graduated from high school, most of the available manpower in our country was in the armed services or in some service-related industry. When I turned 17, I was eligible to join the Navy. But

I didn't like the idea of being on a sinking ship. I couldn't swim. To join the Army, before being drafted, one had to be 18. The one exception was enlisting in a reserve army-training program. I enlisted and the Army sent me to Rutgers University to study physics—my worst subject.

Finally, I turned 18 and was sent to Camp Croft, South Carolina, for 17 weeks of basic training. It was my first experience with discipline, but surprisingly, I didn't have any problem adapting to army life. The war in Europe ended during my basic training, and when its 17 weeks were over, I went to visit downtown Spartanburg one Sunday afternoon. It was raining very hard as I walked down Main Street alone, on my way to the USO. Because of the driving rain, there was no one else in sight. I looked across the street and saw a policeman holding a man by the back of his coat and moving him along. Then I saw another man come up behind the policeman and start hitting him on the head with a blackjack.

I ran across the street to help the policeman. Just as I got my foot on the curb, the policeman wheeled around, drew his gun, and began firing in all directions. I dove for the sidewalk. As it turned out, I was the only witness to the attack on the police officer. This incident occurred at a time when the local newspaper was involved in a campaign that accused the police department of brutality.

The Mayor, the Police Chief, and the City Council members could not do enough for me. They arranged for me to stay at the local hotel. Meanwhile, my unit was being shipped out to the Pacific. The war with Japan was still going on. The city officials took me out for dinner and arranged with the Army for me to stay in South Carolina until the trial came up.

The trial kept getting postponed, however, and they finally had to settle for my deposition. But now the Army didn't know what to do with me. My outfit was overseas so they sent me to a post in New Jersey as one of 40 guards assigned to take 1200 German prisoners of war to France on a liberty ship, so that they could assist in post-war reconstruction. The ship, with its human cargo, docked at Le Havre, France, and we escorted our prisoners into waiting trucks. I found myself in the same truck with the lieutenant in charge.

As we drove, our German driver stopped and started yammering away in German. I roughly understood and what the driver was saying and told the lieutenant. He told me what to tell the driver, which I did in Yiddish—a combination of many languages, but mostly German. The driver seemed to understand, and the lieutenant was satisfied, so much so that when I arrived in Namur, Belgium, a replacement depot for the Army, I had been reclassified from a heavy weapons crewman (machine gunner) to a German interpreter!

This worried me. I had images of General Mark Clark of the 42nd Division using my Yiddish for some important meeting. I asked to be transferred and was reclassified to Special Services, which was responsible for the entertainment of troops. This brilliant reasoning came about because of my background as an usher at a movie theater when I was 16.

I was soon on a train to Vienna, Austria, to join Special Services for the 42nd Division and was assigned, with one other soldier, to Salzburg. We had two duties: audition local talent for the GI nightclubs and assist USO units visiting the area to entertain the Army units.

This Army of Occupation was tough duty. I lived in the Pitter Hotel, the foremost hotel in Salzburg, and had a car *and* a driver. I had an Austrian assistant who, with his wife, helped obtain talent for the nightclubs. We were good friends, and I tried to help them both in any way I could.

One day an investigator began asking questions about the couple. I resented the questions because of how much help my Austrian friends had been and how everyone seemed to like them. Then I learned what they were accused of doing. They, along with others, had apparently stolen the contents of the homes and apartments of Jews who had been herded off to concentration camps. I was appalled. How could two very nice people have done such a thing? Their weak excuses—"You don't know how it was" and "Everyone was doing these things"—were wasted on me. I could not get rid of them fast enough.

I had already learned in a letter from my mother about some distant relatives of my father's family who were at the Displaced Persons Camp near Salzburg. I visited them and brought them a radio and some other gifts. Since they came from the same area as my father (Vilnius, Lithuania) I asked them if they knew anything about his family. They told me that two of my aunts—my father's sisters—had been machine-gunned to death by the Nazis in the woods outside their village.

I never forgot hearing this tragic news. It lives with me to this day. My awareness of this kind of ethnic hatred and horror—from the Holocaust to today's suicide bombers—was one of the reasons I worked tirelessly to improve communication and understanding between countries. If I have learned anything from my career in communications, it is that most strife, hatred and, yes, wars, are a result of inadequate education and lack of good communication, especially between governments. That is why I believed that CNN's satellite broadcasting—covering the earth and reaching its global population—would, by providing reliable and accurate news, educate and inform both the leaders and the general public of all the world's countries.

In spite of my good life in Salzburg—dressing in a tuxedo two or three times a week to see an opera there or in Vienna—I was eager to get home and on with my life.

One incident that occurred before I left remains vivid in my memory and is testament to my "get the job done" personality—a key part of my *modus operandi*.

A USO troupe was scheduled to drive by bus to Vienna for a show, but the bus had a flat tire as it prepared to leave. Changing the tire took time, and I was concerned that the USO group might be late for its performance that evening. By then it was early afternoon, and we had about 250 miles to drive. Half of that was through the American Zone of Austria, and half, which started at the Danube River, was through the Russian Zone. While Vienna itself was divided into quarters and occupied by British, French, Russian and U.S. soldiers, all of Vienna was surrounded by Russian-occupied territory. I decided to go with the troupe and urged the driver to drive as fast as possible on the two-lane highway. This did not please the USO people, and I noticed one woman fingering her rosary beads as we spun around the highway curves.

Finally, we reached the Danube River. Even though there was a line of cars, the guards on the American side were understanding and moved us through quickly. As we neared the bridge, we found ourselves at the back of a long line of cars, trucks, and buses that extended for more than half a mile. I knew we would never make the 7:30 P.M. performance, because the Russian checkpoint guards were well known for their deliberate, time-consuming pace. The Cold War antagonism was only a chill then, but it had already reached the lowest Russian and Allied soldiers. The euphoria following the surrender by the Germans was rapidly replaced by Stalin's paranoia and suspicion, and this was reflected in relations between the Russians and their allies.

I sank back in my bus seat as the vehicle ground to a halt. It could take hours to get through this border crossing. I stood and reached for a carbine rifle above the windows. I put my arm through the shoulder sling so that the rifle was behind my back. "Has anyone got a cigarette?" I asked the now bewildered USO troupe, and several performers held open packs of cigarettes toward me. Although I didn't smoke, I put an unlit cigarette in my mouth, descended the steps of the bus, and walked down the line of cars, trucks, and buses to a single soldier standing at a metal bar crossing the road. Like many Soviet soldiers, he carried an automatic weapon slung around his shoulder. I carried the carbine to establish my status as a soldier equal to him. I walked up and spoke the only Russian I knew, which my college roommate had used constantly: "*Daite mnye spitchka.*" It means "Give me a match." He smiled at my lousy Russian and reached into his pocket and lit my cigarette. "*Sprechen sie Deutsch?*" ("Do you speak German?") I asked. He answered yes, and I knew we could communicate. I offered him my official pass; he took it, studied it, and began copying on his own pad some figures from my pass. In any case, we were allowed to pull out of the line and drive through the checkpoint. The troupe just made it to the theater in time for their show. I'm proud of my creativity and daring that day. I try to find some way to get a job done.

I returned to the United States in 1947 and was discharged. I was a freshman at Clark University in Worcester, Massachusetts, before I enlisted, and now I decided to finish college, then choose a career. At that time, Clark was a very small but prestigious school.

I stayed at Clark, but was put off by most of its liberal arts courses, although I did enjoy the extracurricular activities involving plays and acting. I auditioned and won every part I tried out for and soon realized that I did not care to be a student anymore. For one thing, I did not want to have to learn the two languages required to graduate. I was certain I would never work outside the United States.

A student at Clark, whose father was a talent agent in New York, suggested I contact her dad—perhaps he'd help me get a job. He did. He hired me. In 1948, I started work as a talent agent for the Jules Ziegler Agency on Fifth Avenue. Bill Nichols was the only other employee, and he found stage work for such actors as Sidney Poitier, Lee Marvin, and Eva Marie Saint in Broadway plays. I remember talking to Lee Marvin one day when he was really discouraged about not being able to find work for a long period of time. He talked about giving up acting and "going home." But that magnificent voice told me it would only be a matter of time before he'd get his first big break. My job consisted of going to vaudeville shows to find talent for clubs, hotels, and theaters. Neither Bill nor I handled television—it had barely begun and the demand for talent was minimal.

In August 1949 I went home to Boston to marry Lillian. As much as we both wanted to marry, this was not the smartest move to make at that time, because I still was not receiving a salary at the Ziegler Agency. No pay, just experience. Today, this is known as "interning."

Lillian and I returned to New York and took an apartment on the New Jersey side of the Hudson River where the rent was cheaper. We bussed into New York every day—she to her secretarial job in the garment center and me to my non-paying agent work.

One day at the Ziegler Agency, I got a phone call from the National Broadcasting Corporation (NBC) casting department with a request for an actor for a particular role. I knew just the person for the part and phoned to give him the time and place for the audition. To my surprise, he told me he couldn't make it. I asked why—I couldn't comprehend why an actor would pass up any opportunity to audition. "I'm going to television production school," he said.

"What's that?" I asked, a bit put out that he couldn't arrange his schedule to make the NBC audition.

"It's a school with real television equipment that trains you to be a television director or technician," he replied.

The light bulb went on. I got the name and address of the school, which offered two three-month courses, one in directing and one in studio-technician training for cameramen and audio and lighting technicians.

To make maximum use of the equipment, the small studio was used from 8:00 A.M. to 1:00 P.M. for technician training and from 1:00 to 6:00 P.M. for directing. I was in a hurry. I asked for permission to attend both courses at one time, so I could finish in three months. Lill was pregnant; I had to find a job that made real money. Fortunately, I still had my G.I. Bill benefits for the tuition, and the school gave me permission to eat a bag lunch in class, so I could attend all day.

I was hooked. I thoroughly enjoyed the creativity involved in the preparation and coordination of television programming. I had found my career. I completed the three-month training in early 1950, and decided to look for a television job in Boston first, since that was home. Then I would head west to apply at the television stations that existed at that time. The Federal Communications Commission (FCC) had frozen the first 100 television broadcast licenses and decided not to award any more until the commission could determine the criteria for allocating these valuable "gifts" to the many businesses that were applying. I felt that, if I had to, I would apply at all 100 stations.

But for now, Lill and I were heading home—to have our first baby and to enjoy my first paying job in television.

CHAPTER TWO

The Demise of a Television Station

Even God cannot change the past.

—Agathon

If I were to list five people I have most enjoyed working with over the years, Iran Berlow, the Program Director of WBZ-TV in Boston, would be one of them. He was a thin man with a moustache and a twinkle in his eye. Quiet and unassuming, Iran understood creative personalities and had the temperament for his position, which was developing live programs in an industry that had not yet figured out how to acquire the programs they needed.

It was the era of black-and-white television, and videotape wasn't born yet. Syndication was still unknown; thus the only programming available to a program director, other than the ones he developed himself, came from the network. The motion picture industry was sticking its head in the sand, hoping that the television stations would dry up and blow away for lack of the films that movie studios controlled. Metro-Goldwyn-Mayer (MGM), Warner Brothers, Paramount—they all believed that the lighted box, potentially in every family's living room, would destroy the movie business. What they didn't realize was that they were helping to create a *new* industry that would be, in many ways, more powerful than their own. It also meant that the motion picture industry had a substantial new source of income. First, network television, then local television stations, and finally cable stations and home video companies, made the film studios rich, and in some cases, supported them when a film did not fulfill its promise at local movie theaters.

Iran Berlow had a tough job as Program Director in 1950—he had to create all the programs for the non-network time periods.

He read my resumé in fewer than 30 seconds. Due to my lack of experience, it consisted of one page, which said little. He took a pencil and circled one item. I leaned forward in my to see what he had circled where I had "striven" to show leadership ability. I had been co-captain of the Clark University baseball team in Worcester during my two years there. Now I was really curious—why would that tweak Berlow's interest? I had just thrown it in, desperately trying to fill up the page. As luck would have it, the baseball television director had just resigned. Iran needed to find a replacement in an industry where very few individuals were able to direct baseball games on television, and most of those had very limited experience in sports. Berlow decided to take a chance on me. I was to direct and produce the baseball games on a trial basis. He wanted to be sure I was not exaggerating my ability or training.

It was a historic day for me when my television career began on April 10, 1950, and proves that luck helps, but only if you are ready for it. And was I ready! Like a duck finding its first pond. My job was not only to direct the live action coverage of the game, which involved coordinating cameras placed in different positions around the baseball field, but also to direct the commercial breaks.

In those early days, the remote trucks did not have air conditioning, and on a hot day on the way to the ballpark, the television crew would stop at an icehouse and fill the interior of the truck with large blocks of ice. A folding chair was placed on top of the ice for the director, and I would sit behind the technicians and "call the shots" of the game. Passersby would wonder what the liquid was that was pouring out from the truck and onto the pavement. By the time a double-header was over, most of the ice would be gone, and the chair would be sitting on the floor.

When color television replaced black-and-white, each camera required three color tubes instead of the one in a black-and-white camera. I felt sorry for the technicians who had to set up all the equipment and lay the heavy cable at all the camera locations, particularly during the "dog days" of summer when it was over 100 degrees. Color also required a lot of lighting, and with the low ceilings of an office space converted into a studio, created intense heat. No amount of air-conditioning helped. At Fenway Park, these refrigerator-size color cameras had to be carried by hand up fire-escape-type steps to the upper decks and, along with the cables, returned to the remote truck after each game.

Television technicians at that time, and this included audio, video, tape, and lighting engineers, as well as cameramen, were a special breed. They were required to have a first-class Federal Communications Commission (FCC) operator's license. They were primarily technicians, and didn't have to pass tests for operating their equipment creatively. Some did not understand simple concepts, such as "framing" in photography, and all too often, these people ended up as cameramen for particularly innovative and sensitive television programs.

By 1948, when commercial television first began to reach significant audiences, both the networks and the local stations were more concerned with the equipment operating successfully through a program than with how creative it was. And for the equipment to work, the engineers and technicians were of paramount importance. I can remember the chief engineer at WBZ-TV in the early 1950s falling back on the same phrase over and over again: "It might put us off the air." Thus, another creative idea was lost.

Further down the technical hierarchy was the union. No entity in broadcast television was ever created that was a greater impediment to creativity than the television technicians' union.

Among the television producers and directors at WBZ-TV, there were a few who considered their employment as "just a job." If something prevented them from achieving the maximum creative potential from any program, they did the best they could. But for those of us who were motivated to be creative, and particularly for those of us who felt that even 110 percent was not enough to give the company, the union would be a source of frustration. They were not created to help the company, but were designed to satisfy the worker and to create a power base, which, as often as not, rested with one particular individual. A recalcitrant member of a technical crew could make your life miserable if you crossed him.

I recall an incident during a Red Sox game. One technician was the switcher of the cameras. The switchers at remotes, as well as in the studio, were not supposed to switch to a camera without specific instructions from the director—in this case, me. Because of the speed of action once a ball is hit and base runners and fielders are scurrying to all parts of the field, the technical switcher was asked to switch the cameras on his own to catch the action. On this particular day, the switcher must have gotten out of bed on the wrong side. He was not going to switch to any cameras unless specifically requested to do so. The result was that many important shots were missed, and most of the action was seen a second too late. Both viewers and sponsors were cheated out of a well-televised game. There was no reason even to have a technician to switch cameras, since it required no technical expertise (just button pressing) and could more easily have been done by the director. But the union had jurisdiction it was not about to give up, even if it resulted in poor coverage of a game. (The *button* was attached to technical equipment.) The director was not allowed to touch the cameras. That is why, when I began to work at Turner Broadcasting System (TBS), we were able to develop programs and commercials that had minimal interference with our creative ideas. There were no unions.

When the baseball season was over, Iran Berlow called me into his office and asked me to stay on. My trial period has obviously gone well. Iran asked me if I could create during the "off season" a 15-minute children's program for Bosco, the chocolate syrup.

I had only my childhood motion picture memories of slapstick comedians such as the Marx Brothers and the Three Stooges. I went in search of some characters. I found the Azalea Trio in a local cocktail lounge. Al was the lead singer and straight man; Snuffy was the comedian; a third man who played the bass. Their act was built around visual jokes. I wrote a 15-minute slapstick comedy routine for them to do each week. I gave them the outline of the plot, and they had to fill in their own words. For example: Snuffy has a bad toothache. The boys are going to help him pull the tooth "painlessly." They attach a string to his tooth and the other end to a doorknob so that whoever comes through the door will pull his tooth without Snuffy realizing it. Then the door opens the wrong way.

This show was surprisingly successful, ran for several years, and ceased to be only a winter assignment. I was asked to produce and direct the program 52 weeks a year, as well as direct the baseball games (today, my job at WBZ-TV would require a staff of three to five people). I produced and directed other programs as well, everything from talent shows with cash prizes, and an annual prime time fashion show, to other children's programs. One included a cowboy, Rex Trailer, who woke me up every Saturday morning when he was getting his horse ready at 4:00 A.M., to make sure my alarm went off and I would be at the studio in time for our three-hour morning program.

One unforgettable person, whose televised appearances at our station I directed was John F. Kennedy. He was running for U.S. senator from Massachusetts. I explained to him what was involved in a television appearance as he was being "made up." In the background, his younger brother, Ted, was talking to someone on the phone and losing his temper. I thought at the time how different their personalities were: John, calm and sure of himself; Ted less stable emotionally, less secure of his place in the Kennedy family picture.

* * * * *

I soon earned a reputation for getting the job done, and for not tolerating less than the best effort from everyone. This is still true. Although I have mellowed in style, I have the same determination as I did at 19, when I found a way to get the bus through the Russian Zone in Austria.

Since I cared about results and suffered no fools, I was constantly relegated to professional "Siberia" for "exceeding my authority," and sometimes chastised for insulting union employees or the executives. But I was not fired. I watched other producer/directors, who were less talented but willing to play the game that I was too stubborn to play, advance up the managerial ladder. Iran was very kind and patient with me. He understood my results-orientation and my inexhaustible energy. Yet, by 1957 I knew that I had to leave WBZ-TV, take with me what I had learned, and start fresh.

Fortunately, Boston's WHDH-TV, channel 5, owned by the *Herald Traveler* newspaper, had received its FCC broadcast license and was planning to go on the air. This time, instead of a one-page resumé, I prepared a visual booklet of my work at WBZ-TV. I had an artist draw cartoons to go with the photos, which evidently impressed Les Arries, Jr., Director of Television for the new station. Again, my baseball experience may have been a deciding factor, since the Red Sox were to move their telecasts from Channel 4 to Channel 5, and I, once hired, continued to produce and direct their games. Curt Gowdy and Bob Murphy were the announcers at the time. Gowdy became a major network sportscaster, and Murphy moved to New York to work with the Mets. The Braves left Boston for Milwaukee after the 1952 season. I had grown up with both the Red Sox and the Braves. As a member of the "knothole gang" (we paid 50 cents for a season pass that entitled us to sit in the unsold bleacher seats), I had the thrill of watching Babe Ruth hit one of his last home runs at Braves Field. The Braves had lured Ruth to Boston to increase ticket sales because of the popularity of the Red Sox, in spite of their recent unsuccessful seasons. Forty years later, in 1974, I was at Fulton County Stadium in Atlanta when Hank Aaron hit home run number 715 and broke Babe Ruth's total home run record. Baseball has been kind to me.

I literally signed WHDH on the air on November 26, 1957. When I started there, videotaping had still not come into industry-wide use, and I found myself, once again, doing a considerable amount of live programming.

In looking back, I realize how privileged I was to work with Les Arries, Jr., a man who shared my mindset. Les became my favorite boss and mentor. I studied his methods of handling people and later imitated him in my own management responsibilities. For the 1950s, Les was ahead of his time. He was never authoritarian nor disposed to meting out punishment, something I had gotten used to at WBZ-TV. He understood each person's weakness and took time to discuss each issue so that I, too, learned how to handle my fellow workers and accept their shortcomings. Then I shared what I learned from Les with others.

Years later, one of the most significant projects I tried to do at the station became a lesson for me in dealing with major clients. It was in 1966 when a young man from Montreal, Canada, who represented the Montreal World's Fair (Expo '67), came to Boston and met with me. He had been given the assignment of offering television broadcasters, including the networks, the opportunity to televise the major cultural events at Expo '67, and he didn't know how to proceed.

This was long before agents, television networks, and major sponsors scoured the world for new television program opportunities. Today, we take for granted that we can watch the Olympics or any other international sports or art event on television. However, at that time, the city of Montreal did not even know how to organize the television elements of its upcoming global event. Instead of seeking U.S. network involvement, it offered a legitimate television broadcaster access to the world's most famous entertainment organizations, which had all been invited to Expo '67. These included Kabuki dancers (Japan), La Scala Opera (Italy), Yehudi Menuhin and the Bath Festival Orchestra (England), Bolshoi Ballet (Russia), Vienna State Opera, Czech Philharmonic, and more. They would all be in Montreal with cameras, crews, and remote facilities— all available free. A television producer's *dream.*

All we needed to supply was the videotape. In 1967, videotape was used primarily for broadcast purposes. I estimated I would need $40,000 worth of videotape to record everything I wanted so that I could, in future years, edit this material into a program series or specials, not only for WHDH-TV, but also for syndication throughout the United States and Canada. The international possibilities did not occur to me in those days, but these programs, in fact, could have been shown in any country, and they would never have been dated. At that point, I only had experience finding local sponsors and did not know how to find a national sponsor.

I flew to New York and met with our advertising agency that represented television stations to national advertisers. The agency set up meetings with various clients. International Business Machines (IBM), in Armonk, New York, expressed genuine interest. I asked for $40,000 to purchase the videotape since WHDH-TV was not willing to advance this sum, and a producer's fee to WHDH-TV. For this, IBM would own U.S. and Canadian advertising rights for a specified period of time.

IBM needed their president's approval, and he was out of the country. The interest of the people I spoke to was so genuine that I expected approval. Trusting this sincerity, I did not press the ad agency for meetings with other clients. I just waited to hear from IBM.

The week before Expo '67 opened in Montreal, I received IBM's letter rejecting the project. Lesson learned: Never count on promises no matter how sincerely they are made. The opportunity for recording those outstanding artists was lost. When those groups left Montreal, they soon learned of the enormous monetary value of their individual events and their copyright privileges. Today, taping their performances involves huge sums of money. A television producer must pay union wages, copyright fees, as well as full production and travel costs. Both WHDH-TV and IBM exhibited glaring management shortsightedness, even incompetence. For a "chump change" sum of $40,000, they could have had the television rights, in perpetuity, of what was then the world's premier orchestras, ballet and opera companies, artists, cultural music, and dance organizations. There would have been no end date to their sales value—would you listen to Caruso now if he were available on video? This was the level of management thinking that I dealt with *before* I met Ted Turner.

Another unfortunate lesson learned: One of my responsibilities as Production Manager was to coordinate the shooting of a television commercial with an advertising executive from New York who rented our facilities. Work had started early this particular day, and we broke about noon for lunch. The advertising executive had gone to a restaurant outside the studio, and by 2:00 P.M., I was fidgety since I asked everyone to be back by 1:00 P.M. I complained to Les when he dropped by to see how the production was going. I wanted to know how this man could take so long for lunch when the studio and crew were leased by the hour. Les patiently explained to me that even though it was not fair to the client, it was this man's decision. The executive finally showed up at 2:45, and we finished the commercials. I learned for the first time that some people do not do their best for, or even care about, their clients. As simple and naïve as that sounds, it was startling to me then.

I often had to produce and direct local shows on the same day that I directed the baseball games. If a Red Sox game was played on Saturday afternoon at Fenway Park, as soon as the final out was made and after the game sign-off, I would climb over the steel parking lot fence and drive quickly to the studio to start rehearsal on a local dance program. This show included personalities like Bobby Darin, Fabian, and other recording stars who wanted additional promotion by appearing with Bob Clayton, a favorite local disc jockey trying to make the transition from radio to television.

In 1961, when I had been at WHDH-TV for four years, I came up with my first international television concept. At that time, international programming was inhibited by language and cultural differences, which created a barrier that no one in television was willing to breach, particularly since there were no financial benefits.

Most ideas and inventions are motivated by need. And I had the need to do something that somehow, in some way, might prevent horrific world events like the Holocaust from occurring. The slaughter in Lithuania of members of my father's family continued to haunt me. My father had emigrated to the United States in 1926, when he was 26. One sister and her husband had tried to emigrate to America at the same time, but because of immigration quotas, she had been unable to join my father. She and her husband went instead to Brazil.

My father, long before he died of cancer in 1983, often expressed concern about his sister Flora in Brazil, whom he never saw again after leaving Poland. His concern was transmitted to me, and I felt a responsibility to visit São Paulo, where she lived, now a widow with four daughters.

The eldest daughter, Anita, had married a television producer/director like myself named Alvaro de Moya, and here was the possibility for an exchange of programs. Later, I produced a documentary series on the "American Way of Life," using my own family. We lived a typical middle-class suburban lifestyle in Framingham, Massachusetts in an L-shaped, concrete slab house that cost $16,000. I sent Alvaro the "American Way of Life" series, which was translated into Portuguese. I introduced the program, making it a personal letter to Alvaro, and speaking Portuguese phonetically.

Alvaro's programs were musicals, using locations such as the Copacabana and Ipanema beaches. I then decided to visit Brazil. It was my first trip abroad, not counting my military service.

Alvaro was Production Manager at Channel 9 in São Paulo. When the military later took over the government, the owners lost the license to the television station and the company disappeared. But in 1961, since we both had quick, creative minds, we worked well together. This was my first attempt to carry out a television concept with a creative television person from another country, and I was stimulated by it. Soon after our visit, Juscelino Kubitschek became president of Brazil. When he came to the United States, Alvaro arranged for him to visit WHDH-TV, and he appeared on one of our local shows.

The only other city I visited on my first trip to Brazil was Rio de Janeiro, and I was astounded by the differences between it and São Paulo.

Sid Pike at WHDH-TV in Boston in 1962 with Juscelino Kubitschek, the most famous and popular president of Brazil. In background is the color camera described above on pages 11–12.

Rio was colorful, laid back, with a definite emphasis on *joie de vivre*. São Paulo, with one of the largest populations in the world, was conservative, colorless, and focused on industry and business. It had the quality of a black-and-white movie. However, Rio was sunny and colorful in a way that affected mood and behavior—an infectious blend of excitement and gaiety. As I walked around the city, I felt I was in one of MGM's "glorious technicolor" movies set in Rio. And in 1961, I could walk anywhere in the city. Crime was not the problem that it is today. But that's true everywhere.

Alvaro and I continued to exchange programs, and we decided to take our television exchange on a tour of Brazil in 1963. So, I became determined to learn Portuguese. Learning a language requires the discipline of learning the grammar, and this was not my strong suit. Nor did I have patience with long language courses. I had read in a magazine about "the quick and easy way" to learn languages. All one had to do was buy long-playing language records and play them while asleep, and the subconscious would remember the lessons. Great. Just what I wanted. No muss, no fuss, and I could learn while I slept. So I bought the recordings and began taking afternoon naps on the weekends, with the result that Andrea, my daughter, who was four years old then and just wandering around the house, began speaking Portuguese. I, however, didn't learn anything!

Alvaro de Moya and Sid Pike. In 1961 we started an exchange of television programming between Brazil and the United States.

When I arrived in Brazil, Alvaro and I worked out a routine for our television appearances in which he spoke about the project in Portuguese while I, like the village idiot, pointed out our itinerary on a large map of Brazil. The cities we visited, courtesy of Varig Airlines, in order to introduce the series on the local television stations, took us from one end of Brazil to the other, including Brasilia, the new capital located in the Amazon jungle.

On a Sunday afternoon, as we prepared to land in Fortaleza, a city in northeastern Brazil, I looked out of the plane window and saw crowds of people on the roof of the airport terminal. "Look at the crowd that's come to welcome us," I said. Alvaro deflated my enthusiasm when he told me that people often come to the airport on Sundays to watch planes. It was one of the few sources of weekend "entertainment" in Fortaleza. This city boy had a lot to learn about the limited opportunities in much of the world. I wouldn't forget.

Brasilia was an even greater surprise. I expected to see a city literally carved out of the Amazon jungle. Instead, it was on a barren plateau, and I couldn't find a single tree. I remember being told that the capital only operated Monday through Thursday, after which most of the government officials abandoned this inhospitable environment and flew to Rio for a long weekend. Not many liked Kubitschek's idea of moving the capital from Rio to Brasilia, which he did to encourage the people in the over populated cities that hugged the ocean to move inland and develop the interior.

Although the exchange with Alvaro served my purpose of working toward better cross-cultural communication, it also added to WHDH-TV's public service programming. Later, the U.S. Information Agency (USIA) accepted the series for translation and use in other parts of the world, particularly in Japan. The original WHDH-TV management supported this sort of programming to prove the station's value as a licensee. The new management failed to understand this value.

New management arrived at WHDH-TV after a long power struggle and eventual palace coup among the station's owners and executives. It is a tale of arrogance, ignorance, incompetence, and greed. At root, it is also a tale of monumental stupidity because the post-coup management violated the fundamental writ in the broadcasting industry: *Never fail to comply with your license-renewal promises to the Federal Communications Commission.*

Until the Telecommunications Act of 1996, the U.S. government granted—for free—a television broadcasting license for a renewable three-year period to a citizen or group of citizens committed to operating a station to serve the "public interest, convenience, and necessity" of its market. The costs of operation—legal fees for the license, one-time-only capital investments for technical equipment and studios, film leasing, and station operations—were and are minimal compared to the huge potential profits available to licensees. These lucrative conditions prevailed especially in the 1950s and 1960s, when annual profits of 40 to 50 percent were not unusual, one of the highest profit margin in American industry.

The trick is to receive the license.

On April 24, WHDH-TV received a license to operate a television channel in Boston. It signed on eight months later but there was an opportunity for an appeal by the losing applicants. Those denied a license applied tremendous pressure on the FCC to reverse its decision. To offset this pressure, we in the Programming Department faced an enormous responsibility to provide, as promised, public service programs to convince the FCC to continue to license our station. We broadcasted religious programs, the *New England Farm and Food Show,* and so on. To recapture our audience after the religious show each morning, we scheduled an exercise show hosted by Debbie Drake, a svelte blonde in leotards. (Don't laugh. In those days this was a big deal).

Our most impressive effort to demonstrate our fervor for public service was the show *Dateline Boston,* a catch-all program designed to offer exposure to local public service organizations. We aired this show from 6–6:30 P.M., the prime time for news. Of course, it was a weak lead-in for the 6:30 P.M. local news. Our local news ratings were deservedly abysmal, but there was nothing more to be done. We aired the program because we *had* to appear virtuous, committed, and reliable to the FCC. We were paying for past mistakes. The competition for lucrative broadcast licenses was fierce. WHDH-TV was on probation.

The *Herald Traveler* newspaper owned WHDH-TV. The newspaper's publisher, Robert C. Choate, made the extraordinarily naïve mistakes of twice taking to lunch the FCC chairman, George McConnaughey, while the FCC was reviewing WHDH-TV's license application. McConnaughey acknowledged as much in 1958. Choate's gigantic mistake led to *Dateline Boston*'s place in the broadcast schedule, which led to poor ratings for local news broadcasts. Such ratings were a bitter pill to swallow for the owners of a prominent newspaper.

What followed was primarily a result of internal conflicts at the *Herald Traveler.* George Akerson and Harold Clancy toppled Choate, their mentor, from power. Although the FCC temporarily renewed WHDH-TV's license, in large part because of the presence and professionalism of Les Arries, Jr. at WHDH-TV, the new management team wanted to improve the low ratings for the 6:30 P.M. news and return a lustre to the *Herald Traveler's* reputation. Personal and professional conflicts caused Les to resign. Akerson and Clancy, professional newspaper men, appointed a newspaper colleague as Les's replacement, the News Director at WHDH-TV. With no professional broadcaster of Arries's reputation and experience on the premises, the new News Director unquestioningly took marching orders from Akerson and Clancy. So, while all disgruntled, rejected applicants for the broadcast license watched intently for any opportunity to convince the FCC to rescind WHDH-TV's license, the new management cancelled *Dateline Boston* and the other public service programs specifically produced and broadcast to keep the civic promises the station made during its regular license applications. The new station executives, trained amid the competitive independence of newspapers, felt no accountability to government agencies, if such accountability even crossed their minds.

In September 1967 the FCC rescinded WHDH-TV's broadcast license due to broken promises. Never before had the FCC canceled a station's license. A furor erupted in the broadcast industry. Other broadcasters simply could not believe that an enterprise as profitable as WHDH-TV could fail to appreciate the importance and requirements of FCC obligations.

The chain of events from Choate's lunches with McConnaughey to the rescinded license to further disaster was so profound that Sterling Quinlan wrote a book about the debacle—*The Hundred Million Dollar Lunch*. Quinlan places the burden of the sorry episode in the lap of the FCC, emphasizing changing commissioners and personalities. He interviewed FCC officials and some officials at the *Herald Traveler,* especially the publisher, Herald Clancy, and the CEO, George Akerson.

In my opinion, Clancy was one of the major causes of the disaster. Quinlan doesn't draw this conclusion because he never turns his attentions to the television stations and newspapers where questionable decisions reigned and problems mounted. If Quinlan had looked at the station and newspaper, he would have discovered *why* the problems occurred. In particular, Quinlan fails to note the importance of the mistakes made by the *Herald Traveler*'s new executives concerning programming promises made to the FCC during the licensing process. At the same time, I don't think FCC officials ever fully understood that WHDH-TV *completely lacked* any professional broadcasters in its management after Les Arries left in 1964.

In 1967 the economy took a dive and the station encountered financial troubles as the power struggle at WHDH-TV heightened and confusion engulfed key executives making decisions about advertising, programming, and revenues. They were decisive about one matter, and I guess it became an inadvertent gift: They fired me.

Even though I received a modest settlement, getting fired was quite a blow. As a child of the Great Depression, I learned well the value of money and the importance of finding and keeping a job. Working day and night, weekends if necessary, was common for me, and every year I cancelled my vacation plans because the company needed me.

At that time, for me, work came first and family second. I accepted that I would be loyal and make an all-out effort for the company, even when I was disappointed by something the company did, such as reducing or eliminating a wage increase, or making greater demands on my time.

Lill got used to it. At least I thought she did. She rarely complained, and I felt it was because we both came from that Depression generation. Lill also knew how important work and accomplishment was for me. Much later, I came to realize that my sacrifices were rarely appreciated, and I decided that no one should deny his family or himself whatever time he was entitled to for strengthening personal ties and resting from the daily combat of the workplace. (The one exception was Ted Turner. Although he worried that successful managers or employees would demand more compensation, he let me know how pleased he was. I received handwritten notes on my memos that said "Great job" or "Keep it up." I also heard occasional comments from film salesmen who heard from him how he felt about my work.

Although I got my walking papers, and a springboard to an exciting and prosperous career, the *Herald Traveler* eventually lost everything: the television station, the newspaper, and its 1,500 employees. Stockholders ended up with only an AM-FM radio station. In early 1972, Akerson and Clancy fought their final battle in Washington, D.C., and lost. For some inexplicable reason, Akerson, as a witness at the hearing, refused to concede that the television station was supporting the newspaper, then operating at a deficit, to the tune of a *million dollars* a month. The FCC permanently rescinded WHDH-TV's license, the station went off the air, the newspaper ceased publishing three months later, and Boston Broadcasters, Inc. signed onto the air with their own station, the winner of newly available local license. The *Herald Traveler*'s ghost was taken over by Rupert Murdoch.

The loss of WHDH-TV, which sent terror through the industry like "scissors cutting fabric," was the direct result of arrogance, ignorance, and greed. A fatal combination.

Robert Choate must have been smiling in his grave.

CHAPTER THREE

Only a Fool Would Buy a UHF Station

I think I can recognize a real entrepreneur at 300 yards on a misty day. Like an actor he is full of vanity...He feels alone and knows that what he says matters, so being able to make and carry through on his own decisions is crucial to him. Above all he has this drive to succeed and get things done.

—Sir Peter Parker

The debacle of WHDH-TV was the epitome of managerial incompetence. I witnessed it at WBZ-TV, and I would see it later at TBS. Executives put managers in the wrong positions with limited or nonexistent talent or experience, but with the power to fire the creative people, the very people responsible for the company's success.

Now I was one of the fired ones. Curt Gowdy, the Red Sox announcer, suggested I visit Roone Arledge, president of American Broadcasting Company (ABC) Sports, in New York. I met with Roone, who was then working on a new project called *Wide World of Entertainment,* which was intended to emulate the success of *Wide World of Sports.*

ABC hired me as a temporary researcher to scout entertainment possibilities in other countries. Although this didn't mean I traveled overseas, it did mean I lived in New York. Luckily, I stayed in an East Side luxury apartment (gratis!) belonging to the mother of a writer I hired for the Brazil project. I commuted from Framingham, Massachusetts, every Sunday night by bus and returned Friday night after work for weekends with my family.

It was very difficult for Lill to run the family five days a week—our two older children were teenagers—while I played catch-up disciplinarian on weekends. We were both exhausted at the end of the week, she from managing the household and I from the five-hour bus ride after a busy work week. We bolstered each other as best we could. Lill's support was there when I needed it most, and she never complained when, from time to time, my conflicts with administrators left me emotionally exhausted and temperamental. Our children—Susan was 16 years old, Steven, 14, and Andrea, 8, would accompany Lill when she picked me up at the bus station on Friday nights and when I left on Sunday nights. Often, on the way back to New York, I worried about my family—the children were not coping well with my absence—and I wondered if the future held promise for us. On top of that, my salary was only half of my earlier take-home pay, and it did not include the additional New York living expenses.

While the idea of a "wide world of entertainment" sounded good, as it developed, we soon realized that it could not duplicate the excitement and interest that sports held for the American audience. Since the ABC arrangement was temporary, I continued to contact broadcast-industry associates.

I learned that Pacific and Southern, a recently formed company, had acquired a television station in Honolulu, a very small market among the 100 largest markets of the United States. Pacific and Southern also purchased Channel 11 in Atlanta. Atlanta in 1968 was a city of about 600,000 people, and the seventeenth largest television market in the United States.

When I spoke to the president of Pacific and Southern, we reached an agreement for me to become Station Manager of WQXI-TV. I immediately envisioned myself working in a warehouse in the middle of a cotton field on the outskirts of Atlanta. Yet, Channel 11 was located in a small building in midtown Atlanta and had one medium-sized studio. I began working there in January 1968, living in a one-bedroom apartment that was right in the television station building.

This time, I had no intention of commuting back and forth to Framingham. Channel 11 looked to be a strong station, the company that owned it was expanding, and I was confident I had at least a two-to-three year job in Atlanta before being reassigned. Lill and I decided to make Atlanta our home. After Lill determined where the best schools were located, and since we couldn't find a house we liked in that area, we bought a piece of property and built on it the house we live in to this day. Of course, the move south was not easy on our children. Teenagers hate being uprooted from their school and separated from their friends. Our son had a particularly hard time. Years later, Steven and Susan moved back to Boston, although now, in their middle age, they do complain about the too-cold winters.

* * * * *

Art McCoy, president of Pacific and Southern, was my kind of guy. He welcomed creative ideas and was not afraid of change. He didn't know how much it meant to me to be given full reign in the programming and development of ideas, some of which I had never dared to suggest before. One was a children's show built around two characters similar to my favorite clowns, Laurel and Hardy. Tubby and Lester's show ran daily in the late afternoons, as a lead-in to evening family programming.

Channel 11's news programming had a terrible reputation, partly because viewers considered its local rival, WSB-TV, the "Voice of the South." This reputation and WSB's excellent signal gave the rival almost a monopoly on the news during the early years of television in Atlanta. The only newspaper in the city, the *Atlanta Journal,* owned WSB-TV. Competing with the WSB monolith seemed a hopeless task.

One day I mentioned to George Hagar, the General Manager, a new idea for news presentation. Art McCoy was in the room at the time. My concept was to broadcast the news from a *newsroom environment* rather than from an anchor desk, which always seemed artificial to me. I told George I planned to create a mock-up of the idea the next day.

The next morning I built a makeshift news environment with the anchor and sports director wearing unplugged headsets to look as though they were attached to the world. We thought the interesting concept merited further testing and refinement. Art McCoy, who had been watching from the back of the studio, stepped forward and said, "I want it on this afternoon." I couldn't believe it. A live program like this needed more rehearsal, better set development, and coordination with the control room, director, and newsroom. McCoy was adamant. He knew that Channel 11 news and sports had almost no audience, and an experiment could be no worse than the existing news show. I had about five hours to get everything ready. I needed five weeks.

I certainly understood the discomfit of Art Collier, the sports reporter, who felt strange wearing a disconnected headset. But it did give the feeling of authenticity. Later, in 1980, after others had tried the concept, Ted Turner built an operating newsroom as the CNN set. The idea was so successful that networks and local television stations emulate it endlessly.

I also wanted to improve the image of the station that had no image—worse than a bad image—and so I thought we should have attractive models introducing the programs and the station breaks. I set up a contest to select 11 "Channel 11 girls" from among Atlanta's most attractive Southern belles. Each appeared for a month, identifying the station and introducing programs, and then all 11 returned in the twelfth month. This successful idea gave the station an aura of excitement and sex appeal.

To learn more about the program preferences of Atlantans, I studied old ratings books, but I wanted more information from the man and woman on the street. I was a Yankee who had a sense of what was popular in Boston, but what did they like in Atlanta?

There was a hot dog/hamburger place called the Varsity near the Georgia Institute of Technology that had several separate rooms, each with a television set. I visited the Varsity regularly, counted the number of viewers in each room, and noted the programs being watched. One program that was already on Channel 11, and always had more than one room watching it, was wrestling. I knew it had the highest rating of any local program at Channel 11, but I had no idea it was that popular.

The show was a promotional program to boost attendance at the wrestling matches Friday nights at the city auditorium, but it gave Channel 11 its highest rated hour on Saturday nights. The only problem was that the viewers did not fit the image that advertisers had for their customers. Jim Thrash, the Advertising Sales Manager at WQXI-TV, who was part of the new team, had difficulty selling the time in spite of the ratings until he changed the show's name from "Championship Wrestling" to "Championship Sports." The local clients knew it was wrestling. The national clients did not figure it out until later.

During 1968, my first year with Channel 11, sales increased 100 percent over the preceding year, and ratings were higher than ever. Art McCoy was elated and suggested that I visit the Honolulu station (KHON-TV) to share some program ideas with its management. This was my first trip to Hawaii.

In 1969, the ratings jumped high enough for advertising sales to increase 60 percent over 1968. The success story of Pacific and Southern in Atlanta became known throughout the television industry. The banks were paying attention, too. Soon they were lending Pacific and Southern large sums of money to invest in other broadcasting properties, including radio. Lenders assumed that its management could apply the same magic elsewhere.

However, the stations that Pacific and Southern acquired did not have the quality of management that made WQXI-TV successful, nor did the new acquisitions have the creative programming or sales that we had at Channel 11. Hence, the dramatic audience and sales increases that had occurred in Atlanta were never duplicated elsewhere.

The expectations were too high. Suddenly Pacific and Southern and its banks held properties with only normal levels of performance. By 1970, this included Channel 11, which in two years had finally reached the level where a VHF channel in the seventeenth-largest U.S. market should be. Audience increases after that were much more difficult to attain. WQXI-TV still had a limited signal, and WSB-TV still dominated news broadcasting. Years later, conditions would change as Atlanta grew from 600,000 to 5 million because of the influx of Yankees and Westerners who had no preconceived image of WSB as the "Voice of the South."

I was under enormous pressure to continue the outstanding gains in audience and sales in the third year. Program and news specialists were brought in. Art McCoy and George Hagar must have assumed that I had used up my creative talent and that new blood was needed. I had already learned that an expert is someone who lives out of town. The experts and new managers came and went, but very little changed. Later, after I was long gone, Channel 11 improved its signal and successfully reached a much larger audience.

In February 1971, a local broadcast managers' meeting was held in the basement meeting room of the old Biltmore Hotel in Atlanta. When I arrived and was seated, I looked around the room, nodding to acquaintances. I saw someone I had never seen before and asked my neighbor, "Who is that guy?"

"His name is Ted Turner. He's the one who just bought the UHF station, Channel 17." We didn't have to say what we both thought: Only a fool would buy a UHF (ultra-high frequency) television station.

Back then, very few professional broadcasters would have anything to do with a UHF frequency, unless a particular market did not include at least three VHF (very-high frequency) channels, numbered 2 through 13, that satisfied the needs of the three major networks—CBS, ABC, and NBC. The UHF channels were numbered 14 through 69, and, unlike VHF, no dial clicked into place. Instead, the dial spun, and the viewer had to be seriously motivated to find a UHF channel. It was like locating a foreign station on a short-wave radio.

Most advertisers were turned off by UHF and didn't want to support its high operating costs. Unlike radio, which needed only a handful of personnel, a television operation required a lot of personnel and equipment, as well as programming, to air even a modest schedule. True, large profits could be made, but not until the station had a reliable audience and advertising income. Unlike the situation in many countries, especially the less-developed economies, where television was supported by government subsidy, television user license fees were paid by the consumer, and sometimes also by advertising. All U.S. television channels, including UHF and excepting the Public Broadcasting System (PBS), had at that time only their advertisers to support them.

Both national and local television advertising clients generally buy commercial positions at certain times of day on their local stations. The rate charged for these positions depends on the time of day and reflects the size of the potential audience. Ultimately, ratings, which measure the popularity of the programs, determine the cost to the advertisers.

Networks were formed at the beginning of commercial television in the late 1940s. These were an alliance of stations chosen by the network companies in cities throughout the United States. Local stations competed to be on the strongest and most popular network. All three networks provided programs during the most popular daily time periods—that is, the most desirable advertising times for national companies. Thus, networks controlled the best time block of the day, 8–11:00 P.M.

In previous years, the networks started broadcasting as early as 7:30 P.M., but the FCC insisted that local stations program that time period, naïvely believing that stations would use it for important local programs. However, this led to the success of many inexpensively produced and syndicated game shows, purchased by local stations. In this time slot the local stations, not the networks, charged advertisers to broadcast their commercials. The local stations pocket the profit. During network broadcasting hours, local stations retain only a small portion of the advertising time (hence advertising revenue), usually getting only the advertising breaks between programs. So, the syndicators sold these national programs to the local stations, who then sold all the local ad positions. However, certain programs were so popular that the syndicators could demand payment for the programs *plus* a block of advertising time during the program, which the syndicators sold directly—and quite profitably—to advertisers.

In effect, the FCC's insistence on giving desirable local program time to the stations turned out to be a sham. It meant more advertising money for the local station, but it did not enhance creative local production.

This competition between networks and local television stations for the best advertising time was irrelevant with the costly UHF operations. Major advertisers who ordered their campaigns through advertising agencies did not waste their money on UHF. Through the early 1970s, the outlook for UHF was gloomy. Ted Turner bought UHF Channel 17 in 1970. If he had understood what he was doing in economic terms, he would not have involved himself in a part of the television industry that many considered terminally ill.

Yet Ted was no stranger to tragedy and challenge. Ted's father founded a billboard-advertising company, but then, distraught at over-expanding the business and over-extending the family's financial resources, pleaded with reluctant friends to buy the business. After they did so in a gesture of supportive friendship, Ted's father committed suicide at age 53. Ted, just 24 at the time, demanded the return of the company, so the family friends sold it back.

Ted knew that the billboard company faced serious growth limitations. Communities throughout America were starting to oppose "billboard blight." Ted thought that radio was the road to new advertising opportunities. He purchased stations in Jacksonville, Florida, Charleston, South Carolina, and Chattanooga, Tennessee. Except for the Charleston station, which earned a modest return, he lost money on the other properties.

This impetuous, fiery disposition—the inability to rein in his emotions and energy—was Ted's vital strength and his fatal weakness.

In 1969 Ted wanted to buy a radio station in Atlanta, but nothing of value was available at the right price. Instead, he looked at television and acquired the financially strapped UHF Channel 17, WJRJ-TV. The station had been broadcasting for two years and had lost half a million dollars each year. Jack Rice, who owned a coal company, had put it on the air. He, like the other UHF owners in a VHF-dominated market, did not understand the myriad problems involved.

To Ted's credit, he didn't pay cash, probably because he didn't have any. He swapped $2.5 million in Turner stock (Turner owned other radio stations) for Rice Broadcasting's Channel 17. The station went from one man who didn't know what he was doing to another who had no knowledge of television broadcasting, but who had two important attributes: (1) an understanding of what motivated advertisers, and (2) an uncritical imagination that knew no boundaries. His lack of knowledge about television broadcasting was actually an asset.

To keep his weak radio stations and the losing UHF acquisition going, Ted needed cash. Turner Communications went public and began selling stock on the over-the-counter exchange, and Ted, at that time chairman and president, held about 47 percent of the stock.

The other UHF station in Atlanta, Channel 36, owned by U.S. Communications, was enduring the same problems Rice and Turner suffered. Both stations fought for the few local advertisers willing to buy schedules on programs with such minimal audiences. Between them, they were draining the small pool of support they had. One would have to go. Which one?

During this critical period, Ted learned that General Cinema, a motion picture theater chain and the owner of Channel 6 in Miami, was interested in purchasing Channel 36. General Cinema had a stable business to fall back on. Turner had only a weak billboard advertising company that his father had expanded too aggressively and radio stations that were losing money. General Cinema had one thing that Ted had run out of: money. If it purchased Channel 36, Turner would be finished—his bank credit had been exhausted.

Coincidentally, General Cinema was headquartered in Boston, and one of its executives, Al Tanger, had been the advertising manager of WHDH-TV. Al and I always had a mutual respect, but neither of us knew of the other's place in these unfolding events. I had no way of knowing Tanger was interested in a television station in Atlanta, and he didn't know I had ended up there.

Ted was desperate. If General Cinema entered the UHF market, it could easily force him out. When he realized that he was hanging on by his fingernails, he flew to Boston and met with the top executives, including Tanger. During the discussion, Ted threatened to make all the Atlanta billboards, almost all of which he owned, unavailable to Channel 36. At the end of this fruitless meeting, and in order to demonstrate what their purchase of Channel 36 would do to him, Ted writhed on the floor like a man in his death throes. He scared the hell out of those establishment business executives. Things were bad in Atlanta. Channel 36 was losing money. Who needed to be in the same city with a nut?

Soon after Ted returned to Atlanta, Channel 36 went off the air. Ted later told me it had been a contest to see which one of the two UHF stations would survive. He said, "If Channel 36 had waited two more weeks, I'd have been finished."

Fortunately for Ted, and then for the rest of us, Channel 36 blinked first. However, there were still not enough advertisers to support even one UHF station. Also, Channel 17's management was weak. There were no professional television broadcasters at Turner Communications. The station manager, who worked under Ted, had been brought over from the Chattanooga radio station and had no experience in television.

Ted naïvely assumed that television was the same as radio, *but with pictures.*

Many years later Ted used the same kind of reasoning with me. Atlanta's first electronic scoreboard was built at Fulton County Stadium, home of the Atlanta Braves. Ted put me in charge of the scoreboard on the assumption that it dealt with video and I managed a television station—also video. What's the difference, right? A world of difference, of course, so I found professionals who knew how to operate and manage this new service. I bowed out. I never wanted to create a corporate "empire," as many business executives want to do. I certainly did not want to become King of Scoreboards. I want mountains to climb, not empires to rule.

While Channel 17, now called WTCG, was having its survival crisis in mid-1971, I was facing my own survival problems at Channel 11. The owners, disappointed because we hadn't continued our miraculous growth, gave me my walking papers in 1971.

I sent out résumés and waited at home for a response. The only industry employment opportunity that turned up was with a very small television station in South Carolina. The owner suggested an interview on his upcoming trip to Atlanta.

During the interview, he said, "The local business community has to get along with the manager of the television station." What he meant was that a small Southern community might not react favorably to someone who was Jewish holding that job. I knew I would never hear from him again.

In this case, religious prejudice worked in my favor. Had I received that job, I would have buried myself and my creativity in that market in South Carolina. Instead, I was available for something better. When you have no job and your prospects seem non-existent, it is easy to understand how talented individuals can make a decision that will affect the rest of their lives negatively. They may never know to what level their talents might have taken them, if they had waited.

CHAPTER FOUR

Thirty-nine Employees and a Decrepit Television Facility

Adversity has the effect of eliciting talents which in prosperous circumstances would have lain dormant.

—Horace

A few months later, as I was mowing the lawn, Lill came down the driveway and waved to me. I turned off the mower. "There's a Ted Turner on the phone. Do you know him?" she called.

I thought, that's that UHF loser. Do I want to have anything to do with that station? It could negatively affect my future possibilities in television. I seriously considered not taking the call, saying I wasn't interested. But I walked into the house, picked up the phone, and, for the first time, heard a loud, coarse voice on the other end: "How come you haven't come to see me?"

He knew the reason. I didn't have to tell him. So I changed the subject and asked how he had heard about me. Jim Roddy, who ran Rollins Broadcasting and was a close friend of Ted's, told him that I applied for a position with their Group Broadcasting Service, which was in Atlanta. I had preferred not to move.

I agreed to talk with Ted, and we set a time for the following week. I didn't feel any urgency about finding a job, but I was bored waiting for the right phone call. Since everything I experienced so far in television had been based on timing I figured I had to wait for the right reason to relocate again.

When I met Ted, it became clear that Ted's station had no direction or sense of purpose, except surviving. Ted knew I didn't want to work for him, but he also knew that I had the television station experience that his station lacked. We agreed that I would come on board as a consultant; therefore, I would not have to mention our association on my résumé. The next day, Ted called me. His station manager had just walked out. Could I come in right away and "start the meter running"?

Before Ted hired me in 1971, I had been negotiating for the purchase of a small radio station in Austell, Georgia. I had visions of purchasing other radio stations and, eventually owning television stations. But, as much as Ted wanted me, he didn't feel I could give him the attention he needed and operate a radio station at the same time, and he was right. In which direction did I want to go? I had to choose. In spite of the then-obscurity and seemingly limited potential of Channel 17, I aborted the plans for the purchase of the radio station and never looked back, with one exception. Once during the recession of 1973, I again considered owning a television station, a UHF station no less.

The owner of Channel 26, WGNO-TV, in New Orleans was also in the construction business, and the recession had hit the real estate development side of his company. He wanted to sell Channel 26, located in an office building in downtown New Orleans. I visited the station as part of my Braves baseball network development, and learned of the owner's interest in selling. This UHF TV station, like its counterparts elsewhere, was barely surviving, and he offered the station and its equipment to me for $2 million and made it even more appealing when he said he would take $100,000 as a down payment. I thought it was a great opportunity to own my own station, and I made a serious effort to acquire the financing. I talked to many banks and investors, offering equity in the station, but was unable to persuade them to lend me the money. Most potential investors got cold feet during this severe recession period.

Ironically, only a few years later, Channel 26 was sold for $6 million, then $11 million, and eventually $20 million (I lost track after that).

Timing is everything. In retrospect, I don't feel that I really lost anything by not being able to own the New Orleans station. Yes, I would have entered a new world of wealth after selling or expanding ownership of valuable television properties, but I would not have been thrust accidentally into the pioneering development of news on a global scale that has made my life, at least to me, significant.

* * * * *

In October 1971, Channel 17 had 39 staff people. Only one person was handling promotion and helping out in other areas, such as programming or traffic. This department prepares a daily second-by-second schedule that coordinates programs and commercials. Normally, different people and their staffs would handle each of these jobs. I could see my work was cut out for me.

I was given an office on the street floor in a corner of this small, two-story television station. We had a single studio about the size of a three-car garage. Ted's office on the second floor, about the size of a one-car garage, was above a real garage, which was used to store scenery. Ted had an old legal desk and a couch whose springs had expired years ago. His office opened on to a decent-sized conference room, which we used occasionally for rehearsals. Behind the building sat a 1,042-foot transmitting tower perched on a hill in midtown Atlanta, less than a mile from the downtown skyscrapers.

The other television stations' towers were wired to the ground in suburban locations. Our tower, looming over our building and parking lot, became a serious problem in the winter when Atlanta had ice storms. Rain hovering above the freezing level would ice the tower during the night, and large chunks of ice would fall as the temperature rose. The ice chunks could pierce parked cars and our building's roof. We were concerned that ice chunks could harm our equipment. I stacked used automobile tires on the roof to protect the personnel and equipment, but the weight of the tires sagged the roof. Eventually, I had wire fencing built across the roof to catch falling ice.

The transmitting equipment was in bad shape and frequently failed, putting the channel off the air. It had not been properly maintained, and only the minimum and least costly technical equipment had been purchased. There was never enough money to purchase backup equipment. Going off the air also contributed to the station's negative image. The salaries, of course, were very low. The constant turnover of personnel meant a lot of extra training time and reduced the staff's effectiveness even more.

Two urgent problems I had to face immediately. The chief engineer was an alcoholic who, on one occasion when he forgot his keys, had smashed in a door at the back of the studio. One never knew how much he had been drinking, but his attitude was usually an indicator.

I knew I had to get rid of him. I called a chief engineer at Channel 11 (my previous employer) and said, "I'm going to have to find someone on your staff to become our chief engineer here at Channel 17. Any recommendations?" He surprised me by being very frank. He told me his choice would be an engineer named Jack Verner.

I called Jack, told him of my intentions, and arranged to meet him at Johnny Escoe's, a local restaurant, at 4:00 P.M. Thursday. I was on time and waited for Jack for an hour and a half, but he never showed up.

I then called Gene Wright, another engineer at Channel 11, whom I knew and liked. He accepted my proposal and eventually became Vice President of Engineering for TBS. A short time later, Jack told me that he did show up at Escoe's at 4:00 P.M., but he arrived on Friday. Not long after this, Jack went to work for Gene and was quite happy, even though he missed the top job.

It was now time for me to fire the chief engineer. I expected a violent confrontation. We did not have security guards then and, as a matter of fact, since my office was on the ground floor near the main entrance, the receptionist often phoned me because some strange person had wandered in. I would have to stop what I was doing and ask the intruder to leave.

I don't care for guns, but I learned how to use them during my army years. I purchased a .38 Smith & Wesson while at Channel 11 because I was worried about the Ku Klux Klan. The local free newspaper left on our lawn each week listed a meeting of the KKK on top of Stone Mountain as that week's social event. I have picked up that newspaper each week for the last 37 years and thrown it directly into the trash can. (That's 1,924 bend-overs for anyone who is counting.)

I set up the meeting in my office with the chief engineer. I sat behind my desk as he walked in. My right hand was in the top right-hand drawer, resting on the .38. I told him that he was fired, and I fully expected him to come at me across the desk. To my surprise, he was extremely docile. He even seemed relieved. He handed over his keys without a murmur. I felt his responsibilities and frustrations exacerbated a propensity to drink.

The second urgent problem was our dreadful programming. We lacked a good film library. Since we had no affiliation with any network, we were responsible for all the programming which, at that time, aired from 6:00 A.M. to 1:00 A.M. This, of course, was partly why I stayed with Ted Turner after the initial months of my consultancy. Here were opportunities for creativity I'd never dreamed of. The network affiliates where I worked before were mirror reflections of productions from New York and Los Angeles. All local programming was relegated to the low-audience time slots, including the local news. Of course, at WTCG-TV, I also ran the station, bought the films and programs, and kept the staff happy when they complained or wanted a raise. Yet I managed to create locally produced programs and build a remote production service. Once again, I was doing the job of four or five people.

Occasionally, the networks allowed us to air a single network program or a movie that their local affiliate chose not to carry. Instead, the local network might have carried an inferior program or movie, which had been sold to them by Hollywood film companies as a rerun. The practice of these film companies was to sell a package of 20 to 30 films, which contained 3 or 4 excellent ones, 10 to 12 so-so's, and 4 or 5 awful movies. We call the lousy films "dogs." The affiliates saved the better films for prime time, with the hope of pre-empting a newer network movie in order to capture all the advertising time, as opposed to having only a few station-break commercial spots during an ordinary network movie. Network affiliates needed to make more money—national advertising agencies, as well as their own local sales departments, clamored for greater advertising exposure, especially in prime time. If the local affiliate pre-empted the network program, generally a movie, then the local station enjoyed two extra hours for advertising. The affiliate didn't care whether the network movie was better, or that the movie they were running might have aired six or seven times before.

A station could buy film-rerun packages from salesmen representing the larger motion picture companies, such as Warner Brothers, MGM, MCA-Universal, and Columbia Pictures, or from distributors representing the smaller independent motion picture companies. American International, for instance, sold movies targeted at special audiences, such as horror films or beach blanket bikini films made especially for teenagers. The major studios reaped very high fees for their films. The independents struggled to get decent prices.

Although Ted wisely built friendships with certain salesmen, it was my experience with network affiliates that reassured the film companies, many of whom were suspicious of UHF independents like us. Of course, we wanted the expensive first-run, off-network film packages, but we did not have the resources to pay for them. Broadcasting four movies a day and more on weekends totals over 1,500 movie runs a year. Repeating movies is possible, but if they are unpopular, or if you repeat them too often, even at different times of the day, the audience ratings will suffer drastically. So, in late 1971, I flew to Los Angeles to make a long-term agreement for hundreds of titles with a small company called National Telefilm Associates (NTA). It had a large, older movie library containing some well-known feature films of the 1940s and 1950s. This gave me a small list of promotable films to use. Normally, we ran four or five films a day. By the fall of 1973, I was programming and scheduling a full 24 hours a day and airing almost twice as many films. All my years with local network affiliates had never been this stimulating. My ideas and energies were finally in a creative environment.

Just before I arrived at WTCG-TV, Ted learned that a UHF station in Charlotte, North Carolina, was declaring bankruptcy and would be sold on the courthouse steps. Although he was having financial problems, he attended the sale to buy some of their equipment for his Atlanta station. Ted bought not only the cameras, but also the bankrupt station! Now he had two UHF stations sliding into bankruptcy in the fall of 1971.

The Board of Directors of Turner Communications, which also owned several radio stations and the original billboard company, reacted adversely to the new acquisition. The board, composed of Ted's associates and friends, generally acquiesced in his decisions, outlandish as they sometimes were. Yet they saw no sense in struggling with two nearly bankrupt stations. One was more than they could handle. So Ted created a new company in order to purchase WRET-TV (Channel 36) in Charlotte.

Sandy Wheeler, the Station Manager in Charlotte, phoned me a few weeks after I started working at Channel 17 to tell me that his station was about to go off the air. The various film companies under contract were refusing to ship film because they hadn't been receiving payments. I guessed the reason Sandy called me and not Ted was that he did not relish giving Ted the bad news.

I hung up, climbed the flight of stairs to Ted's office, and told him about the new crisis. He was obviously shaken and began pacing around his small office. "What am I going to do?"

Since I was the only one in the room, I thought he was asking me. Was I supposed to worry about another station's problems? Didn't I already have enough? I quickly realized that I *was* expected to solve the problem and to give it my immediate attention.

I didn't know what to say. I don't think Ted expected me to say anything right then. He was thinking aloud. So I went back to my office. Generally, I ponder the "big ones" overnight. And I often come up with a solution in the middle of the night.

The next day, I went back to Ted's office with the suggestion that he appear on camera that weekend between programs and in prime time periods to say to his Charlotte viewers: "Would you like to have a fourth channel with movies and sports in addition to the ABC, CBS, and NBC local affiliates? In order for WRET-TV to continue on the air, we need your support. Send in five dollars or whatever you can so that we can stay on the air." In other words, I advised him, "Tell the public the truth. Let them decide if you're worth saving."

Ted gave me a puzzled look. "Is it legal?"

"I don't know," I replied. "I'll have to check with the FCC."

"Okay. Let's find out," he said.

I called our Washington attorneys. When I told them what I wanted, they didn't believe me. And they were as surprised as I was when the answer came back that there was no FCC rule that prevented our doing this. I pictured the lawyers and the stodgy FCC bureaucrats looking "stunned," much like the TV managers in Boston that I had arrested and carted off to jail.

So, we had our own version of a telethon—industry insiders would refer to it sarcastically as "Ted's Beg-A-Thon." In effect, we were asking the viewers to pay for programming that was not yet fully supported by advertising (which cable companies did eventually). Today, it is common for viewers and advertisers to support new channels.

To everyone's surprise, including mine, Ted did a pretty good job on the air. I helped write his "pitch." He told the viewers that our creditors had been understanding, but our banks would not extend us any more credit. Due to our losses, we were unable to interest other investors. If the station went off the air, Ted would lose about $800,000. But business was business, and under the free enterprise system, perhaps we should fail. The thought had occurred to us that our viewers had a stake in our operation. The rating survey showed that we had a large and growing audience. Besides our other programs, we could now broadcast about 30 different movies each week. If only a portion of our viewers contributed, then we could survive.

Ted ended his appeal by saying, "I pledge to you that every penny will be used to pay the bills we incur to bring you these programs. If there is a surplus, we will enlarge our film library to bring you more and better movies and other programs not shown on the other stations. I wanted to give you shares of stock in the station, but it is illegal to sell stock on TV. I would like for you to consider this a loan. Please include your name and address with your contribution because, if we are ever able to, I promise to pay you back with interest. A check would be best for your records and ours. This campaign will last one week. We should not have to repeat this since we are close to break-even now."

I slept that night on a couch in the Charlotte general manager's office and woke up stiff, sore, and cranky. I didn't know what to expect. I imagined the local media laughing us out of town. I made myself some coffee, but we were too far from the city to find a place for breakfast. Shopping centers had not yet reached that area.

By noon, I was quite hungry and wondering where to buy food, when I looked out the large lobby window. A few cars were pulling in. People began coming into the lobby, asking where to take their donations. A steady stream of cars followed, and I realized that these people were coming to the station directly from their Sunday church services!

I asked someone to hold the front door open. I hustled into a nearby studio and propped that door open, then ran to the back of the studio and opened the rear door. I found an empty box and placed it on a table as a parade of people began coming in. I stood near the box, pointing to it as people walked up to drop their donations in cash and checks into the box and then left by the rear door. This went on for a few hours. It was a scene right out of a Frank Capra movie. Between what was put into the box and what soon arrived by mail, we collected $26,000. It was enough to pay the film company suppliers something and to keep the station on the air.

More than 3,600 viewers had contributed from 25 cents to $80. By 1975, four years later, WRET-TV was in the black and gladly paid back those who had sent their names and addresses, and with interest. In 1979, Ted sold WRET-TV to Westinghouse Broadcasting for $21 million, which was then used as seed money for CNN.

The week after his appeal to the WRET-TV viewers, Ted called me into his office and gave me 300 shares of the company he had created in order to purchase the Charlotte station. The stock was a complete surprise. No one I had worked for previously had ever made that kind of gesture, and I was very pleased.

A short time later, however, when Ted was in the process of transferring WRET-TV to the control of Turner Communications, he called me into his office again and asked me to exchange the 300 shares for $300, since, as he put it, "It was just an extra weekend's work."

I said nothing and returned the stock. But it was the only time I felt that Ted had been unfair to me. Those 300 shares would probably be worth hundreds of thousands of dollars today, perhaps millions. Later, I purchased my own shares in Turner Communications, Georgia, and have watched them multiply in value over the years. I have benefited greatly from my association with Ted, in more ways than financially. It was a mutually beneficial relationship. He needed my ideas, and I needed the creative drawing board he kept putting in front of me.

CHAPTER FIVE

The Miracle That Won the Braves, Hawks, and Flames

The most rewarding things in life are often the ones that look like they cannot be done.

—Arnold Palmer

When I returned to Atlanta from Charlotte, I went back to the challenge of developing and purchasing programming for Channel 17, as well as strengthening the infrastructure. The 39 employees were stretched pretty thin, and we couldn't afford to hire more people until advertising revenues improved, and that wouldn't happen until the Atlanta viewers could find the signal on their rotating UHF dials. Making them want to find our station was critical, not only for our survival, but also for our future growth. I saw my job as creating an appetite that would overcome our handicap: the rotating dial and the stigma of being a UHF station.

By early 1972, after working four years in Atlanta, I had a pretty good idea of what the viewers wanted. The market now had an audience of slightly less than one million. The great northern migration from Snowbelt to Sunbelt had not yet begun.

My experience, as well as the Nielsen and Arbition monthly ratings, which came out six times a year, told me that the only local programs that had consistently large audiences were local sports events. Atlanta now had the Falcons, a National Football League (NFL) team, the Atlanta Braves, a Major League Baseball (MLB), and the two new professional sports teams: the Atlanta Hawks of the National Basketball Association (NBA), and the Atlanta Flames of the National Hockey League (NHL). Of course, the sports program that consistently earned the highest rating of any local program was Channel 11's wrestling, or as I had renamed it (in my own mind), "Theater Without Words."

These teams needed more television exposure, including the new Hawks and Flames teams. Even the Braves had only a limited schedule of games on WSB-TV, the number-one local (NBC) network affiliate. The Braves had not succeeded in convincing the network affiliates of their value as programming, and so they were forced to buy time on WSB-TV for a 20-game schedule each year. The Braves then created their own limited television and radio network and broadcast the games to other southeastern cities. For many years, the Braves had been the only major league team in the Southeast.

The WSB local radio station did the same thing for all 162 Braves games. The Braves were forced to create their own advertising sales team to sell the television and radio commercials in order to pay for their television time. The team did not usually make money on the advertising after they had paid for their program time and the cost of selling the ads. They had to create interest in the team and bring fans not only from Atlanta, but from the whole southeast to the Fulton County Stadium to watch a professional, if losing, baseball team.

My television industry friends thought an association between the Braves and a UHF station would be a monumental joke. It was apparent to me that a frontal approach would not work. I abandoned that idea for the time being and turned my attention to the two new professional basketball and hockey teams. At first, I encountered only resistance, because we were UHF. But one day a miracle occurred, or perhaps it was a stroke of luck.

I was trying to find a way to convince the teams that they were better off associating with a programmer hungry for material than with a network affiliate that had to convince its network that they should pre-empt their prime time or weekend programming to carry a local sports event. The local NBC station's viewers missed the programs normally shown on a given night when Braves games were aired. Furthermore, all the networks had important programs pre-empted when their local affiliates chose to cancel two hours of prime time to air their own movie.

The networks were at a disadvantage. Thus, ABC, CBS, and NBC had no choice but to place some of their best programming on the weaker, independent television stations, even on the hard-to-find UHF stations like Channel 17. At least they could say to an advertiser, "We got you some coverage in Atlanta." They hoped to make a point with their local affiliates by allowing the pre-empted program, with its strong audience appeal, to be aired on one of the independent stations, thus weakening their own affiliates' audiences.

The rich network affiliates laughed at the networks and told them they didn't care because very few viewers could even find the UHF stations on that stupid rotating dial. So, the networks occasionally offered Channel 17 a movie or a program that their affiliates had chosen not to carry.

It is true that there were times for local public-service programs, such as election returns, when the local stations had to pre-empt network programs in order to fulfill their FCC license requirements of "serving the local community." A television license had to be renewed every three years. Remember that these local stations had one of the highest profit margins in American industry. Although public service requirements were the common excuse given to the public, as well as to the networks, it was the local stations' interest in being able to sell more ads that was the truly compelling reason for pre-empting network programs. Boston's WHDH-TV, of course, had lost its license when it ignored the FCC requirements for public service programming but, by 1971 local station affiliates throughout the country were much more experienced in how much risk they could take with their FCC licenses and still increase their profits.

When Channel 17 carried the pre-empted programs, there was some improvement in our audience, but it wasn't dramatic. The reason: Most viewers didn't want to take the trouble to find us. But a miracle can go unnoticed if you're not paying attention.

ABC decided to air a movie based on a true story about one of the better-known NFL athletes, and it promoted the movie well in advance, especially during the weekend sports programs and most vigorously on *Monday Night Football* the night before showing the film.

The local affiliate had already decided to pre-empt *Brian's Song* to carry a local film. ABC had no choice but to offer this movie to Channel 17 in order to recapture some audience in the Atlanta market for its national sponsors. We accepted, because any opportunity to carry a network program added to our prestige and helped promote our station to Atlanta viewers.

Meanwhile, we had learned that the viewers most successful in finding us on the UHF dial were children. We wanted to encourage them to find the signal, so we began running large blocks of cartoons and situation comedies from 4–6:00 P.M. We provided family programs right after the children's programs, hoping to attract the parents. Maybe they would keep the channel on for our prime time movies.

Then came the highly promoted first run of *Brian's Song*, the true story of Brian Piccolo, a player with the Chicago Bears, who died of cancer. We would not have realized what happened if we hadn't taken a "coincidental"—that is, an overnight survey of that night's programming.

The next day, December 1, we received a single sheet of paper that listed all the programs on each television channel in Atlanta, and the size of the audience based on 320 telephone calls made by the rating service the night before. At first, we did not believe what was typed on that single sheet of paper.

Channel 17 was number one in at least one half-hour period surveyed when *Brian's Song* was aired.

Elation swept through our offices. The advertising salesmen were bumping into each other in their rush to get out of the office to visit their clients. Ted was singing in the hallways and slapping the back of every employee he saw.

After my initial excitement, I sat with a copy of the ratings on my lap and tried to decide how I could use this startling information. I reached for the phone and called Bob Cousins, the General Manager of the Atlanta Hawks, the NBA team that had recently arrived and was still struggling to find fans to fill seats during its home games. I arranged a meeting with Cousins at his office, but I didn't tell him what I had. I wanted to see the full effect of my surprise on him.

The following day I met Bob in his office. Bob then introduced me to the manager of the Atlanta Flames hockey team, which had also recently arrived in the city. Bob had been meeting with the Flames' manager and now invited him to stay and hear what I had to say. They both stared in disbelief at the ratings survey. It wasn't hard to get them to express their interest. Like most teams that contract with network affiliates, the teams made only limited television appearances. Limited appearances mean limited fan interest and limited ticket sales.

While I still had things on the burner with the Hawks and Flames, I phoned the Braves and set up an appointment with Dick Cecil, a vice president, at their offices in Atlanta's Fulton County Stadium. He wondered why I had asked for a meeting, since it had already been established, he thought, that our UHF signal was too weak to reach all of Atlanta and its vicinity.

I didn't have to do much talking. I emphasized my conviction: When the public wants our programming, they find a way to receive our signal. Then I showed Cecil the one-night rating. He, too, was astonished. I reviewed what had happened and how heavily the movie had been promoted. Cecil promised to set up a meeting with the Braves' principal owners.

I took word of this interest on the part of the Hawks, Flames, and Braves back to Ted. He was excited about the prospects and wanted to attend the meeting with the Braves' owners, who had now seen copies of the ratings.

I was worried that Ted might say something outrageous or offensive, and I knew that we would be "fighting the grain." I use the term to describe a meeting with those who are opposed to my ideas. But everyone, including Ted, was warm and cordial. Our timing was perfect. The Braves' owners were dissatisfied, not only with the team and its poor fan support, but also with the amount of game coverage on WSB-TV. The television station had not been "standing behind the team" in order to develop attendance, as it had promised. The Braves were losing considerable amounts of money, and this was long before the players received multi-million dollar annual salaries. The meeting ended with the understanding that we were to make an offer for a one-year contract for the television rights. They still had some doubts, especially about our ability to reach a large audience.

By December 1971, although I had been with Ted less than two months, I had helped him keep the Charlotte station alive and was actively negotiating for and purchasing programs and films from the major motion picture studios. Therefore, I assumed that I would be the one to negotiate an agreement with the Braves. I met with Jack Carlin, Dick Cecil's assistant, to discuss terms, and then we were to meet with Ted to finalize our proposal. I didn't have a figure in mind, but I wanted to learn from our conversation what it would take to make a pact. I knew that the Braves were buying their air time on WSB-TV, and then selling the advertising time. As we talked, it became apparent that the team had decided that an alliance with us would be a favorable business decision. Jack and I agreed on $200,000 for us to buy the television rights for one year.

Ted was waiting for us and pacing about in his office. After the introductions, I sat on the couch with the broken springs as Ted walked behind his desk. Without giving me an opportunity to speak, he said to Carlin, "I'll give you $500,000 a season," and promptly walked out the rear door of the office.

Carlin looked at me in bewilderment, and I just shrugged my shoulders. Should I have jumped up and announced I had already made the deal at $200,000? In those days, a $300,000 difference in price was a lot of money. The station was about to gross over one million dollars for the year, but it was still losing $300,000 a year—the difference between the $200,000 I negotiated and the $500,000 Ted offered!

I don't know why Ted interfered. Perhaps he reasoned it would be a brilliant stroke to prevent WSB-TV from getting the contract. Or perhaps Ted thought we might extract a greater share of the available advertising dollars.

In any case, the one-year contract developed into a five-year contract, finalized in June 1972, to begin with the 1973 season and end after the 1977 one. The total was $3,175,000, an average of $635,000 per season. In 1976, when the contract was up for re-negotiation, Ted realized that the Braves were the most important programming we had, now that we had a signal that could be imported throughout the southeast region of the United States and would be going on a U.S. satellite that would cover the entire U.S. television market.

He knew that the price for the rights could escalate to a million dollars or more a year. Yet the team's standing was still at the bottom of its league, and the owners wanted to sell to get out from under the rain of red ink. They offered the team for the meager sum of $9.65 million, with a payout over 12 years at six percent interest. A sweetheart deal. It was a giveaway, just as the selling of Channel 17 had been six years before. Ted was elated.

"Nothing down and not much a month!" he crowed. He bought the team, thus saving the company a great deal of money in television rights, and the Braves, soon to be seen on cable throughout the United States, became "America's Team."

I couldn't believe that Major League Baseball would permit local market baseball to be shown all over the United States. Evidently new copyright laws allowed independent television stations, no matter where they were located, to show their independent programming nationwide. Around this time, I had a visual image of television sets performing robust somersaults in the living rooms of America.

CHAPTER SIX

Tactics, Tantrums, and Triumphs

You can buy a man's time. You can buy a man's physical presence at a given place. You can even buy a measured number of skilled muscular actions per hour per day. But you cannot buy enthusiasm. You cannot buy initiative. You cannot buy loyalty. You cannot buy the devotion of a heart, mind, and soul. You have to earn these things.

—Ed Liden

Ted, who customarily used the force of his presence to coerce people into giving him the desired results, did everything he could to get fans into the seats of his losing Braves team. The team's public relations man, Bob Hope, had plenty of ideas. Ted sometimes found himself riding an ostrich in races around the field, or pushing a baseball around the bases with his nose. He won, but it took weeks for his nose to heal.

He also acquired a majority interest in the Atlanta Hawks' NBA basketball franchise for $1.5 million, and obtained from the city the management of the new Omni Arena, where the Hawks played. The Hawks, too, eventually became part of the Turner empire. The arrival of the teams affected not only Channel 17's programming, but also our advertising sales. Suddenly, local and national advertisers began to take notice of this upstart channel and its noisy owner.

Ted enjoyed playing David to Goliaths like WSB-TV. In a 1974 article in *Television/Radio Age*, Tom Bradshaw quotes Ted.

> There were about five network shows WSB wasn't carrying on a regular basis. Now you know that when an affiliate doesn't carry a network show, an independent can pick it up if it wants to. Well, that's what we did. We started carrying all five shows on WSB and we had billboards put up which read, "The NBC network moves to Channel 17." And underneath, we listed the five shows.

In that instance I thought the management at WSB-TV would have apoplexy. The billboard was finally removed, but it already had its desired effect. We were, in 1974, ranked as the top UHF independent television station in the United States, and we were in a four-way tie for fifth place, from sign on to sign off, including VHF stations, among all independent television stations. Ted's fearlessness, competitiveness, daring-do, and loyalty were now paying dividends, literally.

* * * * *

In 1972, I did not yet fully understand Ted's intensity and love of risk-taking. For example, Ted was accomplished at sailing, where brains are more important than muscle and coordination, but he was not very grand at tennis. Still, his competitive fire and impetuous personality drove him to invite me to play tennis, my sport. One afternoon, I whipped him soundly. He never forgot it. Only a deeply competitive man would remember it vividly and bring it up again 22 years later when I was 69, when he used the drubbing to convince others in Turner management of my skills and stamina despite my age!

Consider his love of sailing. Ted is not truly interested in any sport except sailing. Lacking good physical coordination, Ted turned to sailing, which involves mental challenge, some physical coordination, and great benefits to those who take risks.

Consider his intensity. Soon after I began working for Ted, he invited Lill and me to a radio station party in Chattanooga, and after the party we drove to Charleston. Ted always insisted on driving, and he performed this relatively simple task with such intensity, not even wishing to be distracted by conversation, that Lill and I began to realize that he was a very unusual human being. Ted never relaxed. He was intense about everything he did. Years later, when Ted was diagnosed with manic depression, many aspects of his personality were attributed to his bipolar condition.

Ted is also deeply loyal. I once saw Ted meet an older employee who was about to retire after working for Ted's father for many years. I saw the deferential way Ted spoke to him. This loyalty to an old timer helped me to put in perspective Ted's highly emotional style and his tendency to unusual behavior. It also triggered an important work motivation within me. Having grown up in the Great Depression, I always wanted to work for an individual who respected my loyalty and returned it with his own.

While Ted and I were similar in our aggressiveness and can do attitude, Ted had one major attribute I lacked, and that was an understanding of money and how it worked. I was two years old when the depression started in 1929 and it lasted through the thirties when I was growing up. I learned about money from watching everyone trying to scrape by and at how appalled my parents were when a relative had to borrow a few hundred dollars; I somehow got the impression he had committed a serious crime.

This borrowing became anathema to me and I avoided it like the plague until I bought a house in the early fifties. But I never really could make the leap into borrowing for business reasons and Ted was a master at understanding the concept and its execution long before I adjusted to it.

Over a period of time, working closely with Ted, I developed at least a partial understanding of his behavior. I never knew on any given day whether he would be merely high or very high. He was rarely down or drained. There was always more than enough energy for the task at hand. Occasionally, in ways I couldn't predict, he could become very angry. Accepting this behavior took its toll on me.

Shortly after I began working for Ted, I realized that most of the station's employees knew very little about television broadcasting. Ted and I worked together to attract a larger viewing audience by trying to hold families in the evening hours once their children had found us in the afternoon. We broadcast situation comedy (sitcom) reruns such as *The Andy Griffith Show* and *Gomer Pyle*. The king of them all was a comedy that ran on CBS for only three years. The 98 half-hour episodes of *Gilligan's Island* air again and again because of their popularity.

Since most syndicated sitcoms consisted of at least 150 or more episodes, a station could broadcast five episodes per week for seven months or more before repeating any episodes. Since *Gilligan's Island* repeated every three and one-half months, each episode would air three or four times per year. Therefore, as popular as the show was, it had to be put on the shelf periodically. We usually brought it out during the important rating periods of February/March, May, and November.

Ratings are measures of the size of audiences viewing individual programs. The higher the Nielsen and Arbitron ratings, the more television sets are tuned to a specific program—whether measured as a proportion of all television sets in use at a specific time or as the total number of sets tuned to the program. The higher the ratings, the larger the audience, and the larger the number of people viewing advertising. Advertisers pay more to air their ads on higher-rated programs. That's why, for example, the cost to air ads during the Super Bowl football game is so staggeringly high. The ratings "sweeps," occurring for several weeks three times per year, significantly affect the rates networks and stations can charge advertisers—usually 15-, 30-, and 60-second ads—over the next several months or broadcast "season." And since national advertisers typically buy advertising "blocks" many months in advance, a program's ratings determine whether the advertiser got good value. If so, the networks and stations may ask the advertisers to pay more. If not, the advertisers may ask for refunds (rare), lower fees in future (typical), or free or cut-rate advertising for a specific calendar period, time slot, or program to make up the difference (not uncommon). To be clear: The foremost purpose of broadcasting is to sell advertising time. Programs exist so that a commercial advertiser can attract the largest possible audience.

I had more flexibility scheduling local and news programs. There were no difficult promises to the FCC to keep. In the case of Channel 17 and other UHF television stations, the FCC was mostly concerned with preserving its existence. FCC officials were well aware of the financial problems UHF stations were having because of limited audiences. We were not expected to carry much in the way of news programs, with their expensive equipment and full-time staffs. Expensive programming was the last thing

Ted needed. He actually came to abhor television news because it cost so much. And since news was available on the local network affiliate stations, we did not offer regular news programs. However, in our license application to the FCC, we promised the FCC a minimal amount of news. This was "technically" satisfied by a comedy news program hosted by Bill Tush, who was a staff announcer.

In an era when we didn't mind trying *anything*, Bill was given the go-ahead, except we told him it had to air at 3:00 A.M. If it didn't work, who would be watching at that hour? You'd be surprised. The crazy antics of this "unknown reporter," with a paper bag over his head, and with the weather report seemingly given by a German shepherd chewing on a bone, earned a devoted cult audience.

In Hank Wittemore's book, *CNN: The Inside Story,* I am quoted by Reese Schonfeld, who was in charge of the development of CNN in the early 1980s, as having told him that Ted "would never do news." Reese apparently misunderstood me. I was referring to Ted's original television station, Channel 17, now WTBS-TV, not to a separate news channel with a 24-hour news concept. As it turned out, I was right. WTBS-TV still does not broadcast news. Its format is entertainment and sports, with occasional documentaries, just as it was in the 1970s and 1980s.

Besides convincing Gene Wright, the chief engineer at Channel 11, to join Channel 17, I also persuaded the organization that consistently had the highest local program ratings to come over. I had worked closely with the World Championship Wrestling Association for some years, despite the strife it persistently had within its local and national organizations. I never got used to the fact that its wrestling events were staged. To most people, it must have been obvious that it was a show, not a sport. Apparently some viewers want to watch a form of violent acting. Playing to these primal needs, as far as the limits of the law, ethics, and good taste allow, often makes for the success of a feature film or television program.

It was my responsibility at Channel 17 to determine which films and programs we bought and how and when they were shown. The success we had had at WQXI-TV, Channel 11, was exceeded in my first year with Ted. We had a 250 percent increase in advertising revenue in 1972 over 1971.

We ran at least four films per day, and more on the weekends, which meant airing over 1,600 films per year. When we introduced 24-hour programming in the fall of 1973, this schedule required televising over 2,200 films annually. Choosing the films was exhausting, all-consuming work. I would lock myself in a hotel room to avoid any distractions in order to schedule three months of films at a time. We repeated some selections, but my choices for when we showed them had to match the potential audience at any period of the day. Once we became more successful, particularly after we obtained the sports teams, the program salesmen came to us, and I no longer had to fly out to Los Angeles and seek them out. I met with Ted two or three times a day to discuss film or program purchases, as well as the station operation.

Buying films and programs means building personal relationships. It is comparable to the fruit stand owner who throws an extra apple in the bag because you're a good customer and he likes you. The film salesmen knew what I had done at Channel 11 and that I had the smarts to do the same with Channel 17, despite its handicaps. They trusted me. In about a year, every company that sold films and programs, including the major film studios, wanted our business.

I was also on the lookout for potential revenue from sources other than advertising. I suggested mobile production, even though Ted felt that contracting the services was cheaper. In Boston I had used remote production vans, mainly for sports. Although Ted refused to allow me to purchase a remote truck, with all its TV equipment for sports and remote events, I convinced him to let me purchase a small truck with used equipment from a television station in Charlotte. I thought we could make money by renting it out. Ted hated the idea and went along with the purchase reluctantly, mostly to shut me up. We had been contracting with an individual who had purchased his own unit but tended to take big risks with scheduling his equipment. He was running it all over the southeast, from Florida to Texas. Finally, one day he didn't show up until the sixth inning of a baseball game in Houston that we wanted covered. I knew this would happen eventually. Clearly, we couldn't depend on him. Not providing coverage for the first six innings is an unforgivable error by a television broadcaster. You fail your audience and your advertisers and leave an impression of incompetence that takes a long time to overcome. It was a hard way for Ted to learn that we needed our own remote trucks. Just because others, including our contractor, were going broke didn't mean we would.

It was an area in which I had a lot of expertise from my baseball days in Boston, and a good example of Ted's stubbornness, even though he lacked the experience. Sometimes I couldn't talk him out of his ideas; thankfully, not often. By then, Ted had enough respect for my opinion; and he never closed the door on me as he did to others.

Now we had not only the mobile equipment to do our own sports programming, but we could also lease the truck and its equipment, sometimes with personnel (even a producer and director) to the networks. I remember spending a weekend in Amelia Island, Florida, producing a women's tennis match live for NBC. It wasn't long before I realized that there was more business than we could handle with the one van we had.

I heard through the film salesmen's grapevine that a television station in Tampa, Florida, had built a special semi-trailer truck at a cost of $130,000. Before installing the equipment, a new manager took over who, like Ted, didn't understand that this was a source of revenue. The new manager announced, "We're in the television broadcast business, not the television trucks business. Get rid of it." I convinced Ted to let me buy the truck. A second unit would greatly increase our leasing income potential with the networks, which had become convinced of our reliability and were willing to spend large sums of money for quality equipment and production dependability. I got a driver and a check for $50,000 and flew to Tampa. We drove the semi-trailer truck back to Atlanta and left it overnight inside a small warehouse I leased.

I was very proud of the deal I had made and the revenue I knew it would produce. I couldn't wait to show it to Ted. I convinced him to drive with me the next day to the warehouse to see it. The technical crew knew we were coming, so they weren't lounging around. I knew they liked the purchase and the opportunity it represented. The crew eagerly awaited Ted's approval and compliments on what a good buy this was for Turner Broadcasting.

Unfortunately, Ted flew into a rage. He shouted at me, "You didn't tell me it was so big!" And he began throwing things against the wall. "What are we going to do with it?"

I answered calmly, "CBS has to bring a unit from Dallas to do the Falcons' games. All the networks need a large truck in the southeast region."

"The networks?!" he yelled. "You know how I feel about them! I don't want to let them use it! Let them bring their own damn trucks in! We'll never find a use for anything this size!" Then he sniffed the air for a moment, and insisted he smelled "pot." Ted raged about this for a few more minutes.

Needless to say, the crew was glad to see us leave, and I was extremely hurt. I knew I had done the wise thing and that good results would come of it. In fact, the remote unit became so successful that more units of the same size were purchased later and were then available for the additional sports enterprises that evolved at TBS.

This kind of battering was not unusual from Ted. Tirades occurred frequently. Working with Ted was not always pleasant. I learned simply to weather the storm, particularly when I knew I was right. There were times when I knew Ted was wrong. I simply tried to find ways to argue him out of his decision. To his credit, he allowed me to argue my positions, and he often changed his mind. Ted's anger was usually brief, and, fortunately, he did not hold grudges. Forty-nine out of 50 times, Ted listened. He might say, "Yeah, but I own the candy store. So let's do it my way," with a shrug and a smile. But look out for that fiftieth time! Once the black cloud of Ted's thunderstorm had passed, the sunshine returned. Incurring Ted's rage was always a risk one had to take, but it was difficult adjusting to it and not bringing it home. It was hard for Lill and the three children when I was distracted and grouchy.

Once I took a job, I tried everything possible to help the company be successful. I expected my loyalty to be returned, not only through my continued employment, but also through future financial security. I had, by 1972, learned to buy stock, and Ted had the company lend me some money, in addition to what I could borrow from a bank, so that I purchased enough shares early on and could watch them multiply and split, and split again, over the 25 years of Turner Broadcasting's growth.

These days, I see young people just out of college who believe their job is temporary. They are looking for upward mobility in the same industry, but not necessarily with the same company. Quite often, I reviewed résumés with "the two-year syndrome": two years with this company, two years with that company. I never hired those people; even if they had skill and talent, their lack of loyalty and commitment overrode everything.

In 1969, the year before Ted acquired Channel 17, the gross income had been $860,281. In 1970, Ted's first year, the gross dropped to $720,170. In Ted's second year he grossed slightly over a million dollars. (I came on board in October.) Then the annual figures started to climb rapidly.

1972: $2,792,821
1973: $5,883,136
1974: $7,076,778
1975: $8,150,324

By 1976, there was no looking back as we headed toward the world that satellite broadcasting would open. The sales figures weren't the only thing heading upwards. Ted Turner was sailing a new sea, into space, as we pioneered the satellite age.

CHAPTER SEVEN

Global Television Equals Endless Horizons

All mankind is divided into three classes: those that are immovable, those that are movable, and those that move.
—Ben Franklin

After Ted's acquisition of the Braves and a majority interest in the Hawks in 1976, Channel 17 flourished. Its audience and its revenue grew steadily. Our weak signal was something we accepted. Ted wanted to be *accepted* as a television broadcaster. But Ted, handicapped by his station's weak signal, his outspokenness, and his outlandish behavior was ostracized by the staid broadcasting fraternity. In his eagerness, the ABC network used him in 1973. It offered Ted the possibility of an affiliation with ABC by setting up a competition between Ted's WRET-TV and the ABC affiliate, WCCB-TV, in Charlotte, North Carolina. Since there were only two VHF licenses in Charlotte, it was possible for a UHF station to carry the third network when VHF stations were unavailable. I believe that ABC never intended for Ted to get the network affiliation, but it used his presentation, which we had carefully prepared, as a means of shaping up WCCB-TV. Not only was the effort an expensive waste of time for us, but it also fueled Ted's dislike of the networks.

By the mid-1970s, a new force in the industry presented itself at the FCC's door in Washington. The cable systems, even where local television stations provided a clear signal, wanted their viewers to be able to choose from a variety of new channels in order to justify the fees their customers paid. This was heresy to most broadcasters, who by then had enjoyed a lock on television rights throughout the country for a quarter of a century. They had fought for years to keep the cable alternative from expanding, but like the motion picture industry before them, they were going to have to concede that they were fighting a losing battle.

To enhance the attractiveness of cable, the FCC decided in 1976 to allow viewers to watch local independent television stations broadcasting from outside the viewers' markets. This was an extraordinary change, which traditional broadcasters like myself ignored. Ted noticed.

Stated differently, the new FCC rule permitted, by any technical means, a local independent station to broadcast on cable television systems in any part of the United States that it was able to reach. This was the first major step in the explosive growth of cable television. The question: By what technical means could WTCG-TV be seen outside of Atlanta? In 1976, the only technical system available to carry a signal any distance was microwave. A small dish sent a signal to a distant dish in the direct, unobstructed "line of sight," and so on as far as unobstructed signals could travel.

By this means we broadcast our signal throughout the southeastern United States in 1976. To the south, we went as far as northern Florida, and to the west, as far as Mississippi. To the north, the signal reached Tennessee and North Carolina. We used a combination of the microwave system and the local cable system's reach in order to bring our 24-hour signal into each cable territory.

Ted, who avidly read all the trade magazines, learned in late 1975 that Home Box Office (HBO) had started to supply its movies by satellite to cable systems that installed antennas to receive the signal.

In January 1976, Ted called the staff into the conference room and showed us a strange-looking mechanical toy that he called a satellite. He said it would beam our signal to cable systems all over the United States. It looked like parts from a junkyard had been put together to create a modern art piece. I had no idea how this floating "debris" in space would affect my work and my future. Ted's discovery couldn't have been better timed. We had assumed that we could only extend the WTCG-TV signal to densely populated areas and that it necessarily ended wherever there was a long distance between these areas. One easily put a dish atop of office buildings and houses, but rural areas would require us to build towers and buy rights of way.

Later, when the networks and other independent stations tried to make inroads into cable programming, Ted promoted his station by putting himself, dressed in his country denims on billboards and in cable magazines: "I was cable when cable wasn't cool." He gave cable systems that picked us up advance promotional materials, such as co-op advertising, billboard and truck posters, ad proofs, four-color sports schedules, and weekly program schedules.

Theoretically, an independent television signal such as WTCG's could be uplinked to a U.S. satellite and distributed to U.S. cable systems by a separate company, not affiliated with any television station. Ted didn't sit around and wait for a distribution system to choose us. He found out that an Atlanta company, Scientific Atlanta, was actively involved in building "send and receive" antennas. He phoned Sid Topel, its president, who sent a group of executives and engineers to meet with Ted. They developed a report to justify the $500,000 cost of this equipment.

Ted didn't want to wait for the study. He wanted to have the first SuperStation—that is, any commercial, independent (non-network) television signal licensed by the FCC and re-transmitted by satellite. He bought the antenna as easily as one might buy a box of cereal in a supermarket. On December 17, 1976, most of the managers and sales personnel of our station drove out to Vinings, a suburb of Atlanta. We came to a wooded area without an access road that had been cleared of trees. Here Scientific Atlanta had constructed a 10-meter (33-foot) antenna. It was my first view of a satellite uplink dish. It seemed so out of place in this beautiful, wooded, as yet undeveloped, green space.

A satellite sketch: It is in geosynchronous orbit 22,300 miles above the earth. Once it is positioned, it remains fixed, relative to the earth's rotation. In 2003 there were upwards of 350 geosynchronous high orbit satellites around the earth, in addition to military and experimental satellites. There is, however, a limit on the number that can be in orbit, because if they are not adequately separated, there is potential signal interference. As time progresses the technical problems will be overcome and multitudes of satellites will cover the earth. However, each country has to arrange a satellite's positioning in advance by a global agreement.

A transponder on the satellite receives a video and audio signal from a ground antenna (dish) that is large enough and powerful enough to send the signal to the satellite. It then returns the signal (reflects it) to hundreds, even thousands, of smaller earth antennas located at television stations, cable systems, hotels, homes, and so on, within that satellite's range (footprint). The size of the receiving antenna is related to the power of the satellite. Today, satellite signals are so powerful that a one-foot antenna placed near a window is able to receive a signal. But in late 1976, large ground dishes were needed to receive signals from the early satellites.

* * * * *

The red Georgia clay had been cleared and graveled over, and a few yards from this glaringly white, huge uplink dish was a small mobile equipment trailer. Ted climbed the few steps and entered the trailer. I was behind him, but could not fit inside, so I stood half in and half out, with my one foot on the steps. I watched as the clock's red second hand circled and pointed to the designated time of 1:00 P.M. At that moment, Ted's finger pressed a button that put WTCG-TV Channel 17 on the air via RCA Satcom II satellite and into television broadcast history. Although we began transmitting by satellite to only four cable systems—in Grand Island, Nebraska; Newport News, Virginia; Troy, Alabama; and Newton, Kansas—we eventually transformed communication, education, religious and civil life, and eventually the whole world. It didn't occur to us then but we had fueled the base for global unrest.

While the dust from this explosive innovation has not yet settled, and global battles are now being fought to stop world terrorism, I believe the ultimate result will be a better educated world population with instant access to all forms of information, organizations, and individuals that can help confront and solve diverse problems. When I began to receive mail from various U.S. cities with the usual questions or complaints, I was not surprised. But when a letter arrived from the Yukon Territory of northern Canada, requesting certain favorite films, I was shocked at just how far our satellite signal traveled. Then letters arrived from Central America and the Caribbean Islands, and I knew that I was participating in one of the most dramatic changes in human history. What this meant to global communications had not yet occurred to me. We had been struggling to reach the outskirts of Atlanta with our 1042-foot metal tower, and now our "tower" was, so to speak, broadcasting from 22,300 miles above the earth. Unbelievable.

I, too, felt transformed—from an ordinary television broadcaster to a pioneer in global television—and no one at that time, including Ted Turner, could measure its future significance. As important as television was in its first quarter century, including its influence on events such as the ending of the Vietnam War, television's effect dramatically increased because of the satellite, which has to be one of mankind's most significant inventions.

Ted created a new company, Southern Satellite Systems, which provided the WTCG-TV signal to the satellite.

Casting a cloud on our euphoria, Ted's attorneys advised him that he could not legally own both a television broadcast service and the means of transmitting the signal to a satellite. Ted and I met with Ed Taylor, Western Union Vice President for Westar Marketing and Development. Taylor wanted to experiment with the new satellite technology and form his own company. Ted then sold the satellite uplink company to Ed Taylor for one dollar, thus fulfilling the legal requirement of separating the two companies.

Ed Taylor's Southern Satellite Systems collected 10 cents per home per month for supplying WTCG-TV to the cable systems. He later provided Ted's WTBS SuperStation programming as an all-night service for those cable companies that wanted 24-hour programming.

By 1983, Taylor's share of Southern Satellite Systems was worth $49.5 million, of which he received $15 million in cash when the company went public that year. Ed Taylor eventually merged the satellite uplink company with Tele-Communications Inc. (TCI) for $50 million (mostly in stock).

Soon after WTCG-TV became a SuperStation—by the way, Ted invented the name "SuperStation"—its popularity among the growing cable systems was apparent, and we expected competition. The success of Ted's SuperStation led another satellite distribution company in 1981 to select WGN, an independent *Chicago Tribune* station as its SuperStation. (Due to legal, technological, and definitional developments, only five other "Super-

Stations," as defined by the FCC, exist: KTLA in Los Angeles, California; KWGN in Denver, Colorado; WPIX and WWOR in New York City; and WSBK in Boston, Massachusetts.) No one, however, grasped the opportunity, as Ted did, to promote SuperStations as a new form of U.S. television network able to deliver programs to American viewers. No local or network television executive cooperated with the cable industry like Ted did. His competitors still considered themselves traditional broadcasters, but Ted had no loyalty to the organizations and individuals that had shunned him.

WTCG's programming in 1977 was based on the proven success of sports and movies. It offered the second largest group of sports packages of any television station in the United States, with major league baseball, NBA basketball, and, for awhile, NHL hockey. It ran as many as 40 movies each week from a library of over 3,000 films, as well as many "non-controversial" sitcom reruns. It de-emphasized sex and violence and operated 24 hours a day.

However, we faced two new and vexing problems. What good did it do to increase our audience outside Atlanta if our advertisers refused to compensate us for the additional numbers of viewers? As if by collective agreement, the advertising agencies refused to acknowledge WTCG-TV's expansion. They wanted to consider the increased viewers as a bonus to their purchase of Atlanta-area advertising. We were caught in the middle between the advertisers and the program suppliers, who refused to sell us programs without compensation for our increased audience. The advertising community had not yet caught onto the new concept, or they chose to ignore the fact that we were pioneering in unmapped terrain. They took advantage of us at a time when we were vulnerable.

Our film and program suppliers were outraged, predictably, because the standard industry contracts expressly forbade WTCG-TV to use such programming anywhere but in the market where the station was located. We were not, however, responsible for the signal being taken out of Atlanta, because we did not actively participate in its wider distribution. The cable systems chose to carry us. We knew that eventually we could more than double our audience size, so we didn't just stay on the sidelines and wait for them to choose us. We actively promoted our programming, attended cable meetings, and sent sales personnel to cable markets throughout the United States.

Our programming costs exploded, but Ted expected it, and even though the advertisers refused to pay for the audience outside of Atlanta, Ted understood the future potential.

Gradually, as the cable systems' audiences grew, in part because of broadcasting SuperStations' programs, advertisers began to pay for the added exposure. What had first looked to the television industry as an "exploitation" of their program signals by the emerging satellite distribution companies became more enjoyable for these stations when the results of the increased audience meant that they could ask for more advertising money.

In 1979, Ted decided to change the Channel 17 call letters from WTCG (Turner Communications Group) to WTBS (Turner Broadcasting System). We tried to convince him not to make this change because we had promoted WTCG-TV for eight years, and the name was now familiar to our audience. However, Ted was ahead of us in realizing that WTCG was unknown outside of Atlanta. To him, TBS sounded more like CBS and suggested the network status he still longed for.

Channel 17 had operated in the red only the first year before I arrived. In 1975, the Charlotte station was also breaking even, and in that same year, the billboard advertising company that had helped provide cash was spun off from Turner Communications, making Ted's long-time friend and associate, Peter Dames, its manager, a millionaire. Peter and Ted met at Brown University when they were students. The billboard company's annual revenue of $6.5 million would eventually become small change to Turner, and selling it made sense. Yet he had learned a great deal from the "street fighting" mentality that rival billboard companies exhibit when competing for prime locations. For example, Ted never hesitated to put a billboard directly in front of a competing company's sign. It was this kind of brashness that he later showed when competing with a formidable foe, such as Rupert Murdoch. He stretched the unwritten rules of conduct in business to their breaking point.

I admired Ted's fighting spirit, and I believe he saw in me a similar spirit, which I exhibited in handling the tough assignments he gave me. I never saw Ted become physically violent, except when we purchased the large mobile truck. But Ted's voice was always booming—he sounded like a foghorn—he couldn't whisper.

After his marriage to Jane Fonda in December 1991, Ted took medication for his manic depression. However, I never saw him depressed, and he always had the will and strength to achieve our goals. In my view, he had two personalities. One was an acting-up child, resisting social restraints and testing accepted rules of behavior. In the early years, he was desperately trying to be "one of the guys" and was thrown out of Brown University for a series of pranks.

The second was a serious, somber, extremely intelligent man who knew the right questions to ask, often the one I had overlooked. Ted exercises his mind like athletes exercise their muscles. He loves to read and often discusses the books he is reading, sometimes in the middle of a meeting. The main attitude we shared was that we believed in loyalty between a worker and his boss. It rarely exists in business today because loyalty cannot be one-sided. A creative worker's results are a reflection, not just of how much he is paid, but also of the comfort and trust in the atmosphere of the company, which becomes, in a limited sense, a second family.

Ted's company, Turner Communications Group, began to buy back its own stock in 1976 and reduced its outstanding shares from the 1.65 million in 1970 to 980,000. Ted then owned 85 percent of the outstanding stock, which was valued at $12.4 million. The company had 240 other stockholders, including me. I, unfortunately, got caught in the buy-back offer of $7 for a $6 share. I quickly realized my mistake and bought back as much as I could, but I never recovered the amount of stock I originally owned. Ironically, I insisted that Will Sanders, the company controller, get an extension on the offer for me when I learned about it past its deadline. I wish he had been firmer when he told me that it was too late to sell my stock.

CHAPTER EIGHT

SuperStation Growing Pains

It is more important to know where you are going than to get there quickly. Do not mistake activity for achievement.
—Mabel Newcomer

In September 1977 I sent Ted a memo advising him that I had not had a contact for months from a major distributor of films and programs. I was buying programming from small distributors only. The big distributors concluded that deals with us would reduce the value of their programs when our broadcast signal arrived in markets where another television station had already bought broadcasting rights to the same film or series. The film and program salespeople, and their managers, were unfamiliar with the copyright laws governing cable television. I had to educate them. In particular, I had to inform them that the Copyright Tribunal of the U.S. Copyright Office pays use fees to the owners of programs each time the programs are broadcast. That is, to shun TBS is to restrict their own profits. To do business with TBS is to earn use fees of pennies per month from each cable-receiving home. Large sums of money are at issue.

A lot of small film companies and producers had been banging on our door ever since the SuperStation went on the air. Desperate for revenue, they took the time to learn about the Copyright Tribunal and were willing to listen to me about the new age of television.

Such are growing pains. I was explaining to distributors that distributing their programs would earn them money!

At first the distribution firms refused to believe me. Copyright law is formidable and dense, I guess. They had already made up their minds that the SuperStation was a poor choice for a business partner. My argument was simple: Cable television broadcasts are simply another lucrative outlet for their products. Television, and now cable television, expands, not reduces, the market for films.

Eventually, I convinced one or two major distributors that the combination of the increased price WTBS was paying for its larger audience, added to the growing Copyright Tribunal payments, made their sales to the SuperStation good business. In 1980, the Tribunal paid $1,000 per hour, and, by 1989, we projected $8,750 per hour for programs and films that we aired. This meant a syndicated series of 100 episodes, if run as much as seven times, would get an additional half-million dollars in revenue in 1980 and over $4.5 million by the end of the decade. This added income, in addition to the inflated price we were willing to pay, eventually tilted the situation in our favor. Once a few major companies started to sell to us, the others did not want to lose out.

However, several film studios, like United Artists (UA) and Warner Brothers, were still dragging their feet. UA's regional salesman and I had developed a 490-film package for $2,450,000; unfortunately UA couldn't make up its mind.

I never convinced Warner Brothers to sell products to the SuperStation. The head of syndication, Charlie McGregor, refused to change the traditional practice of selling only to local television stations. Their syndication sales were strong enough that it could choose to ignore us. Ironically, Time-Warner would eventually swallow TBS because of the SuperStation's success. McGregor was typical of TimeWarner executives that I met as their association with TBS grew; they had limited imagination and a propensity to "coast" on the surface of a successful name.

By 1977, the number of homes with cable television in the United States had grown to 13 million, or 18 percent of U.S. households. Advertisers were beginning to take notice, although by mid-1977, on 465 cable systems,

WTBS had fewer than one million subscribers. Yet 207 more cable systems, representing 307,000 subscribers, had applied to carry the SuperStation.

The traditional television broadcasters, who fiercely objected to our purchase of the same films and programs they aired, succeeded in convincing the FCC to order a "blackout" regulation in the top 50 markets. This meant that if any SuperStation program had already been purchased by a station in a given market, then the local cable service had to "blackout" (not televise) the program. In addition to these exclusivity restrictions, local stations were trying to add 300 of the best films to their protected library.

Also in 1977, the movie industry asked the government to restrict television stations' use of satellites to relay programs to distant cable systems. The government virtually ignored the movie industry's uncompetitive pleas because the SuperStation was fueling the growth of cable.

An editorial in the October 1977 issue of *CATV* magazine (Community Antenna TV Association) noted:

> In Alexandria, Louisiana, the CATV system reported it added 4,000 subscribers (from 13,000 to 17,000) with a sales push that ran parallel to the addition of WTBS. In Jonesboro, Arkansas, one single promotion tied around the WTBS carriage of the Atlanta Braves netted 6 percent new subscribers in a couple of weeks. The excellent backup support fielded by WTBS's cable relations staff is not an insignificant factor in the equation.

The U.S. government, eager to find ways for cable to grow so that even remote parts of America would have access to the many channels of the major urban areas, was, in effect saying to the movie industry, "Prove to us you will be harmed by SuperStations." The industry couldn't do it.

The FCC began studying cable's impact on local television broadcasters as early as 1959. It tinkered with program-exclusivity rules in the 1960s and early 1970s. The 1972 syndicated exclusivity rules can be traced to the 1965 decision to prohibit microwave-fed cable systems from duplicating local-station programming on distant signals, either simultaneously or within 15 days before or after their local broadcast. This program exclusivity was amended in 1966 to "same day protection." In 1976 the FCC finally eliminated its "anti-leapfrogging" rules, which required cable systems importing signals to obtain those signals without bypassing less popular and closer "distant signals." The exclusivity rules continued to be a problem for the SuperStation and spurred Ted to acquire programming any way he could that would not have to be blacked out by local cable systems.

In 1977, the chairman of the U.S. House of Representatives' Communications Subcommittee, Lionel Van Deerlin (D-California), wrote about these issues to Vincent Wasilewski, President of the National Association of Broadcasters (NAB). The NAB is a trade association which sought to function as a broadcasting self-regulatory agency, but, since the advent of cable television, now represents the interests of free, over-the-air radio and television broadcasters. Van Deerlin declared that the document the NAB wrote as a statement of principles for television broadcasters was an attempt to "Keep the gold in Fort Knox. It reads like the report of a committee co-chaired by King Midas and Marie Antoinette." Van Deerlin had the bit in his teeth when he went on to say:

> I have tried to focus on some of the changes which lie ahead for broadcasters, and for communications generally—changes likely to occur quite apart from your ability, and mine, to agree on anything.
>
> It was not Lionel Van Deerlin, but [President] Jerry Ford's Office of Communications Policy which saw the possibility of broadcast services without over-the-air signals by the year 1990.
>
> It is not Van Deerlin, but the courts which have struck down regulatory restrictions on cable (restrictions that the NAB's Statement of Principles would restore as Holy Writ).
>
> It is Ted Turner [of WTCG (TV) Atlanta] whose blend of cable with satellite technology has spread consternation in the smaller TV markets.
>
> It is Paramount Pictures which talks of delivering new offerings direct to broadcast and cable outlets by satellite.
>
> It is the Japanese who will shortly test delivery of satellite signals direct to home receivers via rooftop antennas.
>
> It is the telephone company and its competitors whose sophisticated home terminals could greatly broaden the daily

offering of news and entertainment in the American home. And it is the Texas Instruments Co., whose new television tuner promises absolute parity for UHF stations with VHF—a development which alone could change the economics of television as much as anything in the last two decades.

Finally, not even Chip Shooshan had a hand in the Nielsen rating system's discovery that about one million Americans turned off their TV sets altogether in 1977.

Try to picture this when you're watching the Super Bowl, Vince... A million people would fill the Superdome nearly 14 times over.

That candle still burns brightly.

Sincerely,

Lionel Van Deerlin, Chairman

In its first year, 1971, WTCG-TV's audience more than doubled and was growing by 100,000 homes per month. WTCG's advertising people opened offices in New York and Chicago and offered national rates 30 percent lower than the networks' rates in terms of cost per thousand viewers. The WTCG sales staff, with their pitch about how the industry was changing, fanned out to reach the top 100 advertisers, even though at that time we had only half a dozen national advertisers signed up at the new rates. These included Mobil Oil, Nestlé, and Miller-Morton (makers of Chapstick). Many national companies held back until WTCG reached the number of homes that they felt warranted national advertising attention. We reached 4.5 million homes by the end of 1978, and Ted was spending $500,000 a year to help CATV operators promote our SuperStation.

We had also outgrown our location—our West Peachtree facility with its mini-studio was much too small. Ted asked me to find a new facility. I narrowed my choices to two. One was in Buckhead, an area where wealthy Atlantans had homes near fine restaurants, upscale businesses, and popular nightclubs. Five acres came with the old Brookwood Hotel, but it would be necessary to tear down the building. Also, a railroad line ran alongside the small property. I had visions of a freight train lumbering by as we aired or taped a live program. However, the one-million-dollar price tag was attractive.

The second choice, for four million dollars, was 21 acres at the Progressive Club, located near 10th Street and the campus of the Georgia Institute of Technology (Georgia Tech). Members of the Jewish community in Atlanta built the club, primarily because they were excluded from membership in other private clubs. The building included a large ballroom offering excellent possibilities for studios. The opportunity for growth on the 21 acres, in my opinion, made the extra $3 million outlay worth it. And there were no railroads.

Ted called a meeting in his tiny office over the garage, and all the department heads were present. After I presented the two options, there wasn't much discussion—everyone knew it was Ted's decision. Ted, apparently influenced by the cost, chose the Brookwood location and ended the meeting.

I knew that Techwood was far superior. Frankly, I was shocked that Ted had chosen Brookwood. I was sure he would see the difference in potential growth between the two locations. I had to think fast. After the managers left the room, I stayed behind. I had to change Ted's mind.

Not knowing how he would react (no one did), I said, "Ted, if you take Techwood, we will be able to run our camera cable across 10th Street into the Georgia Tech auditorium, which is located directly across from the Progressive Club, and we can cover any sports event without using a remote television truck."

There was silence in the room. Ted was thinking. Then he said, loudly as usual, "Yeah, Pike. That's a good idea. Let's go to the Progressive Club."

Now, 22 years later, those 21 acres and the building itself, which became the original CNN studios, and eventually the Turner Entertainment Group offices, was without a doubt the best choice. Since 1978 the facilities have been expanded, and 16 more acres have been added, for a total of 37 acres in the heart of Atlanta. It is the center for more than 20 uplinking and downlinking antennas, needed in the 1990s, for the many TBS television channels. Later, when TimeWarner bought the company, it expanded the property on the site even more. It is now the TBS Broadcast Center.

I knew we would not run camera cables across 10th Street to Georgia Tech. We rarely covered an event at the sports auditorium, and when we did, driving a remote truck across the street was still the easiest and best method. By then, I knew how Ted thought.

* * * * *

In early 1979, I appeared at a national programming meeting in Las Vegas. *The Hollywood Reporter* covered it in a front page article, headlined "Pike Defends Superstations Before Hostile TV Executives."

> A panel discussion on superstations drew some angry barbs from an emotionally charged audience estimated at well over 1,000 at NATPE [National Association of Television Program Executives] here as WTCG-TV and FCC licensed common carrier United Video executives presented a defense of the concept while production personnel and broadcasters came out swinging against the superstations. Howls of laughter and booing drowned out WTCG vp Sid Pike's defense of the Atlanta superstation...
>
> WGN, Chicago vp general manager Jack Jacobson (in the audience) revealed that on March 13, the National Collegiate Athletic Assn. revoked its permission to allow WGN to telecast an NCAA-sanctioned Marquette-DePaul University basketball game specifically because of cable TV carriage of WGN's signal in other markets. The NCAA subsequently allowed one of WGN's Chicago competitors to telecast the game, which angered Jacobson and which allegedly threatened WGN's local service...

Further on, the article pointed out:

> Columbia TV Distribution president Norman Horowitz scoffed at the notion that WTCG would pay licensing fees for programming proportional to its nationwide coverage, because WTCG is in a 'semimonopolistic position... They will pay us what they please'
>
> Horowitz opined that superstations would seriously distort existing marketplace patterns. Horowitz attacked [the] assertion that United Video is, as a common carrier, essentially no different from AT&T. Outlining a chaotic future for syndicators' long-term contracts, Horowitz foresees that 'We cannot control our own destinies due to [the uncertainty] of which stations will become superstations.'

And finally:

> NAB (National Association of Broadcasters) President Vincent Wasilewski received applause when he placed blame for the superstation problem squarely on the federal government.
>
> 'Unfair competition created by government meddling in the marketplace,' [as] he termed it, 'is dismantling the structure of the broadcast industry.'

Earlier that year, Sheldon Cooper, Vice President of WGN in Chicago, was quoted in a *Wall Street Journal* article: "We're sitting up here wondering what the hell's going to happen, because we don't know."

The answer, Mr. Cooper, was obvious, even then. You were going to make a lot of money even with WGN's and television broadcasting's resistance to change. Indeed, I received a copy of a one-page questionnaire to cable systems, sent to me by a film salesman who understood the issues, which asked for information so that they could serve the cable stations better and more efficiently. It came from WGN's Public Relations/CATV Department.

* * * * *

By late 1979, Ted realized that he needed help to build the SuperStation into a network with original programming in order to overcome the blackout rules that were decimating our audience and potential advertising growth. He learned that Bob Wussler, the former President of CBS, was available for work. Bob started in the mailroom at CBS and rose in the network's hierarchy. Eventually, he became part of a team sent to resurrect a troubled CBS-owned-and-operated television station in Chicago. After that, Bill Paley, Chairman of CBS, saw Bob Wussler as a "comer," and he became CBS's fair-haired boy.

However, Bob had not been successful as CBS's president. In fact, the network took a downward spiral during his tenure. A CBS Sports fiasco finished him. A well-promoted "winner take all" tennis match had been set up in Las Vegas. Sports reporters from other media learned that it was being "produced," so that even the loser would be financially rewarded.

This use of a misleading title was heavily covered by sports writers, and this would affect the credibility of all CBS's programs, including the news.

After working with him over the years, I believe that Bob's creative and administrative skills are very limited. Just after Bob arrived in January 1980, I happened to be in his office and noticed a copy on his desk of the recently published *Broadcasting Programming—Strategies for Winning Television and Radio Audiences* by Eastman, Head, and Klein. It contained a chapter by me entitled "Superstation Strategy." Bob was a bit embarrassed when he saw me looking at it. He said, "A friend of mine sent it to me when he learned I was going to work here."

I, and others in the company, may have felt that Bob was not the right person to be Station Manager at WTBS, the job I held until he came. Yet he brought with him one very important thing that Ted desperately needed and I couldn't give him: *contacts*. Wussler, because of his CBS experience, knew the key players, particularly in the New York networks and the Los Angeles film studios, and he gave Ted the introductions he needed to build Turner Broadcasting System into a major national television company. Bob could have been the key executive at TBS, second only to Ted, but he lacked reliability, particularly when drinking with his fellow business executives. These details reached the press. For example, in an Atlanta bar, Wussler punched out Bill Bevins, the TBS Chief Financial Officer. A few years later, he did the same thing to an executive of the Organization Committee for the city of Seattle, which had agreed to host the Goodwill Games, Ted's joint venture with the U.S.S.R. and its Russian Sports Federation. Bob Wussler resigned in 1989 and became head of Program Development for Comsat, the private commercial company that was the U.S. representative (or PTT, meaning Postal, Telephone, and Telegraph agency) of the Intelsat international consortium, the worldwide agency governing satellite use. Wussler did that for a few years. Then there were rumors of his returning to TBS, followed by rumors of a "palace revolt" if Ted took him back.

Ted made it clear that I reported to Wussler. To convince me that I need not be concerned about my position at TBS, Ted offered me a five-year contract. As with our other contracts, I wrote it out in longhand on one page. Despite my solidified position, I learned that Wussler was determined to get rid of me.

I have often found that new players have a tendency to want to cut the throats of the team players who preceded them. I have never understood this and always refused to act that way. It seems to me that the new manager's job is to demonstrate confidence and trust in the employees already in place.

Wussler would not be the last person who would try to depose me, only to learn that the roots of my relationship with Ted went pretty deep. I had made too many contributions to the company that paid off too well for Ted to toss me aside. I tried to work with Wussler, in spite of his unwillingness to return my phone calls. I believe he was trying to freeze me out. I finally went to Ted and said, "Wussler doesn't return phone calls." I never had a problem after that. Wussler was very unlike Ted. He wasn't interested in new ideas, only in those that were in place and accepted.

Ted was delighted when Jacques Cousteau, the famous French oceanographer and scientist, who had developed programs for network television of his undersea explorations, found his way to TBS, having more or less run his course on the networks. Cousteau wanted Ted to back his production of some new programs. Ted was so eager to make a deal with Cousteau that he paid much more than necessary.

Later, Ted paid way too much for a series of Cousteau's old network programs. I sent Bob Wussler and Dee Woods, Ted's secretary, a memo to this effect.

> We just purchased Jacques Cousteau's 36 program series from Jim Ricks, Sr., of Metromedia at $15,000 per episode ($540,000). Metromedia has been trying to sell that series for the last 5-6 years in Atlanta and could not give it away. They would have taken $2,500-$5,000, depending on the size of the station. Our price would probably be in the $5,000-7,000 range, depending upon negotiation.
>
> The reason I am saying all this is so that the three of us are aware of the 'end runners'—salesmen, producers, and just operators who know if they can get around the appropriate person or department head, whoever that might be, and get to Ted, it will be a touchdown. Their techniques are very subtle: 'I just wanted to say "hello" to Ted while I am in town.' I suggest we keep a private list of 'end runners'—Jim Ricks, Sr., can start it. Jim

lied to me. We were in the process of negotiating on *That Girl*'s extension and commercial cover for $75,000, and I had asked him (at Bob's request) to give me a price on Cousteau. He said he would get back to me. As far as I am concerned, Jim owes the station $300,000.

By late 1980, one film company asked the SuperStation to pay $30,000 per episode, which was the average price that a New York television station paid. Yet it was quite high for us, since advertising was still adjusting to the concept of a new audience delivery system. We were paying less than $15,000 for all our other programs. We bought original programming and created our own in order to overcome the effects of imposed blackouts. However, what we came up with was still small potatoes compared to the network fare that the public expected by 1980.

* * * * *

Generally, until the 1990s, it was cable systems somewhere in the satellite footprint that redistributed SuperStation TBS by cable directly to the home. Although cable systems started decades earlier and grew slowly, by the mid-1990s they competed with companies offering their programs directly from satellites to homes sprouting satellite antennas and dishes.

The FCC sought to satisfy television viewers in small communities by providing multiple signals, but not to hurt larger local stations that were now showing the same programs. This policy caused a great deal of ambivalence at the FCC, and it drove its decisions first one way and then the other.

The last decision, made in 1988 by the FCC, restored syndicated exclusivity protection to local television stations and remains in effect as of this writing. For instance, if a local television station had bought and was running *The Andy Griffith Show* reruns, then the cable service was prohibited from also running it. If WTBS were broadcasting *Andy Griffith*, then the local cable service would have to import another channel for that time period or program it itself. This is the "blackout" rule and its effect. This is what forced Turner to purchase or produce exclusive programming so that there would not be any blacked-out holes in any market in the United

States reached by WTBS's signal. In order to achieve program exclusivity, Turner paid exorbitant prices that eventually ran into many millions of dollars for movies and programs.

It made sense that Ted own his own films and programs, just as he had decided to buy the Atlanta Braves baseball team in order not to have to continue to pay rights fees. So, in 1985, he purchased the MGM film library and studios and, prior to that, created a film production company called TurnerFilms. He went on to purchase other film production companies, such as Castle Rock and New Line Cinema, in 1993.

In just 15 years, Ted Turner went from riding an ostrich before baseball games to riding a financial roller coaster seated beside the MGM lion.

CHAPTER NINE

CNN Is Born

A man has to choose the battles he will fight, and he has to weigh the consequences of his actions against the importance of the issue.

—Allen Glatthorn

In search of original programming, Ted, because he didn't know much about traditional broadcasting, came up with the 24-hour news concept. Traditional broadcasters like me were steeped in a format that had existed since the beginning of commercial television in 1948. However, Ted was trying to speed up the acceptance of cable, particularly in urban areas where there were good broadcast signals, but people were reluctant to pay for new channels. *Everyone thought 24 hours of news was ridiculous.* Who would want to watch that much news? Well, no one had to *watch* 24 hours. They could watch as much as they wanted and when they wanted. Thus was born the news program that will never end.

CNN—the Cable News Network—officially began on June 1, 1980.

Slowly, the television audience began to realize that news was interesting, regardless of the time of day. There was also the visual appeal, more attractive than radio news, which was broadcast throughout the day. Our concern: Would there be enough news, and how often should it be repeated over a 24-hour period? We solved this not only through a system of domestic and global news bureaus, but also by collecting news from agencies, and later, by cooperating with television stations worldwide. This latter solution was my contribution.

The popularity of CNN grew despite the television network news services' contempt for the youthful, underpaid journalists, fresh from journalism schools, who joined CNN and got their crash "graduate courses" from news veterans like Ted Kavanau, Sam Zelman, and Bill MacPhail, each formerly with CBS. They helped Reese Schonfeld, hired by Ted as president of CNN, design and build the 24-hour network.

CNN had to fight for its position alongside the three major networks. At first, CNN was left out of White House briefings, and Ted had to threaten legal action in order for CNN to participate. It wasn't long before some of the non-affiliated television stations became interested in tapping into CNN in order to augment their news outside of their local markets. I helped develop their interest, but we did nothing to take advantage of this potential market then because CNN's emphasis was on being a premier cable channel. In fact, CNN was causing basic cable service to expand rapidly throughout the United States.

In 1981, ABC/Westinghouse announced plans to build a competing 24-hour satellite news channel. Ted, in a speech at a cable operators meeting in Boston, told the audience, "Your battles are my battles." This was a reference to the networks' attempts to prevent the cable industry's growth and its ability to lobby Congress to change laws favorably. An article in the August 31, 1981, issue of *Broadcasting* magazine comments on Ted's speech:

> And if the ovation he received at the end of his Monday press conference is any indication, not only has 'Terrible Ted' won the hearts and minds of most of that industry, but he's not going to be abandoned wholesale by operators looking to pick up the joint-venture cable news network announced by Group W and ABC.

Ted, in his street-fighting mode, went further and proclaimed: "Anybody who goes with them goes with a second-rate, horse shit service." Those top television executives were not used to this kind of open warfare. They were much more devious. They maneuvered behind the scenes. Ted's out-front stance unnerved them. It worked for Ted because they didn't expect it. The major network presidents and CEOs were flustered and didn't know how to respond.

Ted asked Reese Schonfeld, his head of CNN, to tell him how he thought the rival Satellite News Channel (SNC) would try to emulate CNN. When Reese told Ted that a continuous rotating half-hour was a good way to compete with CNN, Ted immediately ordered Reese to prepare a second 24-hour news channel by the following January, a few months before SNC intended to start its service.

Joel Fisher, Director of Media Research for Compton Advertising, wrote a report on the upcoming competition between Turner and ABC/Westinghouse that was reported in an article in *Backstage* on December 4, 1981, a month before CNN's new channel, *Headline News,* was scheduled to start. Fisher claimed: "Turner will enjoy a short-term advantage, but by 1990, the ABC/Westinghouse joint news will dominate." The article further quotes Fisher's research report:

> By the end of the decade, however, ABC will bring forth and make felt its capital, advertising expertise, affiliate experience, and one of the most formidable news organizations. ABC will then overwhelm the Turner operation…. Just as Captain Ted 'Outrageous' Turner is, undoubtedly, his own best friend, he is also his own worst enemy. Just as he will, undoubtedly, accrue great mileage from his David image (vs. ABC/Westinghouse's Goliath), he will also alienate a great many of his clients. Calling cable operators 'pikers' may seem cute at first, but his unprofessional behavior will soon start proving to be a negative. Once cable operators realize the bonanza that advertising revenues offer, and bring in the personnel who will deal with big-time advertising executives, his behavior and remarks will prove detrimental.

Fisher stated that "merger or outright sale will be necessary for Turner to retain a competitive position." In 1983, ABC/Westinghouse realized that Ted, with his line, "I was cable when cable wasn't cool," had a loyal following, and it decided to fold. Ted rushed in with $25 million and bought out what existed of the ABC/Westinghouse physical plant before anyone got any new ideas. As though they would.

Fisher's words, nevertheless, were prophetic when he predicted that Turner would have to merge to maintain his competitive position, and that his outrageous behavior would prove to be a negative. This came true 15 years later, not exactly for the reasons given by Fisher, and not just for CNN, but for the entire Turner organization.

In September 1981, Ted asked me to form a new division called Turner Program Services (TPS). TPS was to sell or syndicate the original programs now being produced by TBS. This resulted in our first major disagreement. While he wanted me to be President of TPS, he insisted on appointing the Vice President and Director of Sales, and I had a low opinion of the sales ability of the individual he wished to appoint. I didn't want to take on an assignment that I felt would ultimately fail, and so Ted was forced to replace me with Henry Gillespie, a former executive of Viacom, a program and film distribution company. I agreed to stay at TPS, where I played a minor role, such as selling programs to AFRTS (Armed Forces Radio and Television Services), and purchasing programs for WTBS. This purchasing task was soon taken over by the Entertainment Division that was formed to run the SuperStation and develop other channels, such as Turner Network Television (TNT), the Cartoon Channel, and Turner Classic Movies (TCM). I also still produced a half-hour game show called *Starcade*.

Ted and I did not want our disagreement to end our productive relationship. I had known Henry Gillespie during my tenure as Station Manager and program-and-film purchaser for WTBS. Viacom had been an important company to us, and I had often dealt with Henry. He and I worked well together, and he was one of the few executives now joining the company, as it began its enormous expansion in the early 1980s, who was not resentful or intimidated by my relationship with Ted. I continued to send Ted memos on ideas, with copies to Gillespie.

Another executive who understood my relationship to Ted was Terry McGuirk, who started as an intern with the company in 1972 and was, by 1981, head of the Cable Sales Division.

While on a trip to Los Angeles in the early 1980s, I met with an Argentinean who proposed selling CNN in Latin America, in 6-, 12-, or

24-hour increments in Spanish. He estimated potential revenue at $36,000 per day or over $13 million a year. I sent Henry a memo on it, but there was no follow-up. At the time, CNN had not yet reached its full potential in the United States, and that was where our promotion and sales efforts, as well as the financing, were primarily directed. A company must do all this before it considers expansion, or it will risk failure. But this Latin American opportunity gave me much to think about.

In June 1982, Ted announced in a meeting that we were ranked eighty-second out of the 100 leading media companies in *Advertising Age* by virtue of our 94 percent increase in revenue—the highest increase of any company on the list. He also pointed out that our sales were running 75 percent ahead of 1981's. We had, however, projected a 100 percent increase and thus were behind in our own view. Even with these mammoth increases in revenue, Ted, who still held 87 percent of the stock, was beginning to see the need for future capital to continue our enormous growth. Ted requested of us "greater fiscal restraint," and in a memo wrote:

> In my opinion, we are not at all in financial danger. Of course, it may become necessary, at some point, to raise additional capital. This is a situation that has been ongoing for the past several years. If it does become necessary, or I believe it prudent to raise additional equity, I want to make it clear that I have no intention of relinquishing control of the company, nor do I feel that that action would be necessary.

By the end of 1983, WTBS and CNN were the most popular channels on cable, and their selection by each new cable system in that exploding industry had become a given. *Headline News*, the second CNN 24-hour service (CNN2), which Ted had developed to make sure that ABC/Westinghouse's SNC never got off the ground, made its debut in 1983. Gene Wright, Vice President for Engineering, and Carl "Bunky" Helfrich, the company architect, performed their usual miracle and built and equipped a completely new facility in 90 days so that Ted could get a head start on SNC. At the same time, TPS began to sell *Headline News* audio to radio stations as a news service. *Headline News* contained distinct news, weather, and sports segments, so it could be used by radio stations to fit their formats.

Another landmark in 1981: I replaced a secretary, who left for greener pastures, by hiring Joyce Baston, a professional secretary. I could never have managed all the travel I was to do to the far corners of the globe if I hadn't been able to trust Joyce in Atlanta. She always kept me up to date and always found me when she decided that I needed to give a problem my attention.

In 1983, CNN did not yet have the name value to give a television or radio station a promotional boost. I told Wussler that I would like to develop the television markets that expressed interest in CNN news. We always thought of ourselves as a cable system program provider, but now realized that the non-network-affiliated television stations needed access to national and international news to augment their local news reports. CNN2 had cost about $30 million—$20 million in start-up expenses and about $10 million in run-up costs. It would help if we could get some added income from the new news channel.

Meanwhile, Ted was doing everything he could to cozy up to the major film companies in Hollywood, even though they saw him as just a barely tolerable country boy.

He will hate me for saying this, but Ted is the worst deal maker I have ever known. Making a deal is like playing poker. Watching the cards on the table is half the art, but the other half is watching the other players' faces and gestures. I once heard that a diamond salesman in China watched your eyes to see if your pupils widened. Then he knew how much you liked the gem you were looking at. This is a normal part of negotiating. The small talk is part of the strategy. But Ted is an open book. He lets his feelings tell you if he wants what you are selling, and if he wants it, it soon becomes clear that he'll pay any price to get it—like the time he offered $500,000 for the television rights to the Atlanta Braves, when I had already made the deal for $200,000. He'll jump up and pace around the room. He lets the salesman know exactly how he feels. If he played poker, he might as well empty his pockets on the table and leave the room.

Unfortunately, I couldn't be with Ted when Bob Wussler was introducing him to the "moguls of Hollywood," and Ted was trying to convince them what a good guy he was, which he often did by taking their representatives home to dinner. He wanted them to sell him exclusive films and programs, if possible. They gave him exclusive films, all right. I was sent a copy of a note that Wussler wrote:

Yesterday, Ted made an arrangement with Sid Sheinberg, President of Universal, for WTBS's utilization of five feature films that have not been previously sold to nor seen on network television. (They have aired on pay cable networks.)

The deal includes the following motion pictures:

1. *The Last Married Couple in America*
2. *The Conqueror* (with John Wayne)
3. *Somewhere in Time*
4. *The Outlaw* (original Howard Hughes rendering with Jane Russell)
5. *The Concorde Affair.*

We get four runs on each picture over one year. The one-year window in which we receive our runs comes within an 18-month window that starts three months after each film completes its present pay cable arrangement.

The deal is subject to Ted's final approval upon screening each print.

This is a major arrangement between us and Hollywood's leading film studio.

There will be a picture-taking session between officials of Universal and Turner.

What wasn't in the memo was that Ted had agreed to pay one million dollars for each of the five films!

Something was terribly wrong. During the past 15 months, I had been purchasing every public domain film I could find that had a reasonable chance of success playing on WTBS. A public domain film is purchased in perpetuity by paying for the print, which usually costs $300-$1,000. The film, no matter how much it cost to produce, has lost its copyright, usually because someone forgot to renew it. My secretary, Joyce, and I had already purchased *It's a Wonderful Life* (with Jimmy Stewart), *The 39 Steps* (with Robert Donat), *Gulliver's Travels* (animated), *The Inspector General* (with Danny Kaye), *Santa Fe Trail* (with Ronald Reagan), *Strange Love of Martha Ivers* (with Barbara Stanwyck), and *The Stranger* (with Loretta Young and Orson Welles). These films could be played without blackout on any cable system, and the library could be held in reserve in the event the "distant independent" privilege, which we had with regard to cable systems, was again modified by the FCC.

I called Joyce into my office and showed her the list of five films.

Joyce recognized *The Outlaw*. While Universal was "contesting" the loss of the copyright on this film, everyone in the industry with half a brain was buying a print for $500, running the hell out of it, and thumbing his nose at Universal. Fortunately, the deal was subject to Ted's approval upon screening each print. I couldn't wait to tell Ted I could save him $999,500 on that movie, plus he could own the print in perpetuity!

Ted also went to New York with Bob Wussler to make a deal with fight promoter Don King for monthly boxing broadcasts from Madison Square Garden, and for one or two pay-per-view fights.

Electronic Media, on September 2, 1982, reported on Ted's activities:

> 'We snookered ESPN and ABC,' Mr. Turner said with a broad smile. Robert Wussler, Executive Vice President, characterized the contract with Mr. King as 'very, very long term' and being worth 'several hundred million dollars.'

Reading that made me uneasy. I had no way of knowing who was being "snookered." Wussler was no brake on Ted and Wussler made mistakes. He purchased a package of programs from Southern TV in England for seven figures that never saw a run on WTBS; they were largely classical music and operas, too upscale for WTBS. I tried to sell them to the Arts & Entertainment (A&E) channel, but it wouldn't buy them at any price. One of my last program-purchasing efforts was to buy 129 films from Viacom for over $3 million.

Nevertheless, by mid-1983, WTBS and its now national audience had entered a new phase as far as the benchmark criteria for programming costs were concerned. The program blackouts and the advertisers' demand for new and exciting programming was taking WTBS from a channel with largely rerun fare to a level approaching that of the three networks. Although at that time WTBS reached 30 percent of all television homes in the country, it was obvious to me that its popularity would double in the near future.

Despite CNN's continuing losses, WTBS turned a profit in June 1982, with $200,000 in monthly earnings. July earned $500,000. Yet the two CNN networks were still losing one million dollars a month, because the expenses for CNN had increased 90 percent over the previous year due to the start-up and promotion costs of CNN2. Ignoring the CNN ongoing losses, Ted remained farsighted in announcing in 1983 that CNN would be the first television channel to be offered as a news service *around the world.*

By 1983, there were individual departments that gradually took over the jobs I once did by myself: running the daily operation of a television station, buying and scheduling the films and programs, building a sports and remote operation, promoting the station, and creating local programs. I was still working at both TBS and TPS. Those who had come into positions of power wanted their own fiefdoms and did not appreciate my relationship with Ted, and so I was ignored. When I asked for new furniture, I was approved for a discarded lobby couch and chair. I couldn't get shelves for my office. When I ordered television monitors for my office, I was turned down until the new Director of Programming offered me his, because he was getting new ones.

The game was on among those executives to try to force me to leave, but I ignored it. The event with the bicycle club when I was twelve taught me not to quit because I was uncomfortable. I just hunkered down and waited it out. I had done it before when I was "sent to Siberia" in Boston at WBZ-TV; I would do it again.

Producing the California game show kept me busy, but my "motor was in neutral," humming and waiting for the green light. I continued to sell some Turner programs and had to travel to Canada from time to time, but it was not until November 1983 that the light finally changed.

In November 1983, Frank Beatty, who had been trying to sell CNN in Latin America and the Pacific region, resigned. Frank had failed to find a way to interest television broadcasters outside the United States in CNN's domestic news service. When Henry Gillespie told me I was the one "coming off the bench" to replace Beatty, I was quite surprised. I wasn't sure I wanted to traipse around the world, and I thought it was designed as a "fool's errand" to keep me busy—working on something that had already failed. Nor did I have a clue how to begin.

So I decided to do a "handshake" tour of Japan, Hong Kong, Australia, and New Zealand to introduce myself and see what interest there was in CNN.

Little did I know that a Boeing 747 would become my primary home for the next decade.

Before I left on my first trip, Ted said to me, "I guess nobody's interested in CNN outside of the United States." I didn't know then whether he was right or wrong. I only knew that I had always considered myself a poor salesman and stayed away from selling during my television broadcasting career.

I had never forgotten how, when I was seven years old, I had tried to sell *Liberty* magazines. A man would drive around our neighborhood and ask any of the children playing in the street if they wanted to sell the magazine. He would hand a paper shoulder pack with about a dozen magazines to his "prospective salesmen," and we would be off, knocking on doors, asking people to buy our five-cent *Liberty*. I never sold one magazine. My mother felt sorry for me and bought two. I was crushed by my failure. I thought it was my fault. How could I understand at that age that the country was in the depths of the Great Depression and reading even a two-cent newspaper was a luxury for most people, who were having a hard enough time just putting food on the table?

Had I not been literally forced into selling CNN internationally, because no one thought there was any interest in CNN outside the United States, I would never have discovered that I did, indeed, have a talent for sales. In looking back, it seems that the TBS executives gave me what they thought was a hopeless job, perhaps to keep me busy, or perhaps to get rid of me, but I made it work. Between 1980 and late 1983, I had had diminishing responsibilities, but I had refused to quit. Given what I had already done to help Ted, I couldn't walk away.

If I could give advice to someone considering a broadcasting career, I would tell him or her that, with a few exceptions, such "exotic" talents as Larry King and Barbara Walters, the only way to make real money in the broadcast industry (unless you own your own station) is in advertising or program sales. In addition, the sales manager is usually chosen as the general manager of the station, and he and the salespeople are paid bonuses for meeting their projected sales budgets with more bonuses if they exceed their goals. There aren't many program directors who are paid more than a straight salary, even though, in many cases, a creative program director, especially one with talent in negotiating program and film contracts, may have made the most significant contribution to the station. The owners rarely know who is creating the sparks that bring life to a creative environment. They only know who knows how to make money. Could I make contacts, deals, and money for CNN? We'd soon find out.

CHAPTER TEN

CNN International's Flame Is Lit

How to improve your luck. Develop your bump of curiosity.
Acquire a little streak of recklessness. Sharpen your imagination.
Be willing to change your mind.

—Hamilton (Texas) *Herald*

I ended a four-page memo I sent to Ted Turner on January 12, 1983, on "Planning for the Future," with the following:

Future: R&D–For WTBS and CNN:

Our future growth will be limited by the constraints of cable. While cable will give us the economic power during its development in the next 10 years, the ultimate in growth potential is DBS [Direct Broadcast Satellite]–not just in the United States, but worldwide.

The United States is the only country that permits unlimited program development.

All other countries, to varying degrees, limit programming–particularly news. In France, "a true democracy," the government controls all television. Totalitarian countries control all forms of broadcast and newspapers.

I have a dream:

Someday—the metal presses of the world will stamp out foot-high dishes so cheaply that anyone on earth can afford to get one, or receive one free.

There are already enough television sets throughout the world so that DBS can distribute news of the world to every country in any language.

Television—used in this manner—could end war, and preparation for war, for all time.

We have the power and the knowledge to develop this concept.

Whoever accomplishes or even originates this feat will become historically significant.

In early 1982, CNN, through Reese Schonfeld, made a two-year and seven-month agreement with the Sevens Network in Sydney, Australia, to carry CNN as a U.S. news service on a Pacific Ocean Intelsat satellite. The Sevens Network technicians had found a way to carry two different signals on a single half-transponder. Their equipment in the United States would alternate signal information from two sources in the television scanning lines and then restore the two different pictures when it was received at the Sevens Network studio in Sydney. At one time, this was considered innovative. By 1995, the multiple use of transponders through digital systems was accepted practice.

In exchange for the U.S. news, the Sevens Network sent back Australian news to CNN. During this experimental stage, TV-Asahi, Japanese network, was paying the Sevens network 25 percent or ($400,000) of the costs for the transponder it leased on the Pacific Ocean spare satellite. This accommodated the U.S. CNN service, in order to exchange Japanese stories for the same CNN domestic material.

Despite Frank Beatty's efforts criss-crossing Latin America and the Pacific region for a year, and CNN efforts for two years, we had not been able to develop a single formal agreement with any television station or cable service for the use of CNN (then domestic only). Frank had been a United Press International newsman. That agency provided printed news information to its subscribers, newspapers, radio, and television stations, but it contained no video information. Later, it started a service called United Press International Television News (UPITN). Frank was handicapped by his inexperience with video, as well as in understanding CNN's use in television station operations. Nor did Frank have the creative imagination or experience to explain the use of CNN and its potential to television broadcasters, particularly the use of international news to station executives eager to catch up to the sophistication and knowledge of their American counterparts. Frank was a nice guy who had been assigned the wrong job. He became so frustrated that he abruptly resigned. Ted then assumed there was no interest in a CNN domestic service abroad, even though CNN contained not only U.S. stories, but also material from the six CNN bureaus in London, Rome, Tokyo, Jerusalem, Cairo, and Moscow. Since CNN subscribed to the World Television News (WTN) service and had an exchange arrangement with the European Broadcast Union (EBU), no agreements for their non-CNN news could be made without special arrangements. This was only one of the handicaps I faced as I began developing CNN internationally. There were countless others.

I didn't know it at the time, but I was the official representative of CNN. I was CNN incarnate. I would become able to proceed with any plan or any arrangement that I considered favorable to CNN. I enjoyed a tremendous grant from a formidable author—Ted Turner. I was uniquely able to avoid the internal conflicts and jealousies that consume most large organizations.

In December 1983, I was 56 years old, and had worked in television broadcasting for 35 years. For 13 years, I had been heavily involved in TBS's growth from an obscure UHF station to a SuperStation serving North and Central America. I thought I had already experienced more than could be expected from a broadcasting career. While many people my age were preparing to wind down their careers, I would have to prepare myself physically and mentally so that I could criss-cross the world, with long periods spent in air travel or waiting in airports, and still be alert upon my arrival.

I prepared for my first visit to the Pacific Rim. I thought that it might be my last, so I asked Lill if she wanted to come along and share this new adventure. Later, we were so glad we did this, since each year of travel took more and more of my time.

During a trip to New York, I met with several Japanese businessmen from Toei Films, a company that produced animated films. I learned from them that an important protocol when meeting people from Japan was to bring small gifts. Joyce and I searched gift catalogs and settled on a pocket-knife with several different blades, a fingernail file, and scissors. We bought a large quantity, and since I planned to use them as gifts for other trips, I had "CNN" engraved on them. One day, as we were admiring them, we noticed that they were "made in Japan." Nevertheless, I packed a good supply into my suitcase.

I wanted and needed to pick someone's brains on how to organize and proceed with the development of CNN in the Pacific Rim, but I had no one. Nor was I sure how CNN would want me to proceed. Burt Reinhardt had been President of CNN since August 1982, when Ted fired Reese Schonfeld.

I don't think Reese ever learned how to work with Ted, who liked to have a finger in the cooking pot even as late as 1983. In the 1970s, he was, of course, involved in day-to-day decisions, even interviewing the department heads that I hired. As the company grew, he had no choice but to become less involved except with important issues.

But once in awhile, Ted would poke his head into something that should not have concerned him. Most of us had learned to accept this occasional intrusion because we recognized the overall importance of what we were doing, and we wanted to be a part of this innovative broadcasting work. Reese had decided not to renew an agreement with Sandi Freeman—a talk show host of average talent—because he was unwilling to pay the price her agent asked. The agent, determined to get his price for her contract, went around Reese to Turner and Wussler, who, in effect, overruled Reese.

When interviewed after he left, Schonfeld said that he had "numerous policy and personnel differences with owner Ted Turner... [He] became actively involved with the business to the point of scheduling programs and naming on-air personalities."

"That's his right," Schonfeld said in the interview, " but my contract said I was president and chief executive officer, and if I can't name the people on air, then I'm not chief executive officer, and I don't want to work there."

But there were other complications to Schonfeld's tenure at CNN. Reese was unwilling to reconcile his emotional attachment to the success

Photo courtesy of CNN

Reese Schonfeld the first president of CNN and the primary creator of its original organization

of CNN with the fiscal position of Turner Broadcasting, which was in serious financial difficulty at that time, even bordering on bankruptcy. Reese made an agreement with Mike Douglas, the former singer/talk show host, which culminated in a program from Las Vegas that underscored the faded talent of the former television personality. The buyout of the contract cost around $500,000, which made Ted livid.

Unlike me, Reese was not shy about talking to interviewers or the industry at large concerning his success at CNN. Ted was not used to sharing his achievements with others, particularly since he conceived the 24-hour cable news concept. Personally, I gave Reese a lot of credit for CNN's development and day to day operation, while others, including Ted, may have felt he was taking too much credit.

It was very unfortunate for both Turner and Schonfeld that the break occurred, because they needed each other. Reese had hired the key people able to implement his creative vision of Ted's 24-hour news concept, which would end by separating cable and regular television broadcasting forever. Reese was a highly creative person and a hard driver. He knew where his clones were hiding, and he brought them to Atlanta.

One such person was Burt Reinhardt, who became Vice President of CNN Operations under Reese. He had been Executive Vice President of Paramount's non-theatrical and educational division in Los Angeles. Well qualified in negotiations and capable of working with tight budgets, he came to Atlanta to meet Ted, and Ted brought me into the meeting when Burt expressed some reluctance to leave Los Angeles for a part of the country with a reputation for anti-Semitism.

My job was to take Burt to lunch and convince him that Atlanta was safe and a great place to live, which was true. Coming to Atlanta was a big decision for Burt, but he never regretted it. Burt was conservative by nature and better suited as a number-two person overseeing operations, even when he became President of CNN. He realized that CNN's growth depended on imagination and risk-taking, but it was difficult for him to be the kind of entrepreneurial leader that Schonfeld was.

Later, as I became more deeply involved in CNN's international development, Burt cooperated with me, even though there were times when he was concerned that I might jeopardize his relationships with news agencies important to CNN, and with which I competed as I supplied CNN to more and more global television broadcasters.

To the credit of Reese and his pioneering staff, they constructed the basic conceptual framework of CNN so well that it easily continued its growth and development after they were gone. But it was still a mistake for Ted to fire Reese. Whatever reason Ted had, whether it was jealousy of the success of CNN, as Reese claimed, or Reese's overbearing attitude toward his employees (when he was overworking himself), as some had complained to Ted, he never again overruled his division heads. Unfortunately, this fact created a tremendous problem for the company and me later on.

On the day I left for Japan, I met with Ted. He wanted me to hear about his recent trip to Australia. Ted had met with the Sevens Network there, and officials told him that they had not been offered any programs produced by Turner. "That's why I'm going there," I said.

He also told me, "They sold a series to Paramount and didn't know we were syndicating." I told him I was covering all bases for the Australian Channels Seven and Nine—purchasing as well as selling. Ted seemed pleased, particularly when I told him I was leaving that day.

At the same meeting, Ted set up a three-man committee on satellites: Terry McGuirk, President of Cable Sales Division, Burt Reinhardt, and myself. I could tell that Ted was closer to a decision on getting the satellite service in both the Atlantic and Pacific regions. He had hesitated only because of the initial lack of commercial success outside the United States. He also talked about the additional business Charles Bonan, the TPS representative in London, thought he could find in Europe—if we could get a signal there.

Ted explained to us about the one-quarter transponder that the Sevens Network was using on Intelsat. "They are sharing a half-transponder with the Nines Network that costs $2.5 million U.S. annually. The Nines are splitting theirs with NBC/ABC." The Sevens, already getting $400,000 from TV-Asahi in Japan as their share, were willing to do business with anyone who could help them offset their costs.

Ted asked the satellite committee to have a separate meeting, which we did after the regular CNN meeting. I learned that to order a transponder on Intelsat, you had to go through one of their PTT (Postal Telephone & Telegraph) members. These were monopolies held by the individual countries in the Intelsat consortium. Terry McGuirk showed us a copy of the potential "footprint" of the Pacific Ocean satellite. It looked like a flashlight beam that covered one third of the planet.

* * * * *

By the time the plane landed at Narita Airport in Tokyo, I concluded that, since there were no precedents, I would have to rely on my own creativity and my past experiences.

Henry Gillespie, head of TPS, had given me the name of an agent in Tokyo whom he had known when he represented Viacom in Los Angeles. Banjiro Uemura worked for the Tohokushinsha Film company, probably the most respected agency for motion picture representation in Japan. Although Uemura was polite but friendly, and knew exactly how to make Americans comfortable, he didn't quite understand what I intended to do in Japan. Since I wasn't sure either, I told him that TBS was planning to expand the CNN signal (domestic), and that I was on a "handshake" tour to introduce myself and see what mutually satisfactory agreements could be made.

I learned that there were several television networks in Japan: the Tokyo Broadcasting System, Fuji Television Network, Nippon Television Network, TV-Asahi, and the mammoth state television network, NHK. This was my first experience with state or government television which, in many countries, unlike in the United States, is the premier network, with the ability to collect television set license fees and advertising revenue.

My plan was to offer CNN via the Australian Sevens Network satellite signal to any of the television networks that were willing to pay for it. I had no idea what it was worth, but I had my film and program purchasing experience at Turner for the previous ten years, as well as creating news departments for the television stations where I'd once worked, to fall back on.

I decided to do what every salesman does: knock on the door of his customer. It wasn't easy to do this in a city where I didn't speak the language and couldn't read the signs or use the telephone. So, I began to develop a system with the resources available to me.

Every major hotel in Tokyo has a concierge desk. A Japanese woman in traditional costume would write out (in Japanese) the location of your destination for your taxi driver. I then developed a "flash card" system, using the concierge's help, with the names of executives, companies, or other information, which I could use in the taxi, and also show to a passerby when I was lost. Then I took the matchbook of the hotel to show the taxi driver where I wanted to return. Lill used this system, too, when she visited museums and went shopping. I was shocked when she was brave enough to take her "flash cards" on the subway.

I began my visits to the networks with a card that asked to see the News Director or Program Director. I was reasonably certain that an English-speaking person could be found once the introductions were made. My first visit was to the Tokyo Broadcasting System, where I was coolly received. They told me politely that they weren't interested. I went there first because I had been working with one of its programming executives who was trying to interest Turner in carrying the Tokyo Music Festival, an annual, live entertainment broadcast. Even such a small "connection" as this can be an asset when your contacts are nil.

I received the same polite but cool response at the Fuji Television network, and not much more when I visited Nippon Television. My batting average was zero. I then visited NHK and, once more, met with stoic faces, friendly but formal. I saved TV-Asahi for last because CNN had already arranged for a limited exchange of news stories with its news department, and I wanted to get a "feel" for our welcome in general before visiting their facility.

I was met by Keiji Koyama, who had lived in New York City as the TV-Asahi representative, and who spoke excellent English. He immediately took me to Takeshi Kobayashi, the Director of Japan Cable Television (JCTV), a subsidiary of TV-Asahi. Although Kobayashi could speak English, he preferred to have Koyama translate. We had a friendly conversation. I learned that TV-Asahi liked the CNN exchange relationship, and since it was lunchtime, they took me to their favorite sushi restaurant.

I explained that my job was to sell CNN as a news service to any of the Japanese networks. Both Koyama's and Kobayashi's food had arrived, and they were ready to start eating. They looked at me with some surprise. I had just started on my tempura when they both began speaking agitatedly in Japanese. Finally, Koyama interrupted, looked at me, and asked, "How much do you want for the exclusive rights to CNN in Japan?"

I hadn't a clue what I should charge, let alone for exclusivity, but I had some idea of the size of their network, and the revenues they could expect from advertising in certain time periods. "A hundred thousand," I said nervously, not knowing if I was high or low.

"A year?" Koyama interjected.

I did a quick calculation—$100,000 a year was $100,000 we didn't have, since our total present international income was zero. "No, a month," I muttered, not sure if I should have just said, "Excuse me, I have to find the bathroom."

They stopped talking and looked at me as if I were attempting to swallow my tempura shrimp whole. More fast-talk in Japanese, and then suddenly Koyama said, "We have to go back to TV-Asahi."

Suddenly, mid-meal, having barely begun eating, I found myself out of the restaurant, in a car, and on the way back to the network facility. I was very nervous by this time. I didn't want to interfere with any previous CNN arrangements for a mutual exchange of videos from each other's newscasts, and it was obvious that I had upset them by my proposal. But soon I found myself being introduced to the network's executive director in his office. Other than my formal introduction, the conversation was entirely in Japanese, which meant I was a not-so-innocent-spectator.

Abruptly, the conversation ended, and I was asked to follow them into an enormous conference room. There were about 30 soft, heavy chairs around a conference table. I was asked politely to wait. Koyama and Kobayashi left the room. I sat for what seemed like forever. All I could think of was: *I must have screwed up.* CNN will lose its relationship in Japan. And I'm the cause. I imagined all sorts of dire repercussions.

After half an hour, perhaps longer, the door opened, and a large group of Japanese executives entered and sat down in the chairs around the table. A Mr. Narai was the spokesman, and Koyama translated his comments. "We have studied your proposal." I shifted nervously, wondering if I should apologize and make some excuse like, "I lost my head," or "I'm tired from the trip." Perhaps "I'm temporarily insane."

Narai continued. "And we propose a counter-offer." He looked at me coolly. In spite of my desperate thoughts, I sat frozen to my chair and said nothing. "We will pay $50,000 per month for six months and then $100,000 per month; and that is our final offer."

I hesitated only to breathe. "I accept," I muttered meekly. In effect, I had, in this unusual manner, established a price for CNN. When I moved on to other countries, I had a base to work from. I had a sense of excitement and relief once I'd completed the agreement with TV-Asahi. I had made a multi-year, multi-million dollar agreement that none of us in Atlanta, not even Ted Turner, had considered a possibility.

When I returned to Atlanta, however, I had to contend with the CNN executives' perception that charging for the service would interfere with their ability to exchange CNN news for film material developed by local networks and television stations. My answer was to make supplying CNN with local material (upon CNN request) a binding part of the agreement. CNN would not have to pay for any film produced for local use, but would pay the cost of producing news film to be used only by CNN. This arrangement made CNN even stronger because it would now have countless "mini-bureaus" available in many countries. Other countries' television stations became happy to promote their "ties" to CNN and to contribute news material that would be shown worldwide. The cash payments coming in from abroad helped CNN work its way back into the black financially. The "mini-bureaus" would continue to be the backbone of CNN's international news collection well into the new millennium, even though the number of fully staffed news bureaus have increased considerably.

Lill and I were scheduled to leave Tokyo later the next day for our second stop, Hong Kong. I had agreed to meet with TV-Asahi at 9:00 A.M. in the business office of the Imperial Hotel. All major hotels worldwide set aside a working business office within the hotel, staffed with translators, secretaries, and/or typists who supply the office assistance necessary for most business arrangements. These personnel can produce documents in English.

We still needed to negotiate some of the finer details of our agreement. As I casually looked out of the large windows of the hotel at around 10:00 A.M., I saw a light snow beginning to fall. I pointed this out to Koyama, who told me not to be concerned. "Only a little snow falls in Tokyo. Not a problem." Living in Atlanta, I thought I understood. Every few years a thin, white dusting of snow would fall on the city. The buildings, houses, and Georgia pines would poke through, as though thrusting themselves up out of a white blanket. We Northerners would rush to our windows so that we could enjoy the memories of the snows from our childhood. But, in Atlanta, it would melt quickly, and the wet red Georgia clay glistened through.

Koyama and I went back to work. A few hours later, the "light" snow was still falling. "Koyama," I said, "the airport is 60 miles from here."

"No problem, no problem," he said. "Snow stop soon."

I didn't know where he was getting his weather reports, but I did have a sense of urgency about finishing our agreement. I phoned Lill in our room and told her to pack and be ready to leave at any time.

Koyama was wrong, and by one o'clock, the snow was accumulating on the streets in front of the hotel. I phoned the airline—the road to the airport was already closed. Koyama suggested taking the train. "The train is always running," he said to reassure me. We called the train station. The trains to the airport were not running either.

By then it was almost 2:00 P.M., and we had finished the agreement. We had arranged for a late checkout, but still had no way to get to the airport. I would have gladly paid the $150 cab fare, but the roads were blocked. I called Banjiro Uemura, Henry Gillespie's friend, and told him of my predicament. He said that there was only one possible way to get to the airport in these conditions. "What's that?" I asked, thinking to myself that if the cars and trains were blocked, what could he be referring to? I decided I would not take a helicopter in a snowstorm!

"Underground," he exclaimed.

"But the airport is 60 miles away," I said. I couldn't believe any subway would go that far.

"Don't worry," he said. "I'll send someone to take you there." And he hung up.

About an hour later, a young man arrived from the Tohokushinsha office, and we went to the lobby to meet Lill and check out.

There are people who travel light and people who don't. I fall into the latter group, even more so then, since this was my first major trip abroad, and Lill's, too. When the Tohokushinsha car stopped at the subway station to let us out, all three of us were loaded down with suitcases and carry-on bags. The plan was to take us via a series of subways that would ultimately drop us in a town a few miles from the airport. I had seen newsreels of the Tokyo subways. The riders were literally jammed into the cars, like sardines pressed into a can, by the subway attendants. We had the same experience, only worse, as we struggled into the cars with our oversized luggage. Each ride took us a short distance. Then we were jolted out of that car and onto the next as we zig-zagged our way to Narita Airport. I was sure we would be late for our flight, but I was counting on there being a delay due to the snowstorm.

Finally, we left the subway and made our way to a bus for the final ride to Narita. I was right: Our flight had a three-hour take-off delay. We thanked our young guide and tried to unwind in an airport paralyzed by the storm and full of passengers. All flights were either delayed or cancelled. Lill and I were exhausted from the frenzied journey through the myriad subways and welcomed a chance to rest, leaving the responsibility for further travel to the airline.

I thought about what I had accomplished in Tokyo. I had come to Japan merely to introduce myself, but I was leaving with an exclusive agreement with TV-Asahi Network for CNN that totaled $1,500,000 for a year and a quarter. I hadn't expected to arrange an agreement, but had seized the opportunity. I was concerned about the coolness and lack of interest at NHK, TBS, Fuji, and Nippon Television Networks, but I later learned the reason for this. I had innocently disturbed a traditional protocol for doing business in Japan.

Apparently, what I did not know was that programs and films from the United States or other parts of the world were sold via a contract with a Japanese agent. This middleman was necessary. He made the contacts and the deals and, in most cases, the U.S. firm never even met the principals on the Japanese side. My walking up to the front door and knocking on it shocked the Japanese news executives, and they didn't know how to deal with me or my proposals. I later learned as well that the Tokyo Broadcasting System was very interested in CNN, but it hadn't believed in my authenticity and, as a result, their news director failed to inform the executive of my appearance at their front door. Later, when Tokyo Broadcasting System learned from its U.S. office in New York City that I was a legitimate representative for Turner and CNN, it tried to restart discussions, but it was too late. After my first visit to Japan, I encouraged television executives to contact me on a personal basis, which they began doing—I never liked to follow the script.

As I sat in the Narita Airport, I thought about one other interesting fact I had learned. TV-Asahi compensated KDD (a governmentally-decreed telecommunications monopoly, the Japanese PTT) $500,000 a year to downlink its satellite signals and microwave it 60 miles to Tokyo. This was silly and awfully expensive, as well as unnecessary when TV-Asahi could, for a fraction of its annual cost, simply purchase and install an antenna (dish) directly adjacent to the television facilities in Tokyo.

At that time, I didn't fully understand who was in control of satellite up-linking and, more importantly, downlinking. International satellite signals, I was to learn, were under the control of 127 Western countries. This would become my biggest roadblock in distributing CNN throughout the world.

My thoughts turned to how I began the career that had thrust me into such a position of responsibility. How could I think about such formidable challenges with my modest ghetto background and limited education? But I was fortunate that a "spark" I found in a ninth-grade school day sent me in the right direction. If I had been out sick that day, I would not be sitting in the airport wondering how I was going to take on 127 countries without armed forces.

It had happened in Dorchester, Massachusetts, in a class with a teacher that I, and no one I knew cared for. Miss Baker was old and severe-looking, with pinched glasses and never a smile that I can recall. Her standout feature was a brown and gray curled hair bun that stood perched like a coiled anaconda on the top of her head. Her trademark was her cold sternness. I was a gawky, shy, intense, but unsuccessful student. I didn't do any homework because the tough kids in our neighborhood didn't want to be caught walking home with books. I didn't play hooky or cause any problems. I went to school each day and sat passively near the back of the room, mostly daydreaming and hoping I wouldn't be noticed and called on by the teacher.

Then one day in Miss Baker's English class, we were asked to read excerpts from Shakespeare's *Julius Caesar.* Each student row by row, got up and read a paragraph from the play.

I stood up and read mine and sat down. Miss Baker asked me to get up and read the next paragraph and then continue on. And she kept me reading for three or four more pages. When I finally sat down, I wondered what I had done that had made her want to embarrass me in front of the class.

After a pause—this is a moment I will never forget—she said, "You are the best reader in the school." I was stunned. Lights went off in my head. I was never "the best" in anything, not even in sports, even though I couldn't wait for the snow to melt and the field to dry so that a new baseball season could begin.

Miss Baker flunked me in ninth grade English. I've always had a problem with rules, and grammar was no exception. Yet she is the teacher who refuses to be erased from my memory.

* * * * *

The snow stopped soon after we arrived at Narita, and the runways were being plowed. As we taxied for takeoff at 8:00 P.M., a heavy snow started to fall again. The captain announced that he was returning to the gate; he would not take off in such conditions. We were told we might have to spend the night in the waiting area. Lill and I carried pillows and blankets from the plane as we boarded a bus to go back to the terminal.

Most of the passengers of the full 747 decided to try to locate a decent restaurant for dinner since the airline wasn't offering us one. Lill and I had claimed some benches as potential sleep sites when, about 10:00 P.M., the speakers announced that the flight would depart—the snow had stopped again. We didn't think it was possible since we'd been told that Hong Kong would not accept the flight when it arrived at four or five in the morning because of noise-regulated time periods and the unavailability of customs agents. These obstacles, however, were overcome, and we took off, although more than two-thirds of the passengers had not yet returned from dinner.

This first (major) experience with international travel turned out to be not that unusual. I learned to expect conditions that I could not control and to adapt to them. I came to carry books, plus a Walkman with plenty of audio cassettes to help me cope with long delays, as well as the time I had to wait between flights that were on schedule.

After going through Customs in Hong Kong at five in the morning, two brothers, Ronnie and Charles Ling of Adling Holdings, picked us up in a Rolls Royce. The Lings had made a small program arrangement with my predecessor, Frank Beatty, and were the only contacts I had in Hong Kong. They drove us to the Peninsula Hotel, one of the most famous in the world. Unfortunately, our reservation was either lost or had never been received. They were sympathetic, since we had arrived before 8:00 A.M., and gave us a temporary room, with the admonition that we would have to leave if a reservation had to be filled. So Lill and I didn't unpack. We did leave later that day.

I learned in Hong Kong that there were many individuals and organizations that, like the Lings, wanted to associate with CNN. Businessmen, politicians, students, and intellectuals, as I would later discover was true elsewhere, were aware through newspapers and magazines of the U.S. innovations in communications. The 24-hour satellite channels, while relatively new even in the United States, had been discussed, and articles were coming out about them, after tourists and business travelers who came to the United States had observed the revolutionary changes taking place in cable, particularly its use of satellite services.

Lill and I were driven to restaurants in the Rolls, and I was introduced to the television station management of the successful TVB and the not-so-successful Asian Television Limited (ATV). Raymond Wong, Controller of Television News, represented TVB, and we had the first of many conversations over the years on the application of CNN in his news service. Richard Kwang, the Program Director of ATV, and its chairman, Deacon Chu, were very interested in CNN, but were not able to compete financially with the more entrenched and successful TVB in the developing and purchasing of programs.

I also became aware of the potential for the sale of CNN to hotels and cable companies in Hong Kong, as well as to television stations that broadcast to mainland China. Hong Kong, was after all, a thriving tourist and business center that lay at the doorstep of the dormant China giant, where one-fourth of the world's population lived.

I spoke with hotel managers and learned that any satellite signal had to be delivered by Cable & Wireless, a British company that effectively controlled telecommunications by license in Hong Kong. The television stations, and any future cable or multiple distribution system (MDS), could only receive a signal brought to their door by Cable & Wireless. I recalled the $500,000 TV-Asahi was paying each year to the Japanese PTT to bring in its signal. I realized that I had to learn more about Intelsat, the only organization in the world at that time authorized to provide satellite services. *More importantly, Intelsat decided who would receive the signal and how much they would pay for it.* The only other satellite service was the Intersputnik Russian system.

I thought about the early days of short-wave radio broadcasts by the British Broadcasting Company (BBC), and how the BBC signal had crossed all borders, regardless of the politics and usual financial arrangements. For many decades, BBC Radio had provided the only credible news available to countries with dictatorships. Now I saw CNN as capable of doing the same thing on a vastly larger scale and with pictures. But only if the political and financial controls that were in place when I began my international work could be overcome.

* * * * *

Next we flew to Sydney, Australia. Unlike the television stations in Hong Kong, and like the TV-Asahi in Tokyo, the Sevens Network in Australia had tasted CNN news services and were astute enough to realize that CNN represented a novel form of news delivery. For decades, there had not been any real distinction between the newscasts of competitive television channels. Some were faster-paced; others were slower-paced, with friendly chit-chat. Each city's stations studied and copied any improvement or change that seemed to affect advertising rates or the share of the audience. Stealing each other's popular anchor was cosmetic and seldom affected the ratings. By 1984, CNN's 24-hour worldwide coverage held the promise of revolutionizing the way news was *collected and presented* on television in any part of the world.

The Sevens Network and TV-Asahi were leaders with a long-range view, whereas TVB in Hong Kong felt that its position in the market was powerful enough to ignore innovations. It was more concerned with protecting its current system of news gathering and distribution of the videotape by airline. We were forced to think seriously of this tape system when we learned how costly the uplinking and downlinking of satellite signals would be.

Progress at my meetings with the executives of the Sevens Network was not as rapid as in Japan. The general manager was a man in his 50s who looked a bit worn from previous battles, but he was at the top in his profession. As was true with his American counterpart, even when his television station made 30 or 40 percent on its investment, being number one in the market was still his priority.

When I first presented the idea that payment for the CNN service was based on our costs for expanding CNN internationally, I received a cool response. The Sevens was the lead station for a network of Australian television stations (Melbourne, Brisbane, and Adelaide), and having CNN would be of substantial benefit to them as they competed with the Nines and Tens networks.

CNN stories were not available via UPITN (United Press International Television News)–later it would become WTN (World Television News). The most important part of that earlier agreement was that the Sevens satellite signal from the United States was available to CNN customers in the Pacific region capable of receiving it. They would have to pay a pro-rated share based on their market size. This gave CNN 24-hour access for the benefit of its Western Pacific customers at no cost and meant almost $4 million additional annual income for CNN immediately. This was a major discovery on my first handshake visit to the four countries of the Pacific Rim.

I ended my tour with a visit to Auckland, New Zealand, and TV New Zealand, a state-run broadcast service. Bruce Crossan, the Controller of News, was friendly and polite, but he seemed to think that the delivery of 20 minutes of world news each day by satellite was all they needed. I often ran across people with his attitude during my later visits to entrenched news services. They resented new ideas and wanted to hold onto the comfortable status quo, with its handful of news stories coming from WTN or Visnews. When I explained the broad plan of a 24-hour news service, veteran news directors were usually turned off. They saw changes as threats to their positions, or they feared the unknown. I frequently met resistance (initially) that I had to overcome; otherwise, an entire country would be denied the benefits of sharing news and information that was bound to enhance their welfare. In some cases, heads of state thwarted me. I learned later that many British Commonwealth countries were part owners of Visnews, a competitor to WTN and CNN.

Crossan introduced me to Alan Martin, who was Director General of TV New Zealand. Martin was more visionary and understood the failings of the traditional system, and he was more receptive to my proposals and left the door open for future talks. He and I became friends, and over the years he would always visit us when he came to Atlanta.

Before returning home, Lill and I took a few days off and vacationed at the Bay of Islands in the North Island of New Zealand.

Later, I would think back to this virgin beginning, when I didn't know how to proceed because there were no footprints to follow. What had happened was that, like Lewis and Clark, I had become a pioneer. I didn't know what was around the next bend in the trail, whom I would meet, or how we would communicate and come to understand each other. I found this incredibly exciting.

When I returned to Atlanta, I assessed my trip. I had convinced the Sevens Network that CNN should not be exclusive to Australia and that Turner should have access to their satellite transponder in order to carry CNN to the Western Pacific region. I offered Sevens non-exclusive access to CNN stories in exchange for the CNN commercial rights to their transponder. I had met with the Tens Network and made a five-year, nonexclusive arrangement for $4,500,000, if I could provide the CNN signal to them. They were to pay $750,000 the first year and $1,000,000 by the fourth year. I had returned to Atlanta with a total of $6,400,000 in CNN business. That was more than half the amount that CNN was then *losing* each year. What a start! Clearly, CNN was commercially viable outside of the United States.

Burt Reinhardt, CNN's president, was concerned, however, that the CNN material that we provided not include the news from international news agencies like WTN. Reinhardt had carefully, and with much difficulty, convinced WTN to allow CNN to use their daily news stories. Burt feared we would damage his relationship with WTN. The news organizations knew we were the future of news delivery worldwide and that their news was, in effect, strengthening our service.

Fortunately, Burt was not dogmatic. We created guidelines for CNN selling without affecting our competitors' news stories. We identified for each television station the WTN stories that it must not use.

Eventually, I turned this into a plus by convincing some of our television station subscribers, who were already carrying WTN, that they could work out arrangements with WTN to take their stories off the CNN signal. In some cases, I helped persuade stations to subscribe to WTN, and that convinced WTN's president, Ken Coyte, that we could help his business as well.

* * * * *

Many broadcasters, cable systems, and hotels wanted the signal, but under the existing Intelsat regulations, downlinking was cost-prohibitive. As I would soon learn, this had spawned piracy of our unscrambled CNN signal throughout the Western Hemisphere. Broadcasters could install an antenna (dish) and record CNN news stories for later airing on their news programs. Hotels could simply feed the signal from their antenna by internal wire directly to the TV set in each room. This was possible throughout North and Central America, as well as in the Caribbean, because the U.S. domestic satellite signal covered the entire Western Hemisphere.

When I began my international work, I could already negotiate for the use of CNN in Canada, Mexico, Guatemala, Honduras, Costa Rica, Panama, and even in Colombia and Venezuela. The farther away from the United States the signal was received in the Western Hemisphere, the larger the antenna that was required. I would work on these countries between major trips to the Far East, Southern Asia, and Africa over the next several years.

In the case of the Australian Sevens Network signal for the Western Pacific Rim, receiving it required special equipment that was expensive for non-broadcast users, and purchase of it would identify who was trying to pirate the signal. This was, in effect, a form of scrambling, unlike the signal in the northern part of the Western Hemisphere.

I would become involved with a third signal later, but in early 1984, I had my hands full. With my secretary, Joyce, I was responsible for this vast territory. CNN was less than four years old and was still losing money because of the enormous expense of collecting news and delivering it to Atlanta, as well as preparing and editing the material for two 24-hour news channels. Burt Reinhardt, adept at keeping costs down, had only the minimum number of domestic and international news bureaus: Atlanta, Chicago, Dallas, Detroit, Los Angeles, Miami, New York, San Francisco, and Washington. In order to augment the news sent by the six international bureaus—Cairo, Jerusalem, London, Moscow, Rome, and Tokyo—Burt made agreements with WTN and EBU, which delivered 20 minutes of news per day to its broadcast customers worldwide.

We provided printed messages listing in advance those WTN stories embargoed from use by the CNN international television broadcasters, but cable stations and hotels required a different solution. They offered uninterrupted 24-hour service, and it was not technically possible for them to lift the stories that CNN did not own. Fortunately, the news agencies did not object to negotiating a separate fee for the use of their news in cable systems and hotels, but where the television stations were concerned, they were adamant about the blackouts, since we were, in effect, competing for their regular customers. Ken Coyte, WTN's president, not only negotiated rights with CNN, but also was our head-to-head competitor internationally.

Coyte was most concerned with the power of the 24-hour image overwhelming his 20-to-30-minute package that was fed by satellite all over the globe. He was right to be concerned, because my strongest pitch to the stations I visited was: "Do you want continuous non-stop access to 24 hours of today's news or just a few stories of yesterday's news each day?"

In order to allay Burt's fears, I changed my pitch. WTN had another major competitor in Visnews, which delivered its news in the same 20-to-30-minute format and by the same method. When I met with television clients, I found they had both WTN and Visnews. The clients had to cancel one to take CNN's service. I always encouraged the news directors to keep WTN so that they could include its news in the CNN service, and most stations wanted to keep a second news service.

Coyte was delighted, but eventually this success became a problem because my clients wanted to receive WTN's news from the CNN feed and stop paying for a separate identical WTN feed. I had to backtrack and convince our new customers that it was worth the additional cost not to disturb the WTN feeds. Over the years, I was constantly placing my finger in some hole in the dike only to find another hole had sprung a leak, as we grew more powerful globally.

CNN also used EBU stories in its daily programs. The European Broadcast Union was a consortium of European broadcasters that exchanged news stories with television stations through the world. The printed information we telexed out each day contained pages of stories that WTN and EBU had provided to CNN, but could not be used by stations outside the United States unless they had contracted with EBU for these services. CNN's six international bureaus did not supply enough news for CNN on a daily basis. It was years before CNN had sufficient resources of its own to feed its monster appetite. A great deal of the additional international news became available to Atlanta through the agreements I made with individual global television stations, or government entities that provided news bureau facilities, as in China. Arab governments, as well as others, would soon ask us to visit their country for further information on CNN. Israel even sent a delegation to my office in Atlanta.

Due to all the problems, there was no doubt in my mind that neither TBS nor CNN itself would have attempted to sell CNN as a news source to television stations worldwide, in addition to the 24-hour cable and hotel feeds. Yet, I was determined to see it provide a new and lucrative income. Also, the global population would now have access to CNN news and breaking stories that previously could only be seen by those with access to cable, fortunate enough to be registered in a hotel receiving the signal, or who owned a dish.

As a result, the United States came to have a dominant position in news delivery to the world that until now had been claimed by European sources, particularly by the BBC in Great Britain. In the 1980s, outside of the United States, cable reached a very small percentage of the global population.

In 1984, I created the following plan for the sale of CNN globally after my conversations with CNN executives:

Television Broadcasting
A television station subscriber would have:
- Access to individual news stories up to an agreed number of hours per day.
- Access to CNN breaking news for the entire period the story was breaking.
- The right to purchase any CNN programs for local broadcast, including long periods of CNN service, such as all night (example: 1-7:00 A.M., when regular programming began again). This would give a station the opportunity to provide a 24-hour service.

DBS (Direct Broadcast Satellite)
A DBS subscriber would receive:
- A negotiated rate, similar to the rate charged in the United States, of cents per home per month, depending on the rate charged by the cable service, which was minimal. Five dollars a month for cable was typical in less-developed countries.

Hotels
Hotel subscribers would be charged:
- So many cents per day per room. A typical hotel with 300 rooms would pay a day rate of $.06 to $.18 per room, depending on room rates. These rates were based on the premise that there would not be any reasonable advertising income for an extended period.

I explained my plans regarding the use of CNN worldwide to Ted and Henry Gillespie, for whom I still worked in my new role. Later, I had a second meeting with Terry McGuirk, Burt Reinhardt, and Bob Wussler, then Station Manager of WTBS, where I laid out my international plans.

I felt like I was a character in a James Bond movie—the villain plotting to take over the world.

CHAPTER ELEVEN

American Business Guru Visits Japan

Keep away from people who try to belittle your ambitions. Small people always do that, but the really great make you feel that you too can become great.

—Mark Twain

I scheduled a return trip to the Pacific Rim, with the focus on Japan, in March 1984. Ted was planning to be in Japan in mid-March to participate in a goodwill tour of Japanese businesses. He would then head to Hong Kong for the start of the South China Seas sailboat race between Hong Kong and Manila. Neither of us realized what the impact of Ted's visit to Japan would be.

The Japanese culture, as with many Asian cultures, has a deep respect for tradition, "white-haired" elders, leaders, and authority figures. The humiliating Japanese loss in World War II left a tremendous vacuum. Japan's leaders were no longer held in respect. Even the Emperor's venerable image suffered. Through General Douglas MacArthur, the United States quickly introduced democratic governmental institutions.

I believe the Japanese felt a special bond with Americans. The nation of Japan was grateful to MacArthur and to our commitment to militarily protect the Japanese and their South Korean and Tiawanese neighbors.

China, of course, and North Korea, also nearby geographically, were potential enemies at the time. The United States has fulfilled that obligation for over 50 years.

The Japanese population of the 1950s–1970s, particularly the young people, couldn't wait to copy everything that was American. It wasn't possible to live the American dream of a house in the suburbs, because Japan had so little land, but in cars, clothes, music, and even cosmetics, the Japanese couldn't get enough of American culture. I originally walked into this favorable climate unaware of these traits, but now I reappeared with Ted Turner two months later and with a lot more confidence and experience.

The "new" Japanese also wanted to emulate Americans in their thirst for information. The Japanese, especially those in the business world, knew of Ted's reputation as an entrepreneur. They respected his humble beginnings, his ability to overcome obstacles, and his success in "the American way." They wanted to know how he did it. Japanese companies had sent teams to visit U.S. businesses and take photos of their products to copy their success. They ended up improving on American products, as the auto industry discovered to its everlasting regret. Ted's visit meant having an American business hero on their doorstep. Can you believe that in about ten days one young author wrote a 249-page book in Japanese script about Ted shortly after his visit was announced? It wasn't Ted *per se* for whom the normally demure Japanese were expressing such noisy enthusiasm. It was very much a part of that desire to emulate the American style. I would soon discover this to be true in every country of the world. If the United States is a life raft, it may someday sink from the number of people who will sacrifice anything, including their lives, to climb aboard. The distribution of satellite television signals displaying entertainment, documentaries, commentary, news, and displays of democracy, such as voting, globally whets the appetite for a better life. Similar signals in an educational format create a beam of light that will shine into the darkness of ignorance.

The very enthusiastic welcome wasn't just for Ted Turner. It was also an expression of the existing ties between Japan and America and the growing ties between Japanese and American business.

TV-Asahi was thrilled since it had exclusive rights to CNN in Japan. I realized now why I had been able to get the network to go from zero to

In Japan in 1984: Reiko Lewis, unknown man, John Lewis (CNN Bureau Chief in Tokyo), Sid Pike, Janie Turner, and Ted Turner (left to right).

$1.2 million per year. Years later, it would pay as much as $10 million per year to preserve that exclusivity.

During our visit, the Japanese treated Ted as an exalted dignitary but also as a symbol of something august, admirable, and appealing. Our hosts arranged meetings, meals, and interviews with corporate executives from immensely powerful firms, broadcast industry leaders, Japan's equivalent of Babe Ruth, Sadaharu Oh, a prominent yachtsman, journalists, geishas, and the U.S. Ambassador to Japan, former Senator Mike Mansfield.

The meeting with the Ambassador and subsequent press interviews that morning ran behind schedule. A lunch at Maxims at $500 per plate with 60 Japanese businessmen ran late and Ted had a speech at the New Otani Hotel auditorium to an audience of 800 CATV advertising agency representatives and business executives. I will never forget the look on the face of the maitre d! I think he would have preferred a punch in the face to my telling him he had 45 minutes to serve lunch. He turned and walked away, but within minutes, an army of formal waiters began serving food, removing plates, and moving swiftly and silently serving the five course Western style lunch.

Ted left the restaurant 20 minutes late. Ordinarily Ted would arrive early, but our lateness caused Ted to enter from the rear of a filled auditorium to a standing ovation. Without realizing it, we used a psychological trick that Joseph Goebbels used to magnify the Führer's presence: arrive late, build anticipation, arrive from the rear of the hall and walk to the stage to create delayed and growing recognition, respond to cheers and adoration.

I reveled in our circumstances one particular evening, not because of the exalted welcome Ted was receiving, but because I was sitting directly across from the news director at the Tokyo Broadcasting System, the same man who had dismissed me with such an obvious lack of interest when I had knocked on his door. Evidently, by his abrupt dismissal of me he suffered a severe loss of face. The head of the Tokyo Broadcasting System, a Mr. Yamanishi, personally apologized for the misunderstanding. I realized the purpose of the dinner was to try to recoup the network's losses and to demonstrate its interest in CNN. Given my naïveté and ignorance during my first visit to Japan, I had inadvertently short-circuited the traditional system of introductions by agents. I was amazed that I had succeeded at all by merely following the good old American approach of knocking on the door and introducing myself.

Ted was just starting to get used to speaking to large audiences and I was concerned before he spoke to the 800 business leaders.

In the early years, Ted had told us "not to worry"; he was on the debating team in school and was "good at speaking." He wasn't; he was awful. His mind works so fast that his mouth cannot keep up. Sometimes he fails to tell you an important part of the subject he is discussing. He thinks you've heard it simply because he has thought it. We all do this occasionally, but Ted does it often.

It's true that audiences may be more interested in *how* an idea gets expressed. This is where Ted excels—in manner and style. He can capture the sympathy of the audience, then control and play with it as if the crowd were his own personal toy. When you leave a Ted Turner speech, it is folly to try to analyze its meaning. It's best to settle for having been entertained.

At a final meeting with TV-Asahi executives, one man had been telling Ted about Asahi programming that he "must have." One of the programs was a popular animated cartoon called *Doraemon*. Ted insisted that I buy the series. There were 150 six-and-a-half minute episodes, and the cost, including dubbing to English, was $50,000. I didn't like the show and told Ted, but the Asahi people assured him of its good ratings in the six o'clock time slot, and Ted couldn't resist. He had a lot to learn about foreign programs and cultures. As far as I know, no serious effort was ever made to sell or use the program by Turner Entertainment or TPS.

Ted left the next day for New Zealand. I stayed to complete our agreement with TV-Asahi and JCTV and to look for potential programming for TBS. I acquired the syndication rights for some children's animated features made by Toei Films. From a company called Tsuburaya I acquired episodes of a 30-minute program called *Ultra Man*.

Also, I completed agreements for what eventually would be ten Toei animated children's features and later, arranged for RCA/Columbia Home Video to acquire the rights from Turner for seven years at half the purchase price. The dubbing was done at August Films in New York, which was run by Simon Nuchtern. I mention him because he is a very honest person. To

Ted Turner and wife Janie on right of table at Japanese banquet with geishas held by TV-Asahi. Kinichiro Matsuoka, President of JCTV, in center left. Sid Pike at far end of left side..

wit: the Turner company had been expanding so fast, with people being hired who should have had more training, that sometimes there were billing errors. I received a phone call from Simon telling me he had received a check for $17,000 for payment on dubbing services that had already been paid by Turner. The same thing had occurred previously with Simon's company on a $25,000 bill.

On the day that Ted was to leave, everyone was invited to Yokohama Stadium for lunch with the owners of the Tokyo Giants and the Yokohama Whales. One of our hosts was Mr. Oh. The game was proceeding rather slowly, as baseball games are wont to do. I decided to leave. Someone who spoke English wrote out explicit directions on how and where to buy a subway ticket and directions on an appropriate "idiot card" in case I got lost.

I found out later that the Asahi executive in charge of our visit to the baseball game was severely reprimanded for allowing me to return to Tokyo alone. Since he was the same guy who sold Ted on acquiring *Doraemon* without advising me of his intent, I didn't feel too badly about it.

CHAPTER TWELVE

The "Underdog" and Other Concepts

Attitude is the first quality that marks the successful man. If he has a positive attitude and is a positive thinker, who likes challenges and difficult situations, then he has half his success achieved. On the other hand, if he is a negative thinker who is narrow-minded and refuses to accept new ideas and has a defeatist attitude, he hasn't got a chance.

— Lowell Peacock

I used what I call the "underdog" technique to sell CNN. Who knew better than I did that exciting new programming concepts could make a television station succeed? I would convince struggling underdog stations to make CNN a strong new element in their programming and promotions. Station managers would soon be amazed at the attention the station would receive. After all, that's what makes a television service successful—getting attention focused on its programs at the expense of its competitors.

CNN did that. The excitement of watching news while it was happening in different parts of the world could make a station popular almost overnight, particularly if I was able to convince the station to use CNN in some dramatic fashion such as an "all night service." Most television stations went off the air at approximately 1:00 A.M. and resumed telecasting at 6:00 A.M. or 7:00 A.M. Running CNN live during those night hours served two purposes: It made the service around-the-clock, quite often the only one within that country, and it gave the audience a whole new view of the world that they'd never seen before. This created a buzz that kept people up all night (when major stories broke) watching CNN, and resulted in many sleepy workers the next morning.

This idea of first helping the underdog worked in a number of ways. Generally, the most powerful television network was offered program content or film packages first. It could pay the most and quite often it would make "defensive" purchases by buying something not to use for itself, but simply to keep the program away from its competitors (a common practice in the United States). Buying CNN and not using it was not what I had in mind. I avoided this concept like the plague. By strengthening the underdog—an approach not popular with my colleagues, who favored sales with the more powerful television stations—I helped to create a stronger, balanced market that eventually increased all program sales. While this ultimately would help my competitors, who were restricted in their creative thinking by traditional sales methods, we all benefited from it.

* * * * *

In April 1984 I arrived in South Korea, a country whose interest in American democracy and business was similar to Japan's. Seoul, South Korea, represented a strange dichotomy: an ancient language, traditional religion and philosophy mingled with new ideas, new technology and among the younger population, an exploding interest in being entrepreneurs. I found many cities in my global travels had a similar dichotomy—the new order superimposed over the ancient culture. But the people of Seoul more aggressively pursued their interests in this age of technological wonders. Initially, I encountered the same resistance I met in Japan.

South Korea had one independent network, Munhwa Broadcasting Corporation (MBC), and one government network, Korean Broadcasting System (KBS). It was my gut feeling that MBC, while supposedly independent, still had some strong links to the government, making it very cautious about bringing in a news source that was not locally edited or controlled.

This trip sparked my first real awareness of the extent to which some governments seek to control the news that comes into their country. I did expect this kind of control in communist less-developed countries, but it was strange to me that a highly visible, Westernized country such as South Korea, and I would later include Taiwan, would want such tight reins on its own media. Despite a democratically elected government and a capitalist system, leaders were obviously still afraid of freedom of the press. I saw this attitude imperceptibly change as these countries began to compare themselves with other democracies. Watching CNN made this possible. But, in 1984 and for many more years, it was an issue I often had to deal with.

Perhaps the main reason governments all over the world were forced to give up their tight control of news programming was that there was no way they could stop or intercept satellite signals. By the mid-1980s, there were enough direct-to-home dishes that the intelligentsia and elites, at least, were aware of what was going on elsewhere in the world. They were learning that there was such a thing as total *citizen authority* over government. More and more information on what was happening globally would filter down through their societies, increasing the demand for more external information, causing new frustrations for the countries' leaders, and eventually forcing them to accept the realities of global communication.

Ten years later, in the mid-1990s, the global Internet would provide a similar benefit, not only reinforcing the television satellite age, but itself using satellite telephone to enhance television pioneering in communications. It, too, opened the minds of people frozen by repressive cultures. The fresh wind of freedom would finally blow in. Governments had, at last, learned that they could not control information entering the country by satellite, and the Internet could do one thing the television age could not do—it could get answers back to its transmission. Governments were beginning to realize that, in fact, their growth as nations depended on the very information they had always wanted to suppress.

South Korea's leadership made a commitment to the West after World War II, and again after the Korean War, to align themselves against the forces of communism, and those leaders had been rewarded with one of the most successful economies in Asia. North Korea's economic failure, compared with its sister country's success, helped prove that communism was not viable. Still, the South Korean government in the 1980s made a great effort to control information.

I kept going back to South Korea in an effort to convince the KBS and MBC television networks to carry CNN. They claimed the financial costs were too high, but when I found ways to work through that problem, others would pop up, and there would be constant delays. We never really reached a resolution. I kept introducing new proposals and presenting the benefits of CNN, using the evidence from Japan. They would never tell me to "get lost," even though they were afraid of the truth filtering down to the South Korean population. At the same time, I felt they sensed the need for change. At their request, I sent KBS some sample tapes of TV-Asahi's use of CNN. MBC eventually asked for a trial period of 60 days, but CNN had to arrive a day later on tape from Japan because of the excessive costs that the South Korean PTT charged for downlinking the Australian Sevens signal. I was willing to provide the tapes requested, but I insisted that a 24-hour delay did not improve news delivered by air, which had been the standard from the 1950s through the 1970s.

The U.S. Army had 40,000 troops stationed in South Korea, and it had access to the CNN domestic signal 12 to14 hours per day. This was part of an agreement made between AFRTS and CNN before I began working on international sales. AFRTS had arranged to transmit, by various Intelsat satellites, a 24-hour service for the entertainment of American servicemen and women at its various bases worldwide. The other countries with such bases in 1984 were Iceland, the Azores, Italy, Diego Garcia (in the Indian Ocean), Panama, the Philippines, and West Germany.

While AFRTS seemed likely to cooperate in its use of CNN on various global Intelsat satellites, the cost of downlinking was prohibitive and such downlinks are not designed for reception by multiple users, such as hotels, businesses, and individuals.

Not until mid-1988, as I prepared to turn over the Pacific Rim to the Turner office in Sydney, Australia did I succeed in making a small CNN arrangement with KBS in South Korea. A single program, *Sunday World Service,* acquired the rights to excerpt CNN news material for a period of six months. This led to expanded use of CNN a few months later by the KBS network. Eventually, MBC became a CNN subscriber.

Getting that first network in a country on board was always the hardest part of the job for me. Quite often, others would follow for fear of being left behind.

When I visited Hong Kong, I met with Asian Television Limited (ATV), a much smaller and less powerful station than TVB, and the most likely user of CNN, at least in the beginning. TVB was the highly respected giant in the market, the leading proponent of its own Asian news services. It also cooperated with the international news service, Visnews, because most Commonwealth countries did. TVB was historically conservative and had a lock on the Hong Kong market. I had many meetings over the years with Raymond Wong, TVB's news director. I would leave Hong Kong feeling that I had convinced him of its need for CNN's material, only to receive a letter or telex in Atlanta, after Raymond had met with the TVB hierarchy, to learn that we had been turned down. I presumed it was its conservatism or maybe its assumption that, because of its power and size, it could keep CNN out of the region. I wish that I had been responsible for the programming at ATV, its only competitor. I would have taken advantage of TVB's blindness, just as I had exploited WSB-TV's blindness in Atlanta when I took the televised Braves baseball games away from them.

Sitting that April in my hotel room overlooking the beautiful Hong Kong harbor on the Kowloon side of the city, I realized that to bring CNN to every country on earth, I had to overcome many serious problems. The resistance of an entrenched television station such as TVB in Hong Kong was only one of them.

I took a pad of paper and listed frequently daunting problems to surmount.

1. *The intransigence of the Intelsat monopoly of international satellites.* Intelsat's exorbitant fees for downlinking a signal prevented agreements with potential users of CNN news such as television broadcasters, cable companies, or hotels. This monopoly forced the user to use antennas controlled by Intelsat to receive the signal.

Generally, there was one user who contracted with Intelsat to uplink a signal to the satellite and paid both an uplinking and a satellite transponder-use charge. A separate single entity would pay to downlink that signal. If a second party wished to downlink the same signal, it would split the cost, plus some additional amount, and this would go on to third, fourth, fifth users, and so on. This was the case, for example, when one- or two-hour American programs or sports events were broadcast to Europe or Japan.

Under this system, each country could determine its own rate for its part of Intelsat's transponder and the right to bring the signal down into its country.

2. *The size of the task.* A 24-hour news service, certainly one that was relatively new and had not fully developed its own news-collection system, primarily because it was covering was the whole world, was a huge undertaking. CNN had limited resources in 1980, especially money, and had to develop liaisons with existing worldwide news services. At the time these included WTN, EBU, Asian Broadcasting Union (ABU, a group of Asian broadcasters who shared stories) and individual agreements with such groups as the Canadian Broadcasting Corporation (CBC), a government-run television network, commercially operated, but similar to NHK in Japan. These international news services were all reluctant to supply news to CNN, which they knew was becoming a formidable force in the news gathering and distribution industry. The most wary were the long-standing services like WTN and Visnews, as well as regional news exchange services like EBU and ABU, which had survived on their ability to collect, sell, and or exchange news internationally since television's early days.

Fortunately for Turner and CNN, Burt Reinhardt's long-standing reputation in the news and movie industry was helping to "thread the needle," to convince the news agencies that a 24-hour global news service was inevitable, and that it was better to join in its development than to fight a futile battle.

3. *U.S. sports.* The accepted practice in our televising of professional sports was to allow broadcasters to televise a brief segment or play from a game without any rights payment, as long as the source of the covered event was credited. That's why, at the bottom of the screen on local television stations are often the words, "Courtesy of NFL Sports," or in a Chicago Cubs baseball game, "Courtesy of WGN." As professional sports grew in popularity among viewers and advertisers, the sports monopolies became very strict about squeezing revenue from every use of their names. They zealously guarded any use of the same sports plays, which usually lasted only a few seconds, even though this had been accepted practice. The reason: A

"play of the day" was a program event and lasted only seconds, and sports TV producers wanted to monopolize this dramatic play as "exclusive" for their own programs or at least to sell it to sports shows. As a result, when the sports portion of a news period was shown on CNN domestic news carried by satellite (as it was in the early years), television stations in other countries receiving the satellite signal were told they could not carry the sports video on their channels. This was definitely a problem for a station, which then had to cull out the sports items—very labor-intensive, even if it used only part of CNN—but it was a disaster for hotels and cable users, which had no facilities for doing this. JCTV, the cable service in Japan, for instance, was forced to put up a single frame slide (frozen picture) while the sports announcer described a particular event. This was a serious problem and embarrassing. The covering slide was shown only briefly two or three times in a sportscast, but it had a devastating effect on our credibility as a total news service since the viewer in Japan could not see what the sports announcer was describing. JCTV placed the blame on CNN by having its announcer say "CNN was unable to obtain the rights to the picture," which was painfully correct.

4. *CNN was hemorrhaging cash.* CNN was kept alive at that time because the WTBS SuperStation was making money. I couldn't suggest adding to CNN's expenses through the leasing of satellites worldwide. I was back to the problems of the early days at Channel 17: how to make it work when there was no money. Ted obviously still considered me the resident expert in this area.

5. *Language.* How could single-language programming be accepted in non-English-speaking countries?

6. *Credibility and integrity.* Most developing countries, and many fully industrialized nations, endured some governmental control of the news media. For example: Margaret Thatcher, Britain's Prime Minister at the time, refused to allow a BBC interview with the Irish Republican Army (IRA) insurgents of Northern Ireland. I had to convince many governments that controlled their own media that the United States government did not control CNN, an American company. The U.S. Information Agency (USIA) and Voice of America (VOA) were already well known abroad as "voices" throughout the world. Many leaders in other countries did not distinguish between the USIA and CNN.

7. *Reciprocal propaganda.* I had been to only a few countries in Asia, but I already felt some pressure from casual conversations to tell a particular country's story in a particular way to the world. This may have been accepted practice in those countries, but for CNN, it was totally unacceptable. CNN needed to collect news without pressure or interference from any source.

Some of these seven problems had already been addressed in meetings in Atlanta, but I had to solve many of them while I was on the road. My relationship with Ted helped a great deal. Inter-company cooperation can be difficult. We tend to assume that everyone in a company, especially the top executives, all work toward the same goal. Hardly. It depends on the leadership, how projects are assigned and carried out, what kind of relationships the executives have with each other, whether they can overcome personal and professional jealousies, and how strong their friendships are. This is particularly true when a project involves more than one division of a company. The simple truth: Much of what I accomplished at Turner Broadcasting happened because everyone who worked there knew I represented what Ted wanted. Frankly, developing CNN International was so complicated that getting it through the various departments would have been excruciatingly difficult, if not impossible, without Ted's shadow lurking behind me.

When I started the CNN International project, I worked for TPS, headed by Henry Gillespie. TPS existed solely to sell films and programs created by or acquired by TBS. I also worked with CNN and the TBS Legal Department, Advertising Sales (the division that sells commercial time on all the TBS channels), Finance and Accounting, Marketing and Promotion, Public Relations, and, most difficult of all, Corporate Management. Fortunately, in 1984, I could go directly to Ted and be assured of his support.

* * * * *

From my Hong Kong hotel window, I watched the colorful, slow-moving junks as they floated about in the harbor. I thought about how I was taking on an enormous project that could easily run over me unless I kept sailing a true course in, out, and around the huge obstacles, just like a puny junk made its way past behemoth tankers.

In Japan, South Korea, and Australia, I learned about the importance and power of the local PTT and its relationship with the Intelsat satellite consortium. Each country in the Far East and in the Western world not aligned with the Soviet Union had a single organization that acted as its PTT. In the United States it was Comsat; in Japan, KDD. In Hong Kong, it was Cable & Wireless.

When in Atlanta, I had exchanged telexes with A.L. Cooper in Hong Kong, of Satellite Planning and Operations for Cable & Wireless. He suggested a price of $500,000 per year to bring down the 24-hour CNN signal. My telex read: " I doubt that, initially, our total CNN revenue would exceed $200,000 per year, because of present market conditions." Imagine operating a take-out pizza business that relied on its telephone, and then you find out that the phone company wants two and half times the total income your pizza business has projected for the first year.

I wondered later if what they were trying to do was force me into giving them a share of the business. Remember, the real cost of downlinking a satellite signal at that time was the cost of the receiving antenna (dish). This cost could be as low as $30,000 to $40,000.

In the case of Hong Kong, we had to negotiate with Cable & Wireless, because it was the only legal organization permitted to bring CNN down from the Australian transponder on the Intelsat satellite. Yet I began to realize that as CNN grew, particularly in the most powerful Western countries, it would have greater ability to overcome obstacles like the local PTTs. *There is nothing worse for a government or its people than to be left out.* I was not above using this fear in my future negotiations, as I eventually did in countries like India, South Africa, Iraq, and the Persian Gulf states.

* * * * *

Ted and J.J. Ebaugh, his private pilot, joined me in Hong Kong that April. Ted flew from Japan to New Zealand and was now preparing to sail the South China Seas Race. I liked J.J. She was highly intelligent and very dedicated to sane ecology and the future of the planet. The fact that she was a qualified jet pilot also impressed me.

By the time Ted arrived, I concluded that ATV was the most likely user of CNN. TVB, the vastly more powerful station, would eventually acquire

CNN when TVB executives finally realized the extent of CNN's influence. ATV was in a precarious position, its image almost non-existent. Like Channel 17 in 1971, it was operating in the red. A few years later, in 1987, when we were experiencing delays in getting payments from ATV, which claimed they had not received our invoices, Greg Ell, our representative in Sydney, Australia, who routinely sold programs and films in the Pacific, warned me: "The advice that this documentation has not been received is an old ruse used by ATV to avoid payment, particularly when tapes have already been delivered and telecast."

Yet in 1984, I saw ATV as the perfect opportunity for CNN to demonstrate its effectiveness in invigorating a young station's image. I had many meetings and dinners with ATV Chairman Deacon Chu and Raymond Kwang, his young number-two executive. Their relationship resembled Ted's and mine in 1971. The chairman wanted CNN, but unfortunately he was unable to pay for it.

I continued to talk with Cable & Wireless, but its cost of delivering the CNN signal off the Australian transponder remained prohibitive. On the positive side, Cable & Wireless was flexible and willing to negotiate.

I was impressed with the number of hotels in Hong Kong and realized that they, too, could become a good source of revenue for CNN, as well as a pilot opportunity to show other major tourist and business cities with large hotels the advantages of carrying a 24-hour news service for international guests, because English had become the accepted business language. Even when Italians or Germans spoke with Japanese businessmen, they used English.

J.J. and I flew from Hong Kong to Manila, the Philippines, to meet Ted at the end of the race. J.J. and I checked into the historic Manila Hotel and awaited the arrival of Ted's yacht. For the first time in my travels, I noticed a guard outside our doors 24 hours a day. Later, I would encounter similar guards in other countries. I never attributed their presence to my importance, but rather to their desire to avoid any bad news on the next day's CNN coverage.

Ted arrived early in the evening, unfortunately not as the winner of the race, but he didn't seem bothered by the outcome. He was tired and, after a quick dinner, was glad to reach the hotel and get a good night's sleep.

John Lewis, whose Tokyo Bureau covered all of Asia, had arranged some meetings for me. I was about to learn a lot about doing business in developing countries.

Since I was offering an "optional" service, rather than a needed resource, such as the telephone, the time I spent was generally unprofitable. Most of my correspondence, from letters to telexes (there were no faxes available yet), went unanswered.

In the Philippines, not only were the economic conditions poor but the political situation under President Marcos was very unstable. I soon realized that many of the people I was talking to and their companies had some special relationship with Marcos.

When the government is the determining factor in events, and in the ownership of television and radio stations, as well as other businesses involved in international dialogue, it is very difficult to finalize decisions. Too many questions are never answered (and too many answers are never questioned), because the individual businessmen from one day to the next are never sure of their position within the power structure. This was probably the primary deterrent to the development of a business relationship in developing countries with totalitarian power structures. This, in combination with the Intelsat consortium's financially imposed obstacles, made CNN arrangements with those countries extremely difficult, if not impossible.

For years, I worked on Intelsat's prohibitive satellite pricing. The local Manila television stations were collecting 10-to-15 minute satellite feeds daily from WTN, Visnews and others, at rates typical in other countries. In 1985, Philcomsat, the Philippine PTT and representative on Intelsat, charged $650 for the first 10 minutes of a satellite downlink signal and $36 U.S. per minute thereafter. This meant that if CNN planned to feed a 24-hour service to Manila, the shared cost to the television stations and potential cable systems would be $51,840 per day, or $18,922,190 per year. Considering that CNN's total gross income in the Philippines would not reach $500,000 initially, and probably never approach half the cost of 24-hour satellite downlinking, the price was both enormous and unrealistic.

In order to avoid the cost of the 10-minute news feeds at $650 per day in a limited advertising environment that was struggling to pay programming and operational costs, Filipino broadcasters paid television stations in Hong Kong to copy already downlinked tapes from WTN and Visnews made at 9:00 A.M. and then ship them by plane to Manila to arrive by noon.

This meant that Philippine television stations routinely accessed television news after a three-hour delay, provided weather and flight conditions were normal and no airline mechanical problems developed. This was certainly not the intended use of this marvelous satellite invention that, ultimately, would bring instant visual information directly to any home or business in the world.

I couldn't understand why satellites were put in the hands of the least imaginative and most bureaucratic members of the communications industry at a time when satellites were needed to provide information and enhance understanding in a world that was all too capable of destroying itself.

What we had when I started to develop the direct international distribution of CNN was the fox guarding the hen house. Each country's PTT monopoly, in a way similar to the original AT&T monopoly in the U.S., determined the uses of, and the rates for, downlinking. I talked to a former member of the original Initial Communications Satellite Committee (ICSC), who told me that the committee members had no idea how to structure the rates for the use of the satellite services and evolve a system that would be profitable to both the uplinking and receiving countries.

This approach was not new—using an invention as if it had been developed solely for the purpose of making money rather than giving at least some thought to the potential benefits to mankind or to how it might solve the critical problems of wars, overpopulation, and environmental disasters. While my own projected use of the satellites for CNN was motivated by profit, I was well aware of satellite potential.

I didn't know how to approach the Intelsat and PTT problem. I did know there would probably have to be a reformulation of the rate structure that would satisfy the PTT monopolies in the more than 100 Intelsat countries. What I really wondered about, and was afraid to learn, was how much profit the capitalist West would be willing to sacrifice in order to provide mass communication to an extent not yet imagined by anyone, even myself.

* * * * *

When I returned to Atlanta from this second trip to Asia, I analyzed even further my strategy for developing CNN internationally.

There were the obvious difficulties:

1. I was fighting entrenched news services that had, over the years, fostered a high degree of loyalty in local television news departments, particularly with people in decision-making positions. Some of the larger television stations were actually involved in the distribution of these news services and were in powerful positions within important organizations involved in news gathering, such as the ABU and Visnews. They would try to maintain the status quo and would not support new concepts involving independent television news.

2. These accepted news services provided only 10 to 20 minutes of news video per day, making their satellite costs minimal. They had a good satellite signal, the strongest then available, compared to the Australian Sevens signal, which I was negotiating for rights to, along with other countries' television services in the Western Pacific.

3. The Sevens signal was "video plexed." There were two different video pictures on a single half-transponder, and this required special downlinking equipment to bring in its signal.

4. I did not have the rights to sell news from WTN and EBU within the CNN service. Those who took CNN programs live would have to find ways to fill in the gaps where WTN and EBU could not be used. I had to maintain a good relationship with these news services.

5. I had to develop a mechanical means of communicating information to each television unit contracting with CNN so I could advise them daily of the material they weren't supposed to use. This meant finding a company that could provide equipment to send teletypes regarding the embargoed news stories each day.

6. There was no money for CNN to buy its own transponder or to make better joint venture arrangements to downlink the Australian CNN signal than the one we had already worked out with the Sevens Network.

7. I was offering an American service, not an international service, such as Visnews and WTN offered.

8. CNN was in English only.

9. I had no staff to help me cover the world—just me and Joyce.

On the positive side:

1. There was a great deal of worldwide interest in the United States.

The opportunity to peek in on its doings 24 hours a day had a certain appeal, particularly in hotels and via cable services, where they existed. This became true in every country that I visited. Later, I learned that the interest in the United States was an even bigger factor than I had realized in 1984, but even at that time, I decided that I would have to develop this interest in a way so that it would not work against me. I would, later on, discover a tenth negative factor. Some countries, like France and India, where there were strong anti-American influences at work in the government, saw CNN as "too American." Obviously, CNN's American image could be a double-edged sword.

2. I did have one more positive factor going for me: Ted Turner's trust. I knew he wanted CNN to grow internationally, and he knew I was capable of finding a way to get it done.

3. I could go directly to people like Burt Reinhardt, and later to Tom Johnson, who became President of CNN in September 1989. Burt always helped me find a way to solve each problem.

Some individuals in key positions were ones I hired in earlier days. Gene Wright was Vice President in charge of all TBS engineering, and he always gave me the full cooperation of his division, sometimes assigning someone to work with me full time on projects that came along later.

In 1984, Terry McGuirk, who was responsible for the development of TBS on cable and was, in-effect, competing with Bob Wussler for the number-two role after Ted, helped me as I developed CNN internationally. Although Terry and I did not agree on the best initial approach to satellite development for international coverage of CNN (as I will explain later), we did have a strong mutual respect for each other and that helped considerably.

4. Ultimately, what mattered most was that I was used to overcoming obstacles. Despite finding myself (in 1984) much lower in the TBS expanding hierarchy, my relationship with Ted and the "old timers" helped me move the international project forward until its own momentum and success overwhelmed all opposition. The parallel that comes to mind: Ted's original concept of a 24-hour news channel, which everyone else had considered a "dumb idea."

My determination to succeed cannot be minimized, because it became more and more difficult to gain consensus for new and creative developments as the company expanded.

By 1984, there were many people who had to be influenced or coerced to get the job done. Sometimes these people agreed or disagreed with an idea, not because of its merit or lack thereof, but because I was in or out of favor for one reason or another. There were individuals who either could not tolerate my aggressiveness or didn't care for me, but they cooperated because they knew that I was doing something that Ted wanted done. In effect, I could not be ignored.

I realize now, as I write this, how much easier it is for young people with ideas to work in new, small companies, where creativity is absolutely necessary. When the company grows large and full of conservative personalities who do know how to manage such large companies, they tend, in keeping with their operating style and philosophy, to take few risks.

For CNN to grow, I must become a creative risk-taker.

CHAPTER THIRTEEN

A Global Satellite System—On the Cheap

The world is not interested in the storms you encountered,
but whether you brought in the ship.
—Journal of Trade Education

I visited Intelsat at its headquarters in Washington, D.C., to convince officials to lower the satellite downlinking rates.

My first visit to Intelsat was in February 1984, between my first two Far East trips. I met with Joseph N. Pelton, Director of Strategic Policy and Executive Assistant to the Director General. When I arrived at the Washington headquarters, I was taken aback by the very building itself. The severity of its ultra-modern architecture seemed to reflect the spirit of futurism that the satellites themselves represented.

Joe Pelton was a short, friendly, portly man with glasses, who reminded me of a college professor, which is what he was. He had written 12 books on the future of satellite communications and more than 200 articles. He was also a personal friend of Arthur C. Clarke, the satellite visionary and author of the some of the finest science fiction ever written, including *2001: A Space Odyssey*. Pelton convinced Intelsat to develop Project Share, which made available free satellite time in the Intelsat system for health and education purposes. Most important, he, too, was a visionary who understood the potential for good that the satellites represented. We became close friends.

Pelton instantly understood the issue of the excessive downlinking fees and sympathized with our problem, but he was obviously in no position to give me any relief at that first meeting. I had explained that the future use of satellites required a rethinking of the Intelsat rates. Pelton promised to discuss our problem internally and asked me to stay in contact. My impression was that he meant what he said and that he fully understood the issue. The question was whether he could effect any change. I returned to Atlanta hoping I had lit a match but recognizing that, if I had, it would take a while for a fire to start.

In a meeting with Ted and Terry McGuirk, not long after this first meeting with Pelton, the subject of CNN expansion via global satellites came up. Ted looked at me and asked, "Who's going to be responsible for satellites?" The way it was said, and the fact that he stared at me when he said it, clearly indicated that he expected me to involve myself with the companies that CNN used for satellite service. This had nothing to do with CNN's daily use of the satellite for collecting news worldwide. There was a separate CNN department, headed by Dick Tauber, which arranged for occasional use of satellites in order to bring video of news events into Atlanta.

I knew that Terry had been working on satellites as part of his new role at the management level. I'd always had a friendly relationship with him, and I didn't want to declare myself an interloper in his area. I was sure that Terry would cooperate with me, and to show that I wasn't trying to build my own "empire," I said, "That's Terry's area. We'll work together." I also didn't need more responsibility at that point. However, I didn't foresee, because I put too much trust in our relationship, that I had just lost control over a vital part of our CNNI satellite worldwide distribution and the ending of the Intelsat monopoly.

Terry dealt with Intelsat himself and had a good relationship with its sales staff. He and I both wanted to change its system from within, which is what I had already started to do when I met with Joe Pelton. It was only later that Terry and I disagreed about what to do in order to break Intelsat's monopoly. Hindsight being 20-20, I should have taken the satellite responsibility and not ended up facing the obstacles that Terry created for me and the industry's future.

In early 1985, I returned to Intelsat in Washington, D.C. Joe Pelton had set up a meeting with members of their sales team so that I could recount my "horror stories" about Intelsat downlinking rates. I knew Joe had been working behind the scenes for me, and again I felt that each contact or meeting with Intelsat was having its effect. In mid-1985 I inventoried the most urgent problems I faced. They were not new.

1. I had to solve the prohibitive downlinking costs of Intelsat. Downlinking a signal could cost a station between $12,000 and $200,000 per month.

2. I had to find a way around the restrictions on the use of the U.S. CNN domestic signal in areas of North and Central America. Because the signal was domestic, it was not legal for us to sell it as an international service to these countries.

3. There was rampant piracy everywhere, but I was especially concerned with North and Central American countries.

4. I still had limited staff: only myself, Joyce, and Rich Hylen in Hong Kong.

I believed that if the public understood better why there were so many restrictions and limitations on the satellite potential, things would change. I made numerous trips to Intelsat headquarters in 1985, and Joe Pelton did everything possible to help resolve my downlinking dilemma. In 1989, Joe left Intelsat for the University of Colorado at Boulder, to become Director of the Interdisciplinary Telecommunications Program, where, at his request, I participated in the annual World Affairs Conference. In preparing material for this book, I asked Joe for a history of Intelsat. The following is an excerpt from his response:

> One of the first issues the Initial Communications Satellite Committee (ICSC) had to address when it met after the formation of Intelsat was what to charge for satellite services. ComSat had already contracted with Hughes to build the initial satellite (Early Bird) and virtually knew what the initial charges would be, particularly since Early Bird (later called Intelsat I) was considered a prototype. The Europeans wanted the rate for a voice circuit to be on the order of $100,000... Eventually, a rate of $64,000 was established for a voice circuit since this was comparable but

just below the $70,000 rates charged for submarine cable voice circuits, and it was shown that costs could be recouped if a majority of circuits on the satellite were sold. In fact, Early Bird was quickly 'sold out,' and the rate for 1966 was reduced to $40,000. The issue of satellite television was even more of a puzzle. This is because it was a totally unprecedented service. No one knew what the demand would be and what the market would bear. What was known was that there really was no capacity available for television, since Early Bird (and Intelsat II, which followed) had only 240 voice circuits, and these all had to be surrendered to get one low quality black-and-white video channel. Accordingly, what Intelsat did was to set a rate that was essentially pro-rated upon the voice circuit rate, and tariffs were set on the basis that international broadcasts would be limited events of short duration for perhaps major international events.

By the 1968-69 time period, several things had changed. Intelsat realized that coverage of the Olympic Games in Mexico City would generate a lot of interest. (Matt Gordon, who had just come from the United Nations to head up public relations, tried to get broadcasters to use the phrase, 'Live via Intelsat,' and was turned down. He also got the new Intelsat III to be designated 'Olympico,' (and then this became a disastrous launch failure). By July 1969, Intelsat had managed to deploy Intelsat II satellites not only in the Atlantic and Pacific Oceans but also in the Indian Ocean region so as to complete the full global system just two weeks before the moon landing. This live event (Olympics) attracted a global audience of 500 million, establishing the concept of worldwide television. This number was duplicated again at the 1972 Olympics in Munich. (The 1996 Atlanta Olympics were projected to have well over three billion viewers worldwide.)

What was significant at this stage is that the Intelsat III satellite had not only 1,200 voice circuits but also two high-quality color television channels. Even so, the general view was that Intelsat was there to provide voice and data (telex and telegraph) service and that television was incremental occasional-use revenues. The tariff for television was only based on a per-minute rate with a 10-minute minimum, and the service was typically seen as a bilateral exchange rather than a global broadcast. The first broadcasts on Early Bird, for instance, were between Houston and Geneva (open heart surgery by Dr. DeBakey), between France and the United States (the LeMans race), and formal exchanges between heads of state. In short, even though the Intelsat IIIs added a great deal of capacity, the basic concept of satellite television did not change, and the only practical change was a modest 20 percent reduction in charge.

The next big change came with planning for the Intelsat IV satellites. These satellites, which were designed for the upcoming digital service and to boost service capacity, significantly represented a new era. These satellites, with 4,000 two-way voice circuits and multiple video channels, represented the first time when 'spare capacity' was truly available and marketing of service started to be a consideration. In short, with all previous generations of the satellites filled up almost instantly because of latent demand, Intelsat and its system manager set up a special charging policy group, of which I was the leader. We came up with several new charging concepts for digital transponder lease rates. These new transponder rates, adopted in 1973, allowed only for domestic rather than international use (used first by Algeria to connect its regional capitals and by the United States to interconnect the U.S. mainland with Puerto Rico, Hawaii, and Alaska). This precedent was used in subsequent years to allow France to connect with overseas departments (such as Martinique, French Polynesia and Reunion), Spain with the Canary Islands and Madeira, and the United States with its overseas bases via the U.S. Armed Forces Radio and Television network. (Thus, the U.S. AFRTS network operated as a domestic service.)

Things remained rather static within Intelsat as far as international television was concerned until the early 1980s. The key to the change was the rapid evolution of domestic satellite systems around the world. The Canadian (Telesat), European (Eutelsat), and U.S. systems (RCA, ComSat General, etc.) served to create a new paradigm. Suddenly, satellites were not only for telephone service but also for television. (Intelsat, in comparison, was deriving over 90 percent of its revenues from voice.) HBO, CNN, etc., were creating cable television networks via satellite links. The desire to extend these video links to international networks literally forced changes in the Intelsat tariffing policy. There were several key players. There was CNN, which was trying to go global. Western Union and Visnews wanted international video to support news distribution for U.S. and European networks. And, finally there was Kerry Packer, the Australian television magnate. He wanted to get U.S. television programming to distribute not only in Australia but also to reformat and redistribute in the South Pacific. It was the Australian representatives for OTC [the Australian PTT] that first proposed to the Intelsat Board of Governors to establish a new unlimited use of a transponder for international television. Politically, the request from Australia was probably easier to get through the Board than if the request had come from the United States on behalf of CNN.

Within Intelsat, the Finance Department was somewhere between skeptical to opposed to the concept. Several financial analysts suggested that this would lead to reduced revenues and that the occasional-use revenues would drop dramatically. Intelsat had a new Director General at the time who wished to make his mark. He pushed me to develop new digital television rates, to develop 'sales' of transponders to customers, and he particularly supported the idea of international television rates. Although Richard Colino was Director of Intelsat only from 1983 to 1985, he did make a huge impact on the organization. He tried to make Intelsat adapt to a competitive telecommunications environment and revolutionize its marketing and tariffing approaches to the global market. He also tried to allow Intelsat to reach the global market directly and 'end run' its signatory entities in doing so.

On the positive side, Intelsat traffic grew rapidly, and its market agility increased enormously. On the negative side, the organization was politicized and thrown into a chaotic planning mode with satellite procurement process reshaped to Rich Colino's personal interest. In order to personally benefit, Rich Colino and his Deputy Director General, Jose Alegrett, manipulated a number of key Intelsat decisions to get a kick-back on a building addition, receive compensation for planning studies, and otherwise 'feather their nests.' Several of these improprieties and outright illegal acts were designed to increase Colino's power and prestige. Fortunately, an effective and ethical internal auditor (James Malarkey) discovered these actions and reported them to the external auditors and to the Chairman of the Board. In a few weeks, Colino was gone. The Colino years were described in *Business Week* as like living in an environment akin to someone hitting a golf ball in a small tiled bathroom. Ironically, the very positive contribution of Colino's action to move Intelsat aggressively into competitive global telecommunications markets was cancelled by his greedy and Machiavellian manipulation of the Intelsat organization and its Board.

Two years later, after the Board's favorable decision to go forward with full-time international television transponder rates, we had nine transponders under contract and more in the pipeline. I asked the Director of Finance if he was supportive of the decision. He stated that occasional use television revenues were down, and he was not so sure. Incredibly, overall television revenues were up by five times at this point. Today, Intelsat has nearly 40 full-time international transponder leases in effect, and there are dozens more on competitive systems. There were 92 signatories to Intelsat when those key decisions were taken in 1984, and today there are 136 members. Most of the recent and new members of Intelsat have come from Eastern Europe and the entities that were, until recently, a part of the USSR.

* * * * *

The International Satellite Operator Group (ISOG) was formed to foster cooperation between broadcasters, Intelsat, and its signatories. By 1990, this cooperation led to the phasing out of shared downlinking costs and resulted in a rate paid by the uplinking service that covered multi-point downlinking.

Interestingly, none of the Intelsat employees mentioned one other reason for Intelsat's change of direction—one that I believe did make a major difference. That was the introduction of the most important ingredient for effecting change of this kind: *competition.*

Thus, in the mid-1980s, we had one of the world's most significant and truly international organizations (except for the countries in the communist orbit then under Intersputnik), and rather than move in ways that were of maximum benefit to the global population, given that satellites were one of the greatest human achievements, the Board of Governors, representing the commercially avaricious PTTs, failed, in my opinion, to act intelligently until the pressure for independent international satellites began to build. That movement began with PanAmSat and its creative leader, Rene Anselmo (see chapter twenty-nine).

Meanwhile, I was still trying to find ways to get around the various regulations that prevented the distribution of CNN worldwide. For North and Central America, I had come up with an answer thanks to Bob Ross, TBS's General Counsel, and an imaginative attorney who appreciated creative concepts and would try to find a legal way to do what we needed done.

I told Bob that I needed to find a way to allow international users, who received the CNN domestic signal, to pay for it within the legal means permitted by international law. Bob said that was a tough one, and when I didn't hear from him for quite a while, I thought he gave up on my request. Then he sent me a Copyright Release Form.

The form consisted of two legal pages and, in effect, said that since the domestic signal was available in countries outside the U.S., and we did not have the legal right to offer the signal to downlink users (because of Intelsat rules), we did have the right to sue any receiver of our signal(s) for copyright infringement. It was up to some other entity to protect their rights as to how they received the signal. Brilliant. The Copyright Release Form freed me from international restrictions on CNN agreements in countries near the U.S. and within its satellite footprint, and I immediately set about using it in the Caribbean and in Central America.

My third urgent problem, piracy, was also occurring in the United

States. Scrambling and decoding the CNN signal was not successful at first. The decoders originally used by HBO, the first program user of U.S. satellites in 1975 (Turner was the second in 1976), were easy to break. As Wes Hanemayer, Vice President, Distribution Systems, said when I interviewed him on the "sanctity" of decoders:

> It was easy to break it. The original decoder system that was designed under contract to HBO in the early 1980s was designed under the previous assumption that you had control over both the transmission and the reception side. They were trying to make sure that the system could not be broken by somebody who could only intercept the electronic transmission. But what they totally missed was that, being an open-ended transmission, you only had control over the uplink side. With all the boxes going out to consumers' homes, you really didn't have control over the receive side. So the physical implementation of the decoder, and the physical security of people getting in and interrupting the signals and then modifying the hardware—because we didn't have control over the hardware devices — [meant] they could modify the receive hardware. They didn't have to make a device totally from scratch; they just went in and modified the videocypher boxes. So for four years, the industry went through a state of denial, saying, No, no, no; it's not really broken. We put in counter-measures. They finally said there was no security and that it wasn't even keeping the honest people honest. Fifteen years later, there was still no guarantee that 'unbreakable decoders' could be designed. When Scientific Atlanta invented B-Mac decoders in the late '80s, they told me that B-Mac was unbreakable. I'm not so sure any more. Other experts have told me that there is no such thing as an 'unbreakable decoder.'

But, regardless of these technical equipment challenges, my feeling has been that, with the continuing international distribution of programs like CNN by satellite, advertising would sufficiently cover the costs necessary for such program distribution and make profit as well. Ted was farsighted when he predicted that the CNN satellite signal would not need to be ultimately encoded in the international area. A 2001 *Wall Street Journal* article notes that "CNN's viewers outside the U.S. outnumber its domestic audience by about 2 to1," and "CNN's total advertising revenue in 2000 was $1.36 billion, up from $1.19 billion a year earlier." The exception to the rule of advertising carrying program costs, of course, are channels like HBO and Showtime that do not contain commercials. It may be necessary, if decoding equipment integrity is not possible, for these program services also to operate with advertising in some form.

Unfortunately, after the 1996 Telecommunications Act, the amount of advertising per hour has increased substantially over the limits previously set by the FCC for television broadcasters. This was formulated on the mistaken belief that competition would restrict the saturation of commercials. However, the increasing demand for television advertising time resulted in most television commercial channels overloading their programs with ads. The result was in some cases almost double the amount of commercials and an exasperated and exhausted television audience.

Thus, the television watcher is caught between a rock and a hard place: too many advertising channels that steal the viewer's time and a hope that adless pay-channels without commercials will remain. As of this writing, TCM is one of the only commercial free channels. But I doubt it will last long. Its competitor and originator of classic movies, American Movie Classics, has already inserted advertising. It is my opinion that the public will regret the power of the broadcast lobby in formulating the 1996 change in rules.

* * * * *

I wondered where, besides the Far East, I could offer CNN. The fact that the U.S. domestic signal spilled all over North and Central America and reached as far as Bogotá, Colombia, gave me my answer.

Canada, a much larger territory than the U.S., received the CNN signal in all its populated areas and was primarily an English-speaking country. In early 1984, two telecommunications companies received approval from the Canadian Radio-Television and Telecommunications Commission (CRTC) to add CNN and *Headline News* to their existing discretionary pay-television packages. Later, the definition of a discretionary pay package was broadened to include an expanded basic tier of satellite services. The CNN channels would grow rapidly in the late 1980s and early 1990s to a universe of over five million Canadian homes for CNN, and three million Canadian homes for *Headline News* by 1996.

CNN relied heavily on reciprocal arrangements to collect its news. In Canada, CNN had such an arrangement with the CTV network. It worked in much the same way as our arrangements with the Sevens Network and TV-Asahi. As good as CTV was, however, it couldn't compare with the CBC, a commercial government television and radio network. CNN previously had not been able to develop a cooperative arrangement with CBC.

But by September 1983, I decided to broach the idea of a CBC/CNN reciprocal agreement during a film and program selling trip to Canada. By then CNN's stature was growing.

I learned, however, that it is dangerous to play with elephants. They can sit on you whenever it suits them. While I succeeded in bringing the giant CBC and CNN together in a non-commercial arrangement, to my dismay, the CBC demanded some limited exclusivity that made my job a nightmare in Canada for many years. It limited my playing field. I could sell CNN to independent stations but not to other networks, in particular to CTV, the second largest network in Canada, and the group that held the original reciprocal relationship with CNN. In addition, CBC eliminated my sales to Global Television Network in Toronto and Ontario. We could only sell CNN to CITY-TV, an independent station in Toronto. It made me wonder what would have happened to NBC, CBS, and ABC if the U.S. government had decided to build and support its own television network and it had wielded its awesome power the way the CBC was permitted to do.

Despite the Canadian limitations, I was still able to strengthen news collection for CNN, not only in Canada, but in other parts of the world where the CBC had bureaus, including CBC's bureau in Beijing, China.

Burt Reinhardt was ecstatic—because I was now giving him access to news in a most essential country that was closed to other U.S. networks and news services, except for CBS. However, I had, in effect, shot myself in the foot. This lesson was not lost on me, and I learned to deal with giant networks more carefully. The CNN executives were most pleased with the CBC arrangement in Beijing, since Canadian businesses during this period were more easily accepted in communist countries than American businesses, particularly news agencies.

During our talks in that October visit to Canada in 1984, and for a long time afterward, CBC insisted on forming a 24-hour Canadian CBC/CNN channel. CBC's strength in its negotiations was that CNN had, at that time, inadequate resources for collecting news worldwide. But Terry McGuirk felt it would hamper use of CNN in Canada's many and fast growing cable systems.

In a trip to Los Angeles in January 1985, I met with Paul Morton, General Manager of the Global Television Network, and told him of the CBC request for CNN exclusivity. He shrieked, "There's no way that the CBC can get away with it! The Canadian government will not permit them to do it!" While Paul and I were involved in this very intense conversation, water began to flow into his hotel room. He had been running a bath, and when I knocked on the door, he had forgotten completely about it. He dashed to the phone to call housekeeping just as we heard banging on the door. The hotel housekeepers rushed in with towels and mops—it had already started to leak into the room below, and Paul had run into the bathroom to pull the tub plug in his socks and came out embarrassed and disheveled while we both roared with laughter. Once we solved that problem, it didn't take long for Paul to get serious again, and he wanted to act on the CBC information immediately, but I asked him to back off until we completed our arrangement with the CBC. He must have ignored my request because, in the final document, the Global Television Network had some relief from the CBC demands. I wondered why CTV didn't react just as strongly and protest to the government as well.

I continued after 1985 to develop CNN agreements in Canada with independent television stations, as permitted in the CBC/CNN reciprocal news arrangement.

I still don't understand how the CBC, today's broadcast version of *tyrannosaurus rex,* subsidized and supported by the Canadian government, is allowed deliberately to damage the news-gathering capabilities of private commercial networks not subsidized by the Canadian taxpayers. In relationships between television and government in the world arena, I would soon learn that this was only the tip of the proverbial iceberg.

Through the mid-1980s, and in some cases later, every country I encountered, except for the United States, experienced some form of government control over the television broadcasting within their countries. Even the Western democracies of Great Britain, Canada, and France exercise such control. On the other hand, as large and powerful at the NHK network was in Japan, to my knowledge, it made no attempt to interfere with the destinies of its competing, privately owned networks. In Australia, as in the U.S., the networks were autonomous, but I sensed that even there the government had significant political influence.

The Australian government's Australian Broadcasting Service operated as an adjunct television programmer, supplying cultural and educational programs that the commercial networks would not provide because of their limited audience. Australia went further than the United States in subsidizing programs for special cultural groups. The South African Broadcasting Corporation did this as well, even to the extent of forming networks in native languages to augment existing programming in Afrikaans and English. But no competing networks existed in South Africa, and the government-operated network controlled all television programming during the apartheid period.

I concluded an agreement with the owner of a small group of independent stations in central Canada. Then, after numerous trips, I completed a CNN arrangement with CITY-TV, Toronto's most important local news station. I began studying other international opportunities within the range of the U.S. domestic satellite signal. In 1984 I turned my attention to Central America and the Caribbean Islands, and that's when I learned a new meaning for the word *piracy*. Not the peg-legged, swashbuckling, knife-in-the-teeth-eyes kind of pirate. I mean a much subtler and quieter piracy.

CNN was broadcasting in an open, unencoded signal, brought down by cable systems and relayed, usually by wire, to individual homes. Television broadcasters brought the signal down on private dishes (antennas) as well, and relayed selected portions to television viewers. Laws governing the use of private dishes had not been fully developed, but a few private homes and businesses in the United States, and in neighboring countries, were taking the signal without payment to Turner or to other satellite programmers. I doubt very much if laws in any of these countries would have made much difference. Some countries argued that Turner benefited sufficiently from advertising sales, although these sales were only 50 percent of Turner's total income for all its programming channels, as well as CNN. The other 50 percent came from program licensing fees paid by the cable networks, with so many cents paid for each channel per month. Turner could hardly benefit from pirates. Since they didn't admit that they were viewers, we couldn't claim their numbers in our audience statistics for advertising purposes.

In non-U.S. territory in North America, it was *all piracy* in the beginning, even for those who would have been willing to pay, until the mechanism for payment was developed. One could more easily arrange to pay in Canada, but in Mexico, the Caribbean, and Central America, where copyright laws were less respected, piracy was rampant.

I had heard that Jamaica Broadcasting Corporation (JBC), the government television network, was pirating CNN. I decided to visit Jamaica and make a formal agreement. JBC officials were not anxious to see me. Although I finally arranged for a meeting with JBC's General Manager, when I arrived in June, 1984, she was not present. The television network's attorney spoke for her. "It's a lie that we pirate. The signal comes over our country. We have a right to take it down. We were just testing it."

From early in 1984, until the CNN signal became scrambled by stages between 1986 and 1989, I talked to many people in various parts of the world concerning piracy. Most, but not all, piracy occurred in less-developed countries, which usually means less-developed legal systems. Thus, piracy is difficult to enforce because it is not viewed as a serious crime. If I steal your wallet, I am a thief, and the punishment in some of these countries is severe. In Saudi Arabia, it can cost a hand. Yet if I take a satellite signal down with my own dish, and even if I redistribute it for payment in a form of cable service without any further payment, this is acceptable because nothing "material" has been taken and the signal is there—hanging around—all over the place, just waiting to be picked up. In France, the courts ruled that it is legal to take an unscrambled satellite signal down to one's own dish because the satellite is above the country. The counter argument is that the programs are copyrighted material, just as books are, and the producers, writers, and investors have rights to their ideas and programs. There are now, and there were in the mid-1980s, international copyright laws that protect the authors of films and programs.

I returned from Jamaica, realizing that getting CNN agreements in the Caribbean, with its propensity to pirate the signal, would be difficult. Piracy is like looting after a national disaster or when a mob has decided it is acceptable. The rationale is exactly the same, and I heard it over and over: "Everyone is doing it."

Meanwhile, Ted continued to maintain that unless the signal was scrambled, no one would pay for it. And we had to find some way to cover the ongoing CNN losses. Eventually, we would have costs associated with satellite downlinking, but in the early years, I had worked out the agreements with AFRTS and Sevens so that there were no additional satellite costs to TBS.

Another problem with the Caribbean was the size of the market. It consisted of many small islands, sparsely populated and not very prosperous. I would have to spend as much time hopping from island to island as it took me to visit big countries with very large populations. I started pressuring Henry Gillespie again for some staff help, in addition to Joyce. But Henry, in his role as President of TPS, and for whom I still worked, was resistant. No one seemed to think that what I was doing was such a big deal that I couldn't do it in my spare time. After all, we had a signal only in North and Central America and "sort of one" in the Pacific "that no one was interested in but two customers in Japan and Australia. So, what's the big deal, Pike? You can handle it."

Not long after this, I did convince Henry that there was more interest in CNN than he had envisioned. Ted was supportive, particularly if you could show him that the cost would be minimal. But in 1984, no one, including myself, was thinking globally. Our concentration was on the Pacific and North and Central America. We hadn't yet considered adding satellites in other areas of the world.

In July 1984, I attended a Mexican cable meeting in Puerto Vallarta and learned that one reason piracy of the U.S. signals was common was that it was not economically feasible for the cable systems to pay for the service. A typical cable system in this area was getting about five dollars per month per customer and paying a 15 percent tax.

I was concerned when I realized that Mexico was not included in the special arrangements we had made with WTN in the Caribbean for their news on CNN. I phoned Nick Quinn of WTN in London, and he agreed to receive a percent arrangement on the CNN sales that I made.

Another problem we faced in dealing with Mexico was converting pesos to dollars. I spoke with Gordon Kahn, the president of the Mexican cable group, and he proposed that the organization collect monthly payments from the various cable companies for a fee and help in the conversion. However, this meant that more than half of CNN's income from Mexico and the Caribbean went to WTN (18 per cent), our agents in Latin America (15 percent), and Kahn's Mexican cable group (25 percent). I became determined to eliminate middlemen whenever I could.

In August 1984, I flew to Bermuda and made a CNN agreement with Ken DeFontes, who was beginning a multiple distribution service of satellite signals, and he wanted CNN to help support his new service. I was finding that CNN was popular everywhere I went, and in many cases, was the reason a cable or multi-distribution service was formed. Then other signals were added. In Ken's case, access to CNN enabled him to put together a total service. In addition to the contract with Ken DeFontes for a multiple distribution system, I sold three hours of programming to Bermuda Broadcasting.

I returned to New Zealand and Australia in September 1984. Because New Zealand was also an English-speaking country, it represented a good opportunity for CNN. Besides, I was having problems completing the Australian CNN agreement. On the way, I stopped in Los Angeles to meet with the AFRTS people. I started working with this organization in 1979, when it contacted me for permission to use WTCG (WTBS) news and sports programs, then delivered on domestic satellite where armed forces personnel were stationed. I continued this association when I got involved in selling programs. Although technically the AFRTS received programs without charge as a public service, it did pay a management fee, and Henry Gillespie was always insisting that I pressure it for an increase in this fee. Industry producers usually cooperated with AFRTS and authorized the showing of their programs to the U.S. Armed Forces without a fee, so we were rarely asked to provide Turner-produced programs. As the SuperStation developed, we had programs that it wanted, particularly sports programs, such as Braves baseball and Hawks basketball.

I had been asked a couple of times to be a guest speaker at its annual meetings and, over the years, I developed a good relationship with the officers and civilian personnel responsible for its operations worldwide. In 1982, during its annual meeting, we began to talk about their possible use of CNN. By 1983, AFRTS was carrying 13 and a half-hours of CNN per day to armed forces personnel on various satellites covering most of the global population. The oppressive Intelsat downlinking costs were still in effect, so there was no way to use its extensive coverage of CNN for those areas.

Between Far East trips of February and May, 1985, I completed arrangements or continued discussion for CNN with Canada, Bermuda, Aruba (Netherlands Antilles), the Bahamas, Puerto Rico, Curacao, and Barbados. Our Latin American agent in Miami, Florida (Television Interamericana S.A.—TISA), was helping in El Salvador, Belize, Panama, and Honduras. Later in 1985, we added Cost Rica. Mexico was more complicated. Although there were many opportunities, I needed to spend a great deal of time to determine with whom we should align ourselves in their developing cable markets. Television broadcasting in Mexico was under the control of a powerful monopoly called Televisa, and I wanted to know if there were any underdog broadcasters.

I still had a limited staff, but we did have an agent who sold Turner programs to Spanish-speaking countries in parts of Latin America. Tom Todd, working as a TPS associate, offered good advice and helped launch CNN in Puerto Rico. He later concentrated on the Goodwill Games in Latin America. I had hired Tom and watched him develop. He had been a television program director in Greenville, South Carolina, to whom I once tried to sell a schedule of Braves baseball games. He became a fine, successful salesman, only to die of a mysterious brain malady a few years later.

CHAPTER FOURTEEN

Encountering Opposition In a Chinese Democracy

The crime against life, the worst of all crimes, is not to feel. And there was never, perhaps, a civilization in which that crime, the crime of torpor, of lethargy, of apathy, the snake-like sin of coldness-at-the-heart, was commoner than in our technical civilization.

—Archibald MacLeish

In 1984, I returned to the Pacific Rim in November, visiting Hong Kong first. Like most countries faced with the inevitable changes in telecommunications, cable, and traditional broadcast systems, it was having difficulty converting to the new technologies. Entrenched broadcasters, such as TVB in Hong Kong, would often use their political influence to prevent or slow down cable with its dozens, even hundreds, of channels, which would diminish its audience, hence, its advertising income. Hong Kong was a tourist mecca and conveniently located at the front door to Communist China, which, in 1984, was just beginning to awaken to the possibilities of international trade and discourse. Tourists and business executives were flocking to Hong Kong, which is why it had so many hotels. China was forbidden to tourists at that time, so Hong Kong was the closest thing to visiting China. Business interests were attracted by the cheap labor for manufacturing. The Great Wall of China endured, but another, more impenetrable wall separated China and the rest of the world.

Our original plan was to downlink the CNN signal via Cable & Wireless (PTT) and transmit the signal locally to at least 26 hotels via a multiple distribution system (MDS) signal for which, we were told, a license was available. Our application was directed to the Commission for Television and Entertainment Licensing. There were delays, supposedly because the government couldn't make up its mind "whether your application falls within a broadcasting or cable definition."

The potential income from the hotels in Hong Kong, which represented 30,000 rooms, was extremely desirable for Turner. The battle for cable market control went on for years, and by the late-1980s, we decided we had to find a way to connect to the hotels without cable.

We even considered distributing CNN on videotape to hotels as a temporary measure. That meant delivery three times a day with news that was eight hours old—the time needed for taping, editing, dubbing and distributing—which would have been a nightmare. Even though there were no other competing news services that could have provided the news in English (aside from a few television news programs), I'm glad we decided that this was not a compromise we wanted to make. It was the CNN of instant, live news that made our international reputation grow each day. Not long after I turned over the Pacific Rim to others, CNN was finally brought down and distributed in Hong Kong to hotels and cable stations, as well as to television broadcasting services.

Hong Kong, then a British crown colony, was the first place where the local PTT (Cable & Wireless) was willing to negotiate a reasonable fee to downlink CNN. But then the local government delayed it. I found this very strange, given the fact that Hong Kong was a business and commerce model for all of Asia, even for the world.

In November 1984, I went for the first time to Taiwan to see what the possibilities for CNN were there. The existence of Taiwan as an independent country depended a great deal on the United States and its defensive strategies in the Western Pacific. The Vietnam War was long over, but the U.S. government still had concerns in the Western Pacific. The

Soviet Union, the People's Republic of China, North Korea, and Vietnam were geographically positioned to threaten U.S. allies, such as Japan, South Korea, and other parts of southern Asia as far west as India.

Taiwan, a large island with a population of 18 million in the mid-1980s, is just off the coast of China, and is where Chiang Kai-Shek and the remnants of his Nationalist Army took refuge after World War II. Its war with the Communists ended in a stalemate just as the more protracted and costly war between North and South Korea, involving United Nations forces, had.

As China's military strength and arms sophistication grew, Taiwan was forced to provide itself with a military government that would defend the island against an invasion by mainland China. Thus, when I met with South Korean and Taiwanese broadcasters, I had the advantage of dealing with organizations and governments that wanted to learn as much as possible about the United States and its people. But because of the military nature of those governments, I sensed that they wanted to keep all information under their control.

Going through Customs at the international airport in Taipei was a slow, deliberate process. I was carefully screened as to the purpose of my visit. When I arrived in the city, I received an invitation from the Government Information Office (GIO), which I learned from some American friends was a very powerful agency. Anything I accomplished in developing CNN in Taiwan would have to be with its approval.

The day after my arrival, a GIO vehicle picked me up to take me to the GIO offices to meet with certain officials. I was particularly impressed with Dr. Sunshine Kuang. Before the meetings however, I was taken into a room with a single stool and invited to sit down. The door was closed, and I was alone in the room. A film screen appeared, and I had no choice but to watch a propaganda film on the strengths and wonders of Taiwan.

Another reason the United States was very important to Taiwan was the growing business that was developing between the two countries. Access to cheap labor in China was not yet available, so U.S. businesses were flocking to Taiwan until even this small nation became, like Japan, a prime example of what investment capital can mean to a country's economy. This kind of investment meant jobs for the large population, as well as more educational opportunities for their children, and a chance to move up in their society in the future.

This message was not lost on China, which, with the largest population in the world, had the largest supply of cheap labor. It was already looking at Taiwan with envy, particularly after the death of Mao Tse-Tung in 1976. China's labor force had never been wisely and efficiently utilized, at least as far as we know from its written history. China's solution to difficult projects was to use huge numbers of laborers, and communism only perpetuated that philosophy. This was also true in North Korea, where the leader, Kim Il Sung, who lived much longer than Mao, had focused the country so much on military development that it suffers periodic famines on a scale greater than anywhere else in the modern world. Kim built a totally closed and isolated society that forbid any access to outside information and prevented any from going out. Interestingly, he allowed CNN reporters in for brief visits before his death. After he died, his son, Kim Jong Il, has continued the policy of letting CNN in—another example of our success in planting CNN as the world's dominant television news source.

Just as the Berlin Wall still prevented discourse between the East and West in Europe in 1984, other walls, just as effective, kept information from entering or leaving China, North Korea, and Vietnam. I felt like one little ant trying to drill a hole in the concrete of those walls. China was still scary to me, but I was learning how to create CNN proposals that did interest governments and television stations. They wanted CNN to be part of their world, whether in a 24-hour format, by using a portion thereof, or by having occasional stories in their local newscasts. Cable had not yet begun developing in the Far East, except in Japan, and there were formidable forces trying to prevent it, especially in Australia. The television networks were well connected politically, and their clout kept cable from developing for many years.

After Taiwan's GIO had "indoctrinated" me, I held separate meetings with the three Taiwanese networks, but my goal was to sign up all three networks.

I invited representatives of the three Taiwan networks to the Lai Lai Sheraton Hotel, where I reserved a conference room and a blackboard. I laid out what could be done with each of the three networks' use of CNN, including all-night CNN live coverage, either rotated by the three or used by the station with the weakest audience. I knew that the Taiwanese, like the Japanese, wanted to learn English and to "study" America. I had also learned that they had to get approval from the GIO for many programming decisions, particularly those with a foreign flavor. I showed them how all three could share in the live, from-the-scene coverage of breaking news, as it happened 24 hours a day, and explained the individual programs with broad appeal, such as *Science and Technology, Style* with Elsa Klensch, *Financial News* and *Health and Nutrition.*

I estimated their potential income on the blackboard in the "good news" column, and explained that the cost would be $200,000 annually for each television network, or $16,666 per month. I was on a roll, doing a helluva sales pitch. When they collectively said they were in favor of an arrangement with CNN, I was flying high. Then I heard the word *but.* "But what about the cost of downlinking the signal?" one of them asked, and the others nodded. I had hoped the government would cooperate if the group appealed collectively for the "benefit of the country."

"All you have to do is put an antenna next to your television station," I announced. "The cost is minimal, only a few hundred thousand—one time only—and you can watch CNN 24 hours a day." In other words, I didn't want to stop progress by worrying about the small stuff.

"But we must go through our PTT, the International Telecommunications Administration," was the reply.

"How much is their rate?" I asked, already knowing I wouldn't like the answer.

"When we receive Visnews or WTN, the normal feed each day is 10 minutes. The International Telecommunications Administration (ITA) charges us $360 for the first 10 minutes and $30 per minute thereafter." It was the same answer I heard before.

I drew the same figures on the blackboard: 30 x 60 minutes = $1,800 per hour x 24 hours = $43,200 per day x 365 days in a year = $15,768,000 per year to downlink the signal. I was asking the three networks together for $600,000 per year to deliver the news content. The PTT fee was totally absurd when inexpensive equipment was available to downlink the signal. Again, my potential customers and I were trapped by the Intelsat system.

Nevertheless, I continued discussions with the three networks regarding their use of CNN news material. I met with government officials and the ITA regarding the cost of downlinking CNN. I tried to build the pressure on both ends. When I was back in the United States, I made several trips to Washington, D.C., to confront Intelsat directly. In Taiwan and other countries, I put pressure on the PTTs through meetings with government representatives and television station managers. I did this in every country I visited. One way or another, I was determined to make this work.

When I returned to Atlanta at the end of November, I had two plans. First, to encourage Ted and the company to "think long-range" in terms of satellite distribution of CNN worldwide, and, second, to determine what area I could develop in the meantime that would extend the present CNN domestic signal beyond North America and the Australian Sevens Network signal in the Pacific. I believed the AFRTS was the place to begin.

I explored the idea of selling AFRTS's distribution of CNN programs. I alerted him to widespread use of CNN in hotels and through cable, which normally included WTN and EBU news material, and to which we had no resale rights at that time. I had watched a CNN *Headline News* half-hour in my hotel room in Seoul. The hotel, of course, was pirating the signal from the AFRTS satellite, as were many other hotels worldwide. Other methods of pirating cable were also occurring, including the linking together of groups of houses by makeshift wiring, as I had learned was being done in Papua, New Guinea.

Burt Reinhardt could justifiably refuse to cooperate with me in delivering the U.S. CNN domestic signal for commercial purposes. Instead, he merely urged me to be cautious, and he always helped me work through the delicate contractual arrangements, which were possible because of his good relationships with these news providers.

During 1984, while I was juggling the deals in Japan and Australia and plowing the ground in Hong Kong, the Philippines, and Canada, I was still expected to sell programming. I was completing the purchase and the dubbing of the *Doraemon* cartoon series, *Portrait of America,* and ten Toei animated feature films, selling and producing *Starcade* in San Francisco, and keeping up my files and legal searches on all public domain films. Joyce, my loyal staff of one, worked long, arduous hours to keep up with me.

* * * * *

The year 1984 was the most exciting year of my career. I was working for a creative and aggressive company at the beginning of the satellite age, just as the world was poised to share information. My approach of dealing directly with clients—the television stations, networks, hotels, and future cable systems—was working.

On these long flights back and forth to the Far East, I developed a routine. I always arrived at the airport hours early. I hated the hassle of running to catch a plane. I wanted to relax and think about what I had accomplished and what I still had to do. For the first few hours of a long flight I felt very creative—particularly if things had gone well at home or in the field—I wrote poetry and created plans for future CNN development. There was something about the oxygen at 38,000 feet that I found exhilarating.

As CNN's territory grew, I became even more "high" as I traveled. I knew I was on a mission that transcended my job at Turner. I thought a great deal about the possibilities of CNN on a global scale. I believed it could, and hoped it would, change an existing truth: Lack of communication and understanding often leads to horrendous and catastrophic events. I sensed early that the combination of satellites and a 24-hour unbiased news service could provide enough information to make major differences in leadership decisions, particularly in smaller countries with limited access to information.

I didn't know it then, but my world traveling had only just begun.

CHAPTER FIFTEEN

Cultivating the Asian Connection

The wayside of business is full of brilliant men who started out with a spurt and lacked the stamina to finish. Their places were taken by patient and unshowy plodders who never knew when to quit.

—J.R. Todd

I sent a note to Terry McGuirk comparing the cost of purchasing our own transponder with the cost of the right to use the Sevens Network system, which required very large earth-receiving dishes. A small antenna of seven to 11 meters (23-36 feet) would speed up possible agreements with stations in Taiwan and the Philippines, provided we could solve the problem of downlinking costs with Intelsat.

Our ability to expand using the AFRTS signal to other parts of the world also required modifying Intelsat's downlinking costs. As well as meeting with Intelsat directly, I was putting pressure on AFRTS through Colonel Larry Pollack, who was in charge of the distribution of the AFRTS signal worldwide.

In January 1985, I received official notification from Colonel Pollack that AFRTS gave Turner permission to use its CNN signal "on a temporary basis and as an emergency replacement off the AFRTS Intelsat Pacific Spare satellite," with the caveat that "This authorization is valid when it is in concert with the Intelsat agreements." AFRTS wasn't giving me any more than Intelsat was willing to give. This was a gain, even if it did impose certain limits. I was wearing away the wall, albeit with a garden hose. I hoped that my constant pressure would eventually weaken the wall. I did not yet have access to the AFRTS signals in Europe, Africa, South America, and Southern Asia, but I was working on that.

Henry Gillespie continued to insist that we get more than the token management payment for CNN and other TBS programs broadcast over the AFRTS. Although programming sources and networks had traditionally allowed their programs to be viewed free by the armed forces worldwide, the networks and film studios probably did not realize that what had been originally delivered on videotapes directly to the armed services installations was now being relayed on an *open* signal by global satellites. This meant that anyone who installed a dish and aimed it at the proper satellite could watch CNN, as well as recent Hollywood movies and sports events. Only the small number of home "receive" dishes at that time prevented piracy from becoming a major problem wherever the AFRTS signal was available.

By 1985, Hollywood and the networks became aware of the potential drain on their future distribution income and told AFRTS to scramble the signal or lose the programs. The first scrambled signals were easily unscrambled. As I negotiated for AFRTS's cooperation in helping to change Intelsat's downlinking rules (the important issue for me), I also asked for larger payments, the important issue for Henry. Tom Todd, the sales executive at TPS, who was helping me sell programs to AFRTS, and later in Latin America, agreed that we needed to maintain good relations with AFRTS. Henry's "get tough" policy on money would seriously hamper our objectives. So, Tom played "bad cop" to my "good cop," and we were able to keep our balancing act in place. He pressed for money, and I relieved the pressure.

In February 1985, I returned to Taiwan, Hong Kong, Manila and, for the first time, Singapore. The Singapore government, as in Taiwan, had complete control over the television service. But we started another long dialogue. I always hailed access to CNN as the chief benefit, regardless of whether the government controlled the media. I knew that as people watched other countries benefit from information and news coming in and out, access to CNN would have a positive impact. I understood that it would take some countries years to realize that they were being left behind in a way that would inhibit their country's economy and development.

In Taiwan, I continued to chip away at the GIO's hard shell. GIO officials talked with me despite their determination to stay in complete control over the news departments of the television networks. The government was faced with a dilemma. On the one hand, it had to stay in a constant state of military preparedness. The possibility of an invasion by mainland China, which considered Taiwan part of its territory, governed its actions. On the other hand, it wanted to improve relations with the West, particularly the United States.

China Television Service (CTS) agreed to consider the use of CNN news stories in its local news programs. But this meant CTS could selectively use our news. I wanted a broader use of CNN.

A representative of CTS Enterprises, a subsidiary of CTS, was interested in obtaining CNN on an experimental basis in hotels. He believed that there were four or five major hotels that would be interested in carrying English-language news. I was willing, but CTS Enterprises would have to find a way to receive CNN. The only plan we could come up with was again the idea of bringing the signal down (in Hong Kong) and shipping the videos by air to Taiwan. I could just see the distribution of CNN by moped in Taipei, the most congested traffic of any city in the world. Taipei was moped heaven.

I wasn't too pleased with the videotape suggestion, although it would strengthen our position in Hong Kong. My strategy was to find a way to bring CNN in, and then later, when its value as a source of information was apparent, work to expand its service. I used this philosophy to persuade many countries worldwide that were as determined as Taiwan to control the information entering their country.

Y.S. Chin, the CTS Enterprises representative, proposed acquiring CNN by videotape if we would accept the same fee it was paying for WTN and Visnews. We decided to meet later that week to develop a Memorandum of Understanding. Then I met with S.C. Yeh, Director of Traffic and Department of the Commerce ITA, the Taiwan PTT and member of

Intelsat. We discussed the means of getting the signal down. He offered three possibilities: (1) a modification of its present antenna, which was scheduled for 1988 (three years later) but which could be ready sooner for an additional fee. (2) A small dish that it could install more easily, but this would depend on how fast CTS and CTS Enterprises wanted to begin using CNN and the quality of the signal it wanted. For broadcast purposes, it needed a larger dish. It all depended on how eager it was and how hard the television stations' news departments were willing to fight for the extra help and for the quality of dish they were to have. (3) A third possibility took me completely by surprise. A television station might provide a small dish of its own, if it was approved by the Minister of Telecommunications. I also discussed with Yeh the possibility of their delivering the signal, once it had it, to hotels. But I sensed his concern that there was no way to censor the signal.

This brought up an interesting point. If the government was willing to allow the TV stations to bring CNN down without censorship, it could trust that the stations' news editors were sufficiently sophisticated to prevent any damaging news from being relayed to the public. However, if they allowed continuing unfettered news without censorship to be shown in hotels 24 hours a day, they had absolutely no control. I could visualize someone in the GIO jumping up and asking, "Doesn't CNN understand that Taiwanese stay in local hotels, too?"

We discussed one modification that was an improvement on the Hong Kong delivery method. It was to bring the signal down in Taiwan at a central point, where some editing could be done and then delivered by a modified multiple distribution system to the hotels. I wasn't too keen on the editing, but I wanted to see if the GIO would allow CNN in, even with such limitations. And it would be a significant step if I could find a way to break the current downlinking rate of $15 million and actually downlink CNN for a full year.

I couldn't solve just one problem at a time, especially when bringing about any change was so difficult and time-consuming. If I could find a way to get into Taiwan, then I would just have to find a way to bring the signal down. I thought I could, and in doing so our position as a news organization would have greater credibility in China, and I would have laid the foundation for taking CNN there.

While in Auckland, on the last leg of my journey before returning to Atlanta, I received a telex from all three networks in Taiwan rejecting my proposal. It read: "The time is not right yet for them to digest the programs on a daily basis." I assumed the government had made the decision to keep CNN out of Taiwan, and *them* meant the citizens of Taiwan. I was determined to return and include more meetings with the government itself. While I failed in one sense, I succeeded in another. I forced the governmental powers to consider the unrestricted distribution of news in what was then a closed society.

I went to Taiwan three more times in 1984 and 1985, pressuring the GIO and the television stations, as well as government officials, and each time I removed one or two stones. Slowly, more stones began to move, because after I no longer worked in the Pacific Rim, I could "hear" the avalanche as the GIOs and other government bodies in Taiwan, Singapore, Hong Kong, South Korea, Thailand, the Philippines, Malaysia, and later in India and mainland China, finally realized there was no way to prevent CNN from entering their countries. Some continued to try, technically and politically, to keep the CNN signal out. But, ultimately, they were doomed to fail because the satellites sat 22,300 miles above the earth and sent down their signals like sunshine, no matter how hard (or for what reason) the people in power fought the distribution of information and the erosion of ignorance. Regardless of how broad-brimmed your hat is, sunshine always finds your face. The CNN signal was now there for anyone with the courage to install a receive antenna.

After Taiwan and Singapore, I flew to Sydney, Australia, to meet with the Sevens Network and to complete a long-term agreement. It had wanted an exclusive arrangement with CNN, but that would have been too costly. I was able to make an agreement with the Tens Network as well.

On February 28, while in Sydney, I received a telex from Joyce inviting me and all the other "old timers" to a luncheon celebrating Ted's twenty-fifth anniversary with the company. I immediately sent back a telex to be read at the luncheon.

> Greetings from the other end of the world. Sorry can't be present for occasion. Promise to be at the fiftieth anniversary even though by then I'll be bringing CNN to other planets. Sidney in Sydney

Satisfied with the results in Australia, I flew on to Auckland, New Zealand, to continue discussions with Alan Martin and Bruce Crossan of TV New Zealand.

In late May of 1985, as part of a long trip that included Thailand and China, I again went to Taiwan and Hong Kong to continue talks with government officials, local telecommunications executives, and television station personnel. I also met with prospective entrepreneurs interested in distributing CNN to hotels and in developing local cable service if the government approvals were forthcoming.

For five years, we had tried to obtain a license to provide CNN to the Hong Kong hotels, which, as I mentioned earlier, were eager to receive CNN since most of their guests were English-speaking. We hired Rich Hylen, a man involved in the cable industry in the United States and who knew multiple distribution systems well. He opened an office in mid-1985 and worked directly with the necessary government agencies, cable companies and hotel owners, all to no avail. We hired Ogilvy and Mather Public Relations (Asia), Ltd. from June 1985 to January 1987 to assist us in lobbying the government, but to no avail. To this day, I believe that there was heavy politicking to delay and/or keep CNN out of Hong Kong one way or another. Hutchison-Whampoa, a Hong Kong company and the developer of Star TV, which later controlled the available transponders on AsiaSat, in the early 1990s tried to dictate terms to CNN (Turner) for all of Asia.

* * * * *

After my May meetings in Taiwan, I returned to Seoul, South Korea. I already knew from my first trip to Seoul that the major hotels were pirating CNN off the AFRTS signal on Intelsat.

The AFRTS agreements with Intelsat prevented my offering it to my usual customers, despite the fact that some of them were already pirating the signal. KBS, the powerful South Korean government television service, had realized that I was not a visiting dignitary to be handled by its public relations director. I convinced the news staff of the need to maintain a "live feed in all parts of the world," but their superiors were wary of access to so much direct information. I kept finding this resistance to change typical of all the Asian governments, except Japan.

As I continued my talks with MBC and KBS, I monitored AFRTS's broadcasts of CNN in my hotel room. I noted that local television listings carried the AFRTS daily schedule. Apparently hotels and civilian households had access to AFRTS. It was frustrating not to be able to do more in a city so obviously on the move—they were already set to host the 1988 Olympics.

In March 1996, John Major, the English Prime Minister, participated in a press conference—a rare event—with President Kim Young Sam, whose government ministers and son had threatened libel suits against the *Wall Street Journal* and the *Los Angeles Times* after they published articles concerning alleged bribery. After the conference, Major reportedly asked, "Is there press freedom in Korea? I've just come from the most curious press conference in which only two questions were allowed, and they appeared fixed."

A *Financial Times* article points out that foreign satellite broadcasts begun in 1986 were, in 1996, denied access to the cable system "since foreign programming is limited to 30 percent on a single channel. This has been a particular obstacle for Cable News Network (CNN), the U.S. news channel which is otherwise almost unavailable in Korea."

The same article continues:

> Allowing CNN to broadcast would cause serious cultural problems. TV viewers will be made to understand international issues through an 'American point of view,' an information ministry official explained. This view is not shared by the Finance Ministry, which says the decision hampers Korean financial markets by denying them access to information on other markets.

Before I left South Korea, I interested KBS in taking some CNN programs. They liked Elsa Klensch's weekly *Style* show and *Science and Technology.* Both were popular half-hour programs seen on weekends.

The fact that the downlinking authorities were government-controlled and seemed implacable in Taiwan and Seoul, and their executives so rigid and formal, made me realize that the changes necessary to let CNN flow 24 hours a day would not start with the PTT or government telecommunications authorities. I would have to solve it at the center where all the power and control came together and was leveraged. At Intelsat.

Hong Kong's Cable & Wireless was cooperative, but could not change Intelsat's transponder or downlinking rates. We had discussed downlinking CNN there and then shipping it, not only to Taipei and Seoul, but to Manila, and if necessary to Bangkok, where I was now headed after my frustrating trip to Seoul.

Given that CNN couldn't be downlinked legitimately for a reasonable fee, and that certain non-CNN-owned stories had to be blacked out, any sane analysis would have suggested that this was not the time to be selling CNN internationally, especially in the Pacific Rim, with its entrenched resistance to developing a new method of distributing news. I did think that, if I could find enough small countries to share in the downlinking costs of the Australian Sevens Network signal, I could reduce the costs enough that CNN would at least be financially feasible for those countries that, until 1985, couldn't afford the service. Intelsat's excessive rate on the Sevens, and other transponders, was reduced for everyone each time a new user was added on.

The number of WTN stories that had to be blacked out was increasing. I sent Reinhardt a note right before I left for the Far East, with a copy of a daily CNN story schedule listing the number of EBU stories (nine) and WTN stories (18) that had to be blacked out. Furthermore, we had just been informed that we couldn't use ABC sports video, and we already had an embargo on CBS sports. In addition to the 27-plus stories not available that particular day, the heavy CNN coverage of the Claus Von Bulow trial, even though it had limited significance internationally, was pre-empting the *International Hour,* from 3 P.M.-4:00 P.M.

Our customers in the Pacific, in Canada, and in the Latin America countries with whom I had agreements, were beginning to complain. I told Burt that, whereas CNN had been showing nine or 10 WTN/EBU stories a day, we were now airing 25 to 30. This was seriously hampering my international sales opportunities, because many potential clients were monitoring CNN to determine how many WTN/EBU and other embargoed stories we carried in a single day.

While Canada and northern Latin America had a somewhat greater interest in U.S. events due to their proximity, this was not true in other parts of the world. Furthermore, I could not expect CNN to reduce the amount of embargoed stories because of my international sales efforts. At that stage, our international income of $4 or $5 million a year was a pittance compared to the amount of money CNN had to make within U.S. cable systems. All I could tell Burt in my memo was: "I don't have answers or solutions. I am just presenting the problem from our international sales viewpoint."

Another problem, not as damaging to the global sales effort, but fraught with potential repercussions, was the sale of CNN to cable systems outside the United States, generally in the Caribbean, that were in some sort of business partnership with U.S. cable companies.

Turner's satellite channels were sold to cable in the U.S. by a separate sales division. Before our interest in selling CNN internationally, it was not uncommon for this domestic division to "throw in," at a reduced rate or no cost, access to CNN by their foreign subsidiaries.

This practice of trying to satisfy powerful United States cable companies was having a serious effect on our international sales efforts. Not only had the prices in these arrangements been extremely low, or the service given away, there were also no secrets in the cable business. If you charged one company less, regardless of your reason, it affected your negotiations with other companies in the region. Cable operators bragged to their colleagues about how they'd gotten a reduced rate or free service. One example: I had been having a terrible time negotiating with TeleCable Nacional in Santo Domingo. At first, it tried to refer the negotiations to its "big brother," TeleCommunications Inc. (TCI) in Denver and, knowing I was leaving for at least five weeks in the Pacific, I informed Henry Gillespie about the problem.

Evidently, the TCI agreement with CNN, which then had three more years to run, was not very favorable to TBS. TCI probably felt that this difficulty in solving the rate negotiation with TeleCable Nacional would exacerbate future negotiations between CNN and TCI. John Malone, President of TCI, would be asked by Ted to join the TBS board in 1986, but in 1985 neither TCI nor TBS wanted to worsen the situation. Ted often deferred to Malone. During these negotiations, which went on endlessly, TeleCable Nacional continued to pirate the signal.

To complicate the TCI situation further, a CNN domestic salesperson had written a letter to TCI granting "international cablecast rights of Cable

News Network and CNN *Headline News* to Tele-Communications, Inc., Satellite Services, Inc. or other authorized subsidiaries as part of the contractual agreements in discussion." I assumed the contractual agreements in discussion were for TCI domestic cable systems, and the giving away of international cablecast rights to subsidiaries was an inducement to TCI to approve certain domestic negotiations then underway.

When an agreement was finally reached, neither side was satisfied. I would have a similar problem later on in Bermuda and Guam.

* * * * *

I arrived in Bangkok, Thailand, in mid-June 1985, and was met by John Britt who had contacted me on behalf of his company, Far East Telecommunications, (FET), and Pramuan Nitivatana, its chairman. John Britt was a Brit who lived for a long time in Southeast Asia. He had expert technical knowledge of telecommunications, particularly as it related to the new satellite age. John was the one who told me how the Intelsat rate structure was conceived and implemented. Britt said, "They had this marvelous new invention that could transform visual communications on a global scale, and the Board of Governors was in a room literally trying to figure out what to do with it. They finally decided on a method that would give both the uplink and downlink provider a share of the income generated by the use of the satellite. No one present imagined that more than a few users would be interested in downlinking a signal." That failure to foresee the true application of the satellite as a means of transmitting a signal, through a system of only three satellites for the entire world population, was unbelievably shortsighted, although the satellite age had only just begun. It led to the dilemma CNN and I faced in the mid-1980s. We had a news service that was appropriate for mass audiences, yet the satellite video system was designed for only a few prosperous users.

Apparently, the individuals who conceived the use of the service had a "telephone system mentality." In the early years, it is true that as much as 95 percent of the satellite transponders were used by voice. I believe that the decision they made then was partly inadvertent, because the Board consisted of individuals with data or telephone backgrounds who did not understand television, either as an entertainment or communications medium.

John Britt and Pramuan Nitivatana had plans beyond Thailand. They wanted to be agents for the distribution of CNN throughout Southeast Asia—as far north as Hong Kong and Taiwan, as far south as Indonesia. In Bangkok, Rich Hylen joined me. We planned for him to work on CNN distribution to hotels in Asia—he had already concentrated his efforts on introducing CNN to European hotels. Rich and I studied the FET proposal. It was well organized, but it would be meaningless unless the satellite cost problem was resolved. And I did not think that agents like FET were the answer to our global sales of CNN.

My reasoning was that agents represent many clients and sell many products. Even the most conscientious do not concentrate for very long on any given product. They may never learn how different a product like CNN is from other programs or films they represent. My experience with TISA in Central America and the Caribbean proved this. They charged the same amount for a CNN half-hour as for other programs they sold. I was never able to convey to them the difference between news programming and a syndicated comedy or game show.

CNN required constant service to a client, particularly when the client was a television news department. A *Gilligan's Island* episode, once sold, required only a contract and temporary use of a print of the program. CNN, at this stage of its development as a global news resource, required attention to its clients every day.

Problems also came up that involved the CNN representatives, such as how to get a video-plexed signal from the Australian transponder. This required special technical information that the Sevens Network was not willing to provide without some remuneration. Later, it changed its mind. There was constant communication with local telecommunications service monopolies, as well as with government officials who were farsighted and interested in CNN, along with those who resented its intrusion. All this required representatives who fully understood the value of CNN and its importance globally. I did not know any agents who were capable of understanding this or, if they were, could spend sufficient time with CNN and me to make their efforts profitable for themselves.

FET had no experience, unlike TISA, in selling to television stations. I wanted to sell directly, and I had achieved success with my sales effort at

Channel 3 in Thailand. Nitivatana wanted complete control of CNN in the region, but I did not believe that Turner should lose control of it *anywhere, at any time.* And so I decided not to work with agents. These arrangements hadn't worked well in Latin America, Hong Kong, or Southeast Asia, and I had bypassed them inadvertently, but successfully, in Japan. What became clear to me was that Turner and I should develop our own organization, and construct our CNN sales and service independent of earlier models of international program distribution.

To begin this work, we decided that Rich would open our first CNN Far East sales office in Hong Kong. This was a formidable assignment for him. He had to overcome the obstacle of working around Hong Kong politics in order to bring CNN to the thousands of hotel visitors eager to have the channel.

In Thailand, after meeting with executives at two of the country's TV stations, both expressed interest in CNN. One channel wanted exclusivity in broadcasting but offered only $8,000 per month for licensing CNN. We finally agreed to an exclusive three-year license for almost half a million dollars. Pracha Maleenont, Assistant Manager of Channel 3, with whom I dealt, could choose either the AFRTS or Australian CNN signal—both had problems. The question for it was which was the least onerous. It managed to get the cooperation necessary to bring the AFRTS signal down, although Intelsat continued to hamper such downlinking requests.

Then I received a telex from Pracha's assistant, Andrea Cahn, who was working on the satellite downlinking problem:

> Have straightened out most of the satellite connection problems. Main stumbling block is that Intelsat wants concurrence from other signatories of AFRTS signal (Korea, Philippines) before formal approval. Other problem is that everyone I spoke to (C.A.T. [Communications Authority of Thailand], Comsat, Intelsat, AFRTS) has a slightly different understanding of what the connection entails. If there are any more crises, I'll let you know. [She then added,] I would like to complain that the signal we are receiving is not of very good quality. By the time it goes on the air here it is virtually black and white.

So I had another problem to solve.

I was always pleased when I made a CNN agreement in a new country, not only because it was a fresh source of revenue to offset CNN's financial struggles, but because I had also added another news source, which was comparable to having a bureau. Three advantages followed. First, CNN had the right to request any local story without payment to be sent by satellite to Atlanta. Second, if CNN wanted special coverage, it could pay for a crew to follow its requests. Third, if the story was big enough, CNN could send its own team and request local support.

Sometimes, the spirit of cooperation that existed at the television station-management and news-department levels did not always trickle down to the reporters and camera operators. I sent the following message to Andrea Cahn:

> Received complaint from CNN concerning contact with Channel 3 regarding bomb exploding outside hotel in Bangkok where Caspar Weinberger to speak. Your crew covered the bombing but said they were all leaving for the day and we should call back tomorrow, and that was it. CNN forced to contact Channel 9, who refused to deal with them because of arrangement with Channel 3. However, Channel 9 agreed to forward material but asked if CNN was now on Channel 3. Obviously, because of our exclusive arrangement, we must count on Channel 3. CNN is very disappointed with the results of this contact. Can you forward names, phone numbers, as well as home phone numbers, of important contacts for breaking news? Can you advise station personnel to cooperate fully with CNN upon contact?

Even as late as May 1986, I was still struggling to get Channel 3 in Thailand its formal Intelsat authorization, a month and a half after the CNN agreement had begun. I received the following from Andrea Cahn:

> As far as signal permission is concerned, C.A.T. has still received no confirmation from Intelsat or Comsat that what we're doing is OK. AFRTS needs to advise Comsat and/or Intelsat so that this reception can become technically legal on paper. As it is, we are taking the signal with no formal permission from the satellite authorities… We are informed Korea and the Philippines have no objections.

We also had to inform Channel 3, as well as our other clients in the Pacific that might be using the AFRTS signal, that the service was contemplating scrambling the signal because of the on-going pirating. The Motion Picture Association of America (MPAA) was putting pressure on AFRTS to scramble the signal.

By June 23, 1986, I received a telex from Pracha.

> For your information, we are suspending receipt of *Headline News* indefinitely due to schedule instability of AFRTS and satellite authority inflexibility. We do not see this as a permanent situation, but only until we can work things out with C.A.T.

I wasn't worried about AFRTS scheduling. I knew I could solve the problem with Colonel Pollack, but the satellite problem worried me. Terry McGuirk had contacts at Comsat and Intelsat, and I was continuing to work through Joe Pelton. But we still hadn't made enough headway. I sent Pracha the following message:

> We need to discuss CNN situation in Thailand. I understand your problems and am willing to work with you if you can show me the light at the end of the tunnel. I understand your problems and it is difficult for me to maintain an exclusive arrangement that is put on the shelf for too long. Please let me know your thoughts.

His reply surprised me.

> Thank you for your last two telexes. I understand that you want to help, but after much discussing and haggling with C.A.T., I myself can see no light at the end of the tunnel. The only solution would be if a dish ever gets set up, but at the rate things are going I don't see that as a possibility in the near future, even for hotels or a private club. The government is much too concerned about security risks. As such, I realize it is not fair to hold onto an exclusive agreement that we are not using. I therefore would suspend our agreement so that you may proceed with any future

plans you may have. If the situation should become more favorable, I will advise you, and perhaps in the future we may work something out.

Then I realized that the problem was not just the satellite consortium. The Thai government had some concerns about "security" risks—the one word in the English language that has multiple heads.

So much for freedom of the press.

CHAPTER SIXTEEN

Climbing Over the Great Wall

*A man should share the action and passion of his times at
the peril of being judged not to have lived.*
—Oliver W. Holmes

I left for Beijing, China, from Bangkok, Thailand, in June 1985. China was
the prize in Ted Turner's eyes. I had mixed emotions as my flight landed
at Capital Airport in Beijing. I had never been in a communist country,
and China only recently cracked open its doors to business opportunities
and tourism. Several people who had visited China gave me depressing
descriptions of bare hotel rooms with single light bulbs hanging from the
ceiling—quite a contrast to the plush and comfortable hotels in Bangkok,
Hong Kong, Tokyo, and Seoul, with their ornate lobby decor, exquisite
cuisine, and excellent service. This dullness, which I would later experience
in Russia, was a remnant of the Communist party philosophy of only the
basic necessities and nothing to please the senses.

To become a truly significant global news service, CNN had to have
direct access to China. In 1985, we were relying on other news services to
acquire our news. This meant CNN was getting only a "copy" of the China

news that was shared by others worldwide. Occasionally, when a China story required special attention, John Lewis, or a television journalist from the CNN Tokyo Bureau, would travel to China. Indeed, they traveled all over Asia, because they were the only CNN Bureau reporters in the western Pacific region. Quite often, John would make a foray to Manila, Hong Kong, Beijing, or even India, which stretched the personnel and the assets of the Tokyo Bureau. Today, there are CNN news bureaus in Tokyo, Beijing, Hong Kong, Seoul, Bangkok, Jakarta, and New Delhi that cover the Asian continent.

Usually, on my first trip to a country I would try to imagine the attitudes and other obstacles I'd need to overcome, but I knew very little about news opportunities in China, historically or in the present. Burt Reinhardt wanted very much to have a strong system of news collection in China, a huge country that influenced world policy because of its size and population. In fact, China's internal politics and foreign policy influenced the politics of Japan, the Koreas, the Philippines, and other Asian countries, including India, in its relationships with the United States and Western democracies. The West definitely kept an anxious eye on China.

I had four main problems to overcome.

1. CNN was not yet accepted globally as a major news service.

2. The fact that it was an American news service, hence not from a "friendly" country, such as Canada, worked against me.

3. CNN had not yet totally erased its "Chicken Noodle Network" image, even though this image existed primarily inside the United States. *CNN had grown so fast that the perception of it had not kept up with its reality.* It was as if some kid had suddenly jumped out of diapers and demanded to wear pants.

4. CNN had no budget to pay for a news bureau in Beijing.

When I arrived in other countries, I had an outline of possible goals, and at least a superficial knowledge of the broadcasting, cable, and news services in those countries, as well as their government's disposition toward open information from outside sources. In China, I had no clue about what to expect or where I would need to go in order to bring CNN news inside its borders. But I did know that my first priority was to build a CNN news base in China.

Zhang Pengshi, Deputy Director of the China Central Television

(CCTV) News Department, met me at the airport. He was most cordial and friendly. He understood CNN's value to CCTV and China. I would later learn that there were two factions in China—as was true of many countries I visited: those for CNN and those against, the latter usually averse to *any* change. Zhang brought with him a bright young lad as the interpreter. As we rode into the city, I thought back on how I had managed to open this door to CCTV.

After my long trip to the Pacific Rim in February and March a few months before, I had arrived back in Atlanta exhausted. I phoned Joyce to tell her I would need to rest before coming into the office. "No, you can't," she said. "Scientific Atlanta [an info-technology manufacturer and service provider] called and invited you to share a luncheon that's been organized for a Chinese delegation visiting the United States. It's at the Grand China restaurant. And I said that you'd be there," she added emphatically. Joyce knew I was very eager to find a way to make contact with China, and so she had accepted Scientific Atlanta's invitation to co-host the luncheon.

During lunch, I was introduced to a representative from CCTV, and I told him of my desire to visit China. I had been to the Chinese Embassy when I was in Washington earlier that year, but still had not succeeded in getting a visa. My being part of a news service had probably worked against me. Embassy officials promised they would try to get my visa approved. With this contact from CCTV, the only television network in China, I had strengthened my position considerably.

Later, when I was planning my trip to China, CCTV insisted on arranging for me to stay at the Friendship Hotel. This was a complex of buildings built with Russian assistance in the 1950s. It was state-run and vastly different from the new Sheraton that had recently opened, with its first-class accommodations. The Friendship Hotel also had apartments where guest professors and representatives of companies negotiating or operating under contracts with China could stay.

As we drove into the city, I noticed that there were very few cars on the streets, but there was a continuous flow of bicycles, five or six abreast, that never seemed to end, going in both directions on the main thoroughfares. When I arrived at the hotel, I was registered by the interpreter and taken to my room. A single light bulb hung from the ceiling! A small bed in a small room completed the picture.

I found out that a "club" existed on the roof of the hotel and, in the evenings, it was something to do, weather permitting. I hoped I might even find an English-speaking guest whose conversation would give me a break from reading, which was how I entertained myself during non-business hours.

At the club I sensed I was being watched. There was a table in the center of the room with the same male and female Chinese sitting around it each night. When I looked in their direction, every eye was staring at me. The coincidence of at least half a dozen people looking in the same direction was too obvious. Could this be the reason I was "told" to stay at the Friendship Hotel? I must have passed muster. Perhaps my perception wasn't completely accurate, because nothing came of it, and I have no spy story to relate.

This first trip allowed no time to relax. I was continually proposing and negotiating as I learned more about CCTV, what it did for the population, and where it fit into the political picture of the country. I had been cautioned by other Americans not to expect a deal on my first visit. "There has to be a period of adjustment. They have to get to know you and trust you."

There were three key people I met within the first few days: Wang Feng, Director, and Hong Min Sheng, Deputy Director at CCTV. But especially important for me, I met a young man named Sheng Yilai, Manager of World News. I sensed in all three, particularly in Yilai, a desire to be *connected* with outside information sources. It was just a feeling then, but it guided my conversations. The next day, I had a meeting at CCTV to introduce CNN to important staff people. I had prepared a sample "CNN Highlights" videotape and had made the extra effort to bring a Mandarin language version, as well as an English one. This made a good impression even on the more reserved executives.

I listened carefully to all their concerns and offered suggestions or advice when I could. One of their problems was that they didn't have a dish facing the Intelsat Spare Satellite in the Pacific. They had only one dish, and it was facing the Main Path Satellite in the Indian Ocean. I knew I could overcome this problem in some way. I had made many contacts with antenna companies in the region. Fortunately, as was later true in working with the Russians, there was no Intelsat domination to get in the way of downlinking, but I worried that there might be something worse: total government control of any antenna constructed.

I'd learned from a trade magazine that the only CCTV agreement with the United States was a barter arrangement with CBS. I broached the idea of a simpler barter proposal. Instead of cash payment to CNN, CCTV would have access to CNN news, breaking news stories, and feature news, all in exchange for advertising time, which income we would share equally with CCTV. CCTV would also provide a location in its building for a CNN bureau that would include furniture, typewriters, an English-speaking secretary, as well as a car and driver. That's what I wanted. If I could go home and tell Burt that all he had to do was supply a bureau chief, I would know I had hit a home run. They wanted me to draft a proposal.

It was terribly hot in Beijing in late June. The climate is rather like Atlanta's, but without air conditioning. The Friendship Hotel didn't have any, nor did the meeting rooms at CCTV, nor the transportation to and from the hotel. I had been on the road a month, and I was wearing down. Naturally, the heat made it worse.

The hotel had a pool, the largest I had ever seen. It was actually a mini-lake. I couldn't wait to get in and enjoy its cool, refreshing water. I quickly put on my swim trunks, and went to the pool, which had hundreds of guests swimming and sitting around in lounge chairs and mats. I put down my bag full of books, articles and study material, ran as fast as I could and leapt into the pool, eagerly anticipating the cold shock of the water. It felt wonderful. I was so refreshed. I swam around for a few minutes and finally climbed out, found a space to sit, and started to read one of my books. A man who spoke English walked up to me and introduced himself. He was a visiting economics professor from a New York State College, who was teaching at Beijing University and living in an apartment in the hotel complex. "I wouldn't jump in the water like you just did," he said.

"Why not?" I asked, wondering what he could possibly mean. Water is water, and it felt great.

"It's unfiltered," he replied. "They empty the water once a month."

Since the pool was many times larger than any pool I had ever seen, it would take a major effort to empty it and fill it again. I got the message. Unfortunately, I also got an ear infection, which a local doctor treated.

Toward the end of that week, I drafted an agreement, met with the CCTV group, and then redrafted it. In the evening, they took me to dinner again. I love Chinese food and am proud of my dexterity with chopsticks, but I had never tasted the strange dishes placed on a rotating server in the middle of a long table. My Chinese hosts offered their version of a toast, called *ganbai*. It's a glass of wine with a very strong alcohol content, which has to be swallowed in one long gulp; then you raise your hand with the cup turned upside down and shout "ganbai" which means that your cup is empty. Everyone laughs, and the cup is immediately refilled.

In spite of my ear infection, the heat, and my loneliness on this long tour, I finally completed a draft of the agreement that satisfied them. It gave Turner the news bureau I avidly sought, as well as advertising time. Just as I had been forewarned, CCTV was reluctant to give its approval on the first visit. I felt I had enough understanding by this time of what we wanted in China so that, if CCTV accepted my offer, I could close the deal.

One night, I took a walk keeping an eye out for the hotel so I wouldn't get lost. I wasn't concerned about my safety. Crime was not tolerated and there was no recidivism and no "acceptable" excuses for criminal acts, as in the United States. True, sometimes innocent citizens are victims but in a society with a population of a billion and a quarter, there wasn't much room in the legal system for appeals or the re-education of criminals.

I walked as far as a square that had a large television set in the middle of the street. Hundreds of people were watching. I realized that the number of television households television sets would not give a true figure of the size of the potential television audience. Six or seven television sets, set up like this one, might have an audience of one thousand people. I later learned that this "television in the square" was quite common in the villages throughout China and would certainly guarantee a sizable audience until affordable television sets were available to individual families. I later learned that this was practiced in other developing countries. Small rooms resembling theaters were used as well, particularly in bad weather. This reminded me of the early days of American television when most families couldn't afford a television set.

The Chinese negotiation process was snail-paced. The leaders would study everything very carefully, and decisions were made by committee. What a difference from Ted, who would stand up and say "Let's do it!" China, more than any country, was going to be a lesson in patience for me. Ted, who had the same lack of patience, regardless of the circumstance, never failed to ask about China *every* time he saw me. The last day of my eight-day stay, I worked at the television station preparing another draft of the joint venture proposal, and then had several meetings about Turner programming. Naturally, they wanted to see samples. I laughed when they said they could pay only $500 an hour, when they were the only network in a country of over a billion people. "We get more than that from Shanghai alone," I replied. When they asked how much Shanghai paid, I told them $2,500 per hour. "But," I added, "if we make this agreement for CNN, don't worry about it; we'll work out something with the programming."

Some Americans at the hotel said it was customary for the visiting party to host a banquet on the last evening of the visit. It was a good idea, and I made the arrangements. We did the usual *ganbais,* and while I didn't have a final agreement in my pocket, I was certain, thanks to many more toasts and promises of cooperation, that I had made a strong and positive impression for myself and for CNN. I was beginning to feel I was not only a salesman, but a diplomat as well.

I had been traveling in Asia for five weeks. The heat, the long negotiations, the drafting of agreements, the foreign food and accommodations, and the endless ticket lines and flight delays took their toll. I longed for the world of air-conditioning. But first I embarked on what would prove to be my own personal island battle in the Pacific, reminding me of that other, terrible one, some 40 years earlier.

CHAPTER SEVENTEEN

The Battle of Guam

Little men with little minds and little imagination jog through life in little ruts, smugly resisting all changes which would jar their little worlds.

—Marie Fraser

Part I

It all began with an innocent phone call from Representative Ben Blaz's office in Washington. Blaz was a non-voting Republican congressman representing the U.S. Territory of Guam. Joe Mesa, the district director of the congressman's office, had asked me to stop at the island to work out an arrangement for CNN's use by Guam Cable TV. I added a quick stop to this favored Japanese vacation spot to my return schedule.

When I asked Bob Ross, CNN's Washington attorney, if there would be an Intelsat cost for Guam Cable TV to intercept the Australian CNN feed, he said, "The simple answer is, we don't know." He added that it was a very complex situation. Unless there was some real utility and value in pursuing Guam, Bob preferred for us not to waste our time.

I thought about this. I had just left a country with over a billion people, and by this time, I had plans to sell CNN to large countries on other continents. Guam was a small island in the western Pacific Ocean with approximately 120,000 people and about 40,000 television households. But they were U.S. households, and a congressman had contacted me. Even though he was a non-voting member, I was impressed that he had called and asked for help, and I wanted to do something.

Bryan L. Holmes of Guam Cable TV rejected our proposed cable rate. I added an estimated cost of carrying the CNN signal on a separate satellite that covered the Western Pacific area. He wrote:

> At the proposed rate we do not see the cost effectiveness of offering CNN as a basic service and do not believe that it will be successful on a pay tier in a predominantly blue-collar market. The same marketing considerations, specifically price elasticity, which was part of the price determination domestically, cannot be ignored in Guam. I believe the benefits to our subscribers and to CNN warrants pursuing this matter further. CNN stands to gain considerable exposure in the hotels filled year round to capacity with Japanese and Australian tourists, in Guam and Saipan.

What Holmes didn't understand was that CNN was quickly becoming a valuable asset to hotels that offered television news and entertainment to business executives and vacationers; therefore, the hotels quite willingly paid CNN for access to the service.

I had written back to Holmes, advising him of the cost of satellite transmission to Guam, and of the limited number of users of the satellite at that time. I offered CNN free for four months to give them time to determine its value. I had told him that hotel rooms had a separate rate.

So I could see, well before I landed, that I might have to convince them that, even though Guam is a U.S. territory, the cost of bringing the signal across the vast Pacific Ocean warranted additional payment. It seemed to me that this should be obvious. As it turned out, Guam Cable TV knew this fact very well, but it refused to acknowledge it to me.

I had also informed Holmes that a 12-hour-or-less CNN signal from AFRTS's satellite was 50 cents per month per subscriber, and it would be $1.00 for the 24-hour CNN service off the Australian CNN signal. I offered to lower the $1.00 rate to accommodate special equipment that would have had to be purchased for the Sevens video-plexed signal. But I wrote: "A pro-rated fee is unacceptable. The 12 hours or less, or 24 hours is firm. We will make a separate arrangement for the use of CNN by broadcast stations, based on the coverage of the television station."

What I was proposing to Guam Cable TV in satellite program delivery was a dramatic departure from its current system of videotaping its programs on half-inch VHS tape (home video quality; one-inch tape is normal for broadcast purposes) in California, and air-expressing them by bonded courier to the islands of Guam, Saipan, and Rota. An *Electronic Media* article, headlined "Guam Gets Cable TV by Mail," explained this. Holmes is quoted as saying: "We can get a satellite feed on Guam, but it's very *expensive*." [italics are mine] "We can't see any of the domestic satellites, so we would have to pay for additional transponders on Intelsat ...or one of the other South Pacific satellites." The article states that, because of the time for taping in Pasadena, all programs were viewed exactly one week later. Thus, CNN by satellite, live, would have been not only innovative, but also extraordinarily significant for the 120,000 Americans whose only other live link to the U.S. mainland and the world was radio.

When my flight landed on June 29, I was glad to be on U.S. territory, but I was still a long way from home. Joe Mesa welcomed me and took me to the Hilton International Hotel and air-conditioning. I had dinner with Joe, and he filled me in, which was very helpful. Above all, it was a treat to sleep in an air-conditioned room and get a good night's rest.

Although I had corresponded with Bryan Holmes, I was to meet with his father, Lee Holmes, the owner of Guam Cable TV, and a retired U.S. Marine colonel. The meeting included his wife, Joan, who evidently worked there in some capacity, and the radio station manager. I wondered why they were present.

It soon became apparent that Holmes was a "bare bones" manager. There were no preliminaries, no friendly small talk to warm up the meeting—something I had always made a practice of doing as program buyer for the Turner SuperStation. It was also a meeting method used in Japan, Latin American, and Russia, before launching into business, particularly if the salesperson has traveled a great distance. But not Holmes.

His opening remark was adamant. "We're not going to pay more than 18 cents per subscriber for CNN." This was then our domestic U.S. rate, where coverage involved millions of cable subscribers. Holmes went on. "We're part of the United States."

I explained that Guam must receive a special CNN signal on a separate, not a domestic, satellite, and that substantial additional costs are involved.

Holmes arrogantly replied that he didn't care; his offer was firm. I told him that, if he used the 24-hour service, the price was $1.00 per subscriber per month.

Joyce sent me a copy of a telex sent by Holmes to Ted Turner. I received it after I met Holmes.

> Dear Ted:
>
> I'm glad we ran into you on the convention floor of NCTA [National Cable TV Association]. We can now pick up CNN here on Guam from the Armed Forces transponder for over eight hours per day, and understand we should be able to pick it up for 24 hours on the Australian transponder.
>
> Unfortunately, your people's proposed cost of $1.00 per subscriber per month is prohibitive. The people of Guam are solid, patriotic Americans whose love of our country helped get them through two and one half years of Japanese occupation during World War II.
>
> Couldn't Guam be treated like the rest of America and receive CNN for the same price?
>
> Ted, any help you can give me will be most greatly appreciated.

Joyce's note to me also included a request from Terry McGuirk: "Sid, let's discuss. Ted wants me to take a look at this."

Holmes's sudden concern for the patriotic Americans of Guam was touching, but his real motives were related to the very nice profit I later learned he was making. According to the island source, he claimed that Guam Cable TV grossed $7 to $8 million per year, and its expenses were $3 to $4 million. Technically, Guam Cable TV was not a franchise, as are other cable systems in the United States. Therefore, it did not pay a franchise tax to the government of Guam.

When I said the $1.00 for 24 hours of CNN was firm, Holmes began a tirade about how bad CNN was. For almost an hour, he told me what was wrong with CNN, how seldom people watched it, and read me the ratings that it was getting on the mainland. I now knew why his wife and the radio station manager were present. He wanted to impress them with his toughness and how he was going to handle me. Not the best atmosphere for negotiations.

I told Holmes that, in view of our excessive costs in the western Pacific, the prices I had quoted were fair and that, as we added clients to the service, our costs would be reduced. Holmes would have none of it; he wasn't interested in "the full service." "What would we want for 10 minutes of news per day for his local news?" he asked. He had set aside one of his channels, Channel 6, as a television station with its own news service. This was highly unusual. At that time, it was my impression that U.S. cable systems were not permitted to operate in direct commercial competition with regular television stations, as Holmes was doing with the local VHF television station, KUAM-TV. Guam Cable TV received monthly fees from subscribers and charged for commercials on Cable Channel 6, which ran during news programming and at other times. He taped from U.S. network programming and local television stations in California and sent them to Guam. A "Special Interest Legislation" requested by an earlier Guam Congressman, Won Pat, allowed commercials to be added. The act, while it prevented him from putting commercials within the programs, failed to state that Holmes could not put his own commercials before or after these expensive programs. The regular licensed TV station (KUAM-TV) on the island saw its commercial potential drained by Holmes tactics and went bankrupt. It was very hard for a local television station (on a small island) to compete for advertising revenue with a cable system that could not only support itself on subscription income, but had legally found a way to add advertising revenue. The net loser—the viewers on Guam. It appeared to me that the U.S. Congress had failed to properly word the Special Interest Legislation that ultimately applied only to Guam and had not taken the time to study the details carefully.

The meeting ended without any resolution, but we agreed to meet again the next day. Although I did feel some compassion for the people on Guam and wanted to satisfy Congressman Blaz if I could, I had no intention of caving in to Holmes, who was clearly too accustomed to having his way.

The blast of oven hot air that hit me as I left the building was welcome after the temperature of the meeting inside. Nor did I mind riding in the un-air-conditioned taxi back to the hotel. I needed a chance to cool my thoughts and study the situation.

Before I left Guam, I learned that the people on the island knew that a representative of CNN was visiting. There were many talk shows on their radio stations, and the word was out. Many of the Americans who lived on Guam came from places in the United States that had CNN on their cable services. For one reason or another, they were now on Guam, where their television news was limited. Access to CNN as a live news feed would have delighted them. I had to find a way to get the CNN signal downlinked.

It seemed very probable that we would not make an agreement with Guam Cable TV. I knew I would not go below the 50 cents per subscriber for 12-hours-or-less limited service that I had quoted. For the full 24-hour CNN service, I had considered 75 cents as a compromise, but Holmes had refused to budge. "This is U.S. territory, and we'll only pay U.S. cable rates." ESPN, the big sports news network, was receiving three cents per subscriber in Guam and was increasing the rate to 18 cents, the U.S. rate. ESPN, however, was not being received by satellite at that time. I was told Guam Cable TV videotaped ESPN in the United States and air-shipped them to Guam, where they were able to sell ads before, after, and in-between sports events, which U.S. cable systems could not do.

I decided that I had to find a way to talk to Holmes one on one. He was clearly not going to compromise in front of his wife and managers. But any suggestion of a dinner alone or discussions over a late afternoon cocktail—strategies I had used many times before when negotiations were not going anywhere—seemed out of the question.

The same day as my first meeting with Holmes, I met with KUAM-TV, regarding the use of CNN's news as an excerpting service, and it was interested. The problem was payment. It had filed for bankruptcy and was barely on the air.

Then a young, attractive representative of the local Chamber of Commerce picked me up for a tour of the island. I was feeling the effects of those five weeks of traveling. The meeting at Guam Cable TV had not helped. As we drove along, Norine Quinones pointed out the sights. Here was the business section, and over there were the favorite hotels of the Japanese. Suddenly, I spotted a short television-broadcasting antenna about twenty feet tall on a three-story building. "Isn't that a television antenna?" I asked.

"Yes, that belongs to UHF Channel 14," Norine replied.

"Channel 14? I thought KUAM-TV, Channel 11, was the only television station on the island."

"That station is low power and only covers this region of the island," she said.

I knew if that stick could go higher, it could reach the whole island with its signal. I began to feel some excitement. "What kind of programming does Channel 14 do?" I asked calmly, or so I thought.

"They fly in a couple of hours of Japanese programs daily for those few hotels that cater to Japanese tourists," she replied.

I asked if she knew the owners and could find a way to get in touch with them. Norine said yes, and I asked her to take me back to the hotel, so that she could contact them and I could await their call. That's one good thing about an island the size of Guam. If people haven't left it to visit the mainland, they don't have many places to go.

Ed Lee and Dave Larson, co-owners of Channel 14, phoned me a few hours later, and I invited them to the hotel. I was relieved that there was an alternative to Holmes, and the idea of helping another poor underdog UHF, like our WTCG, intrigued me.

I opened my hotel door to two young men who were staring at me in bewilderment. My room was large enough to meet comfortably, and I offered Lee and Larson drinks from the mini-bar. They were engineers by profession, employed in the operation of a large antenna owned by RCA on the island that downlinked satellite signals.

Ed Lee, an Asian American, was the spokesman. He said they were both shocked that I wanted to meet with them. Because, as Ed explained, "We sent you a letter requesting CNN for our low power television station, and you answered that it was going to be shown on Guam Cable TV."

I had entirely forgotten about the letter, which had been sent in early 1985, well before I received the phone call from Congressman Blaz. Guam had been among my priorities as a place to go *after* I had completed agreements in the large, densely populated countries of Asia.

"Well, it looks as though that plan won't work," I said, making clear my disgust with Guam Cable TV. I told them of my meeting with Lee Holmes and that I would be having another discussion with him, but I wasn't hopeful.

Lee and Larson told me of the effect that Holmes's arrogant handling of Guam Cable TV was having on the island. In addition to the local television station's bankruptcy, largely due to Guam Cable TV, all the politicians were frightened of his power in an election because the candidates Guam Cable TV favored had such an advantage. *It was becoming the only television service to cover the whole island.*

I asked Lee and Larson how they got the money to build TV-14. Ed Lee said "The money pretty much came out of our pockets. We put aside money from our salaries working for RCA. We've only been on the air eight months, but it hasn't worked out. We're ready to toss in the towel."

Larson added, "But if we can get CNN and run it full time, we'll keep going."

I liked this. My skin was beginning to tingle. I remembered well when Ted and I were struggling to find an audience for his unwatched UHF signal in Atlanta.

"But what about your signal?" I asked anxiously. "It can't be going very far with that small tower I just saw."

Larson explained, "You're right; it only covers the center of the island."

Lee added, "The tower is painted powder blue, so I guess it stood out enough for you to see it."

I thought about this problem. The area of the island they were presently reaching did not have that many people, except for the Japanese hotels, but I thought CNN might be put on Guam cable anyway.

In 1996, when I talked to Ed Lee on a long distance phone call, and we reminisced about that hotel room meeting, he told me: "I said to myself, 'This is too good to be true!' I didn't know who you were. This was just a first meeting, and I had to decide whether you were on the up-and-up or what. After you left the island Dave checked with our Washington D.C. lawyer who said he never heard of you. I just had to go with my gut feeling. I said, 'Now this guy, Sid, I think he's straight with me.' So I just went with my feeling. And it was right."

When that hotel meeting broke up, I felt the tension leave my body.

But if I had known what was to come in the next meeting with Holmes, I would never have relaxed.

I thought I had the answer to my Guam/CNN dilemma, as well as a chance to help these young guys get started. Bringing in an additional television channel, not controlled by Lee Holmes, had to be good for the island. Plus, the TV-14 people and I needed each other. I wanted to bring CNN to Guam, and they desperately needed programming. Since they were operating on a shoestring and couldn't afford to pay cash, I had offered to take a share of their advertising revenue for CNN. Instead of having to leave the island without having done anything for its 120,000 inhabitants, I had ended up with a fair return for Turner, despite the strange circumstances.

I met with Holmes on July 2, and told him he could have the best of both worlds. He would not have to pay for CNN at all, since he could carry TV-14 on Guam Cable. Holmes and his wife, again present, seemed to be pleased. He reiterated his interest in a 10 minute excerpting service, which I said would be available to him, but he did not like the idea of carrying news that would already have been seen on another channel. He wanted to talk to his news director and suggested I come back the next day. I was sure that he'd have another open meeting at his station to demonstrate yet again what a tough negotiator he was. I suggested that perhaps he and I could meet at the hotel to finalize our talks. Holmes, for reasons I still don't understand, took this as an insult and ordered me to leave the building. It must have made him feel good to do that. True, I was present as an invited guest, but he got his chance to be a U.S. Marine Colonel again. I remained calm. I asked if the receptionist could call a taxi, and I sat in the lobby and waited. Holmes walked by me deliberately, probably assuming I would apologize, but I had no intention of doing so. I took the taxi back to the hotel. I had had enough of Lee Holmes and Guam Cable TV.

In that same long distance phone call years later, Ed Lee told me, "No sooner had you left the island than Lee Holmes called us and said, 'Hey, let's make a deal.' All buddy-buddy. You weren't even off the ground yet, and he was calling us.

"He had a dish already set up, so he was able to downlink the signal," Lee said. "We did not have that capability; we weren't on the cable system since we were only low-power television. The deal he offered was to provide the signal to us from the downlink, which he would send up to us, and then he would put us on a cable channel. That happened within a day after you left. He offered to provide us the downlink from AFRTS, which is where CNN was at."

Lee said they accepted the offer, and Holmes started to carry them immediately.

"He thought he had the thing in the bag with you; he was ready to go with it. Then you threw a monkey wrench in the whole thing, so he had to be nice to us. Using my better judgment, I would never have done any deal with him, because I was always suspicious of him. But Dave wanted to do it. We didn't have to start right away. We could have taken the time to build our own dish to bring in the signal, and we wouldn't have to depend on him." I agreed with this comment but was silent, because I didn't want them to feel bad. Lee also told me that Holmes charged them $1,000 a month to lease the downlinking dish that he had prepared to use himself, and was now getting the CNN signal from TV-14 for free. In addition, Holmes charged another $1,000 a month for the privilege of carrying TV-14 on his cable system. This, too, should not have been charged. While Holmes could hide behind FCC rules that may have allowed him not to carry a low-power TV station, his cable viewers, once they found they could see live news from the States, would demand that he carry TV14 and its five to six hours of CNN daily, and one or two hours of other programs.

Lee went on. "After the second year, we put up our own dish. And in 1987, we decided we weren't going to pay Holmes any more. We were still a low-power television station on Channel 14 reaching a small segment of the island, but we had put in an application with the FCC to change to a full service station that could reach the entire island of Guam."

At that time, there was the "must carry" rule for higher power stations. This was a FCC rule that cable systems had to carry on its service all available local TV channels. Channel 14's decision to stop paying Holmes meant that its signal could no longer be seen on the island.

"He took us off for about a month," Lee explained, "but people were just so irate. He blamed us. He was under a tremendous amount of pressure. At the same time, the FCC processed our papers, and we went from low-power television to full service. That was his excuse, that now he had a 'must carry' obligation. During the month that we were off, he put a flip card up, saying the problem was with us. And he started to carry us again because he has the 'must carry' obligation. He told everybody he had to comply with the FCC."

Again, my experience had shown me that, as difficult as it sometimes was to get through these early negotiations, CNN, when properly utilized as an integral part of a television station such as TV-14, was powerful enough to increase its popularity.

But Holmes was not through with me. Although he had refused to pay a surcharge for getting CNN live via a Pacific satellite and was now getting it *free* because of my efforts, he wrote the following letter to Ted on the day I left Guam.

Dear Ted:

When we have talked with you at NCTA and Western shows since 1972 about getting WTBS for Guam, and then CNN, we wanted help–not Sidney Pike.

Pike arrived in Guam last Saturday night. When he visited us at 1:30 P.M., Monday, he said he had contacted KUAM-TV, TV-14 (an LPTV), and Latte Cable Systems, Inc., which has been planning to overbuild us for two years and visited them before visiting us.

[Did Holmes forget to mention I met with him first?]

He said abruptly he would not budge below $1.00 per subscriber per month for CNN, and would not allow us the lower cost alternative of taking ten minutes of CNN from AFRTS for our one-hour 6 o'clock news (because we were a cable system).

[*Who* would not budge?]

He agreed to meet our marketing manager at 5:30 P.M. Monday at the Hilton to discuss what else could be done, and to meet us again Tuesday at 2:00 P.M. When our manager arrived there and called his room, Pike told him he couldn't meet. He had invited the TV-14 people up to his room for cocktails.

When Pike came by again to see us Tuesday as scheduled, he told us he had already made a deal for TV-14 to carry CNN full-time, probably based on their statements of the past year that they would increase power to be a full UHF–even though the CBS/NBC/ABC VHF affiliate, KUAM-TV-AM-FM, is in

Chapter 11. [I wonder why?] We told him we'd planned an offer, but his deal with TV-14 changed things and we'd like to get together Wednesday. When Pike said we'd have to come to his hotel if we wanted to make an offer, that tore it. We doubt you are aware of Pike's behavior.

It has been an incredible change to go from Bob Ross, Harriet Stopher and Patty Holland's business like efficiency to him. The final irony is Pike's belief that the possible UHF station, TV-14, can succeed in this small market because we'll have to carry them under the "must carry" rule. Do you have someone else who can handle things for you? If so, we would look forward to hearing from him or her.

Regards,

Lee M. Holmes President

P.S. Glad to see you've got Perry Bass, Lee Smith, O.L. Pitts, and the other Fort Worth Boat Club/YYYC boys on the America's Cup Committee.

I received a copy of Holmes's letter and sent Ted and Terry a reply. To their credit, they stood by me. When that strategy didn't work, Holmes contacted TCI, the largest cable system in the United States, shortly to become a partner and major player in Turner. As hard as Holmes tried, he could not deprecate or injure my relationship with Ted.

Ed and Dave were not yet aware, as I was even back then, what CNN's power was. I remembered when I had delivered the Braves baseball team to Ted, and almost every household had gone scrambling to their rooftops to twist their antennas, trying to find a way to get Channel 17. Now there would be a little miracle at Guam's Channel 14.

And a little freedom of speech, for a change.

Part II

I returned in 1987 for a second skirmish. I had been traveling for over a month, and I was tired. I didn't want to go to Guam and reopen the battle with Lee Holmes, but I had been asked by Ed Lee and Dave Larson to testify about the franchising of Guam Cable TV before the Legislative Committee on Tourism, Transportation, and Communications. Unlike most cable systems in the United States, Guam Cable TV was an unlicensed entity; it was operating as an unregulated franchise. It had no official franchise award from the city or the community.

Testifying put me in a difficult position, but I honestly believed that I had a civic duty to testify. While I was not an expert on cable, I was willing to answer any questions I could. True, it might appear that I had a personal grudge against Holmes, and I knew it was not a prudent thing for me to do in any case, given Holmes's power in the cable industry. I felt, however, that he was using his cable system to control television broadcasting on the island and to enforce a dictatorial power that was abhorrent to me and, ultimately, would cause suffering to the people who lived there.

Basically, TBS, although it does have some broadcasting services, such as WTBS in Atlanta, is a cable programming entity. CNN and the TBS channel—the SuperStation outside of Atlanta—are programming services that exist for use by cable operators in the United States. Our cable programming grew as we developed relations with international entrepreneurs who were willing to risk capital to develop their own cable systems.

Later, in the U.S., in addition to TBS and CNN, Turner added new programming channels, such as Turner Network Television (TNT), The Cartoon Channel, Turner Classic Movies (TCM), the Airport Channel, Turner South, and others. Some channels were used internationally and were even created especially for non-American viewers and, in some cases, presented in the language of the region or country.

By 1996, although the majority of the programming was seen only in the United States, TBS had become a worldwide cable program supplier. In the 1980s, I was trying to develop CNN in the areas of the world where cable existed. Outside of Europe, which was not where I was working, Canada had cable, handled by Turner's Cable Sales Division. Mexico, Argentina, and South Africa were the only other countries then actively developing cable. All these countries—in fact, all the other countries in the world, except for a few such as Tanzania in Africa—had some form of television broadcast service. As I sought to expand CNN globally, I worked with television broadcasters, who were the most suited to aid that development at that time, and I had a lot of expertise in this area. We continued, however, to give encouragement and assistance to emerging cable services.

Holmes had already tried to get me out of his picture with his inaccurate letters to Ted and phone calls to TCI. But I had no intention of backing off. The special legislation that allowed him to be both a TV station and a Cable system prevented any television station competition. This was why a session of the U.S. Legislative Committee on Tourism, Transportation and Communications was being held to determine if Guam Cable TV should be regulated. I felt that some control on Guam was necessary to keep the television media in balance and not all in the hands of a single individual. Alternative sources of news were limited to a few local newspapers and radio.

I did testify, but Guam Cable TV remained unregulated.

Later, I received a copy of an article from the *Pacific Daily News* of July 3, 1987, written by Bart Stinson after the hearings, which demonstrates Holmes's lack of candor. In order to receive the U.S. government authorization he needed, Holmes claimed at an earlier time that there were other television signals on the island.

> Sen. Franklin Gutierrez has written the U.S. Court of Appeals in Washington, D.C., to inform judges that Guam Cable TV representatives might have lied to the court about Cable's competition on Guam.
>
> In a brief filed with the Federal Communications Commission, Cable TV claimed its competitors include a full time microwave television station and Armed Forces radio broadcasting from Andersen Air Force Base and Naval Air Station.
>
> The senator wrote Judge Kenneth W. Starr that Andersen's Far East Network station 'ceased operation in September 1986.'
>
> Gutierrez, Chairman of the Committee on Tourism, Transportation and Communications, said his staff determined 'that the Air Force station did go off the air before Guam Cable TV filed its brief, and that this event was well publicized, including coverage by Guam Cable TV News.'
>
> Gutierrez attached a letter from Navy spokesman Greg J. Smith that the NAS radio station went off the air in 1979. Cable

TV president Lee Holmes said yesterday that the brief contains some 'minor errors.'

'The brief in court complains that the FCC didn't hear our case,' Holmes said, 'and any mistakes that are in our attorney's brief will be corrected if we win and it goes back to the FCC.' Holmes said there is 'nothing in there, no errors that will change the basic points we're trying to make.'

The Legislature is considering a proposal to franchise and regulate cable television on Guam. Gutierrez is chairman of the committee holding public hearings on the proposed legislation He sent the appeals court a transcript of public hearing testimony by TV 14 station manager Marie Martin, who accused Cable TV of several false statements in its brief.

Martin said there is no full-time microwave station on Guam, contrary to Cable TV's statement in federal court. Martin said her organization's application for a microwave license is still pending before the FCC. 'They have not given us a construction permit,' she told the committee. 'They have not awarded us a license and we do not have a business license to operate multichannel multipoint distributions service.' 'When we do get the MDS license, if it is ratified by the FCC, we may not use it as a paid TV service. We may just use it as data or an audio type service.'

Martin said TV 14 cannot compete on equal terms with Cable TV. Cable helped drive TV 14 out of the local news business, she said. 'Right now, as it stands, Cable TV is not obligated to carry us,' Martin said. 'Because of that we are currently leasing Channel 25 on the cable system.' She said being on Channel 25 'has put us at a disadvantage and we have repeatedly requested that we be put on the lower band channel.' Cable TV has raised TV 14's lease rates on Channel 25 by 300 percent, Martin said. TV 14's news 'would have been carried for free' in most stateside communities, she said.

Gutierrez forwarded a notarized statement from Guahan Airwaves (TV 14) president Edmund Y. Lee disputing Cable's claim to the court that 'there are two pay television services serving the island's hotels and motels'. 'I am not aware of any other pay TV service currently in operation on Guam other than that belonging to Guam Cable TV,' Lee wrote. Gutierrez also sent copies of the statements to the U.S. Department of Justice and to Edythe Wise, FCC Chief of Investigations and Complaints.'

On July 3, 1987, I left Guam for Honolulu, where Lill had flown from Atlanta to meet me so that we could spend a week together. Despite the "paradise" atmosphere of Hawaii I remained exhausted. The emotional tirades of Holmes, and my efforts to find a way to satisfy the wishes of the Guam population of 120,000 had worn me out completely. I was angry with myself for allowing a two-bit tyrant to drain the energy that I needed for the development of CNN worldwide, a population numbering in the billions. I had just left China with its humanity of a billion and a quarter. This couldn't help but affect me as I tried to paste together the missing time from my relationship with Lill, which was occurring more often than ever before.

I hadn't been back at my desk for a week when Terry McGuirk wanted to meet with me—there were new concerns about Guam. Lee Holmes had telephoned John Sie of TCI, and Terry wanted to know what was going on. I realized that it would be easy for Holmes to make me look bad. After all, I had testified for regulation of a cable company, which was unheard of in view of TBS's association with the cable industry. I hoped I had not put Ted in an awkward position with important people in the cable industry, who might not have known of their colleague's tactics on an island in the Pacific. I explained to Terry the complicated television situation on Guam, and asked if I could speak to Sie directly, which I did, and that was the end of it.

I talked with Ed Lee in 1996 about those meetings. He said, "To this day, I'm still amazed at the slickness of this special interest legislation. Our copyright lawyers told me, after they figured it out, that it was the most perfect piece of special interest legislation they had ever seen because it never hinted that it was special interest. However, when you go through congressional history to figure out what it meant, it was not applicable anywhere in the U.S. but Guam."

Later in our conversation, after Guam Cable TV (many years later) was being overbuilt by a competitor, Lee said, "Holmes has run a monopoly for 25 years and does not know how to compete in a competitive market. He has mistreated his subscribers by offering substandard service at best; using cable news and editorials to manipulate public opinion and bully politicians who are too spineless to stand up to him anyway."

If Ed and Dave had asked me for advice, I would have said: Raise TV-14's mini-antenna, get an audience in the island center, wait until the rest of the island learns that some television viewers are getting CNN *live* from the United States, then sit back and call your shots. They must have assumed that I would remove CNN because of their weak finances. It would never happen to an underdog.

My experience on Guam, except for meeting people like Ed, Dave, and a few others, is still a bad memory. It is a very minor market. But I could not ignore my responsibility as a television broadcaster (as well as a U.S. citizen) when one cable owner was dominating a market, making them dependent on his arbitrary whims. Congress should not have permitted its regulation to be altered so as to permit the monopoly of Guam Cable TV to occur.

In October 1989, CNN became a 24-hour channel on Guam Cable TV, as had been intended. In the meantime, CNN was seen widely in Asia and the Pacific, and its subscribers supported four satellite signals. The cost to Guam Cable TV in 1996 was about 45 cents per subscriber per month. But by then, we had our own transponder in the Pacific and a lot more business to offset its expense.

There is one result of my Guam experience besides my testimony that I am especially proud of. In 1987, the governor of Guam made me an "Honorary Ambassador at Large." I have framed the document, and it hangs on the wall of my office at home.

I had not raised the flag on Guam as the heroes of World War II did on Iwo Jima, but I had fought my own battle with the same moral conviction.

CHAPTER EIGHTEEN

Perseverance and Patience Pay Off

Welcome change as a friend; try to visualize new possibilities and the blessings it is bound to bring you. If you stay interested in everything around you—in new ways of life, new people, new places, and ideas—you'll stay young, no matter what your age. Never stop learning and never stop growing; that is the key to a rich and fascinating life.

—Alexander Seversky

In the fall of 1985, I was working on the renewal of the two-year contract we had with TV-Asahi, which ended in March, 1986. In addition to our supplying news to TV-Asahi, its affiliated cable company, JCTV, was carrying seventeen and a half more hours of CNN in English on a separate channel in Tokyo, which reached about 4,000 households and 50,000 hotel rooms.

During our renewal talks, TV-Asahi offered to help me with China's CCTV, since it had a long-standing relationship with them. It also offered to co-produce some documentaries with CCTV, if that would help.

TV-Asahi was having its own problems, which concerned me. Evidently, it staged a "news" event, and some of its top management might be forced to resign. TV-Asahi's CNN contract was the cornerstone of my Pacific plans.

I did include a new proposal that would ensure TBS increased revenue of almost $3 million annually because of two new programs: *Tokyo Business News* and *High Tech Report.* For CNN, that would be a substantial boost to its financial situation. It would also support the projects I was developing in the western Pacific for smaller countries.

Uppermost in my concerns was China. I needed to resolve the doubts in the minds of those at CCTV who were opposed to a CNN agreement. We considered bringing a delegation to Atlanta to help strengthen our ties. Ted was constantly asking me about China, and I realized how much he wanted CNN to be plugged in there in order to have better access to its daily news. I wanted to give it to him, but the key to our success there was patience. One day I received a telex from CCTV inquiring about our coverage of Africa. Evidently, there was some concern as to whether we only covered the West and Europe, neglecting developing countries. I sent back information to demonstrate our growing news coverage worldwide. Africa was not one of our strengths, but we did have plans to open a CNN news bureau in Nairobi.

I was not responsible for Europe, but I was pleased to learn that in September, 1985, a Ku-band signal (a smaller, more concentrated satellite footprint) began on Intelsat V. This contained a combination of regular CNN news, along with segments of *Headline News,* and some news items prepared especially for the European audience. This was intended to help the London office sell CNN to Europe. There continued to be strong resistance to an American 24-hour news channel, particularly among the French, who resented America's influence as a superpower.

After a two-week trip to Japan to discuss renewal of the CNN agreement, I returned to Atlanta in mid-October 1985 and left two weeks later for a meeting in Rio de Janeiro with Francisco Serrador, who ran the MGM office there and might be my answer to CNN sales in South America. Lill went with me, and we visited my cousin Anita and her husband, Alvaro de Moya, as well as Anita's sisters and their families. I had originally met them in 1961, when I did my first "international project." Francisco was charming and urbane. What's more, his business associates in Brazil, as well as in other countries in South America, respected him. Always elegantly dressed in impeccably tailored Italian suits, he never seemed to gain weight despite all our extravagant dinners with clients.

Francisco brought us prestige. He knew the program buyers for the various television networks throughout the continent, but especially in Brazil and Argentina, where we sought the mass audiences in those countries for our international development. Francisco arranged for me to meet with TV Manchete at its network headquarters, and set up another meeting with the colossus of television in Brazil, TV Globo. Then we flew to São Paulo, an hour away, where the remaining three national networks were headquartered. The TV Globo people were cordial but noncommittal. TV Manchete, a medium-sized network, was struggling to strengthen its position against TV Globo and had a very strong news director who was interested in CNN. In São Paulo, TV Bandeirantes was not news-oriented and did not show interest initially. But I was looking for the *underdog with imagination*, and I found this in TV Cultura and its president, Roberto Muylaert.

TV Cultura, or Cultural TV, is comparable to our Public Broadcasting System (PBS) and was a good place for me to start, particularly since I knew that I'd have a battle with Embratel, the Brazilian PTT and its representative on Intelsat. Embratel had put in orbit its own domestic satellite (BrazilSat) and had lobbied with us to have CNN on it in order to cover Brazil. That turned out to be unnecessary, because I already had access to AFRTS's CNN coverage, and I would learn in 1986, when I was in Santiago, that it reached most of South America.

Muylaert succeeded in bringing down the CNN signal in Brazil in 1988 once PanAmSat was in place. It was then easy for other countries in South America to follow suit.

Since we were pursuing all CNN opportunities within its U.S. satellite footprint in 1985, I had also investigated the possibility of an arrangement to receive CNN in Cuba. I was looking for a way to help CNN collect news from that country. Bob Ross sent me a note explaining the legal problems we would face with Cuba.

> The following is a brief overview of the regulatory hurdles that Cable News Network Inc. ('CNN') would have to overcome before it could provide its program service to Cuba via a United

States domestic satellite. There are two major regulatory constraints, and one minor one.

First, CNN would have to apply to the Treasury Department for an exemption from the 'Trading with the Enemy Act,' which bans virtually all trade with Cuba, including delivery of satellite transmissions. The Treasury Department in the past has authorized telephone and telegraph traffic with Cuba, and has granted requests to transmit video programming of limited duration (*e.g.,* sports events to Cuba.) We do not believe that the Treasury Department has received requests for extended video service to Cuba, however.

Second, CNN would have to obtain 'transborder authority' to serve Cuba via a non-INTELSAT satellite. The State Department plays an integral role in the transborder authorization process, and it has been State Department policy to oppose requests for new or improved satellite services to Cuba. State Department opposition probably would be fatal to CNN's Cuba service proposal.

Finally, CNN would have to determine whether its programming would be re-broadcast over Cuba radio or television stations that could be received in the United States. If it would, then CNN would have to apply to the FCC for special authority. The FCC most likely would grant such an application, if CNN were able to obtain the Treasury Department and State Department approvals discussed above.

There is a blanket exemption for United States news organizations that send news programming from Cuba to the United States via satellite. Transmissions from the United States to Cuba, on the other hand, are evaluated on a case-by-case basis.

Bob was warning me of the likelihood of a negative bureaucratic answer, which seemed to me to be in conflict with the actual purpose of our government. As I understood it, the State Department wanted to send authentic and accurate information to the Cuban population by any means available so that this information might enhance conditions for democracy. CNN should not have been thought of as doing business in the way that a General Motors might if, for instance, it aided the Cuban leadership by selling parts for antiquated Cuban autos.

The U.S. government spent a great deal of money through various agencies, such as the U.S. Information Agency, Radio Marti, and later TV Marti, to reach the Cuban people. But CNN news was freely available via satellite and could not be jammed as Radio and TV Marti often were, forcing the United States to spend even more money to overcome the jamming. It didn't overcome the jamming, but rather than admit Castro had "checkmated" its efforts, the U.S. government continued to spend millions of dollars annually on the operation of a television station that almost no one in Cuba could watch, but which satisfied Cuban expatriate voters in Florida. When TV Marti began airing in 1990, the Congressional appropriations for it were very controversial, and although it has come under severe criticism and has often been called a "waste of money," it still broadcasts, having been supported by Reagan, the Bushes, and Clinton. Hello... CNN, and now other news channels, are taxpayer free...anyone listening?

In addition to the CNN international duties, developing new relationships with MGM program and salespeople, and continuing to add to our library of public domain films, I became involved in selling the Goodwill Games about this time. Ted felt that waiting four years between Olympics was too long in these days of international flight and satellite television, and he wanted to have a form of Olympic Games every four years between the Olympics with the same athletes and sports organizations. The Soviets were willing to expand their Friendship Games, which were similar to the British Commonwealth Games. All the countries in the Soviet orbit participated. The $25 to $40 million each, which Ted spent on the first two Goodwill Games, was a huge expense to TBS, but it was also an indication of the success of Turner in the international arena and his positive relationship with members of the Soviet bloc. I helped by trying to get stations in other countries to carry the games and to pay for them.

As 1985 ended, I felt good about my two years' work laying the foundation of CNN development in the Western Pacific and in the Western Hemisphere. We even had one factor beginning to operate in our favor in the downlinking miasma: the growth of private dishes. But, these would be vulnerable to legal action by national telecommunications monopolies within each country. Still, the crack in the "Great Wall" preventing transborder communications, was growing.

Although, in those years a dish had to be quite large (depending on the

location of the satellite footprint) for CNN reception, as interest intensi-
fied in acquiring access to the open signal programs, particularly in CNN,
I saw more and more of the bowl-shaped dishes when I was traveling. The
international spark was lit, and my job was to set off a conflagration, in
spite of the wet wood called Intelsat.

Sometimes a particular government would announce that the dishes
were illegal, which technically was true, since under Intelsat rules, every
owner of a dish was supposed to be sharing in the costs of downlinking. If
a viewer was receiving a dozen signals, then he was supposed to be paying
Intelsat a fee for each signal. To a large extent, governments that were opposed to the reception of CNN were not so much interested in protecting
Intelsat, or even their own telecommunications systems, as much as they
were determined to control the news available to the general population.

As the world's population grows and legal controls become more limited,
the laws not acceptable to the majority of a given country's population will
sometimes be ignored. This phenomenon helps explain how satellite signals
came to be downlinked throughout the world as more and more satellites
were launched into orbit. But it was CNN's programming that caused more
and more "receive" dishes to be built. Now we have dishes the size of dinner
plates, but I can imagine when an antenna will fit in your pocket.

I refused to give in to obsolete regulations and political games within
countries and international organizations. I just kept putting pressure on
everywhere I could, and I was patient. I spread the word to any organization that would have some influence on international broadcasting about
the obstacles that were preventing a global 24-hour television service.
When international press organizations or magazines asked for interviews,
I hammered away at Intelsat's outmoded rate structure. In an interview
with *Asia-Pacific Broadcasting & Telecommunications,* I reviewed the downlinking fees in Taiwan that would cost CNN or its customers nearly $16
million per year for the 24-hour news. I talked with each country's PTT
and made sure it understood the constraints its Intelsat rates were having.
When asked by the U.S. Information Agency to appear as a guest at their
Washington, D.C., studios and answer questions from television broadcasters all over the world, I made sure that I explained the impenetrable
wall the Intelsat system had constructed around television use. At every
international conference and panel I was on, I told what Joe Pelton still

refers to as "Sid's horror stories." I said what raised my blood pressure was not so much what this was doing to CNN, but that the Intelsat dam was holding back the free flow of ideas that was could eventually lead to permanent global peace.

After the catastrophic terrorist attack on the World Trade Center on September 11, 2001, I realized that the same global satellites that were providing CNN news globally were also disseminating education, information, and Western entertainment to people and regions that had been insulated for many centuries from the rest of the world for religious and cultural reasons, as well as a lack of modern technology. While every conceivable effort was made in certain countries to halt the intrusion of Western ideas and philosophy by modern technical innovations, they failed. Instead of the peace I had envisioned, we are now faced with wars between ancient and modern beliefs, fought not only on traditional battlefields, but also in populated cities and on airwaves.

Meanwhile, in 1985 CNN's advances in Asia, North and Central America, and Europe caused the international news agencies to think about the future. An *Asia-Pacific Broadcasting and Telecommunications* article noted:

> CNN's Europe launch has prompted two major British broadcasting organizations, Visnews and Independent Television News, to announce plans for their own Europe-wide news coverage, expanding to other parts of the world as soon as possible.
>
> Visnews is currently controlled by Reuters, which increased its shareholding from 33 percent to 55 percent at a Board meeting in Sydney at the end of October 1985. The BBC reduced its holdings to just over 11 percent in line with other Commonwealth shareholders from Canada, New Zealand, and Australia.

This last point explained why I was having difficulty in some British Commonwealth countries, particularly New Zealand, where TV New Zealand owned a share of Visnews. It apparently perceived CNN as its competitor. It is true that, although CNN was not a news service per se, I was quite willing for television broadcasters to use CNN stories in their local news programs.

By 1991, the BBC would start its own world satellite news service, encouraged by its owner, the British government, which saw CNN as providing an American voice on a global scale, something no other media had previously been able to do. The contrast between BBC and CNN is interesting, because CNN not only received no government subsidy, but even had to fight its way into White House briefings, and, of course, paid taxes like any other corporation.

Rupert Murdoch's *Sky News,* which had previously been a domestic service in Great Britain, would eventually extend its coverage to Europe and then, as Murdoch expanded his international satellite programming, to other parts of the world as the Fox News network (FNN).

In those early years, 1984-85, I also made mistakes. One's decisions are based on present needs and past experience, as well as on what one can imagine for the future. Turner Broadcasting in those years was having serious financial problems. Not only was CNN still losing money because of Ted's insistence on aggressive expansion, but TBS itself was now paying for that $1.6 billion purchase of MGM. So, I probably focused too much on how to make CNN pay for itself, even to make money. We certainly couldn't add to the debt, even though I believed, as did Ted, that the development of CNN on a global scale would result in enormous financial gain for TBS, and it did. This was another reason I had fought so hard to prevent Guam Cable TV from receiving CNN at the U.S. domestic rates. I tried to persuade Ted to scramble the CNN signal and fought with AFRTS, side by side with various Los Angeles film companies, for them to scramble its signal, as it, in effect, was providing a free service, and we needed that revenue. I threatened to pull CNN off AFRTS if its signal was not scrambled. AFRTS was working on an encoding system, which it did put into place in 1986 for its entire, worldwide satellite network, using the Scientific Atlanta B-Mac encryption system.

At that time, we weren't getting much revenue from advertising in our international programming. Advertising, as it existed in the United States and other Western countries, had not kept up with the global technological advances or CNN's global reach. When Channel 17, WTBS-TV, began to be seen all over the United States, the advertising lagged then too. In 1985, few advertisers were willing to budget for areas not yet within their sphere of distribution. Among the advertising "pioneers" were Bristol-Myers, which committed $25 million to CNN in 1979. Similarly forward-looking was Procter & Gamble, which made a substantial five-year advertising commitment to Turner Broadcasting in 1980. Another exception was Boeing. It advertised in China in order to make its name recognizable long before it sold any aircraft there. Later, in the early-1990s, when I was in Russia, Procter & Gamble was building its distribution system there through advertising. But in the mid-1980s, how was CNN to support itself?

At the time it seemed unfortunate that our unscrambled signal coincided with TBS's period of greatest indebtedness. I later saw that Ted was right in insisting that CNN be an open signal, regardless of our losses. What the open signal did was establish CNN as the lone television news service in lower income areas where it was easily pirated and the antenna costs were shared by many families.

Latin America became the first CNN service to receive a scrambled signal, done with Scientific Atlanta's B-Mac decoder in 1990. Turner Network Television (TNT) Latin America, the entertainment channel designed for that region, used the same scrambling system.

But in early 1986, the piracy of the CNN signal was rampant everywhere, at all levels of society: in a Central American slum, in middle-class homes, in five-star hotels, in the private compounds of Arabian sheiks for the benefit of heads of state, in newspapers, and in various governmental agencies. All were discovering that a six-or seven-meter (20-23 feet) antenna could bring in the day's news, experts' opinions on events as they unfolded, as well as information on an unlimited number of subjects. The same AFRTS signal brought in American films and popular American sports, i.e., baseball, football, wrestling, and boxing.

Some governments did contact us about paying for the CNN service, because they knew that eventually we would scramble the signal, and they wanted to have access to CNN at any cost. Some governments wanted to know what technical equipment was required to get CNN. Others, including many heads of state, wanted to meet me when they learned that I was visiting their country. We heard from oil compounds in Africa and the Arabian desert, and from the government of Israel. They didn't always understand or care about satellites. They just wanted to know "how to get CNN from the sky." We told them how. Everyone wanted to "see it with his or her own eyes." More important, no country, East or West, friend of the United States or foe, wanted to be the one that did not have access to the *eyes and ears of the world.*

CHAPTER NINETEEN

South America—The Hard Way

For all your days prepare.
And meet them ever alike:
When you are the anvil, bear—
When you are the hammer, strike.

—Edwin Markham

On January 9, 1986, I sent a memo suggesting the acquisition of global transponders:

> Because of Intelsat arrangements, I wonder if we should be planning ahead with respect to our own transponder at the end of our present agreement with the Australian Sevens Network on March 31, 1988. I would assume that on April 1, 1988, we will put up our own half-transponder.
>
> Hopefully, the signal could be scrambled with decoders delivered to users. It took the AFRTS over two years to develop this decoding of their signal. I want to be ready and have everything in place when we begin. What do you think?

Terry McGuirk wrote back: "Sid–Good thinking; the further ahead we begin negotiating with Intelsat, the better. Let's discuss."

But a half-transponder of our own was wishful thinking. We remained in a box until 1989, when the whole rate structure changed at Intelsat, largely because of PanAmSat. Intelsat was not budging in 1986. Only the pirates were benefiting. Yet, I believed there would be a change. Despite all my efforts, the PTTs and those who influenced Intelsat seemed to be residing in a soundproof bomb shelter where my barbs and comments could not penetrate.

Meantime, I very much wanted to make an agreement with China. My proposal had not yet resulted in an ongoing dialogue. I wasn't sure if I should return to Beijing or wait patiently for signals from its side.

Some friends at Scientific Atlanta, who had sold technical satellite equipment to China, said that the only way to expedite an agreement in the People's Republic was through a third party who knew the ins and outs of the government's procedures. There were many such companies that provided expert advice and claimed to have contacts within the government, and one of them contacted me. For $12,000 per year, with a five-year agreement, plus seven percent of net revenues received by Turner for the various ventures in China, it would try to sell our joint venture proposal and recommend changes as needed. It advised that it would take two or three more visits on my part to break the logjam.

Frustrated, I sent the proposal to Henry Gillespie, my boss at TPS, and to Ted, too. I didn't receive any answers, which I interpreted as "Do what you think it will take." Fortunately, I did nothing. I wasn't sure that such a third-party contract was the way to go. I had already made good contacts within the Chinese government on the television side, and the proposal seemed designed by a company that had made no such television contacts.

During this period, there was a tremendous amount of pressure coming from Ted's office to sell the Goodwill Games scheduled for that summer in Moscow. Ted was investing heavily in his new Olympics that would bring together the United States and the Soviet Union. The United States had not participated in the 1980 Moscow Olympics (President Carter's decision), and the Soviets had not come to the 1984 Olympics held in Los Angeles. Of all the sporting events in the world, the Olympics was the only one that captured the interest and imagination of every country's citizens.

So, in early 1986 I contacted my international sources about carrying the Goodwill Games. This, in turn, forced me into politics. The Soviets were Ted's partners in the Games. They were responsible for procuring the athletes within their sphere of influence. Ted and TBS were responsible for the rest of the world, as well as for the sale of the television rights and the sale of international advertising required to support the costs of this production and its global transmission by satellite.

I was putting as much pressure as I safely could on my CNN international clients. But I faced problems. After MBC of South Korea expressed interest in carrying the Games, I received a message in late December 1985, advising me that the Korean Athletic Association (KAA) knew nothing about the Goodwill Games. No invitation had been received from Moscow. As a matter of fact, KAA thought the Games were between the United States and the Soviet Union, and it wanted CNN to urge Moscow to extend the invitation to South Korea.

Unfortunately, the Soviet Union did not have diplomatic relations with South Korea at that time. Its ally was North Korea, and in diplomatic terms, for the Soviet Union, South Korea didn't exist. I had to arrange an invitation somehow, but wasn't this what Ted was striving for—to use the Goodwill Games to break down the diplomatic barriers and distrust that existed between the Soviet bloc countries and the rest of the world? Unlike my ongoing CNN work, the Goodwill Games were a "perishable" event. They were to take place in seven months, and Ted's investment was $20 million, which we couldn't afford to lose. I didn't, however, want to slow down my efforts to establish CNN internationally. This could well bring in the revenue to help CNN out of debt and pay for additional news bureaus, so that CNN need not rely so heavily on WTN and EBU news.

Henry Gillespie assigned Tom Todd to help sell the Goodwill Games in Latin America. Tom had been helping to sell special program projects for TPS, and he had assisted me in developing our agreement with AFRTS. In addition, Henry hired Fernando Fernandez, who had originally applied for a Latin American position with me. I had checked out his references and other contacts in San Juan, Puerto Rico, where he had done some business. I found him wanting, and would not hire him. But Henry was desperate. He didn't want to tell me to drop CNN work. He was willing to let me do both, but he teamed up Todd and Fernandez to help me sell the Games in Latin America.

I was concerned about Tom's traveling—he had a mysterious ailment that caused severe headaches and incapacitated him at times. I didn't think he should be flying, but he wanted to continue. When I had seen Tom in office situations, he always looked well. He was tall, broad-shouldered, and athletic-looking. But something was definitely wrong. Nor did I like Tom's working with Fernando, whom I didn't trust.

Over the brief period of time that I was associated with Fernando, I learned that there were discrepancies between what Fernando said and what he did. One of the most important lessons I had learned in program sales was that there were no "quick deals." You will always need to return to the client to sell another product, and your major assets are your character and integrity. I sensed that Fernando possessed neither. His ability to sell was dependent upon his representing a company that had these attributes, as well as having a product that the client felt he could not do without. The Goodwill Games was not such a product. Most of the sports authorities worldwide were still lukewarm, even uncooperative, about providing their best athletes. Competing events at the same time, such as the Commonwealth Games, were attracting the better athletes. Nor did the Goodwill Games have the drawing power that the Olympics had, which caused all sports resources to be focused exclusively on its outcome.

Hence, selling the games, which had no reputation yet in Latin America, as the Pan Am Games did, was difficult. Fernando resorted to smoke and mirrors. I was pretty sure that he would promise anything to make a sale and wouldn't worry about the after-effects. He did, however, do one thing for which I was grateful. I hadn't been confident that he would help Tom if he became ill. As it turned out, Tom did have a seizure in Mexico City while he and Fernando were in a taxi, enroute to a meeting. Fernando instructed the driver to go immediately to a hospital emergency room, and he stayed with Tom during his time there. When Tom was able to travel, Fernando brought him back to Atlanta.

A year later, Tom died, after a series of unsuccessful brain operations. I missed him. He had always given me good advice and encouragement.

After the Games were televised, we had some difficulty collecting payments, particularly from the less-developed countries. Fernando, who had been hired as a consultant and not as an employee during the period we were selling the Games, continued to travel in Latin America for TPS, and was asked to assist in the collection of delinquent Games payments. I received reports that he was telling these clients to make their payment checks out to him rather than to Turner Program Services. I hoped it was not true.

After his consultancy was over, he tried to return to our offices to continue his business relationship. I not only refused him entrance, I instructed our security personnel not to let him in the building.

Years later, when I was no longer involved in Latin America, I was shocked to learn that the new TBS International management brought Fernandez back to sell the Goodwill Games in 1994, when they were held in St. Petersburg, Russia. And again, there were problems collecting the fees in Latin America. Why does desperation force people to ignore history?

* * * * *

In mid-January 1986, I again left for the Pacific Rim. My first stop was Tokyo, to follow through with NHK, the largest television network in Japan. It expressed interest in using CNN on its Direct Broadcast Satellite (DBS) service throughout Japan. Our contract with the TV-Asahi network, while exclusive, referred only to terrestrial (land) television signals distributed throughout Japan and did not include broadcasting directly to home by satellites, which was what NHK was contemplating. This, however, had to be handled very delicately. Having CNN exclusively was very important to TV-Asahi, almost as important as the news itself. CNN's reputation as a door to the United States and its culture had grown stronger in the two years since our original agreement. I knew that both Tokyo Broadcasting System and NHK now had a very strong interest in CNN, even if it were not available to them exclusively.

Unlike in the United States, where competing companies attempt to outbid each other for access to a desirable service, in Japan, a business will respect another business's ongoing arrangement and make no effort to interfere unless that relationship terminates on its own. It was expected to continue, particularly if the Japanese side had spent a great deal of money to promote and develop it.

Although the CNN agreement with TV-Asahi did not include DBS, the network did not wish to lose its image of having exclusive rights to CNN. Its idea was to have its cable station, JCTV, broadcast direct to homes. Unfortunately, this depended on its having a Ku-band satellite not yet built, and there was no way of knowing if or when that would happen.

So, I started talks with NHK about the use of CNN, with the idea of limiting NHK's access to CNN's *Headline News* service, which ran 22 minutes of news in a half-hour period, over and over, collecting new stories as they came in. Because of the time limitations, the stories were brief. There was no opportunity for in-depth coverage.

I also hoped to sell NHK cable rights to programs from the Cousteau "Amazon" series and *World of Audubon*. Documentaries were the easiest of all programs to sell in non-English-speaking countries, since they did not involve lip-synchronization to another language, but merely voice-over narration, which was easy to do.

I kept pressuring Koyama at TV-Asahi to agree to carry the Goodwill Games. He must have been meeting stiff resistance from the television sports division. He wanted detailed information first on which events Japan would compete in.

I left Japan and flew to Sydney for further talks with the television networks, other than the Sevens and the Tens, since our CNN arrangements in Australia were non-exclusive. The Nines Network expressed enough interest to make me want to come back for more talks. I also met with the Australian Broadcasting Company, the government channel, similar to Japan's NHK but not as dominant as NHK in audience ratings. I had meetings with the staff of a small government television service for ethnic and public service programming, Australian Broadcasting Service, which supplied cultural and educational programs, but we never made any agreement with them. And I had public relations meetings with our clients, the Sevens and the Tens Networks.

On this trip, I had my first opportunity, since Turner bought MGM, to discuss CNNI with Bill Wells, who headed the MGM office in the Pacific. At Henry Gillespie's suggestion, I had met Bill on my first trip two years earlier. That meeting had been very friendly, and Bill had gone to some trouble to make me aware of the Australian television world, as well as offering information and advice about other players in the Pacific territory.

But neither Bill nor Greg Ell, his associate, a rather short, very polite man in his 50s had much knowledge about CNN or how I had construct-ed its use for sale to international broadcasters. They were both eager to learn, although neither had much experience selling television news. As MGM field representatives, they had only sold MGM motion pictures and programs produced for the U.S. networks to television stations.

I believed that eventually their Sydney office would take over my responsibilities in that area but, in 1986, I sensed in them some uncer-tainty as to their future, and bewilderment as to how they were to fit into the TPS sales effort. By now I knew that CNN could carry the sale of other film packages and programs with it. Although Bill's manner was formal, serious and unsmiling, I found him gracious and friendly.

I flew from Sydney to Auckland, New Zealand. During my stay there, I received an urgent phone call from Henry in the middle of the night. He was in a panic about the sale of the Goodwill Games. Evidently, Ted was worried about the global sales, and Henry wanted me to catch a plane immediately and join Tom Todd and Fernando Fernandez, who were pre-paring to visit Latin America to sell the Games.

Since the call came during business hours in Atlanta, I phoned Joyce and found that I could meet them in Caracas, Venezuela. It meant flying from Los Angeles to Miami, then taking a Pan Am flight to Caracas. I was able to cancel my appointment at TV New Zealand and start the long jour-ney to South America via the United States, which was akin to flying two sides of a triangle rather than the direct one from New Zealand.

* * * * *

I arrived in Miami exhausted from the long Pacific and cross-country flights, and waited for the flight to Caracas via my favorite plane, a Boeing 747, which I referred to as "my second home." There was the usual crush of passengers at the gate, the flight was finally boarded, and we headed down the runway and took off. Soon after the plane rose, I moved my seat back and relaxed. But just as I got the seat into the position I wanted, I noticed a small cloud of black smoke in the cabin. The plane started to turn around and head back toward the airport. I had a rush of fear. My mind filled with all those images of plane crashes from newsreels as more and more smoke came into the cabin. A female flight attendant appeared near our section of seats after the captain had announced that we were returning to the airport. She was obviously very nervous, and this only increased our anxiety. The captain decided that upon landing he would release the inflatable emergency exit bag so that the passengers could get off the plane without delay. I was sitting next to the emergency exit door, and our attendant nervously asked me to volunteer to go down the chute first and hold it down so that it would not flap in the wind. I agreed to do this as the captain explained how to leave the aircraft and repeated that we should not take anything with us. "Please remove your shoes before exiting so that you will not injure any other passengers," he emphasized.

We waited tensely for the giant plane to touch the ground and brake to a stop. We could see fire trucks driving up and surrounding the motionless monster. Then the emergency door opened and the air rushed into the chute, which was about 12 feet wide. I had removed my shoes, slid down to the bottom and as I prepared to stand so I could hold the chute down, I felt a piercing jab in my lower back. A woman had failed to remove her spiked heel shoes and had slid into me. I turned and looked up. Some passengers had their shoes on and some didn't, but many of the executives were sliding down the chute with their outstretched arms holding their briefcases. Not all of them were leather—in those days, aluminum and even steel briefcases were fashionable. I watched helplessly as more than a few passengers were struck by this "flying shrapnel."

Later, we learned that some internal wires had caused the smoke. Several passengers were taken to the hospital because of a wrenched back or a twisted ankle, but fortunately, there were no serious injuries. I enjoyed having a Miami television station reporter interview me on how I felt about what had happened. Secretly I had often wished that, while I was in some far-off country doing my CNN thing, some important story would break and there would be no English-speaking reporters available. Then I would step in and tell the story, closing with, "This is Sid Pike for CNN in Timbuktu," or wherever. But as it turned out, I was merely a sweaty, dirty, tired executive waiting to board a later flight to Caracas. But I hoped it would at least be another 747.

I met Tom and Fernando in Caracas and helped them plan the trip through South and Central America. I would go with them from Caracas to Bogotá, Colombia, then to Lima, Peru. After visiting Santiago, Chile, we would separate. I would go on to Buenos Aires, Argentina, and to Brazil, where they had already been. Tom and Fernando would return to the United States after a stop in Mexico City.

I helped with some contacts, but my presence seemed largely unnecessary. Henry's response to difficult situations was to take some drastic action. But sending people here and there doesn't effect anything unless the meetings are well planned. Henry, when he had been head of film syndication for Viacom domestic sales, hadn't hesitated to tell a film salesman to go, say, from St. Louis to Chicago and return to St. Louis. But he didn't understand that moving players around the world on a whim was not like moving chess pieces on a board. The travel was a killer. This trip was in particular.

After Caracas and Bogotá, Tom, Fernando, and I arrived in Lima. Following our meetings, I, as usual, insisted on leaving for the Lima Airport early for our trip to Santiago. We had reservations on a non-Peruvian airline whose name I have deliberately forgotten. Call it the Señor Airlines. When we arrived at the airport at 8:00 a.m. for a 10:00 a.m. flight, we found the counter of Señor Airlines, and I remarked, "We must really be early. There are no other passengers here." We walked up to the counter and were advised to go to Air Peru for the flight to Santiago. "But we have reservations and tickets for Señor Airline," I said.

"That's correct," the ticket agent answered. "But Air Peru is taking all flights to Santiago." We learned that it was not uncommon for developing countries, in order to increase business on their domestic airline, to prevent passengers from flying from their city to any other location except on the local airline. Okay, we found Air Peru and flew to Santiago, right? Wrong! We found Air Peru's flight to Santiago, along with hundreds of other screaming *locos* all trying to get on that plane. Air Peru, or the Peruvian government that had made the rule, didn't care that all of these people had reservations and tickets on other airlines and that Air Peru could only carry a small percentage of them to Santiago. The object was to fill up their flight, regardless of the inconvenience and turmoil it caused for passengers who now had no airline to turn to.

I tried to coerce the ticket agent. He ignored me. Fernando tried his Spanish and his best selling job, what I call the "snake oil delivery."

Nothing worked. The plane was full, and there were at least a few hundred more passengers trying to get on the flight. I couldn't believe Señor Airlines hadn't been aware of the situation. Why didn't it warn us beforehand? In any case, the plane pulled away from its platform and was gone. It was now noon, and there were no other flights to Santiago that day.

We had an appointment the next day in Santiago at 2:00 P.M., but we had no guarantee that we could get on the next day's flight. So, we three high-powered but useless executives sat down and contemplated our next move. Fernando wanted to rent a car and drive the more than one thousand miles of rugged coastal roads down to Santiago, but I vetoed that possibility outright. I had learned during our trip that road travel in those rugged areas was dangerous because of bandits.

While Fernando and I were discussing the rental car option, Tom disappeared. An hour later, he reappeared, saying, "I know how to get out of here." He was carrying an air travel directory the size of a telephone book. Tom knew that Peru permitted airlines to fly back to their own country, and he had found an Aerolineas Argentinas flight from Lima to Buenos Aires as part of a continuing flight at 3:00 A.M. that morning.

"Okay," we said. "Why do we want to go to Buenos Aires and not Santiago?"

"Because, at 11 A.M., we can pick up an Eastern Airlines flight, Buenos Aires to Santiago," he replied.

We had about 14 hours, after we had made the necessary reservations. Our plan was to drive back to the city and rent one hotel room so that we could freshen up and have a decent dinner. The military had imposed a 10:00 P.M. curfew, but I made sure we were back at the airport at least one hour before that. I wondered whether the other passengers for the 3:00 A.M. flight would also be five or six hours early.

The mob scene of the day before recurred at 3:00 A.M., but we did take off, and were able to make the Eastern Airlines flight in Buenos Aires. Unfortunately, Fernando and I got very sick right after we arrived in Santiago. We knew it was the food from the flight because Tom hadn't felt like eating. I was furious. I couldn't believe a U.S. airline was responsible for food poisoning. I had been hit hard with some form of tainted food in Hong Kong and Mexico, but never ate unsafe food on an airline before.

* * * * *

The Pinochet government was still in power in Chile in 1986. He had taken over in the fall of 1973 and did not relinquish power until 1990, although some exiles were allowed to begin returning in 1988. Chile had had a strong democratic tradition until Pinochet, and his was one of their few totalitarian regimes. I could feel a certain uneasiness in people everywhere we went. We were watched very carefully as we went through Customs. Generally, when I was asked the purpose of my visit, I answered, "Business," and that was sufficient. I didn't wear CNN lapel pins or say that I represented CNN, unless I was asked in a way that I could not avoid answering. Although I am not a journalist, the average person cannot make the distinction between a journalist and a salesman from a news company. If I worked for CNN, they assumed I had something to do with getting news stories on television worldwide.

When a country is not yet sure of its political position, particularly if it has undergone a political upheaval, then a journalist or anyone connected with a news company, whether print or television, is suspect. CNN people, in particular, seemed to be scrutinized very carefully. At times, of course, any country welcomes a CNN news team. For instance, if an earthquake or some other national disaster occurs, then it is to that country's benefit for the world to be aware of their need for assistance.

So Tom, Fernando, and I went through Customs very slowly. I was used to the hurried, careless pace of Customs in most countries. In Hong Kong, for instance, where large numbers of planes disgorged their passengers almost simultaneously, there was tremendous pressure to get the people through Customs quickly because many hundreds of tired families, businessmen and women, news reporters, along with the zombie-like masses of tourists, were all dumped unceremoniously into a very confined space. That might be the most democratic moment of their lives. For that short period while they retrieved their bags and awaited Customs scrutiny, they were all the same, and treated as so much driftwood floating downstream and out of sight. I have learned that I have some advantages in this situation—my age, particularly, and my white hair, both of which are revered in Japan. Obviously, I don't look like a drug dealer, and for reasons unknown to me, I don't seem to fit any other profile for suspicious characters. But in Santiago, Customs agents took their time, and we did have to admit we were from CNN, but finally we managed to get our prize: We could open the exit door.

As we went by taxi from the airport to the downtown area, on the way to our hotel, it was difficult for me to realize that I was in a country ruled by a dictator who was reminiscent of the fascists of World War II. Two other countries in South America had a reputation for similar governments. One, Argentina, was the only government in this part of the world that had been sympathetic to Hitler. Indeed, it became the final safe haven for many escaping Nazis, most of whom followed an escape route designated by the Vatican. Another such haven had been Paraguay. Chile broke off its relationship with the Axis powers in 1943. But then, it had purged its own "left wing" and Communist Party influences following the Pinochet coup in 1973.

I thought about this as I looked at the beautiful city, with its bright flowers everywhere. As we drove up the driveway to the hotel, the beauty of the colors in the gardens bordering the hotel, and the warm bright sunlight of the noon hour, made me wonder how this part of the world could ever have contained the seeds for such flowers while at the same time, its history had sanctioned such cruel, barbarous behavior.

We had our Goodwill Games meetings with the television stations, but I also met with their news executives to lay a foundation for further talks on the use of CNN news stories in their local newscasts. While I was in the news director's office at Channel 7, I was stunned to realize I was watching CNN on his TV monitor. Incredulous as it sounds, CNN was on a satellite signal that was reaching that far south. I knew that the U.S. domestic CNN satellite (Galaxy I) reached Caracas, Venezuela, and Bogotá, Colombia, if they used a large 11-meter antenna (36 ft.), but that was the extreme northern tip of South America. Yet, there I was in the south central region of South America watching CNN logos and CNN anchor people giving the domestic news service, apparently on an AFRTS signal. But from what satellite? There were no U.S. armed forces in South America that I'd ever heard about after the end of World War II. If Santiago was getting the AFRTS signal, then there was a good possibility that Rio de Janeiro, São Paulo, and perhaps even Buenos Aires, farther south, could receive the same signal. Since my trip was to include those cities, I would have a chance to find out. An Atlantic AFRTS signal had been expanded to reach Diego Garcia in the Indian Ocean, south of India, and it had a range that included a lot of South America and parts of Africa, something I found out later. Transponder signals could be controlled on the ground to reach preferred areas. In its fixed position, a satellite can "see" more than one-third of the earth.

We were in Santiago only two days, and, following our meetings, we had dinner on our last evening together. I would go on to Argentina and then to Brazil before returning to Atlanta, and Tom and Fernando were heading back to the United States, with a stop in Mexico City the next day, which was where Tom had the seizure.

When I arrived in Buenos Aires, I checked into the Sheraton Hotel, and the next morning a taxi took me to the television station, using the address Fernando had given me just before we parted. The taxi drove on and on and finally ended up on an avenue near the waterfront. He rode around and around, but apparently was having difficulty finding the address. He didn't speak English, but he pointed out the name of the avenue and shrugged his shoulders. I didn't like getting out without being at my destination, particularly in a country where I did not speak the language, but I had no choice. I looked at Fernando's address and started to walk in the direction corresponding to the number. I walked for some time until I finally reached the last building on the street, stood there, and stared out over the water. The numbers had ended where I stood, and the number I was looking for would have been about a hundred yards farther into the ocean!

I had relied on a man I didn't trust. He couldn't even get me to the right address. I stood looking at the water lapping against the pilings, wondering what to do next. I had two choices: take a taxi back to the hotel and have the concierge help me locate the television station or try to find it myself. I didn't want to go back to the hotel and then have to return to this same neighborhood. So I started showing the address to people walking nearby. When they spoke to me in Spanish, all I could manage was: "No habla Español." Finally, a man who was rather small and thin looked at my slip of paper and motioned for me to come with him. I hesitated—here I was lost, in a foreign city's waterfront area. Nevertheless, I could tell that the man's desire to help me was genuine. I saw the same light in his eyes that I had seen many times before when I met a truly kind and friendly person.

I followed him down the street and out to a parking lot on a wharf at the edge of the water. He walked up to a small pickup truck and motioned for me to get in on the passenger side. He drove a short distance, and pulled up in front of a building, motioning me to follow him, which I did now without concern. We walked up a few flights of stairs and entered a door with a company name that meant nothing to me. He walked up to a man standing behind a desk and spoke to him in Spanish, while gesturing in my direction.

This man was his boss, and I was now in the office of a Customs bonding company. The boss spoke just enough English to tell me that the television station I wanted to go to was on the other side of Buenos Aires. (Thank you, Fernando!) The boss told me that my rescuer would drive me to the television station in his truck, which he did—right to the front door. I thanked him in Spanish and in English, and he smiled. From the warmth in his eyes, I could tell that he was pleased to have helped a stranger, and he refused my offer to pay him.

After Buenos Aires, I flew to Brazil. In Rio de Janeiro, Francisco Serrador and I had a series of meetings with Zevi Ghivelder, the head of news for TV Manchete. Though something of an underdog, TV Manchete was not a weak station. Along with TV Bandeirantes, it had about a 15 percent share of the audience, but TV Globo had most of the rest.

Francisco and I had approached TV Globo as well, in order to protect his position as the sales representative of all Turner films and programs. But TV Globo's news director was rather arrogant, and while he listened to our description of CNN's news service via satellite, I had the impression that he wanted to keep everything the way it was. That was okay with me. We went back to TV Manchete and made our second non-exclusive CNN television broadcast agreement in Brazil. The first had been with TV Cultura in São Paulo.

Zevi Ghivelter would come to Atlanta often in the years that followed to study the CNN operation and to participate in CNN *World Report* conferences, begun by Ted in 1989 to bring together participants in his *World Report* program from all over the world. This was exactly the right way to maximize the effects of CNN in his country.

When I returned to Atlanta, I told Burt Reinhardt of our new three-year agreement with TV Manchete. Burt, eager to protect his relationship with TV Globo should he need any news stories from them, asked me to inform its representative in New York that we now had a non-exclusive arrangement with TV Manchete. Through Ghivelter, however, TV Manchete was more than adequate to the task of supporting CNN's news coverage in Brazil. I was gradually adding to the list of countries that carried CNN, and they were responding to the requirement built into their contracts to provide local news to CNN. CNN now had seven foreign news bureaus, and was adding one or two a year, so we were gradually relying less on the outside news agencies. I realized that CNN would always need some collection arrangements beyond its bureaus in the event of a story breaking where no bureau was located. However, my agreements with television stations worldwide would more than compensate for this situation.

By this time, CNN was available 12 to 16 hours a day throughout South America, and there were already thousands of private receiving dishes throughout the continent, taking whatever programming they could find. We did have some success in getting a number of South American countries to participate in the Goodwill Games, and my presence on that trip had been helpful because of the relationships I had established with the different stations we visited.

I had now come to realize that the kid who thought he couldn't sell anything because his mother had to buy two magazines to keep him from being a failure was turning into a world-traveling, world-class salesman.

VIDEO DIPLOMACY: Ron Ciccone, Turner Broadcasting System Inc.'s VP-network distribution in the Middle East, chats with Sheikh Isa Al-Kalifa, the ruler of Bahrain.

Ron Ciccone meeting with Sheik Isa Al-Kalifa in Bahrain as he worked to expand CNN distributionin the Middle East.

CHAPTER TWENTY

Expanding in All Directions

It isn't always your words that others listen to,
But the strength and sincerity behind them.
When a sincere man speaks, the world moves.

—Paramahansa Yogananda

I was running into problems negotiating an agreement with NHK in Japan for direct-to-home use of CNN. TV-Asahi and JCTV now insisted that this would violate their exclusivity, although in my original talks with them, Koyama and Kobayashi had no objection to our discussing DBS with other entities. The situation was serious enough for me to fly to Tokyo in March 1986. I had assured TV-Asahi and JCTV that only *Headline News* would be available on the DBS service, and that if a viewer were interested in a fuller report, he would have to seek another television news provider, hopefully TV-Asahi.

A bigger problem was that Gerry Hogan, TBS Vice President for Advertising Sales, had arranged with a separate organization on his own to produce for CNN a half-hour program called *This Week in Japan*. Both Koyama and Kobayashi (the head of Japan Cable) found Hogan's program a burden on them because it confused potential advertisers. Hogan's customers in Japan had a good relationship with the government's Chamber of Commerce, which he thought would help him get around the TV-Asahi exclusivity arrangement. It meant that this other Japanese organization could sell advertising to *This Week in Japan,* whereas TV-Asahi had assumed it had that right regarding all CNN programs telecast in Japan. Hogan had already worked out this weekly program with Burt Reinhardt and, in view of TBS/ CNN's financial situation at that time, I had no choice but to find a way to work around the confusion it caused as to who was the CNN representative for advertising sales in Japan, TV-Asahi or the other entity.

Another problem with NHK loomed: Ted had previously discussed CNN with them, and NHK said Ted had offered CNN to it at no charge. I now had to convince NHK that there was no "free lunch." Ted had met NHK officials in Moscow—he must have been feeling good—(perhaps it was after a dinner) and had too generously offered CNN free, without thinking through the full ramifications. They now insisted on receiving an official letter advising them that they would be required to pay for CNN.

I had to find a way to preserve Ted's honor and my exclusive commitment to TV-Asahi and JCTV, as well as the financial viability of CNN's most popular market outside the United States. The Japanese loved CNN. It was a rope that tied the two countries together.

That spring I also received an expression of interest from a company in Australia that wanted to offer CNN to airlines. There was some resistance from Burt, since any use of CNN in flight would require videotapes and CNN would have no control over how old the news programs were. But Burt's initial resistance waned after I projected the potential revenue of airlines worldwide.

A few months later, I got a note from Mark Henderson in Cable Sales when he learned I would be talking with SeaTel, a company that manufactured satellite-receiving equipment for ships. Mark informed me that the use of CNN on videotape had already been rejected by management and that CNN on ships, particularly cruise ships, had to be live with no excerpting of commercials. I contacted SeaTel and began talks on how to work together to provide seagoing antennas that remained locked on a satellite, regardless of the movement of the ships, whether turning or in heavy seas. This area became an important addition to my CNN sales efforts. It was eventually taken over in 1990 by Irene Heimer, a graduate student I had met at the University of Texas in Austin where I was a member of the Board of Advisors in the College of Communications. Irene helped me in Canada, as well as with ships generally. She had built up the sea business substantially so that now CNN could be seen on land and sea in every part of the globe, except a few areas near Greenland and parts of northern Russia.

* * * * *

Central America was also giving me a nasty headache. The problem with TeleCable Nacional in Santo Domingo pirating CNN wouldn't go away. Because of its business partnership with TCI, it had determined it would not pay more than 15 cents per subscriber per month, and no amount of "cease and desist" threats from my office to stop its piracy had changed its attitude. To Henry Gillespie's credit, he supported me and took it up with Ted. I was surprised when I received a handwritten note from Henry saying, "Fine! Please initiate and discuss procedure." He had just sent a telex to the head of TeleCable Nacional, saying he had discovered that the Goodwill Games, then underway in Russia, were being shown illegally on that service because the rights had been sold to a television station in the Dominican Republic, and not to its cable system. This was clear evidence of their piracy, and he was inviting me to press them for an agreement.

One factor that made my work schedule possible was that few reports to executives were required of me. I sent memos of my results and future plans to Ted, Henry, and others, as needed, but I didn't have to provide monthly or weekly reports and analyses or attend budget conferences. I estimate that as much as 70 percent of some executives' time today is taken up with work that yields no actual results, but is merely part of the intra-communication system of a large corporate structure. More people are employed, more reports are generated, and less time is spent on building a successful company. In the early years, we compared the creative work being done by our "lean and hungry" staff that was propelling us toward greater and greater success to that being done by a network like CBS, which was overstaffed, lethargic, and incapable of diagnosing the future of the industry until *we became the future.*

At a television industry convention in France, I had the chance to meet with Ken Coyte, President of WTN, to discuss further cooperation in using WTN material in our 24-hour service to hotels and cable worldwide. I later learned that WTN had agreed, for an added fee, to allow the use of its news stories on cable and to hotels on a limited basis. This did not include television broadcast, since we were then still competing in this area. If Burt were equally successful with other news and sports agencies, this could be good news.

While we were required to pay WTN based on the size of our audience, I refused to comply with its request for a list of the cable systems and hotels subscribing to CNN. It was our only competitor in television broadcast. Who knew whether it might compete in other areas later on? I had no intention of making its life easy by telling it who our clients were. Rich Hylen was working on an analysis of hotel potential in Asia, Australia, and New Zealand so that I could combine his figures with my projection of broadcast and cable revenue.

The most important meeting at the French conference was with the Deputy Director of CCTV, Hong Min Sheng, who was heading the delegation. The People's Republic of China had a booth there, and I went by to introduce myself. It gave me an opportunity to review our CNN talks. In my note to Ted and Henry, I wrote about this meeting:

> Hong Min Sheng pointed out to me that we need to be more patient with regard to CNN. When I proposed that we take the joint venture proposal and divide it into steps, he was pleased with this. I told him that we would be interested in exchanging CNN on CCTV for bureau space in the new CCTV building, equipment and personnel other than bureau chief and reporters, and technical equipment, such as cameras.
>
> The cost to them of a new dish is $200,000. His main problem in receiving CNN in the near future is deciding where the TVRO (television receive only) will be located—at the new building or the old one. While this seems a simple thing to us, it is obviously complicated for them. Also, I had the impression they lacked funds for the TVRO. Sheng was pleased with the suggestion that we hold up on the hotels until they can determine how to resolve the collecting of CNN for CCTV news: He was very emphatic about not being harassed and emphasized patience.

Despite this caution, Ted continued to put pressure on me to sign an agreement in China. In June 1986, an opportunity surprisingly presented itself in Atlanta. The International Visitors Bureau often asked us to meet with visiting government officials, educators, and businessmen. That June, we were asked to arrange the usual tour of CNN for two visiting television executives, Liu Chi, from Guangdong, and Lu Zigui, from Sichuan Province in China. I was delighted, of course, and arranged a meeting.

Liu Chi got my attention right away because his eyes had fire in them. He was in his 40s, was aggressively interested in CNN, asked pointed questions, and reminded me of Ted and myself in his eagerness to get things done. He wanted to know how the television station he represented in Guangdong Province could use CNN. That was like asking Edison how the light bulb worked. I thought that CCTV was the only television network in China, with all other television services a part of its gigantic, government-controlled network. It turned out that there were some independent stations in various parts of China. Might this be the thread that would help me unravel my Chinese dilemma?

We agreed to continue talks to see if we could work out an agreement. I did not want to risk upsetting the slumbering lion, CCTV, while I played with a mouse right next to him. The lion's displeasure could prove calamitous. But it occurred to me that other independent television stations in China might also be interested in CNN. I hadn't yet decided whether to hire the company that Scientific Atlanta had recommended for China. Generally, I kept my distance from the so-called experts. A true expert is, indeed, very valuable, but I have found that there are too many "self-declared" experts.

* * * * *

My constant badgering of Gillespie regarding my workload finally brought results. Shortly before this, he had sent me a note asking me for my vacation date. I had been with TBS over 15 years and rarely took a vacation, although I was now entitled to four weeks. I answered his memo with three words: "Are you kidding?!?"

Gillespie called one day in June and asked me to interview a woman named Maryann Pasante, who had once managed a television station in

Puerto Rico. Her husband was John Ferris, a writer of novels.

Maryann had an effusive smile. She was also a workhorse with the drive to get things accomplished. She wanted to make Turner more and more successful. I admired her aggressiveness. I had been interviewing others with Latin backgrounds, but when I spoke to Maryann, I knew she was the one I wanted on my team. I hired her in June 1986. With Francisco Serrador in South America and Maryann Pasante in Central America and the Caribbean, I felt that we would have the southern part of the Western Hemisphere well covered.

In July, Maryann and I scheduled a trip to Mexico City, Guatemala, and Venezuela. In most countries, the government television station was the colossus that all other entities had to deal with. In Mexico, a private company, Televisa, had tremendous political power and owned or controlled most television resources in the country. It was able to dictate terms to anyone seeking a television business relationship in Mexico, and as expected, it demanded CNN exclusivity, which I was reluctant to give it. This would be a nail in the weaker stations' coffins. So we went to the weak government station, Imevision, and made an agreement with it to use CNN and, in Maryann's words, "They became very successful overnight." We also had talks with several newly forming cable companies there.

We flew to Guatemala and checked into our hotel, where I told the clerk to make sure we were on the same floor. Maryann looked at me suspiciously. "Maryann, if there is a fire, I don't want to look all over the hotel for you," I said. I was very serious about this. Ever since a major fire engulfed a hotel in Manila on the day I had arrived there (even though I was in another hotel), I always carried a fire mask and flashlights in my shoulder bag.

The next morning, we took a taxi to the television station—military forces surrounded the building, with tanks on either side. I was struck by how young the soldiers were. They looked to be no more than teenagers with machine guns strapped to them. They were definitely too young to be in control of their emotions. Maryann looked nervously at me without saying a word as we showed our passports and were allowed to walk into the rather decrepit building.

Inside, it was dark and dreary. Little light entered. We walked down the corridors to an office that was actually outside the building, where we waited a short time before being invited inside where a colonel sat, wearing the same dark camouflage uniform as the soldiers. He reminded me of Manual Noriega of Panama—he had a similarly pock-marked face. He was polite, but not friendly. He listened to our CNN pitch and expressed some interest. I wondered if anyone ever made a bad deal with this guy and then was dumb enough to return.

We went on to Caracas, where we split up to go to different meetings one afternoon. I had one of my rare experiences where language was a problem. Usually, the companies I met with had an English-speaking executive present at a meeting. In fact, more and more of these executives spoke English, and they were becoming younger and younger. Not only had English become the international business language, but American business methods and its democratic institutions were being emulated by developing countries, eventually including the former Soviet Union and the Eastern European Soviet satellite nations. It would, in the following years, be rare for the company I met with to hire a translator. Although English was the international language in Latin America, too, Spanish was spoken everywhere, except in Portuguese-speaking Brazil. Fortunately, on this trip I had Maryann with me, who not only spoke Spanish but who was culturally oriented to Latin America—she could put the executives that we met at ease.

While the CNN-U.S. domestic signal could reach Caracas with the installation of a large antenna, we were forbidden by Intelsat and the local PTT from building a dish. The Caracas station, Venevision, flew in CNN on videotape from nearby Aruba, which did not have so many restrictions on downlinking an Intelsat signal. Fortunately, this was temporary and lasted for months, not years.

Maryann and I held talks with officials of each of the television stations, as well as with a group of executives who were petitioning the government for a new television network. When we returned home after our whirlwind 10-day, three-country trip, I decided to plant myself in Atlanta for a while to organize what I had now begun to realize was a massive new global undertaking with momentous significance.

Since August of 1984, I had wanted to hire Luis Torres-Bohl, who worked at CBS and was interested in joining a young, aggressive, pioneering company with international aspirations. Luis found CBS too conservative and its management reluctant to experiment, take risks, or change the status quo. U.S. networks (ABC, CBS, NBC) and their local television stations had been making huge profits for 35 years, and they were hesitant to do anything that might change this. Unfortunately, TBS was also exploding in size as it gained more stature, and it, too, would suffer the same malaise almost a decade later.

Luis had a "smiling" personality, a sense of humor, and a great deal of optimism—for Luis, the glass was always half full. In 1984, no one had taken CNN's international expansion seriously (because my predecessor had been unsuccessful), so I couldn't hire Luis then. Two years later, I finally managed to add him to our staff. By now, TBS was beginning to have an international reputation, and Luis astutely recognized the potential.

He was a natural for Latin America. But Maryann Pasante now adequately covered this area, with help from the Rio office. Maryann and I had also visited the MGM office in Mexico City on our recent trip, and the plan was for Maryann to be responsible for that office. Luis began helping me in Canada, where I was offering CNN news stories to television networks there. He also assisted in the Caribbean and in Peru where he was originally from, and where his 96-year-old father still worked as a salesman and traveled by bus from town to town. What a role model for me!

Perhaps I should have recognized in advance that there might be problems between Maryann and Luis. Maryann was highly motivated, very aggressive, and her sales results were impressive. Similarly, Luis more than accomplished the goals I set for him. But the two of them tended to get into confrontations, and no matter how hard I tried to create a pleasant working atmosphere, and carefully avoided showing any favoritism, they just did not get along. My gut feeling was that Maryann was sometimes too confrontational. Even I had tasted her wrath once when I did something she didn't like in Mexico. I said something in a discussion with one of our clients (when she was at another meeting) that she didn't agree with. When I tried to laugh it off by saying, "Just say I'm another stupid gringo," she became furious and refused to let it go. Unlike Ted, who exploded and five minutes later acted as though nothing ever happened, Mary Ann remained angry for several days. Her anger would finally dissipate like a black cloud moving away over a period of time. In a way, I understood this because I, too, had a similar problem, not with anger, but with hurt feelings that lasted for days. Fortunately, both Luis and Maryann operated independently and stayed out of each other's way most of the time. This was lucky for me because now I had a staff of five: Luis, Maryann, Rich Hylen in Hong Kong, Francisco Serrador in Rio, and my faithful Joyce.

CHAPTER TWENTY-ONE

African Adventures, Chinese Checkers, and Other Games

When you cannot make up your mind which of two evenly balanced courses of action to take, choose the bolder.
—W. J. Slim

In May 1986, I received an intriguing phone call from Fanus Venter, head of the South African Broadcasting Corporation (SABC) news bureau in Washington. He and an associate wanted to meet with me in Atlanta. It was the first time I met South African Afrikaners. Both men were very polite and deferential—this was true of most foreign business people I encountered. Venter wanted to learn more about CNN and wondered whether it could be received in the southern part of Africa. I told them I believed that the AFRTS signal might cover South Africa, and I promised to look into it.

Later on, in thinking about CNN's possible contribution to Africa's economic and political development, I realized that it would not really help CNN's cash flow problems, but South Africa was the one major exception. I was well aware of the worldwide embargo then in place against South Africa that lasted until apartheid ended in 1991. I knew of the difficulties athletes had in participating in international sports events. But I also knew that the only way to bring about change there was to penetrate its information barrier. CNN could do that. But I wasn't ready to give the undertaking my full attention just yet. I did send a memo to Ted saying that I was interested in developing CNN in Africa and was looking toward a possible agreement in South Africa. For the first time I sent a copy to Bob Ross, in case he saw any legal problems with our doing business there.

Ted informed me a short time later that he had had dinner with Andrew Young, then the mayor of Atlanta, and Young talked about his contacts in Africa—he offered to help if TBS wanted to penetrate that market with entertainment and news. Soon after I met with Walter Young, the mayor's brother, and with a representative from Scientific Atlanta, the company that had sold TBS its first uplink and receive antennas. Walter Young believed he could find the financial backing to provide this signal to the countries of Africa.

This did not sound practical to me. Had he studied the market? Where would the satellite signal go? *Who* would pay for it? There were no cable systems to speak of. Africa had few hotels, and those that existed didn't have a high occupancy rate. The television broadcasters in Africa were notorious for slow or non-payment for film contracts. *But it was a market that I wanted to work with.*

Charles Bonan, our London salesman, insisted that he had made an agreement with the television service in Gabon, but it had never materialized. Other so-called "experts" on Africa appeared at my office in Atlanta, but nothing ever came of their expertise.

There were a couple of exceptions to this, and one was Dr. Wilbur Blume, then professor emeritus at U.S. International University in San Diego and whom I visited occasionally when I flew to the Pacific Rim from Los Angeles. I first met him when I spoke at the university. Dr. Blume wrote to me in August 1986: "The improvement of communications between African countries is a primary concern. Along with this, training of African broadcast journalists needs to be addressed. Fortunately, both of these concerns fit well with the overall objectives of expanding CNN into a global network." Blume suggested that I contact the Union of Radio and Television Organizations of Africa (URTNA), and he gave me contacts for important organizations throughout Africa. In the same letter, he also cautioned me: "Most African leaders will look at the CNN offer receptively, but with caution. '*Cultural imperialism,*' *as foreign domination of information is called, is as distasteful as any other form of imperialism.*" (The italics are mine.)

I completely understood what he meant. Lack of communication tends to spread mistrust, slow down commerce, inhibit dissent within a society, make it difficult to advance and disseminate ideas that can improve standards of living, life expectancy, and enlighten vast populations. It made me think of the French control over its former colonies in Africa by its language, and discouraging the introduction of English by threatening to end subsidies. Nevertheless, for the moment I had to concentrate on the Pacific and the Western Hemisphere, where the seeds I had planted were starting to grow and needed my attention. I had to organize our resources in order to continue our sales efforts and to provide service for our new clients. By late summer 1986, Ted wanted to use the MGM film library on global satellites. Terry McGuirk, in addition to his cable duties, was now more active in satellite development for future Turner entertainment projects and was giving more attention to the downlinking dilemma.

* * * * *

Back in March, when I was in Japan, I received an urgent message from Joyce, asking that I call her at home, even if was in the middle of the night. Joyce's news was very bad. Henry Gillespie had been diagnosed with a malignant brain tumor which, at that time, was believed to be inoperable. After Joyce and I spoke a few more words and then hung up, I simply sat there in my chair, in stunned silence.

Henry remained a consultant to Ted for another year, working whatever schedule he was able to between his visits to the hospital. Russell Barry, President of TPS, temporarily replaced him in September. Barry had been president of Twentieth Century Fox Television. Russell was very experienced and capable in film sales, but there were problems working with him that I hadn't encountered with Henry. The company politics that I had to deal with became more complex. We had gone from 39 employees when I joined Ted in 1971 to over 3,000 in 1986.

Russ was a handsome, 40-something bachelor, who loved Los Angeles and California. In the beginning, he commuted weekly to and from the coast. True, most film executives were based there or in New York, where most of the high-level film sales action took place. Apart from contacts made at conventions, sales management by this time could be done from almost any location.

Russ had walls around him that only his close associate, John Walden, whom he had brought from Los Angeles to manage local market sales and assist him, was able to penetrate. John was just the opposite: open, friendly, always looking for a funny rejoinder, and always willing to help in any way.

Russ, whom everyone, including myself, respected for his sales executive reputation, was unable to adjust to me and my position in the company, and make it work for him as Henry had. He could not accept the fact that he did not have direct access to Ted and I did. Henry also had access to Ted, but we were now at the point where more management levels were developing, and Terry McGuirk was handling more of the day-to-day activity of the company. Over Russ was Jack Petrik who, like Terry, had known Ted for many years. Petrik understood my special relationship with Ted and had no problem with it. Russ was new and, like many newcomers, had no interest in personal history.

Since Russ could not overcome his personal feelings about my position, he let it affect our relationship. Our meetings were formal, uncreative, and without the easy give-and-take style I was used to with Ted and Henry. Russ was one of three new executives who wished they could dispose of me, regardless of my record. None could do so.

* * * * *

After a third visit from Fanus Venter in October 1986 concerning a South African/CNN proposal, I had to consider how we would proceed in light of the embargo on South Africa. When I discussed the issue with Burt Reinhardt, he thought our position should be that "we provide news and collect news from everyone, regardless of political beliefs." Nor had Bob Ross seen any need for caution. Ross, by the way, had recently decided to change his career and take over the London office to assist Terry McGuirk in developing CNN on cable in Europe.

I felt that this decision on Terry's part was not good strategy, because it divided our CNN global efforts. It put Europe under Cable Sales and the rest of the world under TPS. Further, since Henry had become ill there was no one to represent us on a day-to-day basis in Ted's office, or to help us centralize our sales efforts. This meant I had to make a choice between aggressively working my way into a day-to-day relationship with Ted as I had before, or staying in the field and continuing to sell CNN all over the world. It was not having Henry Gillespie as my advocate on a day-to-day basis that made my work more difficult when I traveled so extensively. But I was determined to work with Bob Ross and Terry. Bob and I divided up the territory of North Africa and portions of the Middle East on the Mediterranean Sea. Later, after Ross returned to Atlanta, I would face the problem of the London office becoming territorially ambitious and unsuccessfully trying to claim all of Africa "because it was closer to London."

In October 1986, it was time to decide whether or not to make an arrangement with South Africa. Steve Korn, a much more conservative and up-tight lawyer, had replaced Bob Ross. Steve not only went by the book, but I felt he went *beyond* the book if there was any question that he might need to cover himself. He was the opposite of Bob, and I was pretty sure that Steve would object to the SABC agreement on the grounds of the U.S. embargo laws. I already knew from Burt that all the different countries were exchanging news, including Africa, although at that time CNN had held back from negotiating with Cuba because of the State Department red tape involved. I felt that I had, so to speak, "waved the flag," and no one was objecting. I reasoned that CNN's presence could only increase information within South Africa about the world's opinion of apartheid, and that had to be beneficial. On October 30, I sent Ted a private note telling him that I had signed a three-year agreement with SABC, to begin immediately. I added, "I looked out my Johannesburg hotel window at the distant sky in the northwest, to see if there were any fireworks in Atlanta." Without the special relationship with Ted, I could never have taken the risk of stepping on the "thin ice" that surrounded South Africa and the new TBS bureaucracy.

* * * * *

In November, I went back to China, stopping first in Tokyo to resolve the dilemma around NHK's desire for CNN on its DBS. I thought I had a solution to TV-Asahi's and JCTV's objections, as well as to Ted's off-handed offer to give CNN away to NHK. I didn't want NHK to look to other major television network news sources in the United States for what it wanted. Again, I made my argument to Koyama and Kobayashi that I would provide NHK only with *Headline News,* informing them that totally free use of CNN, even for experimental DBS purposes, was out of the question. When I wrote them the letter they'd requested, I had carefully chosen the word "compensation." I proposed a non-cash arrangement, whereby CNN would be free for a limited time in exchange for their purchase of programs produced by Turner, and then available in Japan. I also pointed out that NHK would be financially remunerated in this so-called "experiment," since there were a large number of homes awaiting DBS service.

After several years of negotiations, our final arrangement with NHK was made. It provided that CNN would have access to its news material and, in return, NHK would purchase $1,550,000 of Turner programs, which included the 30-hour Cousteau series and the 25 *Portrait of America* programs that Ted was pressuring me to sell in Japan. The agreement also provided $300,000 in cash over the three years of the agreement to cover "handling charges." Through every stage of my daily talks with NHK that November, I had phoned Bill Wells, the MGM representative in Australia, who now was part of Turner's film and program sales distribution in Asia, to recount my discussions. He agreed that it would be an excellent opportunity for Turner to unload some of the expensive specials that TBS was then producing.

I flew on to Hong Kong to meet with Rich Hylen. He was embroiled in an effort to untangle a political morass there that still prevented CNN from being downlinked even when we were able to do so by special arrangements with Cable & Wireless. I left without our having found a solution.

Enroute to Beijing from Hong Kong, I thought back to that informal visit from the television executives, Lu Zigui from Sichuan and Liu Chi of Guangdong. I had been able to get a "Letter of Intent" signed by these two managers of television stations. Their combined provinces were home to 160 million people. That was two-thirds of the population of the United States in 1986. Ted was thrilled when I sent him this information and "Letter of Intent." He wrote back, encouraging me to press on.

It didn't take long for CCTV to learn of this interest in CNN by the two provinces. I soon received a message that CCTV had called Alexandra Kuo, my Chinese consultant, informing her that CCTV "would like to continue discussions regarding the use of CNN on CCTV." A telex arrived the next morning. "You are kindly expected by CCTV to come to Beijing for a visit next month. Please apply for your visa at the Chinese Consulate-General in Houston. Best Regards and looking forward to meeting you. Sheng Yilai, CCTV, Beijing."

Meanwhile, I learned that CCTV had aborted our plans to develop a CNN relationship with the television stations in the two provinces, but I think it had gotten the message that I was not going to give up finding a way into China. It was too important.

Alexandra Kuo was now in continuing contact with CCTV. She received their calls on a 24-hour basis and, at the same time, she maintained liaison with the Chinese delegation at the United Nations. She said that CCTV had a tendency to view the three major American networks as their counterpart, and more important, because of its modest budget, it used only certain news services and already had more international news than its government mandate allowed. She said, "They have no sense of urgency about entering a deal with TBS. Paying for CNN is a luxury that can wait." Interestingly, she added, "If Burt, the president of CNN, had been in charge of CCTV, he would have made a similar decision to wait."

Well, I couldn't wait. Ted was on my back. Every time I saw him, he asked about China. I was determined to overcome CCTV's reluctance to be "associated with CNN." CCTV was the last major link in CNN's development as the first truly global news network. I had to be aggressive but not appear so to CCTV, whose executives kept signaling, "Patience!" It became a joke around my house when I wanted to get Lill to laugh. I'd just say, "my middle name is patience".

Following the visit of the two provincial television executives, Alexandra Kuo had approached her U.S. China contacts in two ways:

1. *Formal Channel.* She briefed the Houston Consulate-General about the intention to establish an agreement between TPS and the Canton and Sichuan television stations, respectively. The Canton television station invited us to visit Guangdong Province. The Consul General was gracious and supportive.

2.   *Informal Channel.* She arranged for the Press Secretary from the Chinese Mission to the U.N. to visit CNN in Atlanta. She kept him informed of the progress that had been made between TPS and the Guangdong television station. Mr. Liu maintained regular contact with CCTV, and he alerted its Director of Foreign Affairs to our pending visit to Canton.

Alexandra wrote to me later:

> The people in Canton are known for entrepreneurship. They are competitive, and their mental outlook is more agreeable with its commerce-oriented neighbor, Hong Kong, than with the 'emperor' in Beijing. As Director of Guangdong TV, Mr. Liu quickly recognized CNN news would benefit its audience and help extend its influence to Hong Kong.
>
> It was generally concluded by all involved that the intent of Guangdong TV to negotiate directly with TPS caught CCTV's attention. They decided to take a second look at TPS. As CCTV sent a telex to invite us to Beijing, we received a message from Canton saying that it needed to postpone our visit to Canton until further notice. With due consideration to Sid's trip to CCTV a year ago, I believed this latest change in Sid's itinerary to Beijing instead of Canton was entirely the Chinese government's decision.
>
> Sid Pike's second visit to Beijing was made at a time when Coca-Cola, the symbol of American 'imperialism,' was allowed to make its first advertisement in China through Ye Sekan's program 'Looking West.' It was very well received in China. The program served as a model in which income may be derived through advertisements. Such potential outlay helped ease its long-term budgetary concern.
>
> Prior to the trip in November 1986, the Consulate Office in Houston had advised me of the long, hard road ahead of us. 'Don't expect a miracle in this second round of negotiations; you are dealing with CCTV, a nerve organ of Chinese propaganda.' So, careful preparations were made prior to and throughout the trip, a reflection of our sincerity. CCTV now recognized Sid as a negotiator with proper credentials to 'make the deal,' and it

[CNN] in turn responded with speed, candor, and openness. This gesture deeply touched those who were involved. The Consulate Office was indeed impressed.

My visit resulted in a finished agreement. The Chinese government still maintained tight control over its propaganda divisions, namely, the Ministry of Television and Radio and the Ministry of Information, and the CCTV negotiators were surprised, perplexed, and impressed by our aggression and determination. One of the negotiators made a remark during a farewell banquet. He said, "The trees I planted today are nourished with my time, energy, and vision. But I will be an ancient Egyptian mummy when these trees bear fruits."

Well, this time the mummy can be unwrapped early because, as of 2003, China's advertising spending increased to $10 billion, and it is the largest growing television market in the world with four major media Goliaths trying to "crack" a market with the highest growth percentage in the world. Two of the four major foreign competitors are TimeWarner (CNN's parent company) and News Corporation (FOX News). It has been reported that TimeWarner has made slightly more progress than News Corporation because it has "a longer history," which can be traced directly to the development of CNN in 1984-87.

After the formal signing of the agreement in Atlanta with Ted Turner in February 1987, Alexandra Kuo helped CNN establish its bureau in Beijing. She later wrote to me:

> CNN served as a wake-up call to Chinese leaders when the events of Tian an Men Square unfolded to the world. By the time the Persian Gulf incident took place, China was fully awake; in fact, CNN became a hero in the people's minds. In a brief five years, CNN had become a household name in China. It brought the Chinese people closer to the world in which they lived.

I returned from Beijing in late November and sent out a memo that included information on the delegation of five or six news and television people from CCTV who would arrive for special training in mid-February. I had enjoyed my visits to China, including my visit to the Beijing Broadcasting

Institute, where I lectured to eager students on my perception of satellite television's role in the world's future. After the painful process of translation, I was surprised to learn that everyone in the class spoke English, and that 50 million Chinese were then studying English.

At last my work in China was over, and Mike Chinoy, Mandarin-speaking and married to a Chinese woman, who had been patiently waiting in the wings for a Chinese bureau, had a new home and base in China, and one of the largest missing links to CNN's global status was finally in place.

Ted could stop hounding me…for now.

Ted Turner congratulating Sid Pike on signing of CNN agreement with CCTV of China in Atlanta. Alexandra Kuo, advisor and translator to Pike is in background.

CHAPTER TWENTY-TWO

Success Can Become a Target

It's a shame when people can't communicate.
When they're managers in your company, it's a catastrophe.
—*Fortune*

By early 1987, my international trips were getting longer and more frequent. One reason for CNN's worldwide success was that the popularity of CNN in the U.S. as a 24-hour news service was now apparent to international tourists, business executives, and government officials, such as embassy staff, who were traveling here. But Washington, D.C., remained one of the few large urban areas that had not yet fully developed its cable service. Most of the officials learned of CNN through word of mouth or during their travels to other parts of the country. They watched CNN in their hotel rooms. When they returned to Washington, they could not understand why they were unable to subscribe to a cable system that existed in other American cities.

Frankly, this puzzled me, too. The nation's capital seemed to be one of the most essential areas to the cable industry, even from a public relations point of view, since it was where the "rules of the game," involving the growth and development of cable, were established. I wondered if the lack of cable in Washington, D.C., was the industry's way of demonstrating that it needed more help from Congress to grow.

Sometimes, I would be contacted by an embassy and asked how the CNN channel could be received in Washington. I would suggest the installation of a dish on the embassy grounds, and if necessary, I would help them contact a distributor. Joyce knew how important these embassies' phone calls and letters were and immediately brought them to my attention, even when I was traveling. Often, my first line of communication with a country's government and its television officials was through the embassy. It was how I developed my contacts in China, India, and South Africa, as well as in Eastern European countries after the Cold War, when I was no longer involved in CNN internationally, but in developing new international broadcasting projects for Turner.

My increased traveling time was very hard on Lill, who had been used to my being at home during most of my television career, the exception having been my commuting to New York for six months after I was fired from WHDH-TV in Boston. The other time was when I first came to Atlanta, and she had to sell the Boston house and join me. During those ten years of constant traveling, the things I had been responsible for in our daily life, as well as family events, from weddings to funerals, all fell on her while I was at the other end of the globe. I missed my own brother's funeral. He had died of a brain tumor while I was traveling in China. Fortunately, I did visit him in the hospital before I left. Lill developed new interests in her volunteer work—including our temple's activities—and became involved in various study groups and classes. Her colleagues at work, as well as our friends, gave her some of the support she needed. My work consumed me, and not only when I was traveling. This naturally added to all the stresses, and there often were times when Lill said she felt like "a single parent." There were many stormy seas in our marriage, but like the crew that feels blessed when sunlight reveals a new calmness, we weathered the storm.

I stayed in Atlanta during the early part of 1987. My office had become a center for information requests about CNN from all over the world. I continued to make frequent trips to Washington to pressure Intelsat to permit multi-downlinking at realistic rates. The private organization, Comsat, which was the U.S. representative on the Intelsat Board of Governors, was obviously not interested in any change in a system that threatened its company's continuing high profits.

The agreement we had for the use of the AFRTS/CNN signal contained the stipulation "that it is in concert with Intelsat agreements." This was my major problem. But I had leverage at AFRTS that I did not have at Intelsat. I continued to meet with Lt. Colonel Pollack of AFRTS, and later with Mel Russell and Jordan "Buzz" Riser, in order to convince them that the use of their CNN signal by television stations and cable systems in other countries was far more important to the whole world than providing entertainment to U.S. Armed Forces personnel, although I did understand it was what mattered most to them. I was also telling myself that it was more important than the success of my own company which had been my original goal.

Like any government bureaucracy, AFRTS was focused on its specific responsibility—they had no political or public agendas. It was true that Turner gave it what it needed to fill out its daily programming schedule when there were no special sports events or entertainment programs to be aired that day. The U.S. network-news offerings were limited to the half-hour evening news, occasional morning news, and late night talk programs. AFRTS had no commitment *per se* to Turner films or programs. CNN, however, was another matter. Once viewers saw it and made it part of their daily routine, they didn't want to give it up. Even though Colonel Pollack and his colleagues in Washington told me that they could always use the network news if they had to replace CNN, I knew that the armed forces would express their displeasure if CNN were not available.

But we couldn't afford to use this trump card of threatening to withdraw CNN if AFRTS didn't allow us to downlink its signal and sell it more widely. We knew what would happen. Ted would get phone calls from members of Congress, possibly from the President, demanding that the U.S. armed forces be able to watch CNN. No one in the industry since World War II, when Hollywood stars began visiting troops at bases all over the world, had failed to fulfill AFRTS's requests for free programs, films, and sports events.

Nor did AFRTS care to take the risk of losing CNN. After all, its commitments from producers, directors, writers, actors, and unions had been made at the emotional height of World War II, and certainly it had been justified during the Korean and Vietnam War periods. There were, however, some, like Henry Gillespie, who felt that entertainment was an industry, with its banks and investors, just as much as those which built tanks, guns, and aircraft. As Henry kept reminding me, "Chrysler didn't donate its tanks at cost." Nor did Lockheed its C-5A, the largest military aircraft. But I was determined to get AFRTS to arrange with Intelsat more downlinking of its 12-to-16 hour daily telecasts of CNN, which now covered almost the entire globe, including the most heavily populated areas.

Of special help to me with AFRTS was Vince Harris, industry liaison director, whose office was in Los Angeles where its global satellite signals were uplinked. Vinnie was an old-timer like me, who had the skills and patience to make things happen, as only those who have worked in a given industry for a long time can. When I had problems with AFRTS and Vinnie called, I listened. When I talked to Vinnie about my concerns, things had a way of changing. We were, in effect, the go-betweens for AFRTS and TBS. Phone calls from Vinnie got my immediate attention, and if necessary, a telex would find me. Vinnie worked as a civilian at AFRTS for 45 years, whereas the commanders of the Broadcast Center in Los Angeles came and went. By 1987, I began to see how AFRTS might achieve what I'd been working toward. It was negotiating with Intelsat to increase the cost of its Atlantic and Pacific transponders, which were costing it between $1.2 and $1.5 million annually, by an additional $300,000 per year so that each signal could include multi-downlinking service. I was ecstatic and waited patiently for the approval of this proposal.

About this time, Ted suddenly got the impression (I never learned where or from whom, but Ted used information he picked up, say, from someone sitting next to him on an airplane) that AFRTS was an impediment to our plans to expand CNN internationally. Perhaps some people had told him that they watched CNN off the AFRTS signal in other parts of the world. In any case, Burt Reinhardt sent me a list of questions Ted had about AFRTS, including when our contract with it ended and where its signal reached. I wondered if he planned to bite the bullet and pay the high cost of putting a 24-hour CNN signal on various worldwide satellites, even though that would still not have solved downlinking costs. I believed that in time AFRTS would succeed in acquiring multi-downlinking permission from Intelsat because it had the ideal "reason," its signals covered the earth, but it was technically considered "domestic." Ted was playing with a grenade. I had to stop him before it blew up in our face.

I fired off a detailed memo to Ted, listing the parts of the globe covered by AFRTS and the reasons we needed to continue to use its signals. I did not even bother to state the obvious effect on our public service image if we abandoned our armed forces. I wrote:

> The contract ends on September 30, 1988. However, I caution against our getting out. I have been advised by AFRTS that they would immediately pick up NBC and carry a morning show and evening news, repeating it as needed. Remember, although AFRTS carries 12 hours of CNN a day, generally each military installation only uses one to two hours per day. It is the hotels that take it all.
>
> To me, remaining on AFRTS is essential. We would be asking for trouble if we discontinued or did not allow CNN on the service. NBC is already being carried to Australia, and the Sevens use it in their arguments (as do other Asian broadcasters) when we negotiate contracts. I don't want to encourage or develop that side.

I knew what would get Ted's attention and make him back off. He saw that our competition could take advantage of us if we lost CNN on AFRTS. On this critical issue, I was prepared to keep arguing, or should I say filibuster, which Ted knew I rarely did. And he trusted my judgment. I had already dodged two bullets aimed at ending or damaging CNN's relationship with AFRTS. Henry Gillespie's insistence (back in 1985) that we try to get more money from it was only the first.

After the CCTV delegates left in February, Maryann and I flew to San Juan, Puerto Rico, and hired her former business acquaintance, Lillian Noriega, to run an office there that would be responsible for CNN and the sale of Turner programs and films in the Caribbean.

Despite my difficulties with Intelsat, CNN was growing everywhere that the AFRTS signal reached. Television stations, businesses, newspapers, and heads of state brought the CNN signal down with or without Intelsat's approval. CNN's coverage when the American shuttle, Challenger, exploded, proved my argument to the global television stations that they needed to have access to CNN in addition to the standard television news services. Our offer to allow any television station to air live, breaking news as it happened was bolstered greatly by coverage of the Challenger tragedy. And more was to come.

Some hotels around the world were paying up to ten cents per night per room for CNN, but many others pirated it. Cable had not yet rooted itself elsewhere, as it had done by 1987 in North America. JCTV and others were pioneering it in Japan, and a few countries like Argentina were beginning to develop it.

The U.S. television networks, and the broadcast industry generally, saw CNN as a Turner product available within the United States. They had no clue as to CNN's international development. When they finally caught on, even with the technical and staff superiority they had in their news departments, they could not compete with CNN's international growth. They simply did not have the entrepreneurial leadership. The Paleys and other visionaries were gone. And while Roone Arledge of ABC represented the new generation of creative managers, and he went on to become its News Division Director and tried to develop a competing news service, he was not in a powerful enough position to mandate its development, as Ted had done earlier, just because he felt that it was the right thing to do.

In January 1987, Henry Gillespie sent a telex to Bill Wells in Australia, saying that his cancer, which had started as a brain tumor, had spread to his kidneys, and a week later he would be having surgery. Henry was at home but was trying to stay in contact with us. It astonished me that Henry had continued to work so long, given the terrible disease that was consuming him. He was attempting to mollify Wells, who wanted to take over the sale of CNN, as well as other TBS programming, in the Pacific region. If this happened, I was afraid that CNN would be packaged like motion picture films or other program products. I didn't feel comfortable giving anyone CNN to sell who could not communicate well with television news directors, our primary source of international CNN sales at the time. Wells was obviously impatient, even though Henry told him in his telex: "It's my intention to lay the complete CNN marketing job in your and Greg's laps. I saw Sid's report on the Pacific and believe it pinpoints our challenges very well. Sid is more than willing to help and double team on calls and give you all the information you need."

The telex implied a gradual rather than a sudden transition, but suggested that Wells would end up with it.

I knew that I could not cover the world alone and that, in order for me to move on to other territories, such as Africa and Southern Asia, I would have to give up some of the territories that I had worked so hard to develop.

In April, as usual, I attended the annual television industry meeting in Cannes, France. The main problem with these conventions was that you met so many people that it was difficult to focus attention on any one country or group. Many agreements were made, however, and relationships begun there continued to develop. For me, it meant a week of exhausting days negotiating with television station representatives from breakfast through late dinners, but Lill looked forward to this trip with the accompanying glitz and glamour of the famous Riviera. For years she told our friends that she caught me photographing a topless bather on the beach behind the convention hall, although I was at least fifty yards away and lacked a zoom lens. *Playboy* photographers did not have to worry about their jobs yet.

A short time before I left for Cannes, Russ Barry officially replaced Henry Gillespie. Russ was now in charge, not only of domestic and international film and program distribution, but of CNN sales as well. Russ was not interested in the international market, and I knew he was hoping that I would quit. But much tougher guys than Russ tried to get me to quit and had failed. Once, on my way to the Pacific Rim, I stopped at our Los Angeles office late in the afternoon, and Russ was there. He said "hello," and I could tell that he was thinking of asking me out for a drink. I sensed that this could have been a defining moment in our relationship, but the moment passed and we, as well as the company, lost an opportunity.

In Cannes, I always stayed at the Majestic Hotel, which was directly across from the Palais des Festivals Convention Hall. Russ stayed at the Carlton, which was a few blocks away. Both hotels were important meeting and dining places during the convention. One evening when I was meeting someone at the Carlton Hotel, I saw Russ and Bill Wells deep in conversation in the lobby as I waited for my client. The next day, Russ pulled me aside in our convention booth to have a meeting with him and Wells. Apparently, Bill was determined to get me completely out of the Pacific Rim and South Asia territory. He said I was refusing to cooperate with him. I told how I had phoned Wells in Sydney from Tokyo when I was putting the NHK/CNN agreement together so that the many less-than-desirable programs Ted wanted us to sell in Japan would be included. To my amazement, Wells denied that I had phoned him. Of course, he was saying exactly what Russ wanted to hear. Russ believed him and not me.

Actually, my work in the Pacific was finished, although not in parts of southern Asia, but I continued to provide Wells with all the information he needed. I resented the lies he had told to achieve his goals. Later, I thought about my personal connections in the Pacific. I knew that Jiro Sugiyama, the Japanese agent who worked with Wells, had strongly resented my by-passing the traditional Japanese agent representation of American film and television companies, and I wondered if Bill Wells and Jiro Sugiyama had decided to remove me and return to the traditional system.

Wells never asked me for any advice on the agreements I had made when he renewed them. While I was doing research for this book, I learned of the CNN rates Wells had given Lee Holmes and Guam Cable TV. Holmes was paying *double the U.S. rate*, which was due to my earlier efforts. In 1992, Guam Cable TV paid 35 cents per month per subscriber (the U.S. rate then was 18 cents); in 1993, 40 cents; in 1994, 45 cents. These rates were reasonable, given the number of CNN subscribers in the Pacific sharing the satellite costs in the early 1990s. This proved that Holmes and Guam were not physically attached to the U.S. mainland.

I wonder what Wells would have done if he had had to *negotiate* as I did with Lee Holmes, "the Marine colonel from Hell."

CHAPTER TWENTY-THREE

Mapping the First Magellan Trip

Great spirits have always encountered violent opposition from mediocre minds.

—Albert Einstein

In the spring of 1987, Ted asked for meetings on global satellite strategies, and we made the decision to forego the Australian Sevens video-plexed signal in the Pacific, which was less than satisfactory. It required expensive equipment to restore the split-video signal into a picture and slowed our sales efforts considerably, particularly in smaller countries. We knew that the income we could anticipate in the area would support our own Turner transponder. I wrote Terry McGuirk about this and also suggested that we seek a satellite signal for India and Pakistan or southern Asia, since this heavily populated area, along with China, would be in the forefront of future international development. In one of the meetings with Ted, he told us of his discussions with the Soviets regarding our possible use of their Gorizont series of satellites. Using them would mean we could avoid the costly downlinking arrangements with Intelsat. Talks were ongoing with Intelsat regarding future coverage of South America and Africa, and Arab, countries, but I couldn't count on their responding to our needs.

Another satellite problem cropped up: Since the U.S. programming was now encoded, it required cable systems, television stations, and other users of CNN to purchase special, inexpensive equipment to decode the signal, which was the same one being received in Central America, the Caribbean, and Canada. The price was $300 to $400 dollars, but the U.S. State Department forbade taking the decoders out of the country because they contained a computer chip that could be used as a targeting device on missiles! Later, the decoders were allowed outside the United States, but only if used for "commercial" applications. I could never understand why the State Department assumed that people who wanted that chip wouldn't get it in the United States or from one of the "commercial" applications. Bob Ross warned me not to authorize any non-commercial decoders outside the country.

We were beginning to have breaks, too. By 1987, because our 24-hour CNN service to hotels or cable systems did not interfere with WTN or EBU marketing, Burt Reinhardt had succeeded in negotiating an additional payment to WTN. Burt convinced EBU (and later Asian Broadcasting Union–ABU) to allow its news to be contained within the 24-hour service, so that we didn't have to embargo those news stories to hotels and cable systems. The one exclusion that Bill MacPhail, head of CNN Sports, could not eliminate belonged to some of the U.S. sports leagues, which refused to allow videos of game action to be shown along with sports results. For a long time, JCTV in Japan continued to cover the sports video with a single-frame picture. This was embarrassing for JCTV and CNN, and it was really unprofessional behavior on the part of the leagues. So when we made an agreement with SeaTel about this time to provide CNN to cruise ships and other vessels, WTN took a large percentage of the payments it made to us. We had no choice. There was no way to edit WTN news stories out of CNN onboard a ship. To delete the sports video, a special "black box" was installed on each ship so that we could command the box to omit a particular segment.

Another problem related to cruise ships that sailed the Caribbean waters and along the U.S. coast within range of the domestic signal was that talent agreements for the commercials only provided for viewing within the United States. Once cruise ships moved a certain distance away from a U.S. port, they were not supposed to air those commercials. Gerry Hogan, Vice

President of Advertising Sales, was reluctant to let me signal the equipment on the ships to cut out the commercials, because it would affect other areas where the commercials could be run. Eventually, we had to find a way for advertising agencies to negotiate with the union so actors received an extra payment for use of commercials "outside" the United States. But I couldn't work directly with the advertising agencies and unions like I did in Washington with Intelsat and AFRTS. I had to rely on my advertising and legal colleagues to convince the unions and potential international advertisers to think globally. This was not a problem if you were Coca-Cola or Procter & Gamble, but if your product were sold only in the United States, you saw no reason to pay actors additional money for international advertising. We finally persuaded the agencies to make some accommodation with the talent unions, but this hurdle took a year to overcome.

By the end of 1987, CNN was developing a separate 24-hour international channel that would be used only by international advertisers. This was an expansion of the European feed begun in 1985. But even then, the domestic CNN signal was still the one used in Canada, Central America, and the Caribbean.

In May 1987, I began planning a Magellan trip—I would go around the world until I returned to my starting point. I would leave at the end of the month for Johannesburg. I learned that Ted had accepted CCTV's offer to visit the People's Republic of China, and he was going to India as well. He would travel to China by way of London, Moscow, Delhi, and Hong Kong. We planned to meet in India and then travel to China and Hong Kong together. This was a very important journey for me, the most extensive I had undertaken so far. I intended to open up Africa and Southern Asia to CNN and thus complete its global circuit.

Rich Hylen was still having a difficult time in Hong Kong. The government was aware of the value of cable, particularly in such a highly populated area, but it kept waffling, refusing to make up its mind, we presumed because of intense political pressure from the two powerful companies (Hutchison-Whampoa and Wharf Holdings) that sought its cable license. Rich was trying to get the Hong Kong administration to allow him to feed a MDS signal (an unwired cable television service) of CNN to the plethora of hotels. The plan was to provide only CNN, but I'm sure there was concern that the CNN signal could prove popular and increase the demand for other forms of programming. Governments and leaders often don't like to have their constituents understand the technical capabilities that have been developed until it has been decided who will share in the resulting wealth from these innovations. The only antidote to this tendency is the media, and generally it is newspapers that inform the public of the particular innovation that they are prevented from enjoying. Governments in many developing countries have control of television. It operates only with their license or permission—whereas newspapers are not usually under the direct control of any government agency except in a totalitarian regime. The Hong Kong newspapers, as well as radio and television, had informed the public about the wonders of cable and its multiple channel potential, but the Hong Kong government had created the impression that it was a very complicated procedure that required extensive planning and preparation. Rich was hoping that Ted's presence in Hong Kong would, through the media coverage of his visit, set off a fireworks display that would affect the political battle of who would get the profitable cable rights. Then, finally, the local government would give the necessary approvals for the MDS-CNN signal.

I would leave Ted after Hong Kong, renew my efforts in Taiwan, then do some public relations in Japan, and finally stop and visit the "battle-field" of Guam to testify for Channel 14. This first Magellan trip took six weeks, but the preparation for it took months.

I didn't know how to approach a continent like Africa. Its southernmost country, the Republic of South Africa, was similar to European countries in its economy and government, but the rest of the continent was quite different. Most African governments were totalitarian regimes; there were a few democratic countries, but those were just emerging. Civil wars were rampant. In 1987, Africa was not, as a continent, attracting business, except for those companies interested in exploiting its vast natural resources. Apart from South Africa, at this time sealed off from participation in the global economy by the embargo, the countries of Africa were still largely agricultural and still using traditional farming methods. Barter economies were common. The cities had little industry and great poverty. Huge numbers of people were still uneducated by Western standards, and most Western businesses were not trying to develop markets in Africa.

But for CNN, it was an important source of news. Gary Streiker had been sent to Nairobi, Kenya, to open the first African CNN News Bureau in April 1985. Africa was important because I was now aware of the power of information distributed by satellite, and I considered Africa ripe for using the satellites for education and medical resources. But how was I to get inside Africa? How was I to plug in CNN and make it function, not only for collecting news, but in order to offer CNN to its television stations and hotels? I turned to my resources, such as Dr. Blume, in San Diego. Blume had already written to encourage me about working in Africa. He was well aware of the significance of the satellite distribution system and always inspired me to continue my efforts.

No matter how strong we are, when others express their confidence in us, it helps us find the courage to overcome seemingly insurmountable obstacles. Dr. Blume was a mentor to me, and when I learned in early January 1990 that he had died, I felt the loss keenly of someone who had so often recharged my intellectual batteries. He was my African consultant in 1987, and helped me hatch a plan, which Luis Torres-Bohl then helped me carry out—to introduce CNN to Africa's relatively dormant television broadcast systems. When I learned that I had scheduling difficulties flying from South Africa to Pakistan, and would have to stay overnight in Europe or in another African country, Dr. Blume and I decided to hold a one-day *seminar* in Nairobi, Kenya. We invited government or television representatives from each African country, so that I could present to them the benefits of CNN. Air travel in Africa often required a flight to Paris or London in order to connect to a city on the opposite side of the continent. Hotels and Customs officials in Africa were not that welcoming to business travelers, which presented another obstacle. Later that year, we were able to open a business office in Lagos, Nigeria, to provide more of a CNN presence and to help facilitate our travel within Africa.

The organizing of our seminar was underway, but first I had to locate an antenna construction company that could demonstrate the technical side of the presentation, while I extolled the virtues of CNN. I found such a company, System Technology Trading in Qatar, an Arab country in the Persian Gulf. Christopher Richardson, a representative of System Technology Trading, agreed to lecture in the afternoon and offered to share some of the expenses with CNN, including air travel and hotel accommodations for the participants.

Sixteen countries, represented by 19 delegates, responded: Cameroon,

Central African Republic, Djibouti, Niger, Senegal, Swaziland, Tanzania, Uganda, Zaire, Zambia, Zimbabwe, Somalia, Ethiopia, Mali, Seychelles, and, of course, Kenya. The seminar was scheduled for a week after I arrived. I planned to go first to South Africa, because our agreement with SABC had been cancelled because of the Intelsat downlinking costs. I hoped to resurrect it. Because of my connection to CNN, the South African Embassy was reluctant to issue a visa to me—they were certain I was an investigative reporter. Finally, Fanus Venter, the SABC Bureau Chief in Washington, told his embassy to issue the visa. South Africa's relentless apartheid policies were causing daily atrocities. If ever a population needed to know the attitude of the rest of the world, it was the South Africans.

I arrived in Johannesburg on May 30 and was met at the International airport by Lionel Williams, a member of the SABC news staff who had traveled a good deal in the United States and had been to various television industry meetings. Lionel drove me to the Johannesburg Sun and Towers Hotel, which was very modern and plush. The hotel, built like ice cream on a stick, had a circular base that rose to a wider round hotel-on-a-stick.

Blacks and whites were now starting to intermingle in the hotels, because the racial "pass" laws had been eliminated in 1986. But the feeling of separation persisted. It was as though neither group acknowledged the existence of the other.

The next morning, I was picked up by a driver for SABC and driven to its broadcast facility. I had expected to see a building that looked like an upgraded warehouse, but its offices were more like a hotel complex. In the lobby I saw, for the first time, the Afrikaner security that I had not seen before, even at the airport. Guards with dogs were everywhere, and only after I was identified at the reception desk was I allowed to enter. There was a single, pass-through revolving door. Once the guards knew me, the locked door would be opened, and I would be allowed to pass.

Kobus Hamman, the Director for News for SABC, greeted me warmly, but when he called in his associates, I could tell that some of them didn't share his pleasure. They liked the status quo and resented the intrusion of outside influences. I was used to this by now.

And as questions were asked, I took in again, as I always did, how the group was divided. Like Kobus, some saw the positive possibilities of an affiliation with the world's first major 24-hour satellite news service. Others were reluctant to change the present system of news affiliation, particularly with Visnews, the London-based satellite-delivered news service that fed them a daily 20 minutes of news. One of those who aligned himself with Kobus, to my good fortune, was an Afrikaner who turned out to be older than he appeared. P.C. (Christo) Kritzinger was the News Director. He had strong Nordic features, typical for an Afrikaner, one of those forever-young looking males, and he couldn't sit still. I was not surprised that he headed up the news staff.

Afrikaners—South Africans of Dutch ancestry who speak Afrikaans, a language that developed from seventeenth century Dutch—particularly those who are educated, speak English well. One might even get the impression that it was their native language, but they preferred to speak Afrikaans. Their white skin and traditional hatred of the English, particularly for the way the British army had treated Afrikaner families during the Boer War, bound them together.

As soon as I made my presentation, the staff used the same method of communication that the Japanese had in my very first CNN sales experience in that country. They spoke in their own language while I was in the room. Sometimes they apologized, but I insisted that they do this, because it saved so much time. If we were all English-speaking, there'd be interminable delays while our clients left the room or asked me to go to another room and wait while they talked.

During the next few days, I returned for more talks with SABC, and I had the impression that there was genuine interest in trying the CNN excerpting service. At this point in time, CNN was not on any satellite that provided a full-time transponder in sub-Saharan Africa, and the only CNN signal that was available was the partial service from AFRTS. The news staff had heard enough about CNN, in addition to having been intrigued by my presentation, to be willing to try it. One reason was their concern about a new, potential rival, a service called M-Net that had been introduced in October 1986 and was growing rapidly, even though it was a one-channel cable service.

A group of the Cape Town Afrikaners, made up mostly of newspaper people from the region, originated M-Net in 1986, which was delivered to various South African cities and transmitted on an encoded system to homes. The technical means for distributing M-Net was provided by SABC, which had control of all television-distribution services in the country.

In the countries that followed the British system of government broadcast monopolies, the viewers now had a thirst for more programming and information. As business travelers and vacationers brought back stories of countries with dozens of channels, the pressure built on the governments of the former British colonies to change their system. In South Africa, the change was slow, almost imperceptible. It began largely because of differences among the Afrikaners. One group had left Cape Town in the nineteenth century to settle in northern South Africa, enduring all the hardships that pioneers suffer. They were the group behind SABC. The other groups of Afrikaners were descended from the Cape Town Dutch colonists. The British had gained more control over Cape Town and had, by the mid-nineteenth century, abolished slavery, and these landowners took their slaves and moved to the interior, where they had to fight with Zulus and other Bantu tribes involved in their own migration south at the time. There were also wars between the Afrikaners and the British—Boer Wars—in the nineteenth century. The Afrikaners living in the interior had a toughness and determination that later shaped the Afrikaner implacability during the worldwide sanctions against apartheid. Some of the migrating Afrikaners had settled in the Transvaal and eventually founded the gold-mining industry and the city of Johannesburg. To make sure that neither side had an advantage, the government was conducted part of the time in Johannesburg and part of the time in Cape Town.

SABC, a government-owned service, following the British model, had four channels: One was part Afrikaans and part English, and one was English only. The other two were ethnic (black). This form of television service collects its revenue from both a government tax and advertising. SABC had to satisfy the Afrikaners who wanted programming in their own language, those speaking English and descended from British colonists (another large group), as well as broadcast in the various tribal languages. I was amused to watch a South African golf tournament and listen to two announcers, one speaking English and one Afrikaans, taking turns describing the play, although all Afrikaner viewers probably spoke English.

Before M-Net, SABC was the only game in town. Their viewers' desire for more programming, however, had been so strong and the challenge of delivering programs in all the various languages was such that they were more than willing to pay for a one-channel cable service such as M-Net. The rate was approximately the same as a U.S. basic cable service of 10 to 12 channels and averaged about 45 Rand ($17 U.S.) a month. In the U.S. in 1987, there were a total of 8,413 cable channels. In addition, the viewer had to buy a decoder. So, in effect, the Cape Towners had achieved parity with the Transvaal group. They also had two sources of income: subscription and advertising.

By mid-1991, M-Net reached 600,000 subscribers. When you count subscribers, you are counting sets in homes or even villages. In the United States at this time, there were 2.2 viewers per television set. In China, where televisions sets were placed in a local hall or village square, there might have been 100-200 viewers per set. In South Africa, 2.5 was the average. So, 600,000 subscribers translated into 1,500,000 viewers. The population in 1991 was 34 million: four million were white, four million were mixed races, and the remaining 26 million were black. M-Net still had growth left when apartheid ended, but it would have to interest new consumers among the black population. In addition, now that blacks were entering the political arena, black entrepreneurs wanted to carve out their own niche in television broadcasting and cable enterprises.

South Africa, having been isolated by sanctions, as well as by its location at the bottom of the globe, was shut out from the information necessary for its citizens to compare their country to other developed nations. A large undeveloped continent lay between itself and Europe. North America and Australia were even farther away. South Africa, as a modern civilized society, was both isolated and protected by this distance. Add to this the xenophobia that developed because of the sanctions, and you have a significant barrier to new ideas.

If fresh concepts and information cannot get through, the governmental infrastructure is no less a victim, particularly if the television system has been set up so that there is no real competition. Afrikaners controlled both SABC and M-Net. Imagine if the Democratic and Republican parties in the United States each owned a television network and were able to prevent any other television or radio service from existing.

To preserve this overall control, there existed at the highest levels of SABC and M-Net mutual cooperation so that the growth of neither service was endangered. The heads of SABC and M-Net met regularly to iron out their differences. Only they knew how the system worked, and they had the technical expertise that the government lacked or didn't want. Ostensibly, they were competing, but they were careful to accommodate each other. This would mean legal chaos in the United States, which has strict, anti-trust laws to prevent just this sort of thing. But I did find similar situations in other parts of the world. Koos Becker, General Manager of M-Net, and Vernard Harmse, Director General of SABC, smoothed out their differences in the same spirit as their governmental Afrikaner counterparts in Cape Town and Johannesburg did. Further proof of how this cooperation worked was that the South African government lacked the ability to provide an independent study of existing radio and television services, not to mention analysis of future technologies and how they might be applied for the betterment of the general population. When the government needed technical advice, it went to the SABC for information. What the government or the ministry in question didn't seem to realize, or maybe they did, was that SABC only provided advice that benefited itself. When a commission was proposed to study a particular broadcasting area, perhaps for expansion of services, quite often, the head of SABC was its chairman.

When the television broadcasting service was first designed, SABC introduced a grid system plan for the allocation of television channels through South Africa. The plan allocated channels along a specified grid that was exactly the same distance from point to point. This meant that the same number of channels was allocated in an area where two hundred people lived as was allocated in a city of two million. The net result of this grid plan was that no additional channels could be added in major cities such as Johannesburg, Durban, or Cape Town, and the multi-channel allocations in small communities were wasted. So SABC was in complete control of all four channels then available in each major market. When M-Net was formed by the consortium in Cape Town, it was SABC that provided the interconnecting technical links to each city.

One could say that this was SABC's function, that it was assigned by the government to provide television and radio services throughout the country. But what the governments in all countries that followed this British television system failed to understand was that it gave two mandates to its broadcasters. One was to act as a government service that provided programming. Their receiving tax money from citizens with television sets compensated this. The other mandate was to make money from advertising; it was in the television service's interest to prevent competing services. In some countries, this was intentional. The government wanted to control the most effective propaganda machine available. Charles De Gaulle of France understood the power of television in its early days and effectively tied its development to the French government.

In effect, SABC, because of its position and power, was able to absorb all creative broadcasting ideas that surfaced within the country.

Within the Republic of South Africa, there were a number of "homelands" that were distinct from the territory which the South African government controlled. They were set aside as areas where blacks could live separately and govern themselves. Most countries in the world and the United Nations had refused to recognize these independently governed areas because South Africa had created them as another means of separating the races. Surprisingly, the governments did function independently of South African influence and, at times, were thorns in the side of their originator, as well as its related entities, like SABC. Sometimes a "homeland" decision interfered with SABC's careful control of all broadcasting and advertising opportunities within South Africa. These homelands were outside any censorship imposed by the government on any of its broadcast services. Although censorship eased up when the DeKlerk government came to power in 1987, the four basic broadcast services in South Africa continued to be controlled by Afrikaners for the most part, and there definitely was editorial influence at SABC.

But in Bophuthatswana, one of the homelands that was carved out within South Africa, President Lucas Mangobe, elected for a seven-year term, had radically transformed this small country into an effective example of how a black government could operate independently. BOP-TV and radio facilities were the best that money could buy. The technical equipment and studios were "state of the art" and were especially designed, particularly the sound studios, to attract recording stars from around the world. Their hope was that artists, particularly black artists, would avail themselves of these studios, less expensive than in Europe and the United States, and that Bophuthatswana would become a mecca for such talent as the color of the South African government changed and blacks increasingly visited this modern country. The chances of their plan being successful were greatly enhanced by President Mangobe naming white Jonathan Procter as Director General of BOP-TV. A resident of Cape Town and of English descent, he was a professor of Business at the University of Cape Town. Two other whites were in management positions and were dedicated to making BOP-TV an effective influence throughout Africa. In order for BOP-TV to transmit to the seven separate "islands" where the Tswana people lived, which constituted its "country," it was assumed that SABC would supply to Bophuthatswana the technical microwave services that it controlled, which M-Net was also forced to use, based on the fact that there was no other facility capable of transmitting the BOP-TV signal throughout Bophuthatswana. This did not happen. Procter decided to use a satellite signal to reach the transmitters that would deliver the BOP-TV signal to its TV homes.

By doing this, which he says he did to prevent SABC's control of the BOP-TV signal, he unleashed a raging lion, the likes of which had never been seen in the jungles or plains of the African continent. Procter's intent was to deliver the signal only within the homelands of that country, but he ended up with a signal that not only covered Africa, but also could be seen as far north as Greece and as far east as Israel. He had, in effect, created a SuperStation, similar to Ted's deliberate creation of WTCG.

Procter and his program director, unaware of the immense reach of their signal, were suddenly shocked by the demand of program suppliers, including myself on behalf of CNN, that the program purchasing agreements be updated. This miniscule market of Bophuthatswana, with its major city of Mmabatho supporting a population of 5,000 potential viewers, including babies, was now reaching a potential audience of 400 to 500 *million*, although many people in Africa did not yet own a television set.

Procter soon realized that he had hit a mother lode and, for the second time, this little country had hoodwinked their Afrikaner founders. The first had been when the South African government had drawn the boundaries. One end of the tiny country had included a platinum field, but at the time, there was no significant market for platinum. As its value increased, the Afrikaners realized their mistake and tried, to no avail, to get the area returned to them. When President Mangobe rebuffed them, they resorted to digging a mine at the border that would enter at an angle into the platinum area. They did not get away with this, either.

To pacify the program suppliers, BOP-TV promised to scramble its satellite signal and offered to pay for any additional audience it was able to reach. Its advertising opportunities were growing exponentially. It had outdone their competitors, SABC and M-Net. I did everything I could to support BOP-TV and Procter, and I made sure that future agreements with SABC did not include black homelands.

As a result of my visit to South Africa in 1987, I was able to convince SABC to try CNN's excerpting service on AFRTS. This provided SABC with ten to twelve hours of CNN every day. Unfortunately, SABC also terminated this limited agreement after three months due to AFRTS's weak signal reception. By the fall of 1988, we again had a Letter of Intent, when the Soviet satellite became a possibility. Intelsat, the Western satellite monopoly, was learning that we had no compunction to use any means available to distribute the CNN satellite signal. The SABC agreement was for 24 hours of CNN, and only Gorizont could provide this at the time. But in 1989, the negotiations to get us on the Soviet Gorizont satellite again were delayed. The system had many interruptions due to lack of proper maintenance. But I would have helped them use *plastic tape* if I could get the muti-downlinking service required for global CNN.

Kobus and I were both frustrated. We saw the benefits of downlinking CNN into South Africa. I saw an entrance into Africa and a chance to break down a wall that controlled a more open view of the world and the status of racial empowerment. Kobus, a mild mannered Afrikaner, with a genuine desire to improve the status of his country, had trusted my efforts to bring in the CNN signal to South Africa.

We both would have to wait for another day.

CHAPTER TWENTY-FOUR

Africa Opens Its Doors

Purpose

I love. I hate. Thus I have power
and am strong.
The only other ingredient is will and
this I have most.
Together we make a human being
for service to all or myself.
The only thing I lacked was inspiration,
and this I have found.
For there is no looking back,
only progressively moving forward.
I know now what is my destiny—
to serve mankind as only I know how.

—Sidney Pike, April 18, 1987

After the plane had taken off from Johannesburg, I tried to relax and concentrate on the upcoming seminar in Nairobi. We had had a devil of a time organizing it. Luis Torres-Bohl had coordinated the event with Dr. Blume and a woman named Naomi Waiyaki of Thuci Associates, who arranged the travel and housing for the participants. One major obstacle was in getting the government of Kenya and the Voice of Kenya (radio and TV) to cooperate. Telex after telex went unanswered. They only responded when we asked Naomi and others to step in.

Even advancing money to Naomi's company was a huge hassle. The money went from the Atlanta bank through a second bank, and was received by the Bank of Credit and Commerce in Nairobi, which failed to confirm the money's arrival. This snafu was typical of the problems we had doing business in countries that were seeking external investment, but had poor coordination among their own officials. They were not used to operations and procedures that involved people and businesses outside their country. I had to learn to go around them or come at them from another direction.

When I arrived in Nairobi on June 3, a representative from Naomi's company took me to a famous hotel, the Norfolk, where big game hunters often stayed. The only thing I was interested in hunting was access to the television newsrooms of the continent. We planned to use the seminar to explain the use of satellites and how the flow of television news between the countries in Africa could be better coordinated. Sixteen countries sending representatives was encouraging and meant, I thought, that they wanted to learn more about satellites, as well as about CNN. The next day I met the delegates, all men, dressed in the usual Western business suits, very serious, even nervous in some cases, perhaps because this was such a new area for them, but friendly toward me. Most of them had heard of CNN. After introductions, I explained that the age of delivering news videotape between countries by hand was over. The miracle of aviation had been superseded by another mechanical device that allowed images to travel through the air all the time. It was not hard to acquire the necessary equipment, but the complexities of the Intelsat consortium represented a difficulty. I explained what was possible at that time. Their Department of State or equivalent would need to demonstrate to Intelsat that neither their local PTT nor Intelsat would suffer financially from this sharing of domestic satellite signals between countries. I used the situation in the Pacific islands to illustrate the benefits of instant reception of CNN by satellite as compared to the two to three weeks for delivery of video information. I mentioned that we hoped to reach the more than 30 hotels in Hong Kong with their 30,000 hotel rooms. I talked about our new agreement in the People's Republic of China and, finally, how CNN was able to reach Africa. I explained AFRTS and the agreement that allowed us to offer 13 hours a day of CNN to other users in the many parts of the world where it could be seen.

I explained that there were now three 24-hour CNN signals: two US signals, domestic CNN and *Headline News,* and CNN's 24-hour signal produced for Europe. While most of the European stories were taken from the domestic service, they were providing non-American news, including foreign financial news. Eventually, by 1991, this service became CNN International (CNNI), with a totally separate organization within CNN providing international news and feature programs, and using American stories only when they were of international interest.

I showed the participants on "The Map" how the AFRTS signals covered most of the world, except for southern Asia, and said that this problem was one of my top priorities. I was determined to get CNN to every habitable part of the globe. I told them the Taiwan "horror story" of how the local PTT wanted to charge nearly $16 million a year for downlinking CNN, but I said that we were on the verge of a multi-downlinking service that would allow the uplinking service to pay a reasonable surcharge for unlimited downlinking. Each country would have to pay its PTT for its service of downlinking through its equipment unless the television station installed its own equipment, and that was why our technical expert, Christopher Richardson, was present. He would explain to them how the equipment could be obtained and its costs.

At the end of my talk, I asked the delegates to fill out a questionnaire. I said, "I want to have communication with the people I work with. I want to know who they are. I want to be able to telex them all the time, phone them if necessary, and maintain a constant flow of communication. We are very anxious to show the news about your country to the rest of the world. Mr. Turner, who owns CNN, has started a program which will consist of the news sent each week directly by countries that are served by CNN and that will go out to the whole world." This was *World Report,* which aired later that year, in October 1987. They were interested, especially when I said that their news material in *World Report* could not be edited.

Then Richardson explained the equipment they would need to downlink. This was too technical for people who were not television technicians, but he gave them the information required to use and purchase the equipment. We had a question and answer period in which we explained how to obtain funds for acquiring the equipment. I discussed barter and said that some advertisers would pay the cost of the antenna in order to receive advertising time. Richardson mentioned that the World Bank had interest-free loans for acquiring high-technology equipment in African countries.

I thought that System Technology Trading's price of $80,000 for an installation was much too high, and I told Richardson that we had to find a cheaper way to bring the signal down. I would soon learn that there were other antenna suppliers in Africa that could provide equipment for $30,000 to $40,000. I wished we had enough cash to purchase the antennas wholesale and install them as part of a long-term agreement, but I knew CNN and TBS could ill afford to do that.

There was one comment that I had heard many times before: "There is the question of bias we have received from many of the Western reporters, the way they cover Africa. In general, it's been very, very unsatisfactory. Now you have been telling us just how much material there is at CNN, but you are not talking about what type of material. If you agree, as many Western people have been agreeing, that there has been a lot of bias, a lot of unfair reporting on Africa, how are you tackling this in your organization? We know some of these biases have not been deliberate—it has been because of sheer ignorance about Africa, but some of it has to do with trying to meet the expectations of someone in New York City. How are you dealing with this question of bias?"

My answer summarized the purpose of the meeting and CNN's evolution into a global news monitor: "The best answer I can give you as to what CNN intends to do about improving these reports, that I agree with you are not adequate, is the fact that I am here. There is a basic decision on the part of Turner Broadcasting and CNN that Africa has remained separate and apart in terms of news. Part of the reason these reports are inaccurate is because Africa has been such a mystery. I not only work for Turner, but I need to watch the news. I am not a reporter but a businessman, but when it comes to Africa, what they report is some kind of mystery. Yes, if there is some terrible explosion or some tragedy, we get the report, but on a general, day-to-day basis, it is unknown, it's a mystery to all of us. So I can only say to you that we don't disagree with your point of view. But there has to be a beginning. The beginning is here today; we are here to make a beginning and to show you how to do it. The fact that we now have a bureau in Nairobi and the fact that, if we make arrangements with each of the countries that are here today, it will increase our ability to bring information from Africa out, and get their points of view during times that are not crises, so that we will have more truth of what Africa is about."

I went on to say: "CNN is not political. It takes no political views; it only reports the news. We don't care what country participates. We have arrangements with the Soviet Union to provide news with the Eastern Bloc countries. One of our projects for the future is that we want CNN to be in Vietnam and in North Korea and every country in the world. CNN is not political for the simple reason it is one of the best opportunities for peace in the world that can exist, because of free flow information going from country to country. It will increase the knowledge of that country's population. And then, those countries—by knowing what's going on in the world—will have less opportunities to misunderstand the other country's point of view. And, in addition to that, it is the policy of CNN and Mr. Turner that any government in the world that wishes to have the right to CNN—I am speaking of the copyright—whether it is the president, the prime minister, or the king, can have CNN free. They only have to provide their own dish, their own downlink, and we give them the right to receive it. It is our philosophy that, if the leaders of the world see what's going on in each country, then they will have better opportunities to make better decisions. CNN is not connected in any way with the government. CNN is not connected in any way with the military. While CNN is carried on AFRTS, and we use it as a means of delivery to our customers who use CNN, that is the only relationship we have with it."

I talked about the need to improve the methods of exchanging news within Africa and, because I had been speaking openly and honestly, I added what had especially irked me in Africa. I had felt rebuffed in my desire to communicate because I often received no reply. Several comments were made about this. Some said that no one had any authority except at the highest levels, which led to their feeling unimportant. I emphasized that communication was a two-way street, and when the other person doesn't respond, the dialogue ends.

I told the participants that, from time to time, Turner would provide programs of a public service nature that were free, such as *The Day of Five Billion*, a program emphasizing a day in the coming year when the population of the world would reach five billion. I also explained how special satellite feeds could provide music without English narrative, so that non-English-speaking countries could offer their own language translations from English scripts.

Perhaps I was caught up in the euphoria of seeing that countries all over the world were, because of CNN, "coming together," and that is why, for the first time, I shared an idea I'd been thinking about: "There are many transponders. A company may buy a full transponder that may be used only two or three hours a day. So that many hours of time are wasted. And so, in a project that I am trying to develop, there would be an organized use of these transponders left with unused time, for countries that could not afford to pay full cost of transponder use."

A transponder on a satellite was like a flashlight that is left on when not in use—it's wasted energy. By organizing this unused transponder time, I have continued over the years, with the help of Joe Pelton, to develop a database that would provide this available transponder information, as well as those organizations that require aid and those that could provide the educational training or medical information needed.

The meeting ended with a spokesman for the group, a Mr. Kangai of Zimbabwe, saying that they had learned a lot in a short time about satellite broadcasting. He made it clear that it "was high time they were exposed to this new technology so that they could use it both for the benefit of their countries, and increased mutual understanding between them and the rest of the world.

That night, we had the farewell dinner that Dr. Blume had recommended at the Carnivore Restaurant, in the hotel where we were all staying. During the dinner, I realized more clearly than ever before that I had something besides experience and the ability to sell ideas and a product (CNN).

It was this empathy that Bob Ross, who was developing CNN in Europe and others at Turner, did not have. Neither did many executives in other industries, regardless of their education or experience.

During my stay in Nairobi, I met with Gary Streiker, CNN's Bureau Chief in Africa. Gary is married to a native Kenyan and one of the most dedicated individuals I have ever met. His subsequent reporting from all parts of Africa about civil wars, famine, and the AIDS crisis made me feel small compared to the huge risks he took going into such dangerous areas. CNN was very fortunate to have him.

Earlier in 1987 in France I met delegates from French-speaking African countries. I thought they might be reluctant to attend the meeting in Nairobi and was, in fact, disappointed because so few of them showed up. But as a result of our seminar, shortly after I got home, I received a telex from Video Presse, advising me that 11 French-speaking countries—Benin, Burkina Faso, Central African Republic, Djibouti, Gabon, Madagascar, Mali, Mauritius, Niger, Togo, and Zaire—were interested in at least two hours of CNN news daily and requested information in French.

Half of Africa is French-speaking, and the other half is English-speaking. When I visited Senegal, the Minister of Information implored me to help him find English movies and programs so that the Senegalese could learn to speak English, the accepted international business language. As he put it, "If you only speak French, who do you do business with?" Could I start an International Chamber of Commerce?

CHAPTER TWENTY-FIVE

Indian Intransigence and Other Hurdles

A country's ability to accept democratic political concepts and an open media is dependant on the depth of its uneducated population and the power of its orthodox religions.
—Sidney Pike

I arrived in Lahore, Pakistan, from Africa in early June 1987. My first trip to Pakistan in 1985 had not been a success. A Pakistani businessman (residing in Australia) had met with me in Atlanta and led me to believe that he had the contacts to bring CNN into Pakistan. I ended up being driven around the country, as far north as Peshawar on the border of Afghanistan—the city from which Western arms and assistance to Afghanistan guerillas were shipped when the United States helped those who fought the Soviet invasion from 1979-89. After the attacks in September 2001 on the World Trade Center and Pentagon and the United States-led overthrow of the Taliban government that ruled Afghanistan, Peshawar continued to be a route for escaping Taliban and Al Qaeda members to Pakistan and other parts of the world. Pakistan itself would be the focus of news during this

270

period as it tried to reconcile its ties to its Islamic roots with its new association with Western civilization.

But in 1985, Pakistan was peaceful when I visited Peshawar. I had some
meetings with minor Pakistani government and television officials, and
finally ended up again in Lahore, a misty city, which always made me feel
as though I were walking through concrete dust.

I parted from this Pakistani businessman, who had been of so little
help, and made my usual arrangements to arrive at the airport two hours
before my flight time to India. At 9:00 AM. when I left the hotel in a
taxi, the temperature was already well over 100 degrees. There was a milling
crowd of Pakistanis at the airport waiting for it to open at noon. By 11 A.M.,
the temperature was almost 120 degrees in the shade, but who could find the
shade? Between the mob and the heat, my best option was just to stand still.
I had never felt so uncomfortable in my life.

I tried to convince the airport guards to let me into the airport. I got
as far as the chief guard but was turned down. No one was going to be allowed to be cool until noon. This miserable experience forced me to learn
exactly what living in an overpopulated country with extreme temperature
was like. We Westerners take a lot for granted.

I arrived in New Delhi and was met by Sudhir Damodaran, whose company, Catvision, built small antennas that could receive the AFRTS signal.
Damodoran wanted an exclusive license to sell CNN to hotels and cable.
There were many others in the cable field who also wanted this exclusivity.
A man named Siddhartha Srivastava, of Tristar, had contacted me in Atlanta,
but after checking his references, I found he did not have as good a reputation
as Damodaran. He was, however, persistent. He barraged me with phone calls
when I got to India and insisted upon a meeting at my hotel. Just to get rid of
him, I saw him briefly.

I also met with Gautam Adhikari of *The Times of India*, who had visited me in Atlanta and wanted to write an article about CNN's international growth. He set up a lunch in Delhi for Ted and me with government
television officials, as well as with Doordarshan, the state television channel. There were no other television services, so it was important that we
make arrangements for CNN with it. It was possible to sell an exclusive
license—because there were no competitors—for television broadcasting
and develop Catvision as our licensee for cable and hotels. Adhikari had

arranged for his newspaper to sponsor the lunch, and he coordinated all the arrangements for Ted's itinerary in Delhi.

I had received a telex from Dee Woods, Ted's assistant, saying that he would be flying in on the 14th from a city in northern India and asked me to pick him up at the airport. I went with a car, driver, Adhikari, and Damodaran to meet Ted and J.J. Ebaugh.

We waited long after his plane had landed and everyone from that flight had left. As in Pakistan, we had to wait outside at the hottest time of the day. Finally, we assumed he had missed the plane. J.J. had convinced him to visit a remote area of the country, a place called Leh, where religious monks meditated on a mountaintop. We went back to the hotel. Sure enough, half an hour after we got there, Ted and J.J. arrived. They had been delayed in Customs at the airport. Ted didn't seem to mind. Perhaps the visit to the mountaintop had made him more peaceful. But I doubted it; I knew him too well.

The first thing Ted said to me, loudly calling out "P-i-i-i-ke" so that everyone in the lobby learned my name, was, "Have you got any money? Someone in Frankfort lifted my wallet." From then on until we separated in Beijing, I paid for everything.

The next day at the luncheon that Ahikari had arranged, and after Ted's speech, I explained CNN and its news services. I opened up "The Map" with blue dots signifying where CNN now had agreements and red dots for countries "in negotiation." For some reason a Hammond map has India at either end. "You must forgive us," I said, "for providing a map with the United States directly in the center. I am told that wherever a map is printed, that country is in the center. We've made up for this, however, by providing two Indias." The laughter that followed seemed to warm up the austere government officials.

As part of my pitch, I mentioned the Goodwill Games, which would be held again in 1990, as well as *The Day of Five Billion*, which ultimately was aired in 100 countries. Doordarshan agreed to carry both events, and I believe Ted's presence made a difference in its interest in the programs. I wanted very much to make an agreement, not only because of India's size and population, but because it was the one area of the world where I did not have access to an available CNN signal. Pakistan, too, was in my crosshairs. Our potential satellite costs would be over a million dollars a year.

In Adhikari's interview with me for *The Times of India,* he pointed out that the Indian government was reluctant to bring outside, unedited news into India and had asked their engineers how the satellite signal could be kept out. The engineers had advised the government that antennas that would deflect the signal could be installed facing the satellite. I was shocked to learn this and had called our Satellite Department for advice. Was it possible? Could the signal be reversed? Technically, yes, they said. The reverse antennas, however, would have to be so close together, and in such proliferation that the cost would more than exhaust the Indian treasury.

I told this to Adhikari, and he included it in his story. It wasn't what the government officials and nationalists wanted to hear, of course. India liked to claim that its population was so large and so volatile that it had to censor their news. I have heard this excuse many times, quite often in democratic countries.

Asia Pacific Broadcasting & Telecommunications magazine stated, in its "India Update," that:

> Television in India will remain a state monopoly, operated exclusively by the government. A spokesman from the Information & Broadcasting Ministry had said, 'No government can dare to give radio and television to private partners. It is not like a steel mill or a paper factory. Any radio and television station can brainwash the people. We have, therefore, decided to continue the state monopoly.'

In the same article, however, a spokesman for the Confederation of Industries said:

> We do not believe that by letting the industry have a go at radio and television stations the survival of a government will be at stake. After all, India is not such a weak country, powerless against the private enterprises. What is really at stake is the greed for power. The government cannot give up what it has got between its teeth. Why not have an organization like NHK as in Japan if you do not want to copy the Americans or for that matter the BBC?

The article went on to say that opposition parties were seeking an equitable allocation of time on radio and television for political campaigning, claiming the electronics media rendered the elections unfair. The high incidence of illiteracy in the country enabled radio and television to serve as the main source of news. Under the existing system, each party was given a 15-minute slot only once during the election campaign to put across its message. But the propaganda of the ruling party almost never ends. One of the reasons given for rejecting the changes requested in control of radio and television by Prime Minister Rajiv Gandhi was that he did not want radio and television to become "as irresponsible as the press."

But a separate article noted: "The Indian government is planning to use satellite technology to link the country's quarter million villages with the television network and radio system." This was part of a $700 million five-year plan. In the same article, Arthur C. Clarke is quoted:

> In highly developed regions like the U.S.A. and much of Europe, communication satellites are a great convenience, but are not absolutely vital. These countries already have excellent cable and microwave links. To many developing countries, however, satellites are essential; they will make it unnecessary to build the elaborate and expensive ground systems required in the past. Indeed, to such countries, satellites could be a matter of life or death.

* * * * *

In the Pacific Rim region, our office in Atlanta was still working with many of the islands that had to rely on radio communications for access to world news. Most of the Pacific Rim work was now being done out of the Sydney office, but I helped develop CNN in Fiji, Tonga, Nuie, and American Samoa. The satellite signals used by the Australian Sevens Network, as well as the satellite signals TBS was planning, covered only the western Pacific and eastern Asia. We still relied on the AFRTS signal to provide CNN to these islands, which were eager for access to CNN.

We arrived in Beijing on June 17, and Ted was scheduled to give a speech the same day at a business conference in the Great Hall, where the Communist Party meetings were held. In addition, he officially was to open the CNN Beijing Bureau. The U.S. Ambassador, Winston Lord, and his wife, Bette Boa Lord, of Chinese descent and a well-known author, invited us to their home for lunch. Alexandra Kuo had arrived before us, had set up the meetings with CCTV, and coordinated the other events as well. The Lords were dedicated to their work, and I sensed immediately that their ideas and abilities were very unusual and impressive. This was also true of Ambassador Mike Mansfield at the U.S. Embassy in Tokyo, whom I'd met in 1984.

Rich Hylen also came in from Hong Kong. He was still optimistic about finding a way to get CNN into the major hotels there. When we arrived at the Beijing Sheraton, good news awaited me. There were messages from Joyce saying that KBS, the state television network of South Korea, had accepted my plan for the use of some CNN material. This was my first success after many trips to Seoul, where I had tried to configure a CNN plan that would not overwhelm either KBS or MBC. I thought South Korea had been backing away from me because the 24 hours of CNN was so powerful. When KBS had suggested that it might want to use some CNN stories in a one-hour program on Sunday nights, I saw this as an opportunity to get my foot in the door. There was also a message that Channel 9 in Thailand was interested in continuing talks.

I attributed these positive responses in part to my face-to-face contact on the home ground of the television management. I listened to all their concerns and problems and gave their resolution my full concentration. Over and over, I had to find a way to prove to them that, without access to CNN, they would be left out, and that they could not afford to ignore this reality.

Ted's speech that June 17 in the Great Hall to the assembled businessmen went well. I stayed backstage to make sure his slide presentation was coordinated with his speech.

Of course, my friends at CCTV, Sheng Yilai and Hong Min Sheng, were eager to show Ted and me their new television facilities. It was a skyscraper not yet fully occupied; they were still in the process of moving from smaller quarters. They showed us an area behind the building where the antenna to receive CNN would be located and, finally, where the CNN Bureau's facilities would be. As I looked at how far they had come, I felt a sense of triumph. All this had grown out of my patient persistence, and Ted's nagging, and would make possible, in two more years, the global telecasting of the events in Tian an Men Square. No one at TBS, except Ted, had believed that I could bring CNN into China, much less construct the first television news bureau in CCTV headquarters.

Rich and I left for Hong Kong on July 20 to prepare for Ted's press conference and cocktail party there. He and J.J. were going to do some sightseeing in China, then fly to Hong Kong. But they never did arrive. I contacted him in Beijing and learned that he had a virus and wasn't coming. Rich and Dietz Ginzel, Turner's International Advertising Sales Manager, were beside themselves. Ted's being there was critical. As an article in *Cable Age* stated in 1985:

> If all the world is a stage, R.E. 'Ted' Turner is the U.S. mass media's most visible and arguably its most adroit global player. He forced CBS to mass its defenses and claimed MGM as his own, he's expanded the reach of his Cable News Network into virtually every continent and many major world capitals. For global citizen Turner, there is no Iron Curtain.

When I called Ted again, he insisted, "You and Rich can handle it." I knew we couldn't replace him. The only thing to do, I told Rich, was to call as many invitees as possible and tell them of Ted's illness. At least they wouldn't think we had deliberately misled them. Many of the guests didn't show up, but we did our best to present the CNN story to those that did.

I left Hong Kong and flew to Taiwan to continue my lobbying with the Intelsat signatory, ITA, and then on to Tokyo, where I needed to use all my diplomacy, since NHK now had the right to promote its use of *Headline News* and we did not want to offend TV-Asahi. My final stop on this long, Magellan trip was Guam, where I helped Channel 14 during the hearings on Guam Cable TV's license. When I landed in Honolulu on July 3 to meet Lill for a brief vacation, I was totally exhausted, but it was also time for me to give some of myself, at least what was left, to my personal life.

I thought of Magellan. All that world traveler had to deal with was a leaky boat, lousy food, scurvy, storms at sea, broken compasses, no indoor plumbing, seasickness and other maladies, no phones, telexes, or computers, in fact, no contact with people except his crew for weeks and months at a time.

In other words, he was just sightseeing, while *I* had to take on dictators, an obstreperous ex-Marine colonel, recalcitrant governments and an uncooperative international consortium.

CHAPTER TWENTY-SIX

Ted Twirls a Lasso—Only to be Lassoed

Innovation is a gamble, but so is standing pat.
—Arthur B. Dougall

The new CNN Center and TBS offices opened in July 1987.

The location selected had been lying dormant for 10 years in the heart of downtown Atlanta. The 350-room Omni Hotel was on one side of the square facility, with two office buildings on opposite sides of the same square. The fourth and final side was the new home for CNN. The complex had been built by Tom Cousins, one of the premier builders in Atlanta and a key player in bringing NBA basketball to the city. It was at the western edge of the business section. I did have to warn business associates who stayed at the Omni to taxi to their destinations because it was near impoverished and high-crime residential areas that would begin to develop into a sports and convention complex over the next decade. The World Congress Center, with its vast cavernous building for large meetings and conventions, is now located behind the CNN Center. There are also two major indoor sports arenas, one for the NFL's Atlanta Falcons, and the other, completely rebuilt and modernized after the 1996 Olympics, for the NBA's Atlanta Hawks. The office buildings were sparsely occupied during the ten years before Ted bought it, and the side of the complex where CNN would now reside had originally been built for Sid and Marty Krofft, the famous television puppeteers, as an entertainment center for children. It had been closed for ten years. The Children's Center was intended as an indoor, Disney-like complex. It had one of the longest escalators in the world. The parents and children were to go up to the top floor and slowly wind their way down, passing clowns, puppeteers and entertainers in the various rooms and theaters until they reached the first floor. It lasted only six months.

Bunky carved this magnificent space into a perfect CNN television studio, with all the necessary offices that its exploding growth required. There was ample room for most of the Turner corporate divisions to relocate, and Ted's office was there. WTBS, TNT, and other international entertainment channels, as they developed, remained at the Progressive Club. In the year 2000, when even TimeWarner, which had swallowed TBS, was itself swallowed by the Internet giant, AOL, announcements were made that there would be further expansion in the Omni area, with more office buildings being taken over and new construction to provide for the continuing growth of the Turner enterprises. The 39 employees of 1971 had become, in the new millennium, 7,800 in the city of Atlanta alone.

* * * * *

Ted had been a spinning roulette wheel from the time he first bought the almost-bankrupt UHF station, WTCG. He always held on until what he was trying to achieve began to show results. He knew all too well that many of his competitors would quit when the going got tough. Perhaps his tenacity came partly from his sailing experience. CBS had given up on a cable venture when it did not immediately succeed. Westinghouse and ABC had sold out to him when their 24-hour news hadn't been able to compete because of the inroads Ted had already made in the market, as well as his relationship with the cable television companies. Westinghouse and ABC, if they'd used their imagination, could have gone for the international market and cut Ted off from future expansion, then turned around and entered the United States through DBS first, and then cable. But there were no visionaries at the U.S. television networks; in fact, they shunned pioneering.

By 1987, any new 24-hour service had to battle with CNN in the trenches for a share of the market, both in the United States and globally. In this country, it was done in the 1990s by the new 24-hour news channel FOX News (Rupert Murdoch), and to a less successful degree by MSNBC, co-owned by Microsoft and NBC. FOX became successful using Murdoch's newspaper formula of sensationalism with dramatic use of music and explosive graphics. Much of its programming was not truly news in the traditional sense, but personality-driven shows. Most of the Fox programming, particularly in prime time, fell into this category. Fox lacked sufficient foreign news bureaus to compete with CNN on an ongoing international scale, although some live reporting during the Iraq war of 2003 was well done, and I consider their 6 P.M.-7:00 P.M. evening news with Brit Hume the best produced news program of the day.

My main concern with American news or information networks on international satellites was the danger they posed to the non-American audience worldwide when they "bang the drums" for a certain point of view. It was particularly true if special international programming was not produced separately, as is the case with CNN. This resulted in problems for the U.S. administration during its preparation for war with Iraq when Fox fed its programs internationally. Turkey, a country that had recently subscribed to its signal, would watch the conservative pro-administration stance of the channel and ridicule of Turkey and its government because it had voted against cooperating with U.S. forces. Their pro-war news bias fed into the Arab frustration and anger. While this news was not misplaced, it should have been presented with international overtones. The Fox domestic (U.S.) news shown worldwide is so one sided that it cannot help but emphasize the neutral position of CNN globally.

Although the CNN loss in ratings to FOX concerned the new Time-Warner/AOL managers of CNN domestic, to their credit, they did not lower their standards, but rather remained the news source of choice. Even in the new millennium, the international version of CNN could not be scratched—a measure of how well CNNI was put together.

By 1987, in addition to my work, Bob Ross in London now had 56 European hotels carrying CNN, with about 400 rooms each, out of an estimated market of 300,000 hotel rooms—thus garnering seven percent of the market. And he was developing the burgeoning cable industry in Europe. Ted was gambling at this time that his expenditure for a seven-year Ku-band satellite lease to cover Europe would eventually more than pay for itself, as well as keep competitors at bay. The monthly cost of the European signal was $210,000. Meantime, the three major networks were cutting their news budgets, and they continued to do so for many years. Ted boasted, "We've taken over news leadership from the networks. They had 30 years to do it, and we did it in only two and a half."

A 1987 article in *Frequent Flyer* magazine noted:

> Turner's astute analysis of the market potential for business reporting has paid off. So has his decision to give business travelers what they need, pursuing them to the ends of the earth to do so. Turner has won the perfect TV audience: sophisticated, influential big spenders who not only watch the news, but also make it. CNN executives, asked to name the network's main target in the international market, understandably begin with 'the business traveler.' These frequent travelers have responded to CNN's blandishments in the best possible way: they have come to expect it in their hotel rooms. And when it's not there, they're starting to demand it. Some conventions now stipulate that delegates must be housed in hotels that offer CNN.

To the London office's credit, it designed a pocket booklet that traveling executives could carry in their briefcases, listing the hotels that carried CNN worldwide. This booklet also helped fight hotel piracy. Hotels were glad to pay for CNN in order to be listed.

In 1987, CNN was showing roughly six times the amount of news as the other major networks for one-third the cost. I was interviewed for the above article and said, "New York is no longer the news center of the world; Atlanta is. When I tell this to people in speeches I give, they look at me like I'm crazy. 'New York has always been the center,' they say. I answer, 'But it isn't anymore!'" Into 2005, TimeWarner would air elements of CNN from New York, but the main news center, including CNN, remained in Atlanta.

True, CNN's international distribution was still losing about $5 million a year, despite my successes, but Ted knew he had to wait. He could see where we were headed.

Cuba received CNN, and Fidel Castro watched regularly, although satellite dishes for the general population of totalitarian countries were prohibited. Turner's predilection for communist countries, in my opinion, existed because he had an innate curiosity about anything he could not understand or that other people shunned, and a conviction that he could convince anyone of the rightness of his ideas. This was combined with his belief that he could bring the enemies of the world together and overcome any inherent political, social or wealth distribution conflicts. Although a man of unusual intelligence and perception, Ted sometimes chose to wear blinders, like a race horse, not because he did not understand the baseness of the individuals involved, but because he knew how to set aside his own convictions and "meet" the level of understanding of his protagonist in order to communicate.

I could visualize Ted coming back from a visit with the Devil and exclaiming, "You know, he's not such a bad guy…just misunderstood." But I knew he knew better. The point here is that Turner now had the power, because of CNN, to be invited to "break bread" with any leader in the world. No longer the "Chicken Noodle News" its jealous colleagues kept out of White House briefings, CNN was now the "official" eyes and ears of the entire world, from palaces of power to hovels in the jungles.

Frequent Flyer wrote:

> Embassies and consulates find CNN appealing because of the convenience of switching on the latest news anytime… Yet a mere half dozen American embassies in Europe are officially licensed to receive CNN, according to Robert Ross. 'The others say that because of the Gramm-Rudman-Hollings balanced budget law they can't afford to subscribe, even though the cost is only a couple of hundred dollars a month.'… He and other CNN executives are well aware that many diplomatic missions—those of the U.S. and of other nations—are nonpaying watchers of CNN. Letters of inquiry, thank-you notes, and phone calls to news headquarters in Atlanta indicate that a first-rate embassy, like a first-rate hotel, operates at a disadvantage without CNN.

All U.S. embassies in the world were receiving the AFRTS signal, for the benefit of the Marines stationed there as guards, so that all they needed was a dish to receive CNN and automatically tune in the rest of the embassy personnel. The one area of international news in which we were seriously deficient was the weather. The domestic CNN signals were acceptable internationally in the mid-1980s because international news was included and the United States was regarded as the business center of the world. CNNI was timed perfectly vis-à-vis to the newly emerging world investment market, stimulated in part by CNN and later dominated by CNBC, part of NBC the network that captured the financial channel that Ted wanted to purchase before it went bankrupt and his board refused. People became emotionally attached to CNN, including the business travelers, often alone in a country whose language they could not speak. But the weather reports covered only North America. I constantly pressured Peter Vesey, Vice President of CNN International, to show the weather in other parts of the world. This was done in 1991.

In a Western European hotel survey done for CNN, by British market research firm AGB, it was revealed that 83 percent of the guests spoke English, 44 percent were Americans or Canadians, and 96.7 percent watched television at some point during their hotel stay and 85.2 percent had watched CNN. Because cable growth was slow in the United States and elsewhere, CNN had yet to reach most television homes in the world and in the United States. Its international popularity began first in hotels, large businesses, and in government institutions, a limited but very influential audience.

When Presidents Reagan and Gorbachev traveled to summit meetings, for instance, to Iceland, special arrangements for a mobile satellite downlinking facilities to monitor CNN were arranged by both American and Soviet staff.

In effect, CNN was supplying for free a service that had been costing governments large sums of money. World leaders and the world population now had a means never before available to observe other countries. *By 1987, CNN was the most important disseminator of U.S. and global information worldwide.* Even the U.S. government, along with other countries, received free propaganda, made more believable perhaps than that of their own manufacture. And in the case of the U.S. it collected an income tax bonus on the multi-billion dollar advertising sales and subscription income from Turner Broadcasting, owners of CNN. Is there a better example of capitalism?

In Europe, CNN and the new satellite technology were changing the concept of state-run television. Richard Reeves wrote in a column in the *Atlanta Journal:*

> The private owners [of television stations] are being sold old and new channels in France, England, and almost every other European country as part of the panicky reaction to multiplying American-driven satellite and cable signals. Watching European establishments try to figure out what to do under the bombardment of exploding video technology is like monitoring research on how to get toothpaste back into tubes. They still think of television as a communications medium. Many Americans understand that it is an environment. Government regulators can control some things but not weather–and television is everywhere now, becoming more like the weather than like a telephone system.

Reeves' final sentences summed up what CNN and future programming on satellites would accomplish:

> The whirlwind of television is touching down here. It will blow through windows and cracks in the society and break down doors. The Old World, like our New World across the Atlantic, will never be the same again.

* * * * *

Amid the political success, social significance, and broadcasting prominence, financial and organizational storms were brewing. The clouds began darkening several years earlier.

For example, in August 1985, Ted made a momentous announcement: He had purchased MGM from Kirk Kerkorian for $1.6 billion. This sale was final in March 1986. Ted's MGM purchase created serious problems with regard to his control of TBS. This became obvious when an article appeared on January 8, 1987, in the business section of the *Atlanta Journal,* suggesting that Kirk Kerkorian, who had sold MGM to Ted, was increasing his preferred stock holdings in TBS beyond the shares he already owned. Ted owned 81 percent of the common stock. That preferred stock was scheduled to begin paying dividends in common stock, and if Kerkorian amassed a sufficient amount of common stock, he could threaten Ted's major stock holdings. I didn't have to be sitting in Ted's office to imagine him pacing around, wondering how he was going to buy back Kerkorian's preferred shares. The article quoted Anthony Hoffman, an investment banker in New York: "Kerkorian appears to be more optimistic about TBS's future than I am." The article also noted that most analysts expected TBS to report about a $190 million loss for 1986.

Ted never held back from extending the company's financial commitments if he thought that an acquisition would improve future prospects. Remember, when he wanted WRET-TV in Charlotte, North Carolina, and needed a million dollars to complete the purchase, he had been willing to borrow the money on his own name until the station was successful enough to be accepted by his Board of Directors. But MGM was quite a stretch and, not surprising to me, the articles reporting on the purchase quoted film and financial executives who claimed Ted had overpaid as much as $300 million for the studio and its motion picture library.

One could argue, based on prices paid for other grand Hollywood studios in later years that the MGM price was not excessive. Most importantly, however, Ted had sold his soul, but he didn't know it.

During the negotiations for MGM, rumors appeared about an Arab counter-offer. I doubt it existed, but in any negotiation, a seller must either find or create a counter-offer in order to get the buyer to pay the top price. This is almost inevitable if he knows the buyer is determined to buy. When Ted is buying something, he should not be in the room with the seller. He will match any counter-offer. The seller has merely to state his price.

Negotiations over the rights to broadcast professional football games also caused financial troubles. Observers generally agree that in 1990 the National Football League (NFL), in order to create a competitive atmosphere, "played" and used Ted because of his interest in bidding for a schedule of games. According to David Lieberman, in a *TV Guide* article, the NFL felt that Ted Turner "was the logical candidate to bid against ESPN since he had tried to win NFL rights during the 1987 negotiations." The fact that John Malone and Gerry Levin, Board members of

TBS, supported Ted's bid of $445.5 million for early season games that included a pre-season schedule—that is, games that didn't count in league competition—is extraordinary. According to Lieberman, "TBS had agreed to pick up the entire season of Sunday night games for around $850 million if Burke (ABC) dropped out." This meant that TCI and TimeWarner had to be very concerned about ESPN's and its owner, Capital Cities's (ABC) involvement in cable and the high rate ESPN was charging cable. I doubt such a tremendous price would have been offered if Turner, Malone, and Levin had not felt that the cost could be passed on to the subscribers. In the days before Congress felt the wrath of the cable subscribers about the growing cable rates, this was possible.

The description in *TV Guide* of Ted's meeting with NFL's Commissioner, Paul Tagliabue, and co-negotiator Art Modell, owner of the then-Cleveland Browns, is vintage Ted and is a good example of his manner in countless other negotiations in which he did not want to lose:

> The meeting started off badly, though. When Tagliabue looked across the conference table, Turner appeared docile, uninterested.
>
> About 20 minutes into the subdued discussion, Turner suddenly awoke from his apparent stupor. He slammed his hand on the table so hard that the 65-year-old Modell says he nearly fell off his chair. 'Well now,' Tagliabue recalls Turner saying as he bolted to his feet. 'Let me tell you what I think about the National Football League and Turner.' The show had begun.
>
> Cable's most famous entrepreneur paced around the room, pumped his fist in the air and banged the walls with the passion of a cheerleader as he made his pitch. Turner needed the NFL, and the NFL also needed Turner. He'd promote pro football throughout the United States on his four cable services–CNN, *Headline News*, SuperStation TBS and TNT.
>
> Turner also vowed to turn NFL matches into worldwide events, something he's trying to do with his Goodwill Games. 'We're in the midst of a telecommunications revolution,' Turner said. 'Sports are becoming international. We're international.' The NFL negotiator had their man.

I believe Ted got caught by his own system, even though it had worked so well before. In the past, he simply bid so high that others gave up and walked away. But this time, ABC and ESPN could not afford to lose the NFL to another cable program service and still call themselves *the* sports channel. They had to outbid Turner. So Turner (TBS) ended up overpaying for its schedule of pre-season and second-choice games. Ted's board members, John Malone and Gerry Levin, wanted him to take some of the NFL games away from ABC and to force it to pay a high price for the regular schedule, which happened. But Turner did not get the important games, and paid far too much for what he did get. A lot of already rich NFL owners got richer, and the exorbitant cost of the games was borne once again by the consumer through increased cable rates or higher advertising costs that are added to the tab for your car or your can of beer. This is the very thing that helped force Congress, not long after this, to seek relief for cable subscribers.

Ted had come a long way since 1971, when I used to accompany him to the Atlanta banks to ask for more time on his loans. The company's cash flow and the new and outstanding loans were no longer problems. However, the excessive purchase price of MGM, at a time when its studio and recent films were suffering from minimal success, introduced unnecessary financial trouble.

I had watched Ted run right up to a precipice many times before, and balance himself on the edge.

He had done it once too often.

* * * * *

While CNN was sweeping the globe quickly, Ted's efforts to develop TBS in the United States faced concerted opposition from entrenched, reluctant, short-sighted, bean-counting members of the TBS board of directors. They were worried about money. I also believe another concern existed: Gerry Levin, TimeWarner's representative on the Turner Board of Directors, wanted to take over Turner Broadcasting and especially CNN. The conflict of interest was obvious and ominous.

In addition to the $1.6 billion debt for the MGM purchase, Ted owed a $38 million dividend to TCI and TimeWarner in April 1987.

John Malone and Gerald Levin respectively of TCI and TimeWarner, and executives of smaller cable companies, put up the money in early 1987 to pay off MGM's Kirk Kerkorian, so that he would not get more stock in Turner Broadcasting. In return, they received 37 percent of Turner's stock and seven out of 15 seats on the TBS board. After this, they could veto any expenditure over $2 million. Ted thought the MGM purchase was important to the future growth of TBS, but it effectively cost him his freedom. Like Faust, he had sold his soul.

Personally, I wondered if Ted needed to give up so much since I doubted that Malone and Levin would have even wanted to allow Kerkorian in the door. But I was no longer asked to share advice on a regular basis.

This veto power devastated Ted, who liked to be in control. While it was designed to keep him from more excessive expenditures—such as another MGM purchase—he was now a caged animal. Gradually, Ted began to spend most of his time at his newly acquired ranch in Montana. He came to Atlanta for two or three days once or twice a month, and received a daily package by Federal Express of all memos and written material, and he worked by phone. Ted "carries a crystal ball in his pocket" and has an uncanny knack for imagining what an acquisition or a business arrangement might mean in the future. Many business executives do not have this kind of visionary ability.

Malone had good business sense, but he did not understand how the entertainment world competed and functioned. He had an excellent reputation as an investor in cable and its growth, but as a member of the TBS Board, he was influenced by the needs of the cable industry and, more important, by the needs of his own company, TCI. Malone was the consummate dealmaker, but he rarely made a deal in which he was not the primary beneficiary.

Levin was also immensely successful in his own field. Clever and manipulative, Levin didn't hesitate to go to Ted's ranch in Montana a few years later to convince him to "merge" Turner Broadcasting with TimeWarner. He promised Ted that he would continue to have operating control over TBS, but Ted had already lost most of his control, and the merger only worsened his position. In 1985, Levin faced turmoil and pressure from within his own company. The stockholders of TimeWarner were impatient with his results and concerned about the corporation's formidable debt.

Once Ted made his MGM purchase, Levin took advantage of the situation by spinning a lasso that eventually ensnared TBS and Turner.

For years, I had worked with Ted on a daily basis. I saw a fire in him that never went out. It was this driving force I could always count on. But after the cable companies took over the TBS board, the fire was no longer blazing, only barely lit and waiting to catch on again.

Turner had theoretically acquired a valuable motion picture library with MGM. I had reservations even about that, because the older, classic films simply do not have great appeal. Their nostalgia quotient is limited, and contemporary audiences are not that interested. Turner Broadcasting, because of that purchase, had lost what it needed most. Ted was its soul.

Two years later, in 1989, Ted tried to buy the Financial News Network (FNN) for $100 million. Reese Schonfeld describes it in his book, *Me and Ted Against the World*:

> Run by Earl Bryant, FNN had dominated the financial news sector for years and was profitable, but Bryant had bought UPI, and the UPI losses were draining his company. Meanwhile, NBC had rolled out CNBC, a business network, a direct competitor with FNN. Bryant couldn't take on CNBC without a partner. First he went to ABC. A contract was about to be signed when Turner called Bryant and offered him a better deal. Bryant dropped ABC. What Ted forgot to mention and what Bryant didn't realize was that Ted didn't run TBS anymore. He needed board approval.
>
> In order to launch CNBC, NBC had bought a failing 10-million-home PR network from TCI. It was believed that TCI had promised NBC it would not launch a competing business channel. Now, TBS, of which TCI as a member of the cable consortium owns a large chunk, wants to compete with CNBC. John Malone, TCI's boss, was on Turner's board. Whether because of a possible noncompete promise to CNBC, or some other reason, Malone adamantly opposed the acquisition.
>
> Through the afternoon of March 23, 1989, the Turner board met in Techwood. Malone and his allies in one room, Turner and his supporters in another. Emissaries walked up and down the

hallway carrying messages, politicking for support. TimeWarner went with Ted, but Malone was the most powerful man in cable. He got the other votes. Ted needed a super majority; without Malone, he couldn't get it.

Bryant, on the edge of bankruptcy, went back to ABC. Once jilted, twice shy, ABC was not interested. FNN failed. The *Wall Street Journal* and NBC bid for the bones. NBC won. CNBC picked up 30 million homes and a financial news monopoly.

This became the CNBC that was not only immensely successful in the United States, but made inroads in the financial news internationally, much to the detriment of CNN.

The roulette wheel kept spinning, and the stakes kept rising. Ted was forced to develop his own contemporary motion pictures in order to overcome the blackout restrictions forced on the SuperStation. But purchasing film production companies moved Ted into a very high stakes gambling arena that had heretofore been the territory of the major television networks. Ted watched the theatrical films that MGM produced flop again and again in front of his eyes. Each theatrical film, which might or might not earn a profit, needed $20 to $30 million for production and promotion. Ted got out of production by selling that part back to Kerkorian, but of course, he kept the large film library.

All of this was exacerbated in the mid-1980s by the fact that the cable systems reached only 65 percent of U.S. homes, while the three major networks reached 98 percent. That 33 percent meant fewer advertising dollars, although the sheer number of channels offered by TBS helped, when combined with the subscription fees paid by the cable operators for the right to carry Turner's television channels.

Meanwhile, I was trying to sign as many cash contracts as possible, without forcing the issue of TBS's adding the cost of satellites worldwide. Ted was willing to budget for these global opportunities. He understood the momentum my distribution of CNN was having.

In 1987, TBS lost $121.4 million on revenues of $400.9 million. Time, Inc., had refused to relinquish its option to buy CNN before it was sold to a third party, and talks between TBS and NBC about a possible purchase by NBC of part of Turner broke off for the usual reason: Both sides wanted control. This was Ted's second attempt to get involved with a network. Ted was supposedly demanding $20 per share from NBC, although TBS stock closed at $10.37 on January 15, up $1.75, and NBC was offering $12. Ted's $20 was a stiffer price than TCI and TimeWarner paid earlier in 1987.

Ad Week in January, 1988, quoted an analyst of L.F. Rothschild & Co.

> You don't want him [Ted] as your chief financial officer, but in cable, he's the best thing going. He's a flamboyant salesman, and even his failures are spectacular. The Goodwill Games were a disaster, but still he got some respect, because people were amazed that cable even tried to do it.

In spite of TBS's debt, Turner purchased the perpetual worldwide licensing rights to 800 feature films owned or purchased by RKO from 1929 to 1959, in addition to 80 TV productions and 50 short subjects and cartoons. Most of the features were produced in black and white. Ted was probably influenced by its colorization opportunities (adding color to old black-and-white films) since it contained several classics such as *King Kong*, *Little Women*, and *Top Hat*. It also contained Ted's favorite film, *Citizen Kane*—most people believe Ted identified with its thinly disguised portrayal of William Randolph Hearst. The film, although not a candidate for colorization because of Orson Welles's contract, probably influenced Ted heavily in his final decision. He tended to buy film packages that contained a movie he liked. This new modern form of coloring by electronic means was relatively cheap and held the promise of turning old popular films into new, promotable television fare. This was true, for a while. The media jumped on it, and Hollywood actors and directors lined up in Congressional committees to object vociferously to the colorization of classic black-and-white films. And then, poof, it was gone.

Ted had never wavered from his belief that the purchase of MGM, despite the debt burden, was an essential catalyst to the success of TBS. He said, "Without MGM, there would have been no TNT or Turner Classic Movies channel." True, but did that compensate for Ted's losing control of his company?

TBS's division managers were more and more in control by 1987. Terry McGuirk was handling day-to-day matters, as well as long-term planning and presentations to the TBS board, although Ted did continue to set goals and suggest methods for achieving them. Although I knew many of the TBS executives, I had trouble getting them to think globally. Most had no experience outside of the United States, except for occasional tourist travel. This made everything I tried to do that much harder.

One of my many obstacles was getting our Human Relations Department (Personnel) to understand the cost of travel and living expenses in countries like Japan and Great Britain. John Lewis, CNN Bureau Chief, and his wife, Reiko had been living under difficult financial conditions for several years in Tokyo. The value of the U.S. dollar was low compared to the Japanese yen. In the beginning of my international work, TBS and CNN had considered non-U.S.-based employees as able to satisfy their individual needs without additional help, but their ability to do so was largely dependent on the local economy. Tight budget demands at TBS, even though CNN itself was enjoying a profit by 1985, meant that supervisors had difficulty making sure that each and every important global event was covered. So John Lewis was not compensated for the extra expense of living in Tokyo, which was in the mid-1980s one of the most expensive cities in the world. When Lill was with me in 1984, she paid $15 for an apple! When I visited John and Reiko, it was clear that, compared to their Japanese colleagues, they were struggling to make ends meet, and had to watch every penny they spent. In the late-1980s, TBS adopted an International Assignment Policy that added income in proportion to the cost of living in each city worldwide. In addition they received round-trip airfare for wives and other travel expenses once a year or for educational expenses for children living at an overseas post.

The annual TBS salary, including international compensation, has more than doubled. But in the early years, we all suffered because of TBS's lack of international experience. The other managers simply didn't understand what this traveling entailed. To correct this, before there was an International Assignment Policy, I sent Bill Shaw of the Human Relations Department a memo to describe the kind of difficulties I was encountering. I described my experience when visiting South America in 1986, and I also wrote:

The differences between international travel and domestic are like day and night, and I am not just referring to distances. The food you eat means that you can count on being ill at least once; the dirty airports, the difficulties in language, the heat—without air conditioning in taxis, airports, and even hotels—contributes to your fatigue. Add these to the distance and time of travel (for me, up to six weeks), and you have one very exhausted person. When I returned from my Latin American trip, I picked up my bag at Miami Customs and ruptured my left side. *Because* I travel overseas, my doctor insisted that it be repaired, or I would risk a strangulated hernia in a foreign hospital. I had the operation, and I paid my share of the medical expense, even though it was a work-related injury. Two weeks after that operation, I was back in the hospital twice with a ruptured disc, which was a result of the intensive travel.

In spite of this, I went to China within four weeks. I know that many will follow me in international travel, and they will require some understanding on the part of both the Travel and Personnel Departments. This note is intended to suggest that some thought be given to this area.

The privilege of pioneering in any form means one must pay a price in comfort and forbearance, whether it be Lewis and Clark discovering paths to the Pacific ocean, living for months at a time in a space shuttle, or building the world's first international satellite television news service.

CHAPTER TWENTY-SEVEN

CNN Replaces the "Drum" in Africa

The man who is not hungry says the coconut has a hard shell.
—African tribal saying

South Africa was a very important news opportunity because of its complex racial problems. The news agencies didn't cover it adequately. I planned to make arrangements with SABC, as with each CNN agreement in the various African countries, so that CNN could depend on the local station to send news to CNN upon request. No other news organization had done this. CNN now had a constant flow of news by satellite from almost every part of the world. We were creating, in effect, dozens of mini-bureaus, which CBS, NBC, and ABC did not have. Our mode of news collection simply overwhelmed the traditional networks and news agencies.

In 1987, I sought a sales representative for Africa. I wanted to follow up the good will that was engendered by our Nairobi seminar in June. What I was looking for was a black person who could open a CNN sales office there. Finding someone with television experience was not easy. I posted the position, now required by our employment policy, and interviewed various applicants. I settled on Patrick Okebie, a young man who had emigrated from Nigeria and worked in our Accounting Department.

I had lengthy talks with Patrick about the positive aspects of CNN being brought down in Africa and how it would revolutionize the acquisition of information needed by the business people and governments there. They would compete more readily with the more industrialized countries that were still taking advantage of their vast, undeveloped resources. I explained that he would face complex political problems, country to country, and that we could not expect much revenue from the poorer countries. Then I sent him to Puerto Rico to take a sales trip with Lillian Noriega in the Caribbean so that he could see how CNN was presented. In September, we both went to Africa, to Gabon and Nigeria, where Patrick was from, so that he could study my sales approach. Patrick asked to leave a few days early—he wanted to visit his family and friends. We arranged to meet at the airport in Lagos, Nigeria.

That airport was memorable. As the passengers got off the plane, we were ushered into the customs area, which was chaotic. The passport inspector was seated on a raised platform that placed him above the milling crowd that refused to get in a line. Passports were being thrust into the face of the inspector. First, he pointed to those who were his friends and, after stamping their passports, he took the ones that suited his fancy. Eventually, I got my stamp and made my way to the baggage area, where Patrick was waiting. Patrick, knowing what I had just gone through, laughed and said, "Welcome to Lagos."

The next day, we met with the news director of the Nigerian Television Authority (NTA), and I made my CNN pitch. Nigeria is one of the richest countries in Africa because of its vast oil resources, but I don't know where the money was going. It was interested, but not willing to pay very much. NTA agreed to "test run" CNN, but like many other countries, it first had to install a dish. Here I wasn't worried about the PTT charges. I was right that most African countries would ignore Intelsat and just take the signal. By this time, African countries were pirating CNN in one form or another and were beginning to wonder how to pay for it. My policy was that no country would be denied access to CNN because it could not afford our rates. We flexed them, depending on the individual country's ability to pay.

Lagos seemed the natural location for the CNN office. Patrick could be with his family, and my only objection was that it was hard to get direct flights to other African countries. I left this decision to Patrick because he was the one who would have to deal with this inconvenience.

We then headed to Libreville, Gabon, which would be an opportunity to approach a French-speaking country. After checking our bags and getting our boarding passes, Patrick was stopped by a very officious Nigerian passport officer as we walked to the gate. The officer waved me through, but was determined to give Patrick a hard time. It was close to flight time, and I was worried that we would miss the plane. The officer acted both meddlesome and arrogant. He knew the time of our flight. He may have expected a fee, but I had a policy of refusing payments to any government official or television manager. At the very last minute, we were let through.

Gabon's president Omar Bongo was a CNN devotee, I'd been told. Charles Bonan had once tried to get a payment from him for the AFRTS signal he was pirating. Charles had led me to believe that President Bongo would be willing to pay for CNN on his television network. By this time, we were allowing leaders of governments to have CNN free.

Once in Libreville, we were taken to the Sheraton Hotel, which was magnificent and ornate, although there were very few guests. We hired a French-English translator and had meetings with the Minister of Information and Telecommunications and the television officials. We made no agreements, but they were interested. There were few cable services at this time, so the only other possibility was the hotels.

Sid Pike with Patrick Okebie, who was responsible for territory of Africa.

In December, Patrick sent me a report listing other countries where he had introduced CNN: Ghana, Guinea, Ivory Coast, Liberia, Senegal, and Togo. He had also begun talks with the east and south coast countries. Delegates from most of the African countries would attend the annual conference of the Union of National Radio and Television Organizations of Africa (URTNA) in Cameroon, in late January 1988. Patrick planned to meet delegates individually there. It seemed Patrick was overcoming his many obstacles.

In March 1988, we hired Ronald Ciccone, who became an effective and important part of CNN's development in Africa and soon after in the Middle East. Ron's grandfather had been one of the last colonial governors of Senegal, and Ron had spent a great deal of time in that country. Ron had been Special Assistant for African Affairs to AFL-CIO President George Meany, and later was Special Consultant to President Carter's Security Advisor for Africa. In 1964-1967, he served in the Peace Corps in Nigeria during the Nigerian civil war.

Ron owned a media consulting company, Vallot International, and his African clients included the heads of state of Nigeria, the Congo, and Senegal, as well as international companies doing business in Africa. Ron was in Gabon working with the president of Senegal when he saw CNN in his hotel room. The president asked Ron why Senegal did not have CNN.

Ron took this as a mandate to get CNN for Senegal. He called TBS and got bounced around because no one seemed to know who handled CNN sales in Africa. He finally reached my office, but I delayed returning the call, because I thought he was an associate of Atlanta Mayor Andrew Young and his brother (I had not been impressed with Young's brother's knowledge of Africa).

In August, I was at the Atlanta airport en route to a meeting. While waiting for my flight, I called Joyce. She told me that a Ron Ciccone had called again and suggested I return the call, since he was being persistent. I thought, well, let's get rid of him once and for all. I phoned his office in New York. As our conversation progressed, Ron's understanding of Africa was coming through loud and clear. He soon became my consultant on Africa. He continued his private consultancy practice, but later he had to leave it to keep up with our growth in the Middle East and Africa. While Patrick was covering sub-Saharan Africa and operating out of Lagos, Nigeria, Ron was working the New York and Washington, D.C. circuit. Over the next few years, he would set up appointments at various African embassies, and we would work together "lighting new fires" during the oppressive heat of Washington summers. Ron brought an unusual quotient to our CNNI development. He was not only experienced in areas of Africa and the Middle East, but well respected.

Part of our development plan was to find manufacturers of inexpensive antennas, ideally in Africa, so that shipping costs could be minimized. A company called Glieman Satellite Services in Zimbabwe manufactured inexpensive seven-meter antennas for as low as $12,000, and we recommended this company to our potential African clients. This didn't please System Technology Trading, whose representative had come to our seminar in Nairobi, but STT was asking $80,000 for an antenna, when the Glieman's antenna was adequate.

Patrick's job was a tough one over the next few years. He traveled on his Nigerian passport (he was not an American citizen) and couldn't go to South Africa at all. Not only might it have been difficult for him to deal with the Afrikaners who operated SABC, but once his passport was stamped in that country, he wouldn't have been able to go to any other African country or even return to Nigeria. The opposition to South Africa was so strong that almost no country in the world would accept one's passport if it had a South African stamp on it. It was foolish to risk it at an airport. I traveled with two U.S. passports, one for general worldwide use, and one just for South Africa and Israel. I certainly didn't want to show an Israeli stamp in an Arab country.

One of Patrick's early problems was just getting a telephone for his office. He told me that he would have to "pay under the table," which was absolutely out of the question, and I reminded him of my firm policy of not paying extra fees for any services, although this payment for a phone was apparently "routine" in Lagos. He did eventually obtain a phone. I never asked how he got it.

I could not fax him at that time, and he had to use a public telex service. He wrote me:

> When there are available circuits to send out messages, the queue
> is usually long (sometimes, it takes close to three hours to send a

single message)... There is a message I have been trying now for one week to put through to Tanzania... I will continue to try to communicate with you more often, but the circumstances tend to frustrate my objective.

Sometimes Patrick arrived at an airport and the customs people refused to let him in. In Zaire, he had to sleep overnight in the airport, even though he had been invited to visit the country by television officials. As a result, he was unable to make his connection to another country.

My foray into Africa opened up another set of problems. I never actually met any member of the French government or anyone from their governmental institutions who was disturbed by my introduction of CNN into French-speaking Africa. But apparently, as far as the French were concerned, I was disrupting the political balance of Africa itself. After World War II, international public opinion forced the English, French, Belgians, and other world powers to surrender their colonies. Other powers basically walked away, but the French did not. These countries were rich in minerals and still dependent on subsidies of various kinds from France. On the surface, their former colonies achieved independence but, in reality, they were still dependent on France, which influenced their governments through economic subsidies and political pressure with occasional military intervention to "restore stability," and through military advisors. The biggest French power play was the strong effort to maintain the French language. The French government did many things to keep English out of their French-speaking countries. The *New York Times* wrote in 1988 about a radio station called Africa No.1 in Gabon:

> With four 500 kilowatt transmitters and a fifth being built, Africa No.1 has become a powerful instrument to further the cause of the French language in Africa. Behind the scenes, French advisors and French government capital have helped create and maintain Africa No.1, a private Gabonese company. Last year the Gabonese government gave the station a $1 million subsidy. This year the directors hope to turn the first profit on projected revenues of $10 million.
>
> Strings to the French aid occasionally appear in public. In

November, Lucette Michaux-Chevry, France's Secretary of State
for 'la francophonie'–the world's French-speaking community–
visited and criticized the growing use of English on Africa No. 1.

In January the station's English programming–six hours a
week–was dropped.

It was about the same time that we learned that the French-speaking
countries were being offered for free the news in French from a French
news service. Ours was in English, and we required payment, so it made
selling CNN more difficult, though not impossible. In my view, there was
no acceptable reason for the French government to prohibit the learning
of English in its former colonies when English had become the recognized
international business language. It was another unnecessary obstacle for
the weak countries of Africa to overcome.

During one of my trips to Washington to visit various embassies, I was
invited to a cocktail party at the U.S. Department of State. In a conversation about Africa, I asked a member of the State Department why the U.S.
government did not object to France's continuing control of their former
colonies, and the answer I got was, "We've talked to them about that, and
they said that was not the case at all."

Really, I thought. How naïve.

* * * * *

Back in late 1987, Maryann Pasante helped us create a new CNN concept: a daily half-hour news program in Spanish for the Telemundo Spanish television network in the United States. She had been approached by
Telemundo because she was now so well known as a CNN salesperson in
Latin America. Normally, our office there stayed away from any involvement with CNN in the United States, but because of Maryann's Hispanic
background, we were able to convince CNN management and Ted that
this first non-English CNN program should be developed by our team.

I flew with Maryann and our attorneys to visit the Telemundo Group,
Inc., in New York for lengthy meetings, and a final agreement was signed
in January 1988. A special unit was created within CNN to produce this

daily half-hour in Spanish. Because of CNN's popularity, Telemundo had a new advantage over Univision, its competitor. We also demonstrated how CNN could grow into new programming areas without a significant investment, important for a company having financial problems. It also signaled the beginning of cross-cultural involvement for both CNN and TBS in domestic and international markets. I knew by this time, the end of my fourth year working internationally, how important access to or association with CNN had become.

In April 1988, because of the success of our daily Spanish-speaking CNN half-hour program, I proposed a similar half-hour in French for French-speaking West Africa. This would help me offset the French government's campaign to keep CNN out of its "former" African colonies, as well as enhance our sales efforts in French Canada. I was certain that Bob Ross in London could use the program in France. I even offered to have the daily program produced in French-speaking Canada so that it would not crowd CNN facilities in Atlanta. Although my estimate ran as high as $30 million gross income annually, I could not stir any interest at TBS for this. C'est la vie.

In countries like Japan that could afford to pay high prices for programming, CNN became the engine for the train. CNN's attractiveness made it possible for TBS to market films and programs, even lower quality films, which would have been difficult to sell otherwise. While I had no objection to this form of salesmanship, I did not want CNN to be kept away from an underdog that needed the kind of "spark" we could provide to them.

One program service that followed my trail globally was ESPN and Andy Brilliant, my counterpart at the 24-hour sports channel. After I'd been to Asia and Latin America, Andy followed. He did not have the large number of hours daily on AFRTS that TBS had. ESPN broadcast occasional sports events, but Andy managed to formulate his system of program delivery. Sports programming can be replayed at a later date; news must be immediate in order to be effective. By the late-1980s and early-1990s, ESPN, HBO, CNN, TNT, and the Cartoon Network would develop combined use of specific international satellites, as they did for United States broadcasts.

* * * * *

Because of Charles Bonan's earlier failure in CNN television broadcast development in Europe and the lack of advertising sales there, Ted and Burt Reinhardt decided in 1986-1987 to keep the European feed on the satellite, but to cut back on its costs. According to Peter Vesey, Vice President of CNN International from 1990-1995: "They were spending a couple of million dollars on this European feed; it looked awful, and it wasn't earning any money." Since Bonan hadn't gotten any subscription revenue and Dietz Ginzel couldn't get any serious advertising revenue, the U.S. commercials had to be covered up. But they used this opportunity to run spots that announced the hotels in specific countries that carried CNN. This, in addition to the "pocket" booklet listing CNN hotels and "on air" promotion, reduced still further the piracy of CNN by hotels. According to Vesey,

> There was still no programming on CNNI that was produced and targeted for the audience. It was all a mix of *Headline News* and some CNN programming. There was one period each hour where material was produced by a small CNNI group.

Nevertheless, Ted and Burt cut personnel down to 12 for the European feed, phased out its anchors, and turned the operation over to John Baker in Atlanta. His main job consisted of working on the rights problems with the news agencies from which the material now came because there was no longer a European staff. This 12-person staff tried to keep a continuous CNN news feed to Europe, but most of it was still *Headline News.*

As Vesey points out, it wasn't until after 1990 that a decision was made to dress up the service. The attention CNN had received after the Challenger explosion in 1986 and the Pan Am flight disaster in Lockerbee, Scotland, in 1988, followed by Tian an Men Square in 1989, increased the desire among Europeans to see more of this 24-hour signal.

From 1990, when Peter Vesey returned to Atlanta from London with the purpose of turning CNNI into a real program service, he focused on internationalizing the programs by building programs aimed at specific regions of the world. With the 24-hour CNNI attracting attention in Europe, circumstances changed: Television broadcasters began to look for CNN stories. Cable operators, beginning a more rapid expansion there, found subscribers wanted CNNI. So an advertising sales office was set up in London, and we finally began to see some success in European and American advertising income. While Ted had been cutting operational costs but going forward in global satellite distribution, he was able to tell Burt by 1989 that they could start to spend some money to produce "special" programming for CNNI. This included the first international business program, *International Business Tonight* in 1990. In 1991, CNNI began using a London-based anchor and a London presence for CNNI.

I asked Peter why it took until 1991 to get an international weather service. He said that everyone wanted this to improve, but nobody wanted to pay for it. "There were so many demands for money within TBS, it was like pulling an elephant's teeth."

The normal growth of TBS and CNN, in addition to the entrepreneurial instincts of Ted and me, was causing a "fault line crack" in the thinking and preservation instincts of upper management. They were not used to the roller coaster financial ride that Ted and I had been attuned to in our past endeavors. It would require Ted's total concentration to lead these nervous executives through the minefield to the success and bonuses that everyone longed for.

CHAPTER TWENTY-EIGHT

PanAmSat and Rene Anselmo

Integrity without knowledge is weak and useless, and knowledge without integrity is dangerous and dreadful.
—**Dr. Samuel Johnson**

In June 1988, the Pan American Satellite (PanAmSat) launched and positioned to cover South America. As a territory, South America was not as important to CNN as Europe or Asia, but PanAmSat was *privately* owned. It was the first big challenge to the Intelsat monopoly, my nemesis for four years.

Like Ted, Reynold "Rene" Anselmo was a dreamer and a risk-taker. I did not know that anyone else was trying to rein in the giant Intelsat's global monopoly. The law firm of Goldberg & Spector, specializing in satellite issues, represented PanAmSat and TBS.

Although I had met with Henry Goldberg on Intelsat problems, it was Terry McGuirk who mainly worked with the law firm before I began asking its advice in 1985. Terry had accepted the status quo as he worked out global satellite agreements with Intelsat, although he was trying to convince it to modify its system of control. I was certain that there could be no changes without some upheaval in the entire global satellite system. While I concentrated on unlimited downlinking globally, Rene Anselmo was trying to break the Intelsat satellite monopoly itself by orbiting his own independent satellite. I wondered why no one told me about another individual seeking redress from Intelsat's perverse monopoly.

I was astonished when I learned about PanAmSat, and prayed that the launch would be successful. It was an unbelievable opportunity for us to get out from under Intelsat's domination. PanAmSat, as an independent, could break the ties between Intelsat and the PTT monopolies in each country that were the main roadblocks to providing direct satellite service, whether to individual homes or to hotels that had their own antennas. While Intelsat fought to keep its control internationally, its most powerful member—Comsat, the U.S. representative to Intelsat and representing 25 percent of the Intelsat membership—also fought to keep the monopoly from changing.

Despite the fact that the White House, State Department, Commerce Department, and the FCC were all in favor of limited competition, Comsat contended that PanAmSat would erode the U.S. commitment to the Intelsat system. So Rich Colino, the Director General of Intelsat, got the membership to pass a resolution stating that it wouldn't enter into business arrangements with separate satellite systems. This apparently was aimed at influencing the FCC, because only it could give final approval to an application after a foreign country agreed to provide downlinking for a given signal. However, other countries now wanted CNN any way they could get it, and if CNN could obtain FCC approval to use a competing satellite, there wasn't much that Intelsat could do. It was trying to cut off PanAmSat from "crossing an important bridge." I was incredulous that Anselmo would risk so much capital when the Intelsat members were powerful enough to influence their respective governments to deny PanAmSat this required direct arrangement. In all those years of my "war" against Intelsat, there had been no one at TBS I could turn to for advice. Terry McGuirk was responsible for leasing long-term satellites and had made the arrangements for Intelsat VA F11—it carried the new special CNN feed to Europe—and he was completing an arrangement with Comsat to acquire a transponder on Intelsat V F8 (the Pacific Rim satellite), so that we could replace the Australian signal. Terry had no real choice but to work within the system. But Terry's weak spot was that he lacked foresight and vision. He favored Intelsat in Latin America over PanAmSat. Neither of us could foresee PanAmSat's eventual global distribution, but I did feel that Intelsat would have a major public relations problem if it denied CNN access to any satellite it required. In addition, to insure competition, I wanted to foster other satellite possibilities, such as the Russian Intersputnik satellites.

CNN's Dick Tauber, who worked primarily with incoming satellite use, was able to afford Intelsat's rate structure, because he only needed minutes here and there for daily use and breaking stories. But I needed 24 hours, 365 days a year.

When I first met Rene Anselmo I was 61 and he was 60, but he looked much older than I. Then again, he had been through quintuple bypass heart surgery, and he was still smoking! He grew up in Medford, Massachusetts, a northern suburb of Boston. I had lived in Dorchester, a southern suburb.

In a *New York Times* article titled, "A Piece of Outer Space to Call His Very Own," which included some quotations from me about Intelsat and PTT abuses, Rene was described as "a headstrong, restless youngster who hated school. He was 16 in 1942 when the principal suggested that the military might be a better outlet for his energies and offered to lie about his age. Anselmo joined the Marines and soon found himself in the South Pacific as the gunner on a two-man dive bomber." He flew 37 missions, and after the war, he attended the University of Chicago, studying literature and theater.

Rene spent the next 12 years in Mexico, having met Emilio Azcarraga Milmo, a theatrical financier whose father was head of Mexico's largest media company, Televisa. The father, Emilio Azcarraga Vidaurreta, one of the richest men in Mexico, was known throughout the country simply as "Don Emilio." Anselmo produced programs and then sold them to other South American companies. Don Emilio was interested in a Spanish-language television network for the United States, and purchased a station in San Antonio. Anselmo operated it for him, as well as a new one in Los Angeles, and received an equity stake in each station. As Don Emilio and his partners bought more television stations, Anselmo bought shares in them.

In the 1960s, when Anselmo reluctantly moved to New York to operate the new Spanish International Network, Inc. (SIN) and open a national sales office for the developing Spanish language television stations, only five percent of the U.S. population was Hispanic. Those stations, which operated on UHF, had the same technical problems that Ted and I had faced in the early 1970s—even more so, because this was eight years earlier. If we had difficulty convincing advertisers that we had viewers, I can imagine what Anselmo's handicap must have been in the 1960s, when only the newest sets could receive UHF. By 1970, Anselmo, Don Emilio, and his partner owned stations in the five markets that represented 50 percent of the Hispanic population in the United States, and they formed a company called Spanish International Communications Corporation (SICC).

While other American broadcasters worked scattered pockets of the Spanish-language market, no one else had Anselmo's national reach or the advantage of his Mexican connection that supplied his stations with inexpensive Mexican programming.

By 1984, the more than 15 million Hispanic people in the United States represented the fastest-growing population segment, and even major advertisers like Procter & Gamble had begun to take notice. SICC revenue, meantime, was approaching $80 million per year.

Don Emilio died in 1972, and Anselmo had difficulty with the other partners about carrying SICC's debts. A group of competitors charged that SICC was controlled from Mexico. Anselmo and the SICC board were charged with financial mismanagement. In 1985 the FCC finished its own three-year investigation of SICC.

Delving into Anselmo's past, the FCC determined that SICC had been the "brainchild" of Don Emilio, without whose financing the stations could not have survived. The FCC also noted the cozy relationship between SICC and SIN (Spanish International Network), which Anselmo ran from a single office on West 42nd Street in Manhattan.

The FCC denied licenses to the five SICC stations and to Anselmo's Phoenix and San Antonio stations. Anselmo wanted to appeal, but his partners wanted to sell. Anselmo walked away from the sale $100 million richer. "I decided this must be God's way of cleaning up my estate problems," he said, "because I'd never sell the TV stations and stock—I'm too stupid. So how are you going to get Rene out of there? You give him all this money and stick him in the satellite business."

As part of SIN, Anselmo had become involved with satellites a few years earlier. He wanted to extend his Spanish programming to Latin America, and he was not satisfied with Intelsat's permitted use of leased transponders. In 1984, he embarked on creating his own satellite for Latin America, encouraged by the new Reagan Administration's policy of "opening the skies" to independent satellite development. This had come about because of the bright, visionary first Director of the Office of Telecommunications Policy, Clay T. Whitehead, who had influenced the White House. Whitehead, the former President of Hughes Communications and the builder of many of the world's satellites, is credited with creating the condominium concept for marketing satellite transponders during his tenure at Hughes. Whitehead's influence on telecommunications led to the enactment of the Foreign Relations Authorization Act of 1985, which put in place a U.S. policy permitting limited competition against Intelsat.

Years of wrangling with Intelsat had left Anselmo frustrated and had cost him financially. "When the President's authorization came out, I counted about nine lobbying firms with plans to block us," he said in an article in *Insight* magazine in 1988. Since Anselmo no longer controlled SIN, he had to find buyers for all the space on his proposed satellite. He created Alpha Lyracom Space Communications to market PanAmSat. His associate, Frederick A. Landman, began working for him in 1973 and had married Anselmo's daughter, Pier. Landman was president of PanAmSat, but he held no equity in the company. He did own 20 percent of Alpha Lyracom. But as Anselmo and others have discovered, Intelsat's real clout was political and international, since it did the bidding for signatories, nearly all of whom are powerful telecommunications entities with political ties to their governments. Comsat, also headquartered in Washington, D.C., opposed PanAmSat's application in hearings before the FCC, which was authorized to consider applications for alternate satellite systems. The presidential determination stipulated that no harm be done to Intelsat, either technically or economically, by allowing others into the satellite communications game. In 1984, Anselmo applied to the FCC for permission to put two satellites into orbit, a primary and a backup, to provide service to South America. Anselmo also proposed to distribute video and audio communications signals between various Latin American countries and ground stations in New York and Miami. Five other firms also applied, but later withdrew.

Those withdrawals were probably a result of the intensive lobbying of Comsat. Only Rene Anselmo was bull-headed enough to continue the fight. In 1984, I had just begun selling CNN internationally. I didn't learn until a year later what he was trying to do.

Comsat asked the FCC to deny Anselmo's application, although the White House, State Department, Commerce Department, and the FCC all supported the concept of limited competition. Comsat argued that the upstart's proposal undercut the U.S. commitment to the Intelsat system and would divert tens of millions of dollars from the international organization, not hundreds of thousands as claimed by Anselmo. Meanwhile, Intelsat had passed its resolution that members would not do business with separate satellite systems. This resolution was designed to destroy competition. And, of course, the FCC could give approval only when an applicant had a foreign partner to provide downlinking facilities. Most of those capable were already Intelsat signatories.

Anselmo, in order to satisfy the FCC requirement and break the boycott against him, offered President Alan Garcia of Peru a deal he couldn't refuse: the use of a high-powered video transponder covering Peru, Ecuador, Bolivia, and northern Chile for $1.00 a year. Garcia jumped at the offer.

In 1985, Pan American Satellite was granted conditional authority to build and operate its satellites. "Conditional" meant it faced two additional hurdles. One of them was "hard to take," says Anselmo, since it required him to demonstrate to Intelsat that his firm's satellite operations would not damage it, technically or economically. "It was one of the real ironies of our license," said Landman. "We had to go to Intelsat, consult and show we would not cause economic harm or technical interference. Intelsat was doing everything to break us. Incidentally, that's when the other early applicants became faint of heart. Intelsat claimed that it entered into negotiations in good faith, but having to consult with its major competitor in drawn-out meetings became costly for Pan American Satellite. Just to agree on service between the United States and Peru took a year. The company's financing wilted."

Ordering a custom-made satellite might have cost Anselmo as much as $80 million and a three-year wait. For about $45 million, he was able to pick up one that the RCA Astro Space Electronics Division had been building for a customer that had canceled the order. Even with this bargain to show bankers, Anselmo had no luck getting financing. Without demonstrated customer demand, PanAmSat remained a blue-sky venture, and his problems with Intelsat and the PTTs were making customer demand virtually impossible to prove. In the end, Anselmo decided to fund the venture himself.

The U.S. government's launch program was suspended in the wake of the January 1986 space shuttle Challenger disaster. Anselmo—like all other satellite operators at the time—had no choice but to turn to the European launch consortium, Arianespace, which had seen its own share of mishaps. Four of the 18 Ariane rockets launched since 1981 had failed after lift-off. The mission scheduled for June 16, 1988, was listed as a test flight, the first launch of a brand-new rocket series, the Ariane 4. No commercial customers ventured forth, except Anselmo, who seized the opportunity to cut ahead of the long line of companies booked for future Ariane launches. "Only Rene Anselmo would have taken that level of risk," said a Citibank vice president who had helped arrange financing for many satellite deals. Often, satellite operators insured a launch for the full replacement value, based on the projected cost of building a second satellite and getting it into space. Their investors insisted on nothing less. But as his own investor, Anselmo could choose to gamble. Rather than insure the flight for $85 million—the $66 million he had already spent on the project and the $19 million he still owed on the satellite—he took out a policy for only $40 million.

English officials held that British Telecommunications PLC, its Intelsat signatory, could not refuse earth-to-satellite uplinks for PanAmSat. London followed with the announcement that it would support an Intelsat consultation for two-way U.S.-British services via PanAmSat. Washington and London invited other European governments to take advantage of the voice, data, and television services being offered by PanAmSat's transponders. To encourage others to join, the State Department launched a diplomatic campaign throughout Western Europe to declare that joining the initiative preserves the option of using PanAmSat's service without undergoing a tedious separate consultation with Intelsat that takes from nine months to two years to complete. In short, Anselmo and PanAmSat encountered the same resistance to change in satellite practice that I had, but his situation was more frightening, because he was investing $85 million. I had to play my cards close to my chest because of the financial problems that CNN was having during the early years.

In September 1985, I was informed by PanAmSat that it had acquired an RCA satellite. The letter I received said in part, "I hope you will agree after reviewing a proposal, that PanAmSat can deliver better service than Intelsat at a fraction of the cost." I was delighted. But I wondered if Anselmo's organization would be able to overcome the obstacles that would be placed in its path. I had one hope. PanAmSat was a rumble. After a rumble come louder rumbles, then often an avalanche. Then nothing is the same any more. I heard the rumble, but I didn't yet understand the strength and courage of Rene Anselmo. I thought I was tough, that Ted was tougher. But I was to learn that Anselmo was amazing, a real magician.

What a poker game. Comsat and Intelsat kept raising the stakes, and all the other players were dropping out, but Anselmo stayed and bet a fortune, using the most unorthodox methods imaginable. Anselmo had powerful allies, such as IBM, AT&T, Citicorp, and the television networks, including TBS—at least as far as I was concerned. Each ally wanted more flexibility and lower satellite rates.

In his book *The CEO Goes to Washington,* Max Holland compares the struggle of Rene Anselmo with that of William E. McGowan, Chairman of MCI Corporation, which challenged the AT&T monopoly with various lawsuits. After 16 years of confrontation with courts, the Congress, and the FCC, McGowan won a $113 million verdict and broke the monopoly.

McGowan's campaign made Anselmo's possible; it introduced the idea of competition into the telecommunications industry. In several respects, though, Anselmo's uphill climb to make PanAmSat the MCI of the satellite world was even steeper than McGowan's efforts against AT&T. The monopoly of "Ma Bell," a nickname for AT&T, was government-sanctioned, whereas the monopoly Anselmo would battle was created by multiple governments. McGowan had only U.S. law to deal with. Anselmo had to contend with the laws of every country in which he wanted to do business, as well as with the Intelsat consortium, which enjoyed special privileges and immunities.

As one industry analyst told *Via Satellite,* a trade publication, Comsat and Intelsat have "held the monopoly position, and in terms of the marketplace there's nowhere to go but down."

* * * * *

In early 1988, I decided to stay in Atlanta until the TBS decision was made about the Latin American satellite. I knew that if I took one of my four-to-six-weeks sales trips, Ted would be influenced to stay with Intelsat. I was the only one who could and would make sure he had the facts.

Terry, in favor of continuing with Intelsat, was having his technical specialist, Wes Hanemayer, prepare comparison information on cost, signal strength, and other pertinent data. I needed similar technical support, and, fortunately, I had been meeting with a Brazilian, Orlando Vallone, who wanted to be a CNN agent in Brazil. We had discussions over a several-month period, but I didn't want to make a final decision until we knew more about the future of the signal in South America. Vallone had an excellent technical background, particularly in satellites. He offered to be a consultant in Brazil or all of South America, but I preferred having him part of our permanent team, and offered him a position in 1988 to help organize our South American sales efforts and advise me on the technical aspects of satellites. It was fortuitous that he appeared just when I needed that kind of support. Terry's and my approach to Intelsat and PanAmSat could not have been more divergent. Terry saw the need for TBS to have access to satellites globally for CNN and future entertainment channels. Intelsat seemed to him the only means of providing the necessary hardware worldwide since no competitors were permitted in most of the world. Intelsat was not averse to using TBS's global needs as a tactic to prevent our using PanAmSat. PanAmSat was also aware of the power of CNN to make the satellite it chose the "hot bird," or satellite of choice, for all the news and entertainment channels that wanted to cover South America. This would assure the success of PanAmSat. I felt certain that ESPN would join whichever satellite CNN chose. This would, in effect, force other program suppliers to seek the same satellite so that a single antenna owner could focus on one satellite. Most antennas were fixed and could only be realigned to another satellite with great difficulty.

Since Intelsat and Comsat were having trouble maintaining their monopoly at the governmental level, their only alternative to prevent the success of PanAmSat was to lower their rates. For the first time in its history, Intelsat/Comsat resorted to creative selling. Comsat convinced Terry of its support for TBS global satellite needs, even offering special rates, such as $45,000 per month, when Embratel, the Brazilian PTT, wanted $150,000 per month just for the Brazilian use of transponder space. Terry used these price drops to argue for Intelsat, while I fought for PanAmSat. I was sure that if Intelsat kept PanAmSat from succeeding financially by forestalling its potential clients, then it could more than make up any money lost after it had rid itself of its competitor.

More important, an independent satellite could permit unrestricted downlinking. Intelsat's representative PTTs had to be remunerated for *each* downlink antenna, even though the continuing piracy of satellite signals by anyone who could afford to install a six-or seven-meter antenna made its policy a joke. Our broadcasting and cable clients had to pay these prohibitive rates, however. They couldn't risk piracy as a policy.

I saw PanAmSat as the first of many independent satellite companies which would offer far lower costs than those Intelsat was proposing. Then again, I do like fighting for the underdog. I'd been doing this for Ted since 1971, and he respected what I had accomplished. This gave me some leverage in the satellite decision that Ted would have to make.

I contacted Fred Landman at PanAmSat in March 1988 to tell him of my need to present an acceptable financial plan to TBS. Fred answered me, attaching a copy of PanAmSat's proposal to Terry in September 1987. I had not seen it. Since I had previously spoken of the financial difficulties at Turner, its proposal suggested a sharing of CNN income until the cost of the satellite half-transponder at $100,000 per month was paid off, and then it would get a smaller share of our income. It had also offered service to Great Britain at a rate 20 percent less than we were then paying Intelsat. It was an unusual offer in that PanAmSat, having its own cash problems, was willing to help start the CNN feed to Latin America without *any* cash payment on Turner's part. It was not the final agreement I would want, but a good place to start negotiating. It also gave PanAmSat a share of our income during the years that the initial contract ran.

Landman sent me a cash payment offer of $500,000 per year for a preemptible (occasionally other programs could be given precedence) and $800,000 for a non-preemptible, half-transponder. This was less than half what we would pay Intelsat. Terry's assistant on satellite affairs, Suzanne Detlefs, received a copy. That same day, I sent copies to Terry, Jack Petrik (Director of Programming and Executive VP of WTBS), and Russ Barry, TPS President, but not to Ted. I wanted to sell Terry first and then have him recommend PanAmSat to Ted.

Jack Petrik sent a memo to Russ Barry informing him that Ted wanted to proceed with a PanAmSat transponder that summer, with a possible operational date of September 1, and that he wanted the signal unscrambled for the first year or two. Ted also wanted a business plan for a possible entertainment channel for South America. He wanted me to spearhead the project and Terry to make the financial arrangements with PanAmSat. I was given responsibility for CNN sales in South America, along with my team of Serrador, Pasante, Vallone, and Torres-Bohl. Terry phoned to tell me that Ted had directed him to move on the PanAmSat transponders and that Ted was "gung ho" on the project. Then another note from Terry's assistant, Suzanne, with a copy of the proposal to the Turner Board, recommended the PanAmSat $500,000 per year proposal, with increases in years two and three to $700,000. This was an outstanding offer and was approved by the TBS Board of Directors at its next meeting.

In the spring of 1988, many CNN global projects were on my mind, but before I closed my eyes each night, I couldn't help thinking that if the PanAmSat launch is a failure, then we will have to go to Intelsat with hat in hand, begging forgiveness for blowing up their monopoly. Then I thought, oh, well, for me this is only a bad dream. Look what Anselmo is risking!

Meanwhile, Landman verified that all of the Latin American countries' PTTs would permit unlimited downlinking, with the possible exception of Brazil, and this was being worked on. I wasn't concerned, since I had already learned that once CNN reached an area, it was almost impossible to keep that country's citizens from finding a way to receive the signal, particularly if other countries in the region were receiving it. It would take draconian methods, such as were used in Iraq, to prevent people from watching CNN.

As the power of satellites increased and smaller dishes were used, then CNN and other satellite news services could be watched surreptitiously, just like the BBC radio broadcasts had been listened to during World War II and, later, behind the Iron Curtain. I was confident that no Latin American country's government would even *try* to prevent CNN from being watched.

In May, I received a phone call from HBO trying to "pick my brain" on South America and its potential development. This convinced me, along with discussions with ESPN, that if CNN were on PanAmSat, I would have helped build a coffin for Intelsat's monopoly.

Arienne rocket blasting off with first PanAmSat satellite from French Guiana, South America.

But Intelsat was determined to keep CNN and PanAmSat from getting married. The Turner Board didn't really care what satellite TBS used. It approved PanAmSat because it would cost less. Suddenly, Intelsat was back in the picture, trying to better the PanAmSat offer and throw in some benefits on other global satellites that obviously were not available to Anselmo.

In mid-1988, I sent Ted and Terry a memo, attaching Orlando Vallone's comparison of the Intelsat and PanAmSat transponders. He pointed out that PanAmSat actually had a stronger signal in the most populated areas, so that the cost of antennas for PanAmSat would be $1,000 versus Intelsat's $2,000 and most important, there were far fewer regulatory issues with PanAmSat.

Two days later, I bought a bottle of champagne and telexed Francisco Serrador in Rio: "PanAmSat successfully launched this morning (on a French Ariane rocket in French Guiana, South America). Preliminary testing will be completed by tomorrow. Will advise." I told everyone: "There must be dancing in the streets of Greenwich, Connecticut, or at least in front of the PanAmSat offices and Anselmo's home."

I think my champagne would have turned sour if I had been at Intelsat and had heard its reaction to the successful launch. It definitely had its first competitor. In fierce fighting mode, it went after Terry McGuirk and Wes Hanemayer. Even though PanAmSat had been approved, no contracts were signed (the satellite was still in a testing phase), and we were determining whether to uplink to PanAmSat from Atlanta or, if necessary from Miami, where its uplinks were located. I realized I had a problem when I received a memo from Wes Hanemayer that "Every effort is being made to allow immediate activation of the service while *retaining a strong negotiating position with each supplier.*" Intelsat was still negotiating with Terry!

Wes went on to apologize for Comsat:

> As the signatory for Intelsat they are required to conduct business in a combined regulated and deregulated world. The result is a company trying very hard to compete with their hands tied by tariffed pricing and treaty defined relationships. Nonetheless, they were able to provide us a competitive bid both in price and technical features. They were also able to discuss some of your other demands, such as eventual coverage of Africa with a feed directly from Atlanta. Though this east hemi feed may not be available until later in 1989 or early 1990, it could be financially and operationally beneficial to us to wait since this same feed could be used by CNN International in Europe and the Middle East for transportation and primary coverage. Resulting in a major savings to both parties by sharing the transponder costs.

I couldn't believe anyone—especially Wes Hanemayer—could think the Intelsat monopoly operated with "its hands tied." Exactly the opposite was true. Intelsat's long arms and thuggish hands were choking the life out of the fledgling satellite industry and the prospects for improved global communications. The 100 or so member countries banded together to direct the potential benefits of satellite technologies only toward increasing profits of national telecom monopolies.

I sent Vallone a copy and asked him for an updated analysis on the two competing satellites, and the answer was still the same. *PanAmSat had a better signal at half the downlinking cost.*

Yet the debate continued in the TBS office, and Jack Petrik asked Hanemayer for a point-by-point comparison. The only major benefit to using Intelsat was that we would have to construct an uplink for PanAmSat. Hanemayer claimed it would cost $1,400,000, but Vallone said it would be less than $1 million and, if we used our existing building, only $500,000. Hanemayer's memo had been written to favor Intelsat, while questioning PanAmSat's acceptance in South America. It was unfair but, fortunately, I had Vallone to help me. Hanemayer was supposedly completing negotiations with PanAmSat. All that was pending in July were certain out-clauses and a few other minor points. Gene Wright was taking engineering tests on the proposed transponder for performance evaluation. On August 29 he reported the satellite was performing very well for our proposed use. Brazil, Uruguay, Chile, and Peru were participating in the tests and were sending back word that they were receiving very clear video pictures. Nevertheless, the negotiations with Intelsat continued. So there I was, still trying to put an elephant through the eye of a needle. I had had enough. I called Terry and asked for a private meeting.

I had never considered us adversaries. I liked Terry. I knew his father. I thought that Terry would be like him. I realized he had played a more conservative role at times than he may have wished in order to offset Ted's tendency to make quick and sometimes emotional decisions, perhaps failing to understand the difference between one risk taker and another. He lumped all risk takers in one group, and Ted and I were both in it. Many who take risks fail. But others, who take similar risks, succeed. Why? Because some people, such as Ted and me, are *determined to make it work*. We can *force* a potential failure to succeed. Not 100 percent of the time, but often enough to make a growth company keep on growing. There can be no creation, development, or growth without risk, and key executives who are too timid or conservative should not be in positions of *future planning*.

Terry and I sat across from each other in the executive conference room to discuss the two satellite companies and the obvious fact that most of the points favored PanAmSat's. I knew Terry was under considerable pressure from Intelsat—I believe it was using its satellites in other regions of the world as leverage in negotiating with Terry. Intelsat was in a serious battle, a last-ditch effort to maintain its monopoly, and it had an extraordinary adversary who was willing to try any form of public promotion and lobbying to win. For the first time, Intelsat/Comsat must have realized they might lose at the governmental level. Their only way to prevent that was to keep PanAmSat from becoming a "hot bird," a working satellite. The only way to do that was to keep CNN off Pan-AmSat because, if we were there, the other programmers would follow.

I faced Terry and called in my marker. I said, "When we were in Ted's office four years ago and he asked me who would be handling the leasing of satellites, he expected me to say that I would do it. But I didn't. I pointed to you and said, 'Terry will handle it,' because I felt we could work together, and I knew it was an area you wanted to be responsible for."

Terry looked at me and said nothing, but he knew I was right. I was not seeking power, and I had no interest in "ladder climbing." I loved taking on impossible projects and making them happen, and Terry knew it. I didn't expect an answer then, and I had no way of knowing if I had tipped the balance back toward PanAmSat, even after I had reiterated the importance of breaking Intelsat's monopoly and control by the individual PTTs in each country. I had emphasized that Intelsat would have no choice but to sell us transponder space on its other global satellites, particularly once its stranglehold was broken. And I made clear that I intended to press the issue.

If I had not chosen to go that far, or if I had not been involved in CNN internationally, or even if I had not had the relationship with Ted that I did have, then TBS would definitely have made an agreement with Intelsat. That doesn't mean that PanAmSat would not have succeeded eventually, but it would have delayed the opening up of CNN services globally and kept Intelsat from providing multi-downlinking services to anyone with a dish in order to compete with PanAmSat. Months went by, and still no decision had been reached. I knew that Intelsat was pressing every button it had, and evidently it was succeeding in keeping us from completing an arrangement with PanAmSat.

Reuters News Agency reported:

> PanAmSat was suing Comsat for $1.5 billion for operating an illegal monopoly. In its suit, Pan American Satellite said it has been blocked in its efforts to find customers for its own satellite

launched last year at a cost of $100 million. The small satellite concern charged Comsat with predatory pricing and other actions that it said hindered Pan American's efforts to provide an alternative satellite service.

Comsat countered that the antitrust suit was groundless, but Rene Anselmo was quoted as saying, "We want to bust open their monopoly." The lawsuit claimed that Comsat had interfered with PanAmSat's less expensive service. Comsat officials argued that they were trying to help PanAmSat! You could have fooled me.

PanAmSat was concerned about this delay, since we were the linchpin to the immediate success of their project, as well as to its making good on its investment. Landman and I decided that desperate times called for desperate measures. The law firm of Backer & McKenzie in Brazil had just confirmed that an agreement for downlinking the PanAmSat signal with its PTT, Embratel, was necessary only if the signal was being transmitted by the Intelsat satellite system. There were other minor obstacles, but it was now clear that Brazil, the most important country to receive CNN in South America, would have unlimited downlinking access to PanAmSat. This was a strong point for PanAmSat, but Landman and I agreed that we needed to strengthen their proposal even more, so that it would be very difficult for Intelsat to improve upon it. Wes Hanemayer's final negotiations with PanAmSat had been completed and sent to Landman but had not yet been signed by TBS.

A week later, Terry McGuirk received the following letter from Rene Anselmo:

> Dear Terry,
> Allow me, in order to impress upon you how critical it is that TBS use PAS for its Latin American service, to turn the table on this matter. We will pay TBS to come on board PAS!
> Specifically, this is what we are prepared to do:
> 1. We will pay TBS $250,000 up front upon commencement of CNN's service. This will help defray your marketing and development costs in working with us to implement CNN in Latin America.

2. We will provide TBS with a 15 meter dish, free of charge, for your uplinking from Atlanta. TBS will be responsible for all electronics and installation.

3. We will provide TBS two 36 MHz Latin Beam transponders, free of charge for a period of 12 months commencing January 1, 1989. At the end of this period, we will continue on the basis of the deal we have already negotiated. You may commence now at no charge.

4. We will provide TBS with one hour per day, free of charge, 36 Mhz of Ku-band space segment on a Europe to US transponder for backhauling your European news feeds.

This space segment will be provided free of charge for 12 months commencing January 1, 1989. (You may start earlier if you wish, the 12 months are from January 1st.) At your option, TBS can continue the Europe and US service afterwards at our regular low Ku-band rates.

Terry, the broadcasters in Latin America are united to a man in wanting to free themselves from dependence on Intelsat and their local PTTs. I have already stated your decision is going to make or break PAS; and if we do not make it, none of the other proposed alternative satellite systems are going to make it. So yours is not just a decision that will affect TBS, but will have a major impact on the future of telecommunications throughout Latin America and the world. And I do not believe I am exaggerating the importance of this decision one bit.

I know that Comsat's pitch is that they offer instant access, whereas with PAS it is going to take 6-12 months to gain access in Latin America. (I do not know the legality of Comsat making these offers in concert with the declared boycott of PAS by the Latin American PTTs, but I intend to pursue the matter.)

Mr. Dreyfuss will be visiting Sid Pike this week. Dreyfuss claims absolutely that his TV station has the authority to pick up and retransmit signals from PAS in Brazil. This is true of many other countries. You have a report on the status of these countries. With your signal up, and working together, believe me we will crack all of Latin America. Further, our original proposal allows TBS to cancel if certain levels of penetration are not met.

PAS beats the Comsat/Intelsat service on technical quality, flexibility and price hands down in Latin America. I do not know what Comsat is offering you on a world-wide basis, but I hope the above will show you how important your decision is to me. In theory, with the above offer, it should cost you nothing to help us out. And you will feel better about it. I send you my best.

Sincerely,

Rene Anselmo,

Chairman

I couldn't believe it. Anselmo was offering to *pay* Turner instead of being paid by Turner for the leasing of a transponder. It was as if you went to an auto dealer and he gave *you* $20,000 to take the car! It was brilliant when you thought about it. Anselmo was offering not just one transponder for CNN free, but a second for the proposed entertainment channel for one year, plus one hour per day free to backhaul news feeds from Europe to Atlanta, plus saving us $250,000 in marketing and developments costs, *plus* a 15-meter antenna for uplinking!

Intelsat could not even think about matching it, let alone improving on it. With CNN on PanAmSat, its success was virtually assured. Anselmo had already invested $85 million, so what was another couple of million to guarantee the investment? It reminded me of his $1.00 proposal to the president of Peru in order to assure himself of a downlinking partner.

A brilliant stroke from a brilliant, fearless man. It was bound to end the battle at TBS. *It was the sort of thing Ted would do.* Only a man like Anselmo could have defeated a global monolith like Intelsat. This offer shifted the balance overwhelmingly in favor of PanAmSat, but just to be sure, I sent Terry a memo comparing the proposals, point by point. Again, I did not send a copy to Ted. I wanted Terry to propose PanAmSat.

I knew we had finally succeeded when I got a copy of a memo from Wes Hanemayer:

Further discussions with Fred Landman have resulted in his improving the long term incentive. Using the provided information, we need to draft a new letter of intent for PanAmSat proposals.

Given the regulatory approval by the FCC on part of the proposal
I recommend that we commence service by January 1989.

The Intelsat monopoly was broken. I was proud to have played a role,
but the leading warrior had been Anselmo. I found out later that Intelsat had
been asked to match the offer. It couldn't do it. I wonder if they teach this
example of business acumen and courage at Harvard Business School?

A year later, in October 1989, after I had sent Anselmo a letter expressing my feelings about what had taken place, I received this one from him:

Dear Sid:

Well, your letter has been lying around my desk now for six
weeks begging for an answer which has not been forthcoming.

I guess what I wanted to do was to write something as equally nice and moving to you. Since I am viewed as some Typhoid
Annie, or an ambulatory AIDS virus by the established telecom-
muncations industry, it is comforting to know that somebody
appreciated what we are doing.

That you, Sid, have managed to interconnect the whole
world for CNN is no small feat. Knowing what you've had to go
through, it is more like a miracle.

Someday, what we are pioneering will be commonplace, and
it's going to be one hell of a lot better world for it.

I send you my warmest regards.

Sincerely,

Rene Anselmo,

Chairman,

ALPHA LYRACOM Space Communications

There is only one other letter that comes close to matching it that I
have received in my 48 years in television broadcasting, and that was from
Edward R. Murrow, then head of the U.S. Information Agency, thanking
me for providing USIA with my American documentaries in Portuguese
for distribution in Brazil in 1963.

Anselmo fought other battles, one of the most remarkable being when
he wanted PanAmSat to have the same rights as Intelsat to international
telephone connections. The FCC denied him access to Public Switched

Networks (PSN). These connecting circuits were responsible for almost three-fourths of all satellite revenues. Anselmo believed that this protected revenue allowed Intelsat to develop a form of predatory pricing. In July 1990, he filed a petition with the FCC to access PSN and thus to effectively end Intelsat's monopoly on another front. His lawyers wanted him to lobby Washington himself. They got more than they bargained for. It was described in Holland's *The CEO Goes to Washington* this way:

> Phil Spector, one of Anselmo's lawyers who accompanied Anselmo to a meeting-on-the-run with [Senator] Danforth, recalled the occasion. It took place literally in the lobby outside the Senate chambers. The idea that somebody put in $80 million of his own money—essentially cashed out on his life's work and put the money, double or nothing, on a new satellite project—was just shocking.

On May 6, 1991, Anselmo took out an ad in the form of a cartoon in seventeen panels showing him and his dog Spot, as he plays Don Quixote against the Comsat/Intelsat monopoly. Anselmo tried to buy ad space in the *Washington Post* and the *Wall Street Journal,* as well as the *New York Times.* For $15,000, the *Times* accepted the ad, even though Spot urinated twice in the cartoon. Holland writes:

> Anselmo's team was accustomed to his blunt letters but feared that publishing his cartoons would destroy their efforts to depict PanAmSat as a 'company of stature' recalled Anselmo. 'Everybody was squeamish [about] a respectable corporate image and all that horseshit. This was the only time I said, 'I don't want a discussion. Lay off.'
> Anselmo's team was dumbstruck by the impact; the cartoon's appearance accomplished more than a dozen soberly reasoned briefs. All anyone in telecommunications could talk about was Anselmo's unusual tactic. While the results of the ads were having their effect on the media and the government, Anselmo wrote 'comedy letters' to telecommunications executives, members of the U.S. Congress, and President George Bush. There

were people in the government who came to boast of having a complete collection of his letters.

Anselmo's persistence paid off. On November 17, 1991, seven years after the Reagan Administration issued the original determination that private satellite systems were in the national interest, the Bush Administration ruled that all PSN restrictions be eliminated by January 1997 and allowed PanAmSat limited PSN rights during the interim.

Anselmo is a great model for young business people. He fought ferociously to succeed, first in a pioneering environment, as Ted and I had done, and then made an incredible investment when an organization with over a hundred governments behind it, including his own, was arrayed against him.

Rene Anselmo died on September 20, 1995. He had accomplished a goal to which we all aspire. He left the world a better place.

Rene Anselmo, originator of PanAmSat, first independent satellite

CHAPTER TWENTY-NINE

CNN's Vital Link: Africa and Turning to the Soviet Union for Satellite Help

They are decided only to be undecided, resolved to be irresolute, adamant for drift, solid for futility, all powerful for impotence.

—Sir Winston Churchill

Before I could further extend CNN globally, first I had to fix the existing leaks in the plumbing. Canada had sprung a major leak.

Burt Reinhardt insisted on keeping a strong relationship with the CBC because of the excellent news material it provided to CNN. Their news executive, Bill Morgan, was again demanding exclusivity of CNN material in English-speaking Canada. (The Canadian government was very careful to respect the language needs of its French-speaking citizens, to prevent the appeal of secession.) I never liked to give exclusive arrangements, and the CBC, like the BBC in Great Britain, already had the playing field tilted in its favor.

We finally got Morgan to allow independent stations, if not networks, to use CNN services. I simply leaned on the definition of independent stations to arrange CNN agreements, although some *were* part of networks.

I let Paul Morton, the General Manager of Global Television Network, express his displeasure directly to the Canadian government back in 1985, and that took care of it. I ignored CBC's Morgan as much as I could and pacified him when I had to, but nothing substantial changed.

During the satellite crisis, I made quick trips to Quebec to discuss agreements with Télé-Metropole and Pathonic Communications. Pathonic's owner, Paul Vien, was relatively new to the television world but very progressive in his thinking. He was determined to succeed and smart enough to realize that CNN would give his small network coverage of the United States and the world, equal, if not superior, to what the government-funded CBC was providing for all of Canada. I liked Vien, and he invited me to join his family at their summer lake cottage, where I surprised them and myself: I could still jump wakes on water skis. After Paul made his agreement with us, he built his own receiving antenna. Then the Royal Canadian Mounted Police told him that he had to take it down or they would arrest him. He refused on the grounds that the government of Canada would be preventing him from keeping the French-speaking population informed of world events. They didn't arrest him.

I turned my attention to Africa and planned a trip for late November and December, first to Brazil and then across the Atlantic to South Africa. Ron Ciccone and I had been working with the ambassadors in Washington and at the United Nations, while Patrick visited television stations from our office in Lagos. We were on course. By late 1988, we had made progress in English-speaking Botswana, Ethiopia, Ghana, Kenya, Nigeria, Swaziland, Tanzania, Uganda, Zambia, Zimbabwe, South Africa, Bophuthatswana, and Gambia. There were no television stations constructed at that time either in Chad (French-speaking) or Malawi. Certain countries were politically unstable, and although Ron and Patrick kept up communications, we knew it would take time before we could introduce CNN to Angola, Central African Republic, Mozambique, and Namibia. There was, of course, piracy still going on. But we were moving forward even in the French-speaking countries. I was well satisfied since only a few years earlier the distribution of CNN in Africa had seemed unattainable. We already had agreements in Zimbabwe and Nigeria. Ted told me that if I could get a half million dollars annually out of Africa, he would go for a 24-hour CNN signal in the region of Africa and South Asia, which would cost $1 to 2 million a year.

It was very hard to get agreements in Africa to provide enough cash to justify a permanent 24-hour transponder. Any use of the AFRTS signal was usually a stopgap measure until a full 24-hour satellite signal could be obtained. And all available satellites were getting crowded—and some had no room from time to time, such as the Indian Ocean Intelsat system. After the Intelsat experience, I wanted to encourage any country or independent organization to use satellites that were available for commercial use worldwide, such as satellites from Russia, Indonesia, China, and PanAmSat. However, the lack of money on the continent weakened my position for regular service. This problem made me look for other sources to satisfy my Africa requirements.

Bob Wussler was negotiating with the Russians about leasing space on the Gorizont satellite, since there was no room for us on Intelsat's Indian Ocean bird. If Gorizont had an acceptable signal, I preferred it to Intelsat. The Russians were not preventing anyone from downlinking. I wondered if Intelsat's not having room for us had anything to do with our support for PanAmSat.

Africa presented some internal CNN obstacles for me. Russ Barry, now head of TPS, sent me a memo questioning what I was doing in Africa and whether it was worth our expense. He didn't understand: *CNN could not be a preeminent global service without Africa.* I told him that CNN would bring a part of the world still living in the Stone Age into the present, before all their precious resources were stolen from them by former colonial countries, such as the French, aggressive Western businesses, and even their own corrupt regimes and dictators. I gave Russ some figures to show him that it was a promising road to take. Of course, we couldn't work on a purely business basis there, but I had more in mind than just selling CNN. Our work on the continent was important to the development of CNN as a global entity, and, at the same time, we were contributing to the improvement of communications between its developing countries and the world. Some economically weak countries could not convert their currency into U.S. dollars, which irritated Russ, and he wanted to know why we were doing business in Third World countries, anyway. I came up against this lack of foresight in Russ and other executives, who were not familiar with developing new territory. Russ was also not happy about my taking on Ron Ciccone as our African and Middle Eastern consultant. He challenged the

$60,000 we were paying him and wanted to know what he was supposed to accomplish. Of course, Ron was essential to our efforts in those regions. He had the ear of the African ambassadors, United Nations representatives, and even heads of state. He was so important to TBS that after I left CNN international development, and a new management team was developed in London to service Africa and the Middle East, Ron was invited by Bill Grumbles at TBS to write his own ticket. He was reluctant to stay because he wanted to return to his consultancy business, but then TBS made him a financial offer he couldn't refuse. Once again he set aside his business and worked full-time for TBS. Until 2002, Turner International offered Ron more incentives because of his excellent contacts and well-developed trust within the Arab and African countries.

Ted, of course, stood by me as I developed Africa. So did Burt Reinhardt, and later, Tom Johnson. Certain others also understood the magnitude of what I was accomplishing and helped to keep me on track.

A few months before I left in November, I had completed arrangements with SABC to carry our American election coverage for $25,000, and I was on the verge of a new agreement with it. I'd been in continuous talks with Kobus Hamman, who would be retiring soon, and we were both eager to complete the SABC agreement before he left. I was aiming for a $500,000 annual fee, which would cover a bit less than half the cost of the Soviet satellite, with unlimited downlinking, and fulfill Ted's minimum requirement so that CNN could go ahead and pay for its own signal. Kobus and I thought we would succeed by the end of the year, and Kobus assured me that CNN would be broadcast without editing.

At the end of November, I flew to Rio de Janeiro and met with Francisco Serrador, who was doing a competent job in South America. I also met with news executives at TV Manchete and TV Cultura regarding their downlinking of CNN on PanAmSat. A private company was also interested in developing cable in Brazil.

Fortunately, by this time, we solved the problem of working with Embratel. These companies found a loophole in the law, which was written so that Embratel was in charge of satellites. But since the legislators thought that Intelsat would be the only international carrier, there was no reference to non-Intelsat entities. This was the string we pulled to go around Embratel. CNN was already being downlinked by many Brazilians who were simply pirating it. The Brazilian government realized that this practice would grow and there would be no way to stop it. When I left Brazil, it was ready for CNN.

I always felt somewhat uneasy when I went to South Africa because of our problems with the signal and our domestic-U.S. news. This time when I arrived in Johannesburg, I was optimistic because shortly the CNN International news would be redesigned to be truly international. And it would be broadcast, we hoped, via the Soviet satellite, which covered half the world, including Africa. I was able during this visit to complete an agreement that provided CNN excerpting rights to SABC for all of South Africa for $1,100,000 per year for a five-year period. Although SABC insisted on exclusivity in order to prevent M-Net access to CNN, we compromised. They would have exclusivity for the first three years.

I wanted to talk to M-Net, but had difficulty arranging a meeting with the general manager, which I interpreted as his lack of interest in CNN at that time. I hoped that eventually I could place CNN with a cable service in South Africa, which was why I persisted. Later M-Net did pursue us, trying to get CNN exclusively to foster its cable growth.

During my meetings with SABC, I told officials of the new international signal and that it would provide more worldwide news. So they had to decide which format they wanted. In February 1989, Kobus Hamman and his wife, Jeanette, visited Atlanta to study the differences between the 24-hour international service and the U.S. domestic service on AFRTS, which they had already received, though only for a short time. We provided Kobus with two television sets in a private office, with both services being shown, and he studied them, while members of the staff took turns taking Jeanette shopping and sightseeing in Atlanta. In the evenings, Lill and I had dinner with the Hammans. After watching both services for a week, Kobus agreed with me that the international version was the one that SABC would prefer. I admit I had some misgivings as I watched CNN on my own office monitor and saw South African police using force to quell various disturbances. There were also comments from different parts of the world asking for stronger sanctions against the South African government. Kobus never said a word about this to me. When he made his decision, I was relieved. It was a million dollar per year account, and it was not unusual for countries to complain about CNN stories that were unflattering to their governments. After a while, they had begun to understand that we were not going to be influenced by their remarks. Throughout the world, at that time, it was not unusual for the news media within a given country to change their news presentation when the government complained.

I had delivered double what Ted had wanted in order to lease the transponder on an Indian Ocean satellite. When he got my note about this in December, and the good news that TV Cultura in Brazil was about to test their law by downlinking CNN from PanAmSat, he was delighted and scribbled on the memo, "Terrific, Sid. Merry Xmas."

After Johannesburg, I was on my way aboard a South African Air 747 to Cape Verde, a strange island country in the Atlantic Ocean that was treeless, barren, and bleak. Truly a moonscape. Ron Ciccone had corresponded with the ambassador and arranged for me to visit the television station on Praia Island, the capital. The small island of Sal that the giant 747s landed on was not much bigger than a couple of golf courses. The television network had expressed interest in CNN and ordered an antenna from Cuba. It arrived with a part missing, and it took almost a year to get it.

My plan was to meet Patrick on Sal and continue together to Praia. Our plan was to work together in presenting CNN and then have a meeting to discuss other African problems.

I was met by Fernando Rodrigues Carrilho, a friendly young man with a warm smile, who had been asked by the Praia government officials to welcome me to Cape Verde. He drove me to my hotel, and we arranged for him to come by for dinner that evening with his wife. I was scheduled for a local commuter flight to the main island the next morning so that I could meet the television executives.

Fernando picked me up and drove me to the airport, only about a mile away. I arrived at 8:30 A.M. for my 10:00 A.M. flight. At 9:30 A.M. I walked to a desk and asked about the flight to Praia Island.

"Oh, that plane has left, sir," the clerk said.

"Left? What do you mean? It's not 10. How could the plane leave?"

"Oh, but it was full," was the reply.

"But I have a confirmed reservation, and I was never informed the flight was leaving early," I said, my voice now rising an octave or two.

"But it was full by nine A.M.," the clerk explained.

Evidently there were no reservations. The plane waited until it was full and then took off. No one had warned me that in Cape Verde passengers were on a first-come, first-served basis. Fernando's wife worked at the airport, and she found me a later flight. The next one was at 4 P.M., but I decided to meet with Patrick first on Sal and let him carry on with the scheduled meeting since it would add to his experience and reinforce him as our CNN salesperson. He, too, had been delayed in Senegal, the closest country to Cape Verde.

The English-speaking Carrilhos took good care of me while I waited for Patrick. They were extremely hospitable and treated me like a member of their family. On my second evening with the Carrilhos, after dinner, I was taken to meet Fernando's parents. Everyone in this family gave each other such undivided attention, were so concerned for one another, that I was reminded of my early years. Some of those qualities, which I remembered from my childhood, had somehow evaporated. And I realized why. On this tiny island, with this loving family, I was in a time warp. It was pre-television. Although there were TV sets on the island, there weren't many. Thus it simply wasn't an important part of family life, as was the case for my family, and others of my generation when our children were young.

Once again, I worried about my efforts to develop a global interconnecting and simultaneous news service that I believed was critical to the world's survival. Was there a terrible downside? Was I helping to export violence by increasing the importance of television? Would more traditional countries look through this window at a highly civilized country, like the United States, and see it as a detriment to their culture and values? Was this stirring Al Qaeda and other fundamentalist groups to hate Western civilization even more?

I came to believe that what I had been doing was speeding up the process of people using television to connect with the modern world that would eventually envelop them. The world could not have separate societies, those with television and those without. One culture would overwhelm the other with faster learning and instant information.

Unfortunately, international television had been misused because it had been placed in the hands of a fairly small and powerful group of countries that were accustomed to approaching any invention in terms of its market value rather than considering its significance for mankind. This was understandable, but even when it must have been clear to that august body of the Intelsat Board how important satellites were to the future of the world, they still didn't "get the message."

All this begs the question: Would the world be better off *without television*? I watched the Carrilho extended family, so truly loving and happy, and wondered, could my efforts be misdirected? I thought about who I had become, and where I stood in my own life on this tiny, treeless, lava-based, barren island with its simple happy families. Then I realized that the answers to both my questions were simple: We cannot halt progress, or eradicate the human desire for self-improvement.

Fernando picked me up every day in his jalopy, the island's version of a jeep, and we would careen around the black, hardened lava to his favorite fishing places. After a day of baiting and casting, with no luck at all, I realized I was not a fisherman. I had gone deep-sea fishing off the North Island of New Zealand once; now I was fishing in the Atlantic, and the only fish I caught in either ocean was five inches long, and no one knew what the hell it was.

When Patrick finally arrived, we worked out our plans for developing CNN in Africa, and I asked him to continue to Praia and complete the mission, because I needed to get back to Atlanta.

As I flew home, I thought about how much of the world we had covered. We now had our own 24-hour signal in the Pacific. On PanAmSat we covered all of South and Central America, and our CNN domestic signal took in all of North America. We had made substantial inroads in sub-Saharan Africa, and Bob Ross in London was developing Europe and northern Africa with the new international signal. But the 24-hour CNNI feed still needed a lot of work. It had too much U.S. news, and it was, at that point, hampered by stringent budget cuts.

I still had to fill in the gaps that existed in southern Asia; India had the second largest population in the world. As my fifth year of working on CNN came to an end, I felt that we had made giant strides with a paltry operating and personnel budget. There had been no five-year flow chart because no one had had any idea where CNN was going. There was no map. Only after we had covered an area like the Pacific, Latin America, or Africa, could we start to project figures on potential sales.

I sent Bob Wussler a memo answering his request for income projections in the Soviets' offer of its Gorizont service on Statsionar-12, which reached from the eastern tip of South America as far as China, the Philippines, and western Australia, and as far south as Antarctica:

> While you advised that $1.8 million Gorizont figure is negotiable, it is substantially higher than our estimate of an Intelsat transponder which we expect to be in the $1.2 million range. We are advised that Soviet satellites have problems in geosynchronous orbit. They 'drift' and sometimes the earth stations have difficulty in picking up the signal. When we talked about this possibility some time ago, I think we were hoping for a bargain basement price, particularly due to the condition of the satellite and their lack of use by international customers.

I had estimated that we could more than pay for this new Soviet signal with our income from sub-Saharan Africa, the Middle East, India, and Pakistan. But not at Wussler's price.

When my plane touched down in Atlanta on December 15, I looked forward to spending the closing weeks of the year with Lill and our friends. There was still work to do, but we had cleared much of the jungle.

CHAPTER THIRTY

Complications and Tian an Men Square

The world hates change; yet it is the only thing that has brought progress.

—Charles Kettering

Harold Schindler, television columnist, wrote in the *Salt Lake Tribune:*

> I wonder if Ted Turner ever sleeps? His broadcasting empire closed a deal with Pan American Satellite to transmit CNN on a round-the-clock basis to Latin America on PAS's new international satellite. According to Terence F. McGuirk, president of Turner Cable Network Sales, who executed the agreement for TBS, the deal marks 'the first time a major television organization has utilized an international satellite transponder on a non-Intelsat-operated satellite to distribute programs.'

Schindler didn't know the half of it and, as in almost all my work for Ted, the press never learned who actually made it work. While PanAmSat had resolved many issues, there were always new ones. For example, in order to offset FNN's influence on the stock market news, Ted decided to overlay the bottom of the *Headline News* picture with a rolling tape of up-to-the

335

minute stock prices. We couldn't talk him out of it, and I began to receive threats of contract cancellation from television broadcasters in Canada if a clean picture wasn't restored. We had a number of income-producing agreements there with stations that used the CNN news segments of *Headline News.* We were eventually forced to use a separate, clean feed via satellite to Canada. Somehow no task was ever completely finished. I had to keep protecting what we had already accomplished. Of course, we were still competing with network news feeds in Canada and in other parts of the world.

All three major U.S. networks were active in different areas, but none had Ted's nontraditional vision. They could not put it all together and develop their own 24-hour news service. Westinghouse/ABC's abortive attempt earlier, and Ted's cable influence, which reached a growing percentage of U.S. homes, had kept at bay further encroachment domestically and globally. The networks were, in fact, unhappily preoccupied with their own decline in the face of the growing influence of cable and independent television. The heads of the networks were wondering whether their share of the audience would keep declining—it had gone from 80 percent in 1984 to 68 percent in 1989. Perhaps they would even fall as low as 55 percent, which NBC's President and Chief Executive Officer (CEO), Robert Wright, called "bottoming out." The other network CEOs, Thomas Murphy of ABC and Lawrence Tisch of CBS, were also concerned, but they weren't about to spend money on developing wild global news concepts. Actually, the networks began to cut back on their worldwide news gathering, which had grown enormously expensive. Tisch was determined to eliminate certain CBS bureaus in the world, even if it "cut into muscle." Remember, he was the "white knight" brought in to save CBS from Ted Turner. But, most significantly, the network behemoths were too distracted to pay attention to the future of international news delivery and collection. Later, in the 1990s and into the new century, other television broadcast services, such as the 24-hour FOX news channel would compete with CNN, but for the moment, our competition was limited. Our main problem in 1989 was distributing the signal globally and collecting the revenue to support this growth. Cable was still relatively weak worldwide.

To enhance the use of breaking news stories for the broadcasting stations, Jon Petrovich of CNN created a special news feed customized for a station willing to pay satellite costs and a modest fee. This was typical of the kind of cooperation I received from CNN's key personnel, who were well aware of what I was doing.

By 1989, CNN's name was synonymous with global news, like Coca-Cola's is with soft drinks. Its recognition internationally had supplanted BBC radio as a source of authentic and accurate news reporting. I received new requests from many places. Sometimes embassies in Washington, D.C., or individuals from countries all over the world phoned or telexed inquiries about representing CNN in their area. Each one required careful consideration. Entrepreneurs had to be checked out, plans studied, and meetings held. Every morning when I was traveling, I examined the messages from Joyce and FedExed or phoned her if something was urgent. (There were no cell phones in those ancient times.) All the balls had to be kept in the air. I couldn't afford to drop one unless I had determined that another one offered a better course of action.

The only "black hole" I had left—my term for where there was no effective CNN signal—was India/Pakistan and nearby countries. The Prime Minister of Pakistan, Madame Benazir Bhutto, was eager to bring CNN into her country, as well as to participate in providing Pakistani news to CNN. Nepal Television contacted me and wanted to bring in CNN. This wasn't possible yet, and it added to the pressure I felt to cover southern Asia. I had heard from Sri Lanka and Bangladesh, too, but India was still trying to keep CNN out. I couldn't be in all the places where people wanted CNN, even though I now made many long trips to negotiate for its use. Since we still did not have the signal in southern Asia, I postponed a trip there and decided to concentrate on the Arab countries in the Persian Gulf region.

Bob Ross and I had worked out an arrangement so that he would handle all the countries bordering on the Mediterranean, including North Africa and Jordan. I was to work from Syria and Iraq south, including sub-Saharan Africa. I would also handle Lebanon, probably because there was a devastating civil war in that country, and no one, including myself, wanted to go there.

Ron Ciconne had organized a visit for us in May 1989 to Oman, Iraq, and Bahrain. Ron had very good connections in Oman and Bahrain. I had asked him to add Iraq to the trip, because after studying the comments by Saddam Hussein in the media, I believed that the Iraqi dictator was making momentous decisions based on limited information. I learned that he had *never* traveled outside of the Middle East. While he was a secularist who shunned Islamic fundamentalism, he chose, when he wanted favorable propaganda, to use the media so that he could be seen praying. I would learn later the extent of protective religious fervor and frustration, compared with Western civilized growth, that had been festering for over a thousand years, not only in Iraq, but in the entire Islamic world. Bringing CNN to his country and making it available to him personally would correct what I perceived as an extremely narrow view of the world. I also asked Ron to advise each country's embassy that I was Jewish—I wanted to prevent any unpleasant surprises while I was there. Ron reported that he was told: "We respect your advising us. Please do not bring it up again." Evidently, the prospect of bringing CNN into these countries, as far as their leadership was concerned, overcame even this obstacle.

Ted was interviewed by global journalists on *Worldnet,* a USIA television program, in early March, when it was announced that CNN would soon be available to every nation on earth 24 hours a day. By this time, we had agreements in nine countries in sub-Saharan Africa. He explained to the reporters that TBS was completing negotiations with the Soviet Union for satellite space to give CNN full global coverage. I hoped that Intelsat heard that—as it was widely covered in the news—and realized it had failed their responsibility to supply satellite services worldwide, which was its mandate. CNN was being transmitted to 75 countries with 150 million viewers, and it had 20 news bureaus around the world, which helped to address the concerns of journalists in other countries about global television being controlled by privately owned media based in a few dominant countries. Ted said such worries were exaggerated and that globalization was a positive force. *Variety,* in March, 1989, reported that "a number of U.S. companies have recently introduced international ventures, such as ESPN, MTV, Walt Disney, NBC, and Radio Vision International." MTV was reported to reach "five continents in 23 countries and more than 90 million households." The same article pointed out that the Turner organization, and particularly Ted, had a special relationship with the Soviets "via such programming as *The First Fifty Years: Reflections on US/Soviet Relations,* the Goodwill Games, and *USSR: Portrait of the Soviet Union,* an extensive look at the people, geography, and culture of the country."

Ted followed in the footsteps of Armand Hammer, the American businessman who had dealt privately with the Soviets since the days of Lenin and Stalin. Ted met with Gorbachev in Moscow, and he was convinced that Western good will could remove the barriers that had been created between Russia and America during the Cold War.

Ted's position was courageous since TBS depended on advertisers, public acceptance, and sometimes government approval. But Ted's timing was right. Gorbachev was more conciliatory to the West than his predecessors had been.

I was concerned that Ted may have spoken too soon on the matter of the Soviet satellite. Tests showed that because the satellite had been launched years earlier and flew in a lower orbit, it had a tendency to drift, causing viewers to constantly reposition their antennas. But there was no alternative—the decision had already been made to go with Statsionar-12, and I had informed SABC that we were now able to offer it the 24-hour international service it wanted, as long as it didn't mind moving its dish every few hours.

In March 1989, Terry McGuirk received a letter from PanAmSat:

> Dear Terry:
>
> Who was it who said, 'Pan American Satellite would never get into Brazil?' The Intelsat Board meeting in Nairobi unanimously approved the Brazil coordination today. France, Guatemala, and Honduras have also been coordinated at this meeting. There may even be a few more before the Board meeting ends. We think that the end result of the Brazil consultation is that your customers in Brazil won't need to pay a penny to Embratel for the right to access PAS. I believe that's our idea of a perfect satellite world.
>
> Best Regards,
> Fred Landman, President

Our support of PanAmSat, along with the agreement to use Statsionar-12, had done what we'd hoped for: It convinced Intelsat that its monopoly was no longer acceptable and that other satellite organizations, which had reasonable rates and unrestricted downlinking services, could legitimately be supported. As I look back on this effort, I realize that we never received credit for removing the Intelsat obstacle because no one ever reported it *or even knew it existed.* It was obvious that many satellite television channels, such as those mentioned in the *Variety* article, were waiting in the wings for us to solve their problems at our expense. Ted didn't care, and I certainly wasn't going to wait until all interested parties got together and contributed to a legal fund. We were not only changing the behavior of entrenched entities like Intelsat, but also changing attitudes and laws all over the world. Roberto Muylaert, President of TV Cultura in Brazil sent me a message: "We tried to have part of the news in English and that was forbidden by Dentel, the government agency. We were forced to stop it. That started a new series of articles in favor of our constitutional right of presenting it. Till now we didn't succeed, but we are sure that our battle here is deciding the future of CNN in Brazil." It wasn't just CNN's future that was at stake; it was Brazil's.

The first CNN *World Report* meeting was held in Atlanta on May 8, 1989. Delegates from broadcasting organizations in more than 80 countries attended the meeting. They were all contributing stories to the three-hour *World Report* program that aired every Sunday at 3:00 P.M. and repeated at midnight. The *Atlanta Journal* reported that the senior editor of television news for the Soviet broadcasting system remarked, "I have a Bible in my hotel room, and it says that once all people spoke one language, but we lost that. I feel that now we're developing a common language. It's the language of information and truth."

The conference, which emphasized international unity and cooperation, also gave rise to clashes reflecting the different ideologies present. A heated public argument erupted between the director of Voice of America, which beams Radio Marti to Cuba, and the director general of Cubavision television, who said Radio Marti is a "violation of the rules of communication." Voice of America responded that Cubavision just didn't like what was being said about Cuba since it represented the U.S. government's view of Castro and communism. Greek and Turkish Cypriot representatives confronted each other and swapped charges over whether the Turkish Cypriot station should be represented at the conference, while Ted Turner, sitting in the back of the room gleefully exclaimed, "This is great! Let them be heard. This is what *World Report* is all about."

* * * * *

While I was on my Persian Gulf trip, a pivotal event occurred that strengthened CNN's credibility worldwide and further enhanced my global endeavors.

In the spring of 1989, the CNN News Bureau in Beijing, which was part of the agreement with CCTV that I had worked out a year earlier, augmented its local staff in preparation for Soviet President Gorbachev's visit to China to cement good will between the two neighboring communist giants. CNN had on hand a crew of 40 people for this Sino-Soviet summit when a wave of protests began, something unprecedented in China's 40 years of communism. It started with four university students protesting the lack of democracy in China. Others joined them from 40 different universities. Soon, hundreds of thousands of demonstrators swarmed through Beijing's enormous Tian an Men Square and congregated in other cities in China. For awhile, the situation seemed to be out of control, and the news coverage, which demonstrators always want, increased the number of participants. The government finally sent in troops and tanks to quell the uprising, and this, too, was shown on CNN via satellite to a global audience.

The three major American networks had maintained costly staffs to cover international news since their origination in the late-1940s, but they had been cutting back. And now CNN's 24-hour service was available to more than half of all American television households. The only thing that had been keeping CNN from dominating news in the United States was providing global news coverage as good as that of the three networks, which were now slipping.

The first time I had noticed this was in 1986. CNN was the only network covering the Challenger shuttle launch, thus the only one that immediately aired the news of its disastrous failure. At Tian an Men Square, NBC and ABC had minimized their coverage of the Sino-Soviet summit, and only CBS and CNN were giving it total coverage. It was Tian an Men Square that helped establish CNN as the preeminent global news entity and gave new credibility to my reasoning that every country, its citizens and its leaders, *needed access to CNN.* It also demonstrated the power of this access to news when the oppressed citizens of repressive governments saw it. Tian an Men Square was the first time the whole world and its leaders saw the effect of open and uncensored news. The image of a young man standing in front of a tank to deter its movement was seen not only worldwide, but also in *China* itself via CNN. While the worldwide coverage was not unexpected, the China reportage was extraordinary in that CNN had just breached the "Chinese Wall" of controlled news to the general population that was as traditional as the history of China itself.

Particularly striking was the moment when, *on camera,* CNN reporters questioned the Chinese government's right to stop them from feeding the events they were covering onto the global satellite. This democratic perception by the CNN staff was "revolutionary" to the Chinese authorities who were not used to having news coverage limitations questioned. The Chinese government then decided to take back control of the news images within China that were being viewed both inside and outside their country. Some commentators claimed that the networks "failed to look at the deep-seated Chinese aversion to chaos, a suspicion that too much freedom is a threat to domestic peace. 'Water can float a boat,' said a Chinese feudal emperor, 'but water can also capsize a boat.'"

China's government would not again risk letting the rest of the world see what was going on. Richard Falk, a professor at Princeton University's Center for International Studies, said, "Historically, China doesn't care what the outside world thinks. Chinese leaders recognized that world public opinion had been activated against them by the American media. So they think, 'If we can control our own cameras, we can reshape internal public opinion.'" That was the main reason for cutting foreign uplinking to international satellites. They didn't want uncensored news about China to come back into the country.

The televised events at Tian an Men Square affected the relationships I was developing in key countries, such as India, which was already worried about the effect of uncensored news coverage. Even so, by the 1990s, CNN global coverage was so complete that any country refusing to allow both coverage and distribution stood out like a Russian wolfhound in a pack of poodles.

Meanwhile, I was concerned that Ted, who was in more and more demand as a speaker, would say something that would force the networks to compete more strongly against CNN. Ted's mind wandered sometimes when he spoke, and he tended to make outrageous statements. He did this in May 1989 when he spoke to the Washington Metropolitan Club at its monthly luncheon and called General Electric (GE), the parent company of NBC, "the most corrupt corporation in America." He said that some of its top executives were "thieves" and "convicted felons...who belong behind bars." He was referring to a publicized indictment of a GE unit the previous year.

Ted was worried about NBC's plans to launch a new cable service that would offer financial and consumer news. Ted pointed out that GE had offered to buy TBS in 1988 but had balked at the $20-a-share price. A year later, the same TBS stock was worth $27 a share. Ted added that, even if GE had met his price, he would not have sold, although his back had been to the wall, and he was forced to sell part of the company to several cable operators. He claimed he was better off with "the Devil you know than the one you don't."

Remarks like this hurt us. They emphasized CNN's growing dominance over the network news and forced them to compete both globally and domestically with Ted, the man who had caused them too many problems with their affiliates, and embarrassed them publicly. And it didn't help when he tried to convince the owners to allow him to buy or merge. The ultimate "bomb" in the Washington Metropolitan Club speech was when he referred to those who take a pro-life stand on the abortion issue as "bozos and idiots," thereby alienating half the American adult population.

CHAPTER THIRTY-ONE

Sheiks and Satellites

The average person puts only 25 percent of his energy and ability into his work. The world takes off its hat to those who put in more than 50 percent of their capacity, and stands on it head for those few and far between souls who devote 100 percent.

—Andrew Carnegie

Ron Ciconne and I left for our first visit to the Arab world in the spring of 1989. We flew to Oman, on the edge of the Persian Gulf, because the country's leadership was receptive to Western media. Ron had been communicating with Ahmed bin Suwaidan Al-Balushi, the PTT minister and his British advisor, Peter Sullivan, General Manager of Al-Balushi Limited Liability Corporation (LLC). They were interested in developing cable in Oman and wanted to use CNN in order to have a good "start-up." Even though Al-Balushi was an influential minister, he still needed to proceed carefully. A satellite channel was still very new to the area.

Ron and I stayed at the Al-Bustan Hotel, which was my first experience with accommodations in the Arab world. The beds and the rooms tended to be small, and the walls were painted with beautiful and very intricate designs, similar to those on Persian rugs. I was always disappointed when I was traveling and could not arrange for weekend singles tennis matches, and sometimes I substituted a swim in the hotel pool. The Al-Bustan had an excellent, large, ornate pool, which afforded me a relaxing swim on a beautiful afternoon in a country where one individual or one family made all the major decisions—and I would have to figure out how to deal with this unique situation.

We met with the news executives at the television network, and I went through my usual dog-and-pony show, but I had the feeling that the decision to use CNN would be made in a different place and at a different level. In all Arab countries, the television systems are part of the government and run at the ministerial level. When Ron contacted each country, the decision to invite us was made by the heads of state. In the Arab and Islamic world, there has always been a curiosity about things Western. In the fifth and sixth centuries AD, and for many centuries after, this Islamic world was in the forefront of civilization's achievements. In the eighth and ninth centuries, the Muslim world conquered Spain and Portugal and parts of Europe and Russia. At the same, time the Arabs were the economic power worldwide while achieving intellectual and artistic leadership. However, Europe and Russia, even before the Renaissance, began to make significant progress in the arts and the military. Such progress passed almost unnoticed in the world of Islam, and soon Muslims were left far behind. As more than a thousand years passed, strong fundamentalist religious forces took control because there were conflicting views of the interpretation of the Koran, the Islamic holy book, among Muslims. Those who believed in peaceful evolution and compatibility of their religion with others were overwhelmed by the violent methods of religious orthodoxy and conversion of non-believers by the sword. Commerce and education with the Western world diminished and the Arab crescent became even more insulated and withdrawn from day-to-day contact with the rest of civilization, except for a small coterie of traders and military advisors. It was a changing form of this protective isolation that the leaders of the Islamic world allowed CNN and me to step into. Despite the walls that Islamic fundamentalism had built, there was growing demand, because of traveling Arab students to the West, for more understanding of the outside world.

The introduction of CNN on satellites that covered the entire world could not be kept out by these or any other walls, and the leaders knew it. On May 21, we flew on to Iraq. In all the countries we visited, we were treated as special guests because we represented CNN. Even at the airports, we were always ushered into a special and very ornate waiting room and served refreshments while we waited for our flight. The room was the Bahranian version of a Delta Crown Room, only there was no alcohol, of course. Ron knew what had to be done to gain CNN approval, and he arranged the meetings, making it clear that I was the *official* representative of CNN.

Baghdad was one of the most beautiful and modern airports I had seen so far in my travels, but no one met us at our arrival. It felt like a cold welcome in a hot country, and I knew that my task of bringing CNN to Iraq would be formidable. The airport was surrounded by a high, concrete, supposedly tank-proof fence that made me wonder. Was it to keep people from leaving the country or from getting into it? The airport officials scrutinized my passport carefully and asked me a question I didn't understand. But by the time Ron intervened, they had stamped and returned my passport to me. The Al-Mansour Hotel was spartan, but the people at the reception desk were friendly, as was our translator/guide (called a "minder" in Iraq), who arrived the next day to take us to the television station. He was young and thin, one of the few Iraqi men who didn't have a small square "Groucho" mustache. I instinctively liked him, and later, when he learned that I was a stamp collector because I had asked him if there were any shops that sold them, he said he would bring me, as a gift, part of his own Iraqi stamp collection. I was very touched by such generosity.

When we arrived at the television station, I was surprised, although perhaps I should not have been, to see it ringed with large, ominous concrete tank traps (huge concrete blocks placed in front of the building), as well as by a group of the largest tanks I had ever seen. This was not the first time I had visited a television station around which there was a military presence with a great deal of menacing hardware visible. I thought of my meeting with the army colonel in Guatemala, and in Thailand there was a separate network run by the military. But Iraq's television service, at that time, was a single channel network, like that in other Arab countries. Since these countries were small, they were able to receive each other's signals. Not surprisingly, Israel's television broadcasts could be seen by its Arab neighbors, and the Arab stations could be viewed in Israel. The Iraqi tanks surrounding the station appeared especially sinister to me. Saddam Hussein was threatening Israel and had already committed atrocities against his own people, and had begun a costly war with Iran.

Ron and I were escorted into the television station's lobby and asked to sit while a military crew approved our credentials. When our turn came, after a few minutes of explanation, Ron looked at me and asked, "Do you have your passport?"

"No, I didn't bring it," I replied. I had left it in the hotel. But what difference did it make? They knew who I was. "No one asked me to bring it. How about my driver's license? It gets me into Canada," I added flippantly.

Ron looked perplexed and, after more exchanges between him, our minder and the guards, Ron turned to me. "They would like you to go back to the hotel and get your passport."

"Hell, no," I said. "They know damn well who I am. Either they want me to visit or they don't." I could tell that Ron, ever the diplomat, was not pleased with my language. He knew that Arabs quite often understood more English than they cared to admit.

After another long conversation in Arabic, Ron turned to me, exasperated. "They'll let you in, but they are not pleased." In other words, I had not been a hit with the military. But I had no intention of allowing myself or CNN to be insulted by anyone who simply wanted to put me through some ritualized entry procedure. As I think of it now, I realize that I was not my usual self in Iraq. Normally, I would never have been discourteous, even when provoked. I think I was reacting to the friendliness and courtesy we had received in our present tour throughout the Arab Gulf that seemed to end at the Iraq border. Except for our minder, I felt a coldness and unfriendliness I was not used to in my travels. But I also knew I was beginning to experience exhaustion. The long trips, the battles with the ex-Marine colonel in Guam, the internal company warfare, all were taking their toll on my patience and usually compassionate demeanor. I realized my years of training to control my emotions were showing "fault lines."

Our minder escorted us through the entrance, and I noticed a faint smile on his face. Ron, however, was frowning as we entered the office of the director, Said Al-Bazzaz. I immediately felt relieved because he seemed genuinely friendly. I explained honestly and openly that CNN was a 24-hour global news service that could help any country, especially its leadership (I didn't mention Saddam Hussein) to know what was going on in the world. Mr. Al-Bazzaz had heard of CNN and was sincerely interested. He listed some of his government's requirements. First, the Ministry of Information had to approve, then it needed to acquire an antenna. The country had one antenna, trained on an Intelsat satellite, but it did not carry AFRTS's CNN signal. I advised them that the Russian Gorizont satellite was going to be carrying CNN. It had a small 4.5 meter (15 ft.) antenna and, when I gave them Statsionar-12's coordinates, they said they would make a test that night. If a larger antenna was needed, I offered to help find a supplier in the region, and asked if I could meet with the Minister of Information. After more discussion in Arabic, our minder turned to me and said, "It will be arranged."

Then, they gave me a tour through the television station, which I saw as a part of my diplomatic duty, and I wanted to please my host in spite of the misunderstanding with the military earlier. Mr. Al-Bazzaz was operating the television network, but he obviously was not able to make substantive decisions, and, if CNN could come to Iraq, it would have to go through the Ministry of Information, and probably only Saddam Hussein could give final approval. I also wanted to make sure Saddam had access to his own CNN monitor. We were to be told sometime during the day when the meeting with the minister would take place, and since we were staying several days, I was asked if I would like to visit the military hardware convention that was taking place in the city. I didn't want to show an interest in things military—my mission was a peaceful one—so I declined and asked for the name of a good restaurant instead. Years later, I regretted not having gone when I watched a documentary on Gerald Bull, the Canadian designer of long-range guns, who was presumably assassinated by the Israelis. He had constructed the largest gun muzzle ever built, and it was supposed to have been able to reach Israel from Iraq. Bull had been present at that fair, demonstrating his super, long-range gun to the Iraqi military. As we drove back to the hotel, I noticed that in many streets and at many corners there were pictures, posters, and statues of Saddam Hussein, some very large. In some he wore Arab robes and headdresses; in others he wore Western suits or military uniforms, but always with the same smiling countenance.

Later that day at the hotel, Ron got word that we would be able to see the Minister of Information the next day, surprisingly at 9:00 P.M. This gave us time for some sightseeing and shopping. At the Martyr's Monument and Museum, I became quite depressed and angry seeing the exhibition, proudly displayed, of the helmets of fallen Israeli pilots and pieces of their aircraft. And of course, there was a huge exhibition glorifying Saddam's life, beginning with his childhood. There was also a monument to the soldiers who had died in the Iran-Iraq war, along with a display of uniforms, pistols, knives, and automatic weapons. The Martyr's Monument held a dead soldier, who rested overhead with "scientific preservation methods," the guide proudly explained. Both monuments were extremely ornate in design, and one cost $100 million.

The next morning, at my request, we were driven to Babylon in over 100-degree heat as part of our "tour." Babylon was under reconstruction, and I was very interested in seeing the ancient biblical city. Unfortunately, the car had no air conditioning, the driver drove too fast, which seemed to be a common practice, and we just missed colliding with a car that was traveling too fast behind a truck that had stopped. The other car made a 180-degree turn, but still hit the truck. They drove like nuts. There seemed to be no comprehension of car speed, physical size, car weight, and the serious potential for damaging collisions.

Babylon was fascinating, and I was impressed with the restoration. I looked for museums but was disappointed that I couldn't locate one. I did, however, find sort of one inside a postcard stand that was more like a mud hut by the side of the road. To my amazement, it held exhibits from 3,000 B.C., although I was no expert as to their authenticity. As we looked at the exhibit, Ron got stung by a wasp. I told him he was in good company. Alexander the Great, one of Ted's favorite heroes, who had conquered the then-known world in the 300's B.C., had been felled not by a sword, but by the proboscis of a malaria-bearing mosquito in the swamps of Persia.

On the way back to Baghdad, we had to stop because of another accident. A car had hit a young girl and her mother. The mother was not seriously injured, but the car had literally stopped on top of the girl! We all ran over and lifted the car off her, and she actually got up and walked away.

When I met again with Mr. Al-Bazzaz, I was exuberant in my praise of the Babylon restoration, and told him that tens of thousands of tourists would flock to see it because of its biblical significance. I added that their opportunity on CNN to provide stories for *World Report* would be an excellent way to tell the world about one of the most famous cities of antiquity.

Perhaps the television executives thought that I was "putting them on." There was little reaction to my excitement. Perhaps they didn't want tourists. I didn't know, but I had the feeling that they were being polite and couldn't say what they were really thinking. I failed to persuade them to make Babylon a tourist mecca; I don't think the Iraqi people understood my need to get things done.

That evening, we met with the Minister of Information in his office at the Ministry building. He manipulated his "worry beads" constantly as we spoke. "Yes," he said, "having CNN is a good idea, but perhaps this is not the time." It was not a firm "no" nor "yes." I thought of my father, who never said "no"—just "we'll see." It meant the same thing.

It was clear to me that the Minister of Information was under a lot of stress. I had been in other situations where people stayed late, not because of the amount of work, but to *prove* that they worked late. I sensed that this man was simply afraid. Saddam was not above killing people who angered him on the spot. He had done this many times.

I didn't know then if my presence in Iraq helped bring CNN into the country or if it was already being watched by Saddam. But I could tell that Iraq's government did not understand world opinion at the time, and particularly not Western opinion. I have in the years since my visit felt great concern for the Iraqi people. After I left, I kept the dialogue going with Mr. Al-Bazzaz, and he and other journalists from the television network visited Atlanta and attended the *World Report* annual conference several times.

After Ron and I checked out of the hotel, we went to the station for a final visit and our good-byes. As we were leaving, I asked our minder if I could take a photo of the station with the tanks in front of it. He said no, which I'd expected. But I really wanted a picture, so I did something stupid. I cocked the camera, which was hanging on a strap over my shoulder, and I heard it go "bzzz" and then I clicked it behind my back as I walked away, which caused another "bzzz." What I'd done was obvious, and it made the minder furious.

I didn't know what he was going to do. Would he take my camera? Take the film out? He was extremely upset, and I regretted what I'd done.

Ron was not pleased, either. Since we were on the way to the airport, the minder chose not to do anything, but he wouldn't let me take any more photos, not even of the enormous Saddam pictures on the streets and on the facades of buildings. I respected our minder's wise choice not to make an issue of the photo, but to focus on getting me on a plane and out of Iraq. When we got to the airport, Ron let me know how angry he was.

A month later, when I was back home in Atlanta, I found out that a British journalist had been arrested for taking photos at a "military installation." He was eventually hanged for doing so. When I had my roll of film developed, it turned out that I had completely missed the television station, but I did get a good shot of the cloudy sky. I have earlier accused Ted of his mouth and brain being uncoordinated. Well, put me down for having my brain "frozen" that day.

In Bahrain, Ron and I had meetings with the Minister of Information, Tariq Al-Moayed, and Dr. Hala Al-Umran, the Under-Secretary. Both seemed the most willing of anyone we had met to bring in CNN to an Arab country. Bahrain has often been called the Switzerland of the Arab world. When I asked Minister Al-Moayed about this comparison, he asked me if I had driven around the country. When I said that I had, he asked me if I had seen many oil wells.

I said, "A few."

He replied, "Precisely. Our oil is running out. It is almost gone, and we must develop other sources of income."

Ron had explained to me in a memo that he thought of Bahrain as a "working model." He emphasized: "One working model is worth a thousand words. Bahrain is indeed the flagship. This is not accidental. The Minister knows exactly what he wants and has the clout to get Cabinet approval for his ideas."

Ron pointed out that Al-Moayed was also the most media-savvy Minister of Information in the Gulf, and his Ministry was the best organized and best equipped in the Middle East. For the sake of Bahrain's future, they had to be innovative. Soon, the oil would be totally drained from beneath the sand, and the tiny island would have to realize its plan to become the banking and tourism center of the Persian Gulf.

We promised to help them acquire an antenna to bring in CNN, and when we left, we had laid the groundwork for an agreement that included the government's participation in all the uses of CNN, including hotels and cable in the future. As usual, when we left, we were escorted to the special waiting area at the airport, but this time Al-Moayed and Dr. Hala came with us. They were waiting for other Gulf Ministers of Information, who were coming to Bahrain for a meeting. In these special rooms, I always felt I was given the "royal" treatment. After I returned from the Persian Gulf, I learned that, although discussions and testing continued with the Soviet satellite, no decision had yet been made, so I still couldn't do much in southern Asia. I had offers from companies in the region to distribute CNN on videotape by bicycle, but this would be like getting a daily newspaper several days late.

Bob Wussler, who had been station manager of WTBS since January 1980, was resigning and joining Comsat as president of its Program Development Division. Fortunately, our plans to use the Soviet satellite were far enough along not to be disrupted by Bob's departure. He had been the primary executive working on that project. Wes Hanemayer was trying to find equipment that would follow the aging Gorizont satellite's drift, which required an antenna to be adjusted every five or six hours. By this time, I didn't care if they had to use a Model-T Ford in order to complete CNN's coverage by satellite.

The good news that summer of 1989 was that CNN was going to make an operating profit of about $100 million. Since Ted's philosophy led him to expand rather than pay taxes on the profit, this gave CNN the funds to form a team of investigative reporters and to set up additional bureaus. He also instructed Scientific Atlanta to install a receive antenna in North Vietnam. He had met its television network Director General at the CNN *World Report* conference.

I was not only working to bring CNN to every country on earth, I wanted to include the oceans as well. With the help of SeaTel, which had created an antenna that picked up the satellite while the ship was rolling or turning, this became a possibility. There were, however, vast areas of the ocean not covered by satellite footprints that had been designed to cover land. By the early-1990s, we developed a profitable cruise-and naval-ship service that promoted the use of CNN because on ships it was the only source of news available to this captive audience. It took time and effort to overcome various problems, just as it had on land, but it added up to complete world coverage.

In 1989, CNN's growing domestic service was developing innovative concepts, some of which I hoped to see used internationally. *Newsource,* for instance, allowed local television stations, including network affiliates, to show live, breaking news stories that CNN was covering. CNN provided a television journalist who did an individualized report for the local station, as well as organizing the delivery of the story by satellite for an additional fee over the cost of licensing the service. This further eroded the networks' relationships with their affiliates and sparked the belief in many industry insiders, including myself, that the networks' period of control over U.S. television was ending. FOX (the fourth television network) would develop, but so would cable 24-hour program providers, and other forms of entertainment in the home, such as computer games and the Internet. That massive audience the networks had counted on was eroding, except for big events like the Academy Awards, the Super Bowl, the Olympics an so on. CNN was also experimenting with using film made by amateurs with camcorders, as were all local television stations.

In September 1989, Burt Reinhardt retired as CNN's president. There was the usual speculation about who would succeed him. Tom Johnson took over soon after and remained CNN President until a TimeWarner executive replaced him in 2001. Burt has stayed on as advisor, consultant, and handler of special developments that have enhanced CNN's growth.

No company ever stays the same. Although a French philosopher once said, "Change is the very essence of life," I would add, "in business, only if properly considered and executed. Change for the sake of change means nothing, and can be detrimental."

CHAPTER THIRTY-TWO

Gulf Revisited and Meeting a Satellite Visionary

The long-heralded Global Village is almost upon us but it will last for only a flickering moment in the history of mankind. Before we even realize that it has come, it will be replaced–by the Global Family.
— Arthur C. Clarke, February 14, 1987

Ron and I returned to Kuwait in November 1989. Ron would go to other countries in the region, and I would travel to southern Asia and open up our new territory in advance of our plans for the Soviet satellite. I had been in continuing communication with Pakistan, but I would also see what I could do in Bangladesh, Nepal, India, and Sri Lanka. Ron had very carefully prepared our visits to each country with the ambassadors and embassies.

As CNN spread worldwide, more entrepreneurs contacted us. Some countries had several firms wishing to represent CNN. I had to determine which were financially able to support CNN's development and to build the infrastructure CNN and TBS's future program channels would need.

We hadn't realized the extent of the proliferation of private antennas throughout the Middle East until AFRTS encoded its signal there in 1989. This forced into the open a large number of antenna manufacturers and distributors, and increased the calls to Atlanta. They wanted to get decoders and to represent CNN in their country or region.

Many affluent and educated people of the Middle East and Africa considered CNN an essential part of their lifestyle since television news was so carefully controlled either by government censorship or by its operating station in their countries. CNN had become the only news source they trusted. In the Gulf countries, the leader was on the front page of the newspaper every day. The local television service and radio followed the same pattern. The various members of royal families and those high in the business and professional world had their own antennas, even if they were illegal for other citizens. For instance, a member of the Saudi royal family wanted a decoder in order to receive CNN. In a royal family compound there might be 15 to 20 television sets. Getty Oil, which was in the same region, also wanted CNN. I received a fax in 1989 from a rich Gulf merchant that read:

> We are willing to pay any subscription fees that are required. We will need three descramblers:
>
> 1.   For my personal use in Kuwait.
> 2.   For my personal use in my summer villa in Cyprus.
> 3.   For my cousin's personal use in Kuwait.
>
> We are very eager to start receiving the signal since the NBA playoffs are right around the corner. Right now we are completely cut off. PLEASE HELP!!!!

While I could help them get decoders, these customers were disappointed to learn that their equipment would only provide 12 to 15 hours of CNN on AFRTS, but not the sports events and films that AFRTS carried during its 24-hour period. The decoder only decoded CNN. By this time, hundreds of hotels, both large and small, had also installed antennas so as to provide the AFRTS signal in each guest room or on a single set in the lounge. Travelers had begun to depend on CNN and sought out hotels that provided it. We had laid the groundwork with the unscrambled signal of the 1980s for the work our marketing departments in Atlanta and London, and later in Rio de Janeiro, Hong Kong, Sydney, Tokyo, Lagos and New Delhi, would do in the 1990s.

Our second trip to the Gulf states took place during this period of intense interest. In Kuwait, Ron and I met with antenna distributors and companies designing cable and pay-television services to clarify what the relationship with CNN involved. The hotel association arranged a meeting for us with six major hotels. They told us that several of our non-exclusive sub-agents had proposed to provide CNN to the guest rooms and that they would select one to contract for all six hotels.

Ron and I worked with Kuwait's Minister of Information to develop an agreement for the use of CNN material on the television network and arranged with Sheik Salman Al-Sabah, Director of the Media Documentation Center, to use CNN. This center, as Ron explained to me, was a special unit with its own budget, which served as the archives for the Ministry. Another function was to prepare extracted footage for the country's ruler. Following our meetings with the two competing agents in the Gulf region, Ron pointed out that each one wanted to be CNN's exclusive agent. He was afraid there would be a real tussle as each tried to outmaneuver the other. It was important to make our position and expectations perfectly clear.

One of my concerns in every country I went to was copyright protection for CNN. While I was in Kuwait, I met with local lawyers and was surprised when I found a bright young African-American, Ernest W. Alexander, working for a local law firm. Alexander and I studied his company's proposal to represent CNN legally in any future copyright issues. He told me that, to his knowledge, there had not yet been a case involving broadcast copyright. Ours would be the first. This didn't surprise me, since that had been true elsewhere.

During our visit to the television station, I met with Mahmoud Al-Hennawi, a Palestinian, who was head of television news. He invited Ron and me to his home for dinner with his extended family. We arrived at a comfortable and spacious home in the suburbs of Kuwait City, similar to an upper middle-class home in the United States. Mr. Al-Hennawi's mother was the first to greet me. This Palestinian grandmother reminded me of my own effusive Jewish grandmother. The first place she led me (where else?) was a table at the end of a large dining room, where a huge array of special Palestinian dishes were laid out. This room opened into a living room where various cousins, uncles, aunts, and other family members were gathered and enjoying each other's company. They welcomed us warmly and, surprisingly, many spoke passable English. I enjoyed the "home cooking" and found it similar to Israeli dishes that Lill's cousins prepared for us. Gratefully, the subject of the Palestinian/Israel conflict never came up. While I doubted they were aware of my religion, and they were too polite to ask, we had promised the information minister in the region never to mention it. I had one of the nicest evenings in all my travels for CNN.

I thought often of this family when the Iraqi invasion struck Kuwait the following year, and the Palestinians made the politically disastrous decision to support Saddam Hussein, which Palestinian leaders repeated during the U.S.-led coalition war on Iraq in 2003. After the war, they suffered greatly at the hands of the Kuwaitis for this error. Many Palestinians had been employed throughout the Gulf region, particularly in Kuwait, but after the war, they were largely expelled.

From Kuwait, I flew on to Dhaka, Bangladesh, while Ron went to Bahrain and Saudi Arabia. About the latter, he told me that it was strange, but in spite of their enormous wealth, the Saudis were not keeping up with media development in the other Gulf countries. It was clear to Ron that the Saudis had become very concerned about their isolation and what it boded for the future. Thus, some of the senior princes were working to start opening the gates. As far as CNN was concerned, he was told that the king had asked the Ministry to find a means of using it to enrich Saudi television. If CNN were firmly established in the Gulf, the strictest, most conservative region on earth, we would have little difficulty elsewhere.

Kuwait was still skeptical, but Ron believed that it would try to figure out how to use CNN from the model in Bahrain. He recommended that we use Aga Ali's efficient firm. Ron believed that if we proceeded based on his recommendations, then we could deliver the entire region for CNN.

I separated the countries to which we were selling CNN into two categories: (1) those that could not afford more than a token license fee and (2) those that could afford to pay what was necessary to cover our satellite costs, to contribute to the overall costs of CNN, and even to provide a reasonable profit for the company. The countries I visited on this trip fell into the second category except for Bangladesh, and my approach there was similar to what I'd used in Africa. The previous July, I had met with a representative from Bangladesh's National Broadcasting Authority (NBA), who had been in Atlanta with a group of international visitors. I offered him six months of CNN service to his country's television broadcast system free, with a token fee thereafter. I made the same proposal to guests from Maldives and Liberia, and even tried to get the antenna distributor in Kuwait, Aga Ali, to supply a free antenna to that country. I had earlier asked him to supply and install one free in Ethiopia. Aga Ali quoted me $30,000 for the tracking equipment needed for the Gorizont satellite, including computer and London technicians, and Glieman Satellite Services in Harare, Zimbabwe, which we had been using in Africa, quoted under $6,000. In the end, we used neither in Bangladesh because the huge population meant cheap labor. The television station needed only to hire someone to go out every five or six hours and swing the antenna.

The people of Dhaka, Bangladesh, were warm and friendly, and both the chief news editor of NBA and the deputy director general of news wanted very much to work with CNN. I had successful meetings with the chairman of NBA to discuss its network's participation, including handling CNN arrangements for hotels. When I left three days later to fly to Kathmandu, Nepal, I couldn't help but feel compassion and concern for the fine people of Bangladesh, with their egregious problems of overpopulation and vulnerability to flooding, since they lived in one of the world's worst flood plains.

Flying into Kathmandu is scary. The plane skims over the hills and mountains that include the highest peaks in the world. I stayed in the Everest Hotel—where else? I was welcomed by the Manager of International Affairs for Nepal television, and he wanted very much to find a way to receive the 24-hour CNN service. He was disappointed to learn that there was no CNN signal in his area, and he, too, proposed shipping in videotapes. I advised him and the station's general manager to wait until CNN was available on a satellite. I explained that my trip to the region was to determine CNN's potential revenue so that we could assess whether the cost of the satellite, over $1 million a year, would be an acceptable investment. We worked on a preliminary agreement that could develop into a four-year contract when the CNN signal was finally in place on Statsionar-12. The agreement included Nepal television's development of CNN for hotels and cable. But, ultimately, the television station was not the proper organization to develop these opportunities, and private businessmen, who were more entrepreneurial and less bureaucratic, did it.

In mid-December, 1989, I flew to New Delhi. I hadn't been there since my visit in 1987 with Ted Turner. Certain managers at the government-controlled television network, Doordarshan, seemed interested in a CNN agreement, but the government itself was still blocking CNN growth in India, seeing it as an unnecessary Western influence. When we did finally provide an open signal on Statsionar-12 in 1990, there was, initially, an increase in piracy in India by those with private antennas, as well as by large numbers of small, unsophisticated cable operators. The government insisted at the time that it was necessary to obtain a license (which it was reluctant to give) in order to downlink CNN. Eventually, between the piracy and the media's exposure of the government's unwillingness to satisfy the appetite of its citizens for global information, the bureaucracy had to look the other way.

I settled on Catvision, a public company that constructed and distributed antennas, to represent CNN, hoping thereby to organize other forms of distribution with other organizations. I had met with its principal, Sudhir Damodaran, on my earlier visit. In certain parts of India, Damodaran could receive CNN on the AFRTS/Intelsat signal designed to reach Diego Garcia. But he had some technical problems. For example, the

Sid Pike with television executives from Nepal.

CNN anchor people's faces appeared green. Damodaran told his customers that green was a common skin color in the United States! I didn't ask any more questions.

With Damodaran's help, as early as 1986, CNN was being seen in many parts of India, either direct to home or business or through the burgeoning cable system. In remote townships, companies bought antennas and installed their own cable system for the sake of their workers. Hotels, too, began to downlink CNN on AFRTS in 1986 on 7.5-meter (25-foot) antennas. I was under intense pressure from businesses and individuals who wanted to represent CNN and develop it in this vast, English-speaking country. The government's reluctance didn't help. A company called Tristar continued to press me hard to be the exclusive representative. It was already supplying local stories to Stu Loory, Manager of CNN's *World Report*. My research turned up negative information on Siddhartha Srivastava, Tristar's owner. He had been one of the defendants in a video cassette piracy suit brought by Indian film producers.

Srivastava conducted a campaign to discredit Damodaran and Catvision, cleverly using his relationship with *World Report* to his advantage. He falsely claimed that he represented CNN, and that, since he contributed stories to *World Report*, he had the right to use the program for his own purposes. I pointed this out to Loory and urged that Srivastava stop supplying film on India to *World Report*. I offered to have Catvision replace his work. Loory was uncooperative at the beginning. Only after I provided proof of Srivastava's piracy difficulties did he send messages canceling his efforts with *World Report*, but Srivastava continued to undermine our efforts in India. He contacted CNN executives in London and Atlanta to "end run" my decisions. However, Loory would continue to cause me more problems after I finished my work with CNNI.

The biggest concern, however, was India's *size*. We simply did not have adequate staff to meet this mammoth sales challenge. Catvision was doing a good job, but it was a small company. India's population, approaching 900 million at the time—it has since passed one billion—was the second largest in the world. Its middle class alone was 200 million. I decided that the only answer was to involve cable and hotels with Damodaran and to find an Indian company to help develop CNN in other parts of the country. Many of the cable systems we sold CNN to were former "pirates" but had evolved into legitimate businesses. We also sold CNN direct to homes and made hotel agreements with selected representatives. The fact is, we just had too few people on our staff to develop the *world*, much less give India the attention it needed. But I knew that one day CNN would profit greatly in India.

Before I left, Shahid Ahmad, our agent in Pakistan (at the Information and Systems Corporation), arrived for meetings. His lovely wife accompanied him and joined us for dinner, which was unusual in a Muslim family. Ahmad is one of my favorite people, and our arrangement with him was one of the most successful business agreements I'd made for CNN. Ahmad had what I needed most in these CNN relationships: integrity and honesty. Evidently, the Pakistani government shared my opinion. CNN relationships in Pakistan, whether broadcast, cable, or hotels, were of the very highest quality because of Shahid Ahmad.

I was now on my final lap of this trip, and it was one I had looked forward to for quite a while: my visit to Sri Lanka. The country (formerly Ceylon) had been shaken by a long and nasty civil war, involving the Tamil population in the northern part of this large island off the coast of southern India. Once it achieved independence from the British, it found, just as Russia did upon the demise of the Soviet Union, that many of the country's small ethnic groups demanded their independence, too. Government leaders and highly visible news personnel were routinely assassinated.

Although I would be selling CNN in Sri Lanka, I was most eager to visit Arthur C. Clarke, the father of the communications satellite concept and the author of countless science fiction novels, including *2001: A Space Odyssey*.

It is my belief that many parents, particularly American, send their children to look in the wrong places for their heroes. Sports figures provide a very limited and short-term model. The real heroes are those who work for the betterment of all humanity by challenging and developing their minds, not their biceps. Arthur C. Clarke was certainly my hero. And I had an appointment to meet him in Sri Lanka. Joyce insisted that since I was in the region, I should see Clarke.

I thought it would be a quick trip from New Delhi to Colombo, but there were no direct flights. I had to go through Bombay, and since I arrived in mid-morning and didn't leave until late afternoon, Sudhir Damodaran arranged for his colleagues to pick me up at the airport and take me on a whirlwind tour of the city. My impressions of this city's huge population gave me a great sense of unease. What would happen to the human race in the future if we couldn't collectively control our exploding population? The poverty and squalid living conditions were unlike anything I had ever seen before, even in Brazil. It helped me understand why China and India were so concerned about outside influences and information crossing their borders. It was not easy to control the immense poverty-stricken masses. In effect, the governments of China and India were relying on the ignorance of these people in order to maintain their authority over them.

As the plane prepared to land, I looked into my carry-on bag to check the birthday gift for Dr. Clarke. Prior to leaving Atlanta, the Sri Lankan Embassy, which had helped me acquire a visa, had called Joyce at least three times to remind her that Dr. Clarke would be celebrating his 71st birthday on the day of my visit. Joyce knew of my excitement about meeting Clarke and had helped me select a silver desk clock, engraved with "CNN," which I had carried everywhere with me.

Sid Pike and Arthur C. Clarke, science fiction author of 2001: A Space Odyssey, in Sri Lanka, Clarke's home.

I was met at the airport by Uoosoof Mohideen, a member of Dr. Clarke's staff. The Sri Lankan government honored that Arthur Clarke chose their country as his home, provided research facilities for him. Uoosoof drove me to the Hotel Ceylon International, where the rather rotund, gray-haired, hotel manager and members of the hotel staff were waiting for me. The manager was a CNN-aholic. I was spreading the disease, but most victims enjoyed their sufferings. Its symptoms were red eyes, but the effects were beneficial: an understanding of events as they unfold. Uoosoof also took me on a tour of the island and to the Arthur C. Clarke Centre for Modern Technology—Clark's research laboratory. Its goal was to be the focal point of future high-end technology transfer in Sri Lanka and the region.

We arrived at Dr. Clarke's home in the early afternoon. I had been told to dress informally, but I wore a sports jacket. As I entered Dr. Clarke's study, this tall, gray-haired man, who, at first impression, appeared conservative—he wore glasses and was sitting behind his desk—stood up and walked toward me with his hand outstretched. I stared in astonishment. Dr. Clarke was wearing a bright, red-flowered *sarong*, a skirt-like garment of colored silk or cotton typically worn by both sexes in the Malay Archipelago.

I tried to act nonchalant, as though I were used to meeting people in their offices in sarongs! Dr. Clarke was warm and cordial. "Art," as he wanted to be called, insisted on a first-name basis. He extolled the virtues of a 24-hour news service by the satellite, which he had helped create. I asked him why he had adopted Sri Lanka as his home. He said he had never enjoyed the cold, raw English climate and had often visited Sri Lanka to go scuba diving, one of his favorite hobbies. Finally, he decided to stay.

Clarke worked on radar at its inception during World War II, and from that experience, his theories on satellites evolved. He was a member of some of the most prestigious scientific societies and occasionally traveled to England and the United States. We talked for awhile on the effects of the satellite on the global population and its traditional values and customs. We agreed that changing the direction of the world was an awesome responsibility. While Clarke seemed accustomed to accepting the results of his work, I had to admit that I felt that I was untrained and unprepared to do something that was so significant to the world's future welfare. Clarke's remark was "While the technology was accomplished, it needed something like a CNN, and someone who knew how to utilize the two concepts, to develop its potential." For this, I credited Ted, whom Clarke knew personally. I gave Dr. Clarke his birthday gift, and he was "delighted" that I was aware of it. Joyce had been reminding me in her morning faxes and telexes not to forget or—heaven forbid—lose the gift. As I was leaving, we walked past a wall of scientific awards and mementos; Clarke explained their significance with pride, but with humility. My visit with him had rejuvenated me at the deepest level about the importance of CNN globally.

Uoosoof arranged for a meeting the following day with the television network, Sri Lanka Rupavahini Corporation (SLRC), and he expressed interest himself in developing a UHF channel that would carry CNN. There were six major hotels with 3,000 rooms on the island, and all were interested in CNN, especially now that CNN International was mentioning the names of the hotels that carried our network.

Because Sri Lanka was another English-speaking country important to CNN, Uoosoof suggested that CNN donate two antennas, one for the president and the other for the Minister of State for Information. I told him I would consider this, and when I did get approval for them, Dr. Clarke presented the antennas on our behalf. Then came the hard part: paying for the antennas via Sri Lankan banks.

I had this problem in most developing countries that I traveled to. I was forced to carry large amounts of cash so that I would have enough money for my personal needs, because credit cards were not always accepted and I was wary of depending on the banks. Another problem was trying to get money out of a country that was paying for CNN. For obvious reasons, developing countries are reluctant to convert their local currency into dollars and see the capital flow out of the country, so they create all sorts of legal barriers to prevent this. In some countries, the government will not permit any remittance of profits, even after a large portion of the transaction has gone to taxes. When Ted bought MGM, I learned there was money from previous film distribution still held in Indian banks, and I contemplated using it if we were able to extend our operations there. Such decisions would be left to my successors.

When I visited a country, I tried to meet with government officials to foster good will on behalf of CNN, and to answer any questions as to how CNN news was collected and selected for airing. My background in television broadcasting came in handy, because when I was a station manager, one of my responsibilities was to protect unbiased reporting. I knew that any apparent bias would mean a loss of credibility with an audience that might have difficulty forgetting a lapse.

In Sri Lanka, I met with A.J. Ranansignhe, Minister of State for Information. After our meeting, we went directly to the television station, and I was ushered into the office of a young, dark-haired man. He was Air Commander A.P. Samarakoon, the Competent Authority (General Manager) of SLRC, the television network. The former Competent Authority had been assassinated earlier that year, perhaps as a way for the Tamil rebels to terrorize the city of Colombo. No civilian had been willing to accept the position of Competent Authority, and it had fallen to the Air Commander to "volunteer."

Commander Samarakoon spoke softly, slowly, and succinctly, with emphasis on the business points of the proposed agreements. To my surprise, he had arranged for me to address the entire television station's staff. I was escorted into an auditorium and talked extemporaneously about television in the United States and other parts of the world I had visited. I answered questions later. Most of the staff seemed to have the same kind of dedication I had observed elsewhere. To these people, working for a television station was more than a job; *it was an opportunity to serve.*

Commander Samarakoon was genuinely interested in a CNN agreement, but rather naïve about television broadcasting. He thought that the three minutes of news he could send to *World Report* each week could be used anywhere else on CNN, and I had to point out that that privilege extended only to *World Report,* and when that program ended, so did the three minutes of Sri Lankan news.

For some agreements, with countries that could not afford to pay our usual fees, I substituted local advertising in prime time so that international advertising would be available to Turner as a special bonus to its sponsors or for cash. But the Commander didn't understand this barter system, and that giving free advertising time would be their way to pay for CNN. When he asked for reciprocal time, I had to send him a long telex explaining the difference in costs and what our barter agreement meant in cash terms.

Samarakoon was very interested in our journalistic training programs offered to CNN clients, and asked me if I would send him the names and addresses of schools that taught electronic engineering. I was happy to do this when I returned to Atlanta, particularly when I read a copy of a memo from CNN about this same television station.

> Our communications with SLRC broken down earlier this year and we have not yet reestablished contact. According to Huma-yan Choudhury, News Coordinator for the ABU [Asian Broadcasting Union], there has been an incredible turnover at SLRC with some journalists even being killed. Shirley Perera, Deputy Director General, was our contact and came to the CNNWR conference with his wife. He has since written us about the situation at SLRC and has left his job. We also used to work with Mr. Pathirana, Director of News and Current Affairs, who has since resigned.
>
> We would be most interested in getting new contacts in their newsroom.

While I was in Sri Lanka, I also met with Asoka Malimage, who was the general manager of a new television station called the Independent Television Network, Ltd. I believe that later Malimage became manager of SLRC. I don't know the circumstances of his appointment, but I hope it wasn't because Commander Samarakoon was "eliminated."

I returned to Atlanta on December 20, in time for the holidays with my family and above all, with a much better understanding of the dangers involved when working at a television station in those areas of conflict that exist in too many parts of the world.

CHAPTER THIRTY-THREE

Gulf War Puts CNN in Spotlight

We can communicate an idea around the world in 70 seconds, but it sometimes takes years for an idea to get through one-fourth inch of human skull.

—Charles Kettering

By 1990, the era of paying a PTT for each and every signal received by an antenna was finally over. The Intelsat arrangement—using a single receiver in each country to distribute an international signal within the borders—was in shambles. The countries that were still determined to keep out unwanted information were realizing that this was futile. All over the world, round white and black metal and mesh dishes were appearing in varying sizes against every conceivable landscape. I was elated that I had something to do with this effort. The sad note for me at this time was that the indomitable Rene Anselmo of PanAmSat had died. I visited him earlier at his Connecticut office and was astonished to see that he was still smoking profusely after his serious heart attacks. To me, he was no less than an army general who had fought a brilliant campaign and had been victorious. At the time, neither Rene nor I were aware that we were digging a tunnel from opposite ends of a mountain made of ignorance, selfishness, and greed, and that we would meet somewhere in the middle and celebrate what we both knew was now inevitable: the dissemination of information worldwide that would, ultimately, be for the greater good.

For Turner, AFRTS's signals of 12 or more hours of CNN daily on various global satellites had more than paid us back for TBS's free programming supplied to AFRTS. I had been able to offer CNN even in areas of the world where the local companies were unable to generate enough revenue to pay the $1-2 million annual lease fee for satellite transponders. By 1990, CNN had its own 24-hour signal on satellites worldwide, and we no longer needed AFRTS. Finally, the Statsionar-12 signal was broadcasting to an area from the east coast of Brazil to the Philippines. Statsionar-12's wide signal was weaker than that of more narrowly focused satellites and required antennas as large as 11 meters (36 feet). In Europe, the Ku-band signal could be picked up, for non-broadcast use, with an antenna of less than a meter (3.3 feet) in size in some countries, such as Germany and France.

Except for those on AFRTS, CNN signals were left unscrambled and remained that way until later in 1990 when TBS began experimenting with decoders in Latin America.

I could see now how valuable CNN was to TBS, and I wrote to Ted in January 1990 to say that CNN's sales for global television broadcasting, cable, and hotels, would exceed, in my opinion, our international film and program syndication sales, which were in the $100 million annual range at the time. *I thought that we would do better than that in India alone.*

I estimated worldwide potential gross revenue of a billion dollars. In broadcasting and hotels, I had over $31 million in present or planned contracts, despite my still limited staff: Joyce, Irene Hiemer (who handled Canada and cruise ships), Patrick Okebie, Maryann Pasante, and Francisco Serrador in Latin America. They also still sold Turner and MGM programs and films in the same region. I did not include Europe, handled by London, or the Pacific and Asia, now done through Bill Wells and Greg Ell in Sydney. Collectively, we were approaching $100 million, all of this from a market that hadn't *existed* six years earlier, and that Ted and others at TBS had given up on.

Most of the growth internationally was being done with a domestic CNN signal, but slowly more and more non-American news stories and weather reports were being added to our 24-hour CNNI signal. A concerted effort was being made to find non-American anchors. By 1991, CNN International had taken on a life of its own and became a separate unit within CNN. Plans were underway to develop 24-hour entertainment channels worldwide. In short, TBS had proved itself the pioneer in satellite television broadcasting on our planet. And I had experienced one of the wildest rides of my life, since I'd taken over the international work in late 1983. It had felt like an untethered space walk.

CNN was functioning as a major communications system between countries. Governments could monitor the world without cost to their taxpayers. And now, international advertising was following, enhancing businesses capable of worldwide distribution. CNN also tended to reinforce English as the international language. I thought that CNN would be a means to promote democracy as the preferred form of government in regions of the world that had not yet been given a choice. As much as CNN, as a tax-paying entity, did to promote Western civilization globally, it was paid in full by the promotion it received as the sole television news provider during the Gulf War.

* * * * *

I was now entering the final phase in CNN's global media revolution.

In February 1990, Ron Ciccone and I visited Senegal and the Ivory Coast. We planned to end our trip with a stay in Gabon, but Ron, ever careful, called ahead and found out that there was civil unrest and rioting in Gabon. We decided to return to Atlanta.

The headline that greeted me on arrival said that Ted Turner had spent $450 million to televise 47 National Football League games over a three-year period. TBS was now in 53 million U.S. homes, but I couldn't believe we were paying almost $10 million per game for pre-season games that were glorified practice events. Ted had two business gurus, Malone and Levin, each with his own cable interest to protect, coaching him in the negotiations. They must have been paranoid about ESPN's control of televised sports events, particularly since they were owned by the ABC network. Had Ted overpaid again? Nevertheless, I realized more clearly the level TBS had achieved as a broadcasting entity.

In February, I sent Ted a memo titled "An Off-the-Wall Idea." I attached a recent article from the *International Herald Tribune* on private television development in Poland. I also attached an article from *The Wall Street Journal's* European edition discussing Federal Reserve Board Chairman Alan Greenspan's comments on the need to find capital to modernize Eastern Europe. He said that it was "the most important financial issue of the decade." He also said, "Eastern Europe's anticipated appetite for capital—and the eagerness of the world investors to satisfy it—is forcing up long-term interest rates around the world."

I wrote in my memo that the people of the Eastern Bloc countries would become the new consumers of the world:

> It seems to me that this would be a good time for a broadcasting company to become involved in the development of Eastern bloc commercial television. It appears that the opportunities are there and the governments are willing to make concessions to foreign enterprises, particularly with those organizations that have television broadcasting know-how. With our reputation of cooperating with the Soviet Bloc, I think we would have an advantage with those countries. Whether we elect to participate as partners in these broadcast entities or perform management services, it could be a future profitable enterprise.
>
> The situation reminds me of the late 1960s when UHF television was considered a joke in broadcasting in the United States (as though we can forget). I can see where the Eastern Bloc television growth will eventually parallel, for example, West German television. The value of a West German broadcasting entity I can only guess at, probably $500 million+ U.S.
>
> It goes along with my feeling that we should have a separate international division that formulates policy and coordinates international efforts relative to other divisions involved in selling Turner products worldwide.

I sent copies to Terry McGuirk and others. I didn't hear about the subject of Eastern Europe again until two and a half years later. But Turner International was created a year later, in March 1991.

In June, I traveled to Toronto and Montreal to renew and develop new CNN broadcast agreements. In November, I returned to South Africa by way of Rio and met with Francisco Serrador. From South Africa, I flew to Harare, Zimbabwe, to attend an African technical convention, and for meetings with Zimbabwe Broadcasting Corporation and the Gliemans, who were helping me build inexpensive antennas in Africa.

I stayed at the Harare Sheraton Hotel, which is the only hotel I know of that can claim 200 percent occupancy. Here's how they do it: I arrived in Harare just after sunrise, exhausted from a British Airways flight from Johannesburg. When I asked for my reserved room, I was told that it was not available. I finally got it at 10 P.M. I found out later that the hotel used my room as a separate check-in for the British Airways crew that arrived with me that morning. They were sleeping and getting ready for their flight that evening. Thus, two guests used a single room within the same 24-hour period. The hotel management knew what was going on, and let the desk clerks lie to us all day and evening when the dozen or so paid reservations kept annoying the clerks demanding to know why the rooms were not available. The least they could have done was give us a discount.

* * * * *

In 1990, CNN became the victim of a business power play. Although the signal to Latin America was scrambled in 1987, the signals in other areas of the world went unscrambled until 1995, when TBS was forced to use an Indonesian domestic satellite to cover Southeast Asia.

In 1990 international satellites were used again as business "muscle." This time the strong-arming firm was not Intelsat, but was instead Hutchison-Whampoa. This Hong Kong firm leased all eight video transponders on AsiaSat, the new and powerful independent satellite covering Asia. Once the Intelsat monopoly was broken and independent satellite firms took root, some companies took advantage of limited transponder availability in order to force other companies into business arrangements they did not want, particularly when there were no severe government restrictions on monopolies in place in international commerce, as there were in individual countries.

Hutchison-Whampoa, controlled by local Hong Kong businessman Li Ka-shing and his family was a minority investor in AsiaSat. The eight transponders they controlled serviced 38 Asian countries and 2.7 billion people, more than half the world's population. Despite the poverty of over 90 percent of those who lived within the satellite's footprint and wouldn't be able to afford dishes, the opportunity for future program service was extraordinary. Li Ka-shing attempted to use his control of the AsiaSat transponders to force CNN into a partnership. Star-TV, Hutchison-Whampoa's television service, wanted to control CNN in its Asian and southern Asian footprint, including handling CNN sales within the area. Turner International (TI, begun in March 1991) and TBS did seriously consider giving in, in order to ensure coverage on the only available satellite in such an important region, but finally they decided not to capitulate to Star-TV.

I'm certain Li Ka-shing and his executives were surprised at TBS's refusal. They probably thought they had cleverly boxed TBS into a corner. Our alternative was to continue with the drifting Statsionar-12. It would be years before another satellite was put into orbit in the region. One of Star-TV's threats had been that it would replace CNN on its satellite with the BBC, which was eager to get into global competition with CNN.

While we waited for a new satellite, however, we were able to get on Palapa, a Southeastern Asian regional satellite originating in Indonesia. In order to get approval from the Indonesian government, TI promised that it would scramble CNN's signal at some future time.

This power play by Li Ka-shing and Star-TV failed, and it considerably weakened their own programming on AsiaSat. Advertising was not yet supporting the cost of the many transponders reserved for Star-TV, not to mention its other expenses. In 1993, Li Ka-shing sold Star-TV to Rupert Murdoch for over $500 million. Murdoch then became a major new player. Until then, he had been a minor player with European satellite interests emanating from England. Murdoch controlled the Star-TV AsiaSat monopoly when the Chinese failed to launch a competing satellite, Apstar, in 1994.

* * * * *

Most of the countries and continents where my pioneering efforts were focused had, by 1990, entered into an advanced stage of development. Exceptions were Africa, the Middle East, and southern Asia. I had just been to the last two. Before I headed to Africa in February, I asked for and got Ted to approve $1 million to aid in downlinking equipment for the poor African and Middle Eastern countries. I used the French government's installation of free antennas in French-speaking African countries to promote French-language programming and to forestall CNN's development as an example of the kind of resistance I was encountering in Africa. I was, in effect, asking Ted to do something the U.S. Department of State should have done, but, unlike France, the United States had no particular interest in Africa.

Ted had passed on to Russ Barry this request for $1 million to buy antennas for the 25 poorest countries. I sent projected income figures to show that we would get our money back. I explained that, since we wanted CNN to be seen in every country, and we wanted to be able to collect news from those countries, we had to assist certain ones in obtaining antennas. I mentioned also that CNN would be promoted in the Third World as the only news service that could supply information on a fully global scale:

> Worldwide commitment will enable TBS to be the only broad-cast entity that can supply total global advertising.
>
> The position we take with regard to these poorer nations will reflect in any ongoing statements that we might need to make relative to our relationship with South Africa. At the moment, our income from South African Broadcasting Corporation (SABC) is $1.2 million annually. In two years, I project an additional $6 million annually from hotels and cable. We have just been asked by a member of our Internal Audit department with regard to our relationship in South Africa regarding anti-apartheid sanctions laws in California, since we sell stock in that state. Troutman, Sanders, et al, has to prepare a report on our South Africa business relationships.
>
> My position has always been that there are two reasons for our involvement in South Africa. One is to bring CNN to the population, as we do in all other parts of the world. While this can be justified to a certain extent with regard to SABC, we may have difficulty in justifying it as far as hotels and cable go because of the amount of money involved. Second, our position is that

the money we receive from SABC funds the Soviet signal.

Pointing out our assistance to other African nations may become necessary.

Uganda is an example of how the present antenna expense is justified by looking at future income projections:

Uganda offered to pay $1,500 U.S. per month. Uganda is an extremely poor nation that has suffered a virtual holocaust under Idi Amin, who murdered hundreds of thousands of his own people. The country is struggling to recover from the devastation. Here, I would not want to accept the $1,500 U.S. I would prefer to reduce the license fee to $500 U.S. per month. The Ugandans would thus feel that they are making a contribution now that could be gradually increased as the economic situation improves.

I also sent Ted an article from *Broadcasting* magazine, pointing out that NBC had introduced an International Strategic Planning Unit. I knew it would not be long before our competition would surface. My plan was to finish most of the race while our competitors were still listening for the starter's gun to go off. All of my reasoning about the poorer countries was in line with Ted's personal goal of improving life on this planet.

Ted, had, in fact, launched a cartoon series, *Captain Planet,* in which the hero fights environmental villains. Ted also offered $500,000 in prizes for unpublished works of fiction on the subject of saving the planet. He forbade TBS employees from using the word *foreign,* which he said implied something unfamiliar and tended to create misunderstanding. Employees were to be fined $100 if they used the word, but I never heard of anyone being fined.

In July 1990, Ted received a letter from the Iranian Ambassador thanking him for the CNN coverage of a devastating earthquake in which thousands had been killed or injured and 500,000 left homeless. I immediately asked Ron Ciccone to contact the ambassador, since we had been trying to find a way into Iran.

In South Africa, CNN's talk show host Larry King was so popular that his program was moved from 5 A.M., a throw-away timeslot, to noon. This popularity enabled CNN to add other programs on SABC. Ted appeared on *Larry King Live* show and spoke with a caller from Johannesburg who was concerned that his signal would be scrambled. Ted explained that there were no plans at that time to scramble the signal in most of the world. Further, Ted didn't consider taking down CNN's unscrambled signal a case of pirating. It was no crime to watch CNN on a satellite dish.

Ted's comments changed our direction, since we had been moving toward scrambling the signal everywhere. Our financial survival was no longer in jeopardy. So I concentrated on expanding CNN regardless of how it was received, which did prove to work best for enhancing its global reach.

* * * * *

The Gulf War, which was to have major ramifications for CNN, began with Iraq's invasion of Kuwait on August 2, 1990. I had been there a year earlier and was convinced that Saddam Hussein did not understand world events. *Time* had put him on its cover, and he was considered by many to be the most dangerous man in the world. I had offered an antenna to Iraq-TV in the hope that CNN would convince the Iraqis of the problems they would face if they started a war. I believe Hussein watched CNN before I came to Iraq, but in May 1989, I didn't know that. I wanted get CNN news to him. Without Ron Ciccone I couldn't succeed. An arms dealer who wanted to be a consultant for CNN in the Middle East informed me that he could arrange for me to attend a dinner with Saddam for $U.S. 200,000 cash, later increased to $U.S. 400,000. I could just see the Accounting Department's reaction to: "Dinner with Saddam Hussein and his military advisors–$400,000."

So, for a change, I gave up on an idea. I'd wait for another one to come to me. In July 1990, after watching Diane Sawyer's interview with Saddam on ABC's *Prime Time*, I wrote to her. I explained our policy of permitting and encouraging heads of state, governmental bodies and so on to watch CNN:

> I was most impressed with your coverage and especially your handling of President Hussein. What you brought out, more than anything else, is something that I have learned throughout the world, and that is the lack of information and general understanding of

simple global news by major leaders. When President Hussein obviously did not know that President Bush could not punish those that speak harshly of him, it was shocking to your audience; but I understood. When he thought that American Indians were still kept on reservations, he exposed himself as a leader whose knowledge of the world ends at his own boundaries.

She sent me a handwritten note:

Fascinating letter–my thanks to you–and forge ahead in Iraq. I never underestimate what CNN can do.
    Best, Diane Sawyer

Shortly after this exchange, Iraq invaded Kuwait. I was appalled by the cruelty and slaughter of the invasion shown on the tapes that were smuggled out. Then, the diplomatic haggling began between Iraq and the United States and its allies over whether Iraq's armies would remain or leave Kuwait. There was concern that Saddam would invade Saudi Arabia next or stir up Islamic fundamentalists dissatisfied with secular governments, such as those in Iran, where the Shah had been toppled a decade earlier. The West had a sense at the time of impending turmoil in the Middle East.

Saddam tried to get media attention to offset the horrific stories about the invasion by staging press conferences in which he would pat the head of a nervous child to show how harmless and friendly he was. It was about this time that Jesse Jackson met with Hussein. And *he* didn't have to pay the $400,000 to dine with him! Jackson wrote in the *Boston Herald*:

As I stood in the lobby of the Kuwait International Hotel, across the street from the U.S. Embassy, I watched Iraqi soldiers, business people, civil servants and others gathered around television sets viewing and studying events as they unfolded live on Cable News Network television.

This is a totally new phenomenon–international diplomacy by live television. When President Bush conducts a press conference in Kennebunkport Maine, carried live by CNN, it is beamed straight into Kuwait and into the government palace in Iraq to Saddam Hussein.

This was when I knew for sure that Hussein was watching CNN. Then something strange occurred. I was in my Atlanta office one morning when Joyce buzzed me. "You're not going to believe this, but Iraq-TV is on the phone," she said.

I quickly picked up the phone. It was the Director of Iraq Television, Said Al-Bazzaz, whom I had met during my stay in that country. "Mr. Pike, His Excellency, the President of Iraq, the Honorable Saddam Hussein, wishes to speak to the American people."

I couldn't believe it. Suddenly I was the contact Saddam was using to fulfill his wish to appear on CNN. I had no problem getting them to hold while I spoke to the CNN International desk, on the other line.

It was only minutes after I connected Iraq Television with the CNNI news desk that I saw "The Honorable President of Iraq" on my television monitor justifying his invasion of Kuwait. When I transferred that call to the CNN International Desk, I thought that was the end of the part I would play. It wasn't. The next day, Iraq Television called me again. I couldn't understand why it hadn't taken the International Desk's number, but, apparently, since calling me had given it the results they wanted, it repeated the ritual.

Some might ask: What are you doing helping a tyrant get propaganda access to the world? But that is precisely what CNN is all about: a conduit for all sides to air their views. Years later, just after the start of the new millennium, when Palestinian leader Yassar Arafat refused Israel's generous offer at the Camp David meetings with Prime Minister Barak and President Clinton, Arafat instead embarked on a new "*intifada*" of murderous suicide bombings in the misguided hope that he would force Israeli Jews to relocate to another part of the world. CNN was accused by Israel of favoring the Palestinian side by the amount of reporting of Israel's reprisals. There was even talk of removing CNN from the cable systems in that country. Eason Jordan, Senior Vice President of News Gathering, made a personal visit to Israel in 2002 to assuage the delicate situation.

What was not reported by the news media following the story: numerous Arab television stations submitted biased news to CNN while Israel's singular efforts were minimal by comparison. Again, in 2003, after the Iraq war, Jordan ran into a buzz saw when he wrote in an op-ed article in the *New York Times* that he held back stories that would put

CNN reporters or their Iraqi associates at risk. Franklin Foer, in a *Wall Street Journal* piece on April 14, along with other news organizations, lambasted Jordan for not pulling CNN out of Baghdad and trying to work around the dilemma. This is a serious problem that must be confronted by all worldwide news media. Outside certain Western countries there is no legal redress. CNN should have accepted the results of its refusal to conform and become a martyr in the eyes of the world when they were forced to leave and report from Kuwait and Jordan. There were still enough tie-ins from other sources to maintain competent coverage from Baghdad.

The *real* bottom line: What are the global news organizations going to do collectively to insure that such manipulation and use of power by a host government is not used against any legitimate news service? I didn't see any of the letters and editorials that criticized Jordan address this unresolved issue.

During the five months of troop buildup in Saudi Arabia called Desert Shield, until the final and inevitable stage of the Desert Storm military assault in early 1991, CNN remained the primary source of information about the conflict. In many ways CNN provided governments with intelligence previously obtained only by other means. It was mixed with propaganda and often delivered in self-serving speeches, but it was not hard for either the viewer or the intelligence expert to separate the wheat from the chaff.

In January 1991, after the Allied Forces had begun their offensive against Iraq, something else occurred. The CNN International Desk received another call, this time a request for Libya's Moammar Gadhafi to address the American people. The person on the Desk thought it was a crank call and hung up. The caller rang again. "Don't hang up! Don't hang up! We will put Moammar Gadhafi on the satellite, and you can see for yourself." Sure enough, there he was. The fact that he rambled on and on wasn't the point. Both Gadhafi and Hussein knew CNN was *their access*, to the United States and the world.

During the war we received a phone call from Bahrain's assistant to the Minister of Information asking if Bahrain television could extend its CNN signal outside the Bahrain borders and into Saudi Arabia so that certain Allied military units could watch CNN. We sent back a fax immediately:

Permission granted. U.S. and Allied military personnel contacted our office for the same reason and received the same answer. When the 101st Airborne in Saudi Arabia asked for permission to carry CNN and it was granted, it wanted to know how much it cost. No charge, of course. During Operation Desert Shield and Desert Storm, we granted requests worldwide to watch CNN and asked no remuneration. "I'm sorry," the Airborne caller said. "I'm not permitted to accept free gifts." "Okay," I replied. "The cost is one dollar per month."

Do you know what we went through to invoice the U.S. Department of Defense for that $1.00? We had to study the *Code of Federal Regulations.* There are 50 titles in 200 volumes. The cost in paperback is $620. Plus, we had the Billing Department's overhead. Why couldn't they just have taken CNN when we offered it free?

Frequently, Joyce was forced to make decisions in my absence. As she tells it:

> Desert Storm had just started. All of the executives left to go to a meeting in San Francisco. The phone rang. It was Shahid Ahmad calling from Pakistan. He said that Pakistan Television (not a CNN affiliate) had called him. They were going on the air with their news in exactly 20 minutes and wanted to know if they could carry Desert Storm from CNN. There was no one I could ask. Sidney Pike, as well as everyone else, was in the air on a plane. So I told Mr. Ahmad to keep talking for a few minutes while I decided what to do.
>
> He did exactly that, chatting about inconsequential things. I decided that we had to do this and told him to advise PTV they could carry CNN Desert Storm coverage. He graciously thanked me and hung up the phone.
>
> Mr. Pike called me as soon as he arrived at his hotel and I told him what I had done. His response? "You were exactly right. It's precisely what I would have done." Then Mr. Ahmad called me back and said, "PTV is amazed that CNN could make this decision in such a short time!"
>
> Later in the day Ron Ciccone called in, and I told him what I had done. He advised me to send Mr. Ahmad a message so

that the permission would be in writing, and he suggested I use my official (payroll) title—Manager of International Administration. I did this.

Hey, I got to make an executive decision!

No Iraqi requests were received during the war, but the same permission would have been given. CNN had to be *neutral. It must show at all times that it is not an American news entity.*

In the past, our CNN breaking-news service to television systems, which was part of our agreements with them, had meant a few minutes or hours when a global event was unfolding. We had covered a volcanic eruption, an assassination and the Tian An Men Square protests. A television station could interrupt its programming and carry CNN for as long as it chose. We never imagined that breaking news would last for weeks!

I and millions of others couldn't get away from the television screen when CNN was presenting the events from Baghdad as they happened. Bernard Shaw and his colleagues, Peter Arnett and John Holliman, were reporting *live from under the bed in their hotel room in the midst of the Allied bombing in Baghdad!* Daily at 10:00 A.M. we got the Allied military updates. CNN was being watched by the world.

I couldn't take my eyes off the screen, not until the Allied Forces had driven the Iraqi Army from Kuwait, decimated Saddam's Republican Guard, and the conflict had abruptly ended. The abrupt end turned out to be a political blunder allowing Hussein to remain in power and lead directly to the U.S. invasion in 2003. For me, it was more than an event on CNN. It was the culmination of more than seven years of developing CNN globally. If we had done nothing else, we had accomplished what I had seen as the reason, the *need* for CNN on international satellites. CNN had become a forum where the principals in a war could communicate. For the world's population, it was a way of seeing immediately the horrors and consequences of armed conflict.

This major event, which the media types said was "ideally suited for television," was the first profound demonstration of what news coverage could mean in the age of global satellites.

The fact that the Gulf War, in effect, promoted CNN beyond our wildest dreams and extended it even farther globally didn't hurt either.

CHAPTER THIRTY-FOUR

The Management Shuffle and Other Dance Steps

Every human being, but especially the adult, prefers to keep on believing what he already believes, and to accept ideas only when they reinforce the ideas he already has. He tends, in other words, to become less and less intellectually curious, to have a more and more closed mind as he grows older.

—Charles Adrian

Ron Ciccone arranged for Ted and me to attend the African-American Institute Awards Dinner held at the United Nations in October 1990. Ted was seriously involved with Jane Fonda, and she and her daughter were with him at the dinner. It was the first time I met her. We were seated next to each other and chatted during the evening. I did not bring up the fact that when she had traveled to Atlanta during the Vietnam War and had sought opportunities to appear on television, I had been the one responsible for her *not* appearing on Channel 17. It happened this way: We invited her to appear on a local talk show. As station manager, I insisted that the local Congressional representative, Fletcher Thompson, a strong pro-Vietnam War advocate, appear with her so that Ms. Fonda's views would be balanced. When Jane learned of my intent, she refused to appear. (If she reads this book, she'll know who prevented her first association with Turner Broadcasting).

* * * * *

In July 1990 we added three countries to our growing list: Kenya, Kuwait, and Pakistan, where Shahid Ahmad was our representative. When Shahid came to Atlanta, we always had a rug available so that he could say his prayers after lunch in a room we set aside for him.

The Pakistan agreement was with People's Television Network (PTN). It could take eight hours of CNN per day, any eight hours it wanted, as a block or spread out over the day. The Pakistanis, who spoke English in a sing-song way, used CNN as a means to improve their English. Many people stayed up most of the night just to watch CNN.

One time, People's Television Network decided to run the entire hour of *Larry King Live.* The program that day happened to be about lesbians. The Pakistanis watched it carefully. As soon as the program was over, Ahmad's phone began to ring; the Pakistanis had no idea what this program was about. Apparently, they have no language equivalent for the word "lesbian." The English newspaper felt called upon to run a front-page article the next day explaining the program.

* * * * *

In October 1990, a management shuffle took place. Gerry Hogan, President of Turner Entertainment Network (TEN), left to join Whittle Communications. Hogan had been the Number Two person after Ted. Hogan's duties were taken over by Terry McGuirk, who was named Executive Vice President of TBS. Scott Sassa took over Hogan's duties as head of the SuperStation and TNT, became President of Turner Entertainment Network (TEN), and received a seat on the Executive Committee. Another new member of this committee was Julia Sprunt Grumbles, in charge of TBS advertising and promotion and married to Bill Grumbles, head of TPS. The Grumbles family had a powerful two-vote bloc.

McGuirk's new position made him titular head of the Executive Committee and responsible for day-to-day operations, especially in Ted's absence. Ted also gave McGuirk the responsibility for directing the flow of company information to the public, so that news of profits and cash flow would help Wall Street brokers look favorably on TBS stock.

Knowing Ted, I'm certain there was no question in his mind that he was still running the company, but by this time, especially after this shuffle, it did not seem that way to me. The year 1991 began with Bill Grumbles in his new role as president of Turner Program Services, which, in March, became Turner International. Bill Grumbles had a limited background in the motion picture and television industry. He had worked in cable and for Home Box Office (HBO). He was a thin man with a pasty white complexion and reddish hair who spoke in a soft voice and never seemed confident about what he was doing. Marriage to Julia Sprunt brought him to Atlanta. Rumor held that Terry McGuirk did not want to lose Sprunt, who headed TBS Public Relations, so he offered her husband a position at TBS. Grumbles was hired in 1989 as executive vice president of Turner Network Sales, responsible for selling the company's channels to cable operators. In 1991 he replaced McGuirk as head of Cable Sales, in addition to taking over TPS.In 1993, Grumbles was sent upstairs as vice president of World Distribution, and John Agnoli was hired as TI president.

Neither Russ Barry, whom he replaced, nor Grumbles himself, knew very much about international sales, but in the early 1990s, not many executives did. When John Agnoli was hired in 1993, Turner searched for an executive with international experience, and Agnoli's had been extensive with Citibank, R. J. Reynolds, and Colgate-Palmolive in Europe. He had no television experience, but his function was primarily administrative.

I liked Agnoli. He listened, which was all I asked, but he didn't last long and was later replaced by Bob Ross, TBS's legal advisor, and to whom I turned for support in the early phase of CNN's global development.

When I first met Grumbles in 1991, I offered to help in any way I could because he so obviously lacked international experience. I analyzed for him everything I was involved in, as well as detailing what each member of my team did. He was bright and a quick learner, but he had no imagination whatsoever. I doubt that he had ever had a new idea. He didn't like controversy. His office was impeccably clean; there were no pictures or objects on his desk or wall shelves.

It wasn't long before some key people left, whom I thought Grumbles needed, but he couldn't accept their idiosyncrasies. The people who replaced them had MBAs and were sound administrators, but like their new boss, they were visionless and uncreative. CNN's growth internationally contin-ued, but it was mainly due to earlier momentum.

Unfortunately, by the early-1990s, TBS had reached the point where ideas no longer had value. Conforming to company policy did. Our execu-tive parking lot had the usual number of BMWs. One day, Terry McGuirk parked a new Jeep Cherokee in his spot. A month later, I noticed a spank-ing new Range Rover in Bill Grumbles' parking space. My eight-year-old Chrysler New Yorker didn't fit in anymore. The era of SUVs had begun. Had I applied for a job at Turner in the early-1990s, I would have been rejected. No college degree. Nor did Ted have one. He had gone to Brown University but been kicked out. Fortunately for Turner, in 1971, the issue was whether Ted and I could *save* the company. And we did, largely because of my experience in broadcasting. The qualities I brought to Turner are dif-ficult to assess on the standard job application today. The requirement of a college degree ignores the fact that many talented people with imagination, stamina, aggressiveness, and a dedication to work are the best people for the job.

* * * * *

Once the 100-hour Persian Gulf War ended in late February 1991, there was never again a need to explain what CNN was in any part of the world. Although current affairs pundits and editors wrote glowing commentary about CNN's coverage, there was criticism, too, especially of Peter Arnett. He had remained in Baghdad when other journalists had either been forced to leave or had voluntarily run for the border when the air bombardment of the capital was about to begin. Some paid $1,000 for a car ride to Jor-dan; $100 had been the going rate. But Arnett stayed, armed with the new satellite phone, although his reporting was done under the scrutiny of Iraqi censors. Even though the CNN screen flashed this fact, some com-mentators objected to Arnett's reports because of it. His coverage of the bombed milk factory particularly irked the Allies, who claimed the factory was merely a front for biological weapons manufacture.

Unfortunately, Arnett, who left CNN and worked for National Geo-graphic and the CNBC network at the time of the Iraq War in 2003, ran into even more serious problems when he allowed himself to be interviewed, at the request of the Minister of Information, by Iraq Television. Arnett gave answers to questions that presumably satisfied the ministry and what he may have thought was Iraq local television, but the interview was broadcast by the Arab 24-hour television service, Al Jazeera, worldwide. He was dismissed as a result.

In 1991, a bipartisan group of 39 lawmakers in Washington attacked CNN's war coverage from Iraq. Senate Republican Minority Whip Alan Simpson charged that Arnett was a "sympathizer" to Saddam's cause. Not only Arnett came under fire in 1991. CNN's anchorman Bernard Shaw, who was also in Baghdad when the war began, refused to be debriefed by the U.S. Intelligence Service in Jordan. Shaw said it was not his role to give information to either side. Shaw was one of the first African-Americans to hold a leading anchor position on a major news network, and he became known for his intelligence, hard work, and dedication. He soon became a role model for Africans and other aspiring black reporters worldwide.

In a *Variety* article, Shaw said he would do the same thing, "again and again and again," adding that he would "not want the world to think I am a spy or our CNN people are spies."

While no one in Congress was advocating censorship of the media, even in wartime, it appeared there was a difference between censorship and advocacy. The prominent U.S. mainstream media conformed to a recognized practice during war of supporting the government's decisions, because their signal was only seen in the United States. In the 2003 Iraq war FOX News and CNBC were seen outside the United States. CNBC had its own international news channel seen mostly in Europe and Asia, but Fox presented in its many interview shows a perverted view of America with its emphasis on crime and pornography. This warped view shown throughout the Middle East and the world aided the terrorist recruitment considerably. All American TV media seen outside the U.S., including CNN, in constantly reporting visually the strength of the anti-war movement in the U.S. strengthened the terrorists resolve to recruit and fight because the American history in Vietnam and Somalia proved that the American public could not withstand a protracted war and continuing losses in personnel. Can a free nation support a television news service dedicated to unbiased reporting on an international rather than a national level? The answer better be yes.

CNN bears an awesome responsibility not to be forced into *conforming* to the propaganda control of countries that threaten to force them to leave. Nevertheless, Gulf War I was the first war ever, internationally speaking, in which the news was presented in an unbiased, or at least non-nationalist, way. Prior to this, neither CNN nor any other international news service had been challenged about its loyalty to its own government. During World War II, all the news services were loyal to the Allied or the Axis powers. The BBC certainly was.

By 1991, CNN had worked for a decade to reassure the world that its coverage was world coverage, not U.S. coverage. We needed those television and cable services all over the world to trust that we were unbiased. I had always insisted, wherever I went, that CNN was neutral. *I had rarely been believed.* Gradually this changed, but it was the coverage of the Gulf War by CNN that proved it beyond a doubt to the rest of the world. It was CNN alone during the war in Baghdad. It was Shaw refusing to be debriefed. In both Gulf wars, CNN reported both sides of the story, despite the handicap of Iraq's censorship. In 1991, the air time given to Saddam and Gadhafi to express their views to the world, and the criticisms by governments and media services of Arnett and Shaw, put an end to any need on my part to claim that CNN was a truly international service. Of course, all this was new, and it was hard for the Congress and most Americans to understand that the world needed a neutral news service.

* * * * *

Despite CNN's determination to report the news objectively all the time, there were still individual countries that tried to censor live news feeds. A letter appeared in May 1991 in the *Pakistan Times*:

> CNN was coming with a lot of fanfare and of all things my TV set was just out of order. Then with more pain than expenses, I could get it back to life. But something went wrong with my antenna or the direction or both; I could not watch even the trial runs. Fortunately, or unfortunately, everything was ready and I was now able to watch the much awaited CNN programs. I sat

leisurely on my best sofa in an expansive mood. A new world was about to take shape.

In fact, I caught up with Mr. Bush looking hale and hearty after a brush with his hospital. All right, very fine. Then some news from here and there. But suddenly, a very beautiful young lady with somewhat low neck dress appeared and in a split second some multi-colored cubes covered the screen. I thought naively that this must have been a part of the show as these cubes were moving up and down, right and left but did not make any sense, at least to me. After 10-15 seconds these cubes vanished and a male was seen making his good or bad comments. The programme continued on various topics and then, after a few minutes, another young lady appeared but some cubes again covered her totally. This game continued for 10 seconds or more. I felt deprived of the sight of a shapely lady, a rarity in this part of the world, although no offence is meant.

While I continued to watch TV for about two hours, this game of hide and seek continued but now it penetrated my thick neck that these cubes were not somebody's display of aesthetic sense but some thicker necks had decided to censor God's best creature from their own points of view and protect other mortals from further moral bankruptcy.

No wonder why people call us fundamentalists and we are galled by it, rather we must be grateful to them for calling us just that because we are simply worse. What is obscenity and what is not is entirely a matter of relativity.

But in my case if I have to watch these cubes most of the time, then my TV set is for sale.

That wasn't the only surprise I had from Pakistan. A clothing tag was mailed to me that had been removed from underwear. It read: "CNN International. Excellent Quality. Innovative Style. 100% Guaranteed."

There were still some countries—India, Saudi Arabia, Iraq, Iran—that did everything possible to keep their people from having access to any information besides their own propaganda. In an article titled "The Karachi Line—The Freedom to Know," Dr. Mervyn Hosein wrote in 1991:

In the Third World, where basic human rights are either denied or suppressed, the most effective method of keeping a people subjugated (short of actual physical intimidation) is to limit access to information. This is done in four ways. One is to provide a progressively poorer quality of education. This restricts the development of talent and increases the pool of incompetents, ignorants and the poor. The second method is to censor or restrict the publication or airing of material that the leaders feel is 'undesirable' or 'harmful' for their people. The third technique is an extension. The 'ban' in the 'national interest.' What you don't know won't hurt us! The fourth aspect is disinformation. This can range from the subliminal and utterly subtle to the grossly crude. What we preach is gospel truth; what the other does is propaganda, lies, fabrication.

It is only when people are aware that they can make conscious and rational decisions based on choice, fact and having options. That they may not make rational choices is their option but that is what 'informed consent' is all about. It is for the people to make those decisions not for hustlers who sway the mobs with promises of glory or threats of damnation. But people can only pause to think when they have alternate options to think about. That is where access to information is so vital for the people of Pakistan and so damaging to the interests of those who would keep us in the Middle Ages. Information is Education. The greater the sources of information the greater the educational impact. The greatest thing that has happened to Pakistan is this information explosion that has reached out to millions of our homes and is battering its way into our closed and shuttered minds. The gyrating, fleshy, Pakistani heroines or the multi-colored squares that are the censors' replacement for what would otherwise corrupt us only make the obvious or unattainable more tantalizing. Calls for a ban on CNN have been numerous, largely from religious and feudal quarters. Not because they fear that information, however biased, can destroy us but because, if allowed to flow in freely, that very information will soon make them redundant in a more aware nation. People

see and hear what they wish to believe. Let them have the choice
to see and hear more and more. 'Then it must follow as the night
the day,' that belief will be tempered with logic, understanding
and reason. That is the base for progress. That is where the real
power lies. And for those who still wish to stay in the dark there
remains the choice to switch off the television.

I could not have said it better. This had been *my* vision—that the people of the world should have free access to the information that affected
their lives.

* * * * *

Although I added two more to our small staff in 1992 to help cover Africa
with its many emerging nations, most of the development of CNN internationally was now being done on the administrative level. I hired George
Amoah, a native of Ghana, who had received permission from the Ghana
government to build a cable system. He called us initially to arrange to
have CNN on his cable service. He worked diligently building his system,
and the day he turned the service on, he was so excited he called us to say
that it worked perfectly the first time. He was ready for CNN.

Less than a week later, the Ghana government took over his cable system and never reimbursed him. George was, in effect, tricked into establishing a cable system when no one else in Ghana was capable of doing it.
He said his satisfaction came from knowing that he had built it and that it
worked. In 1992, I also hired Edward Boateng, another native of Ghana,
who had been working at the Coca-Cola world headquarters in Atlanta.
Boateng moved with Ron Ciccone to London and worked on our team
developing CNN in Africa. Amoah eventually left us for Black Entertainment Television (BET).

I took one final field trip in November 1991 to southern Asia. In Pakistan,
in order to keep the support for CNN strong, Shahid Ahmad had arranged
for me to meet with Prime Minister Mian Muhammad Nawaz Sharif, the
successor to Benazir Bhutto, who, unlike her counterpart in India, had
been determined to make CNN a means of access for Pakistan to the international community. Bhutto had wisely understood how CNN and the

Pakistan Prime Minister Mian Muhammad Nawaz Sharif invites the author to dinner at the palace. Shahid Ahmad on the far right and his wife second from left.

satellites' two-way connection could strengthen her country internationally in its business, education, and political relationships.

The Indian government still resisted us, but its efforts were doomed to fail. The construction of antennas and the pirating of CNN continued unabated. Whereas Ahmad in Pakistan had been close to those in power, Damodaran, in India, was an ordinary businessman with nothing like Ahmad's influence and unable to persuade his prime minister of the need to become part of the global picture.

By late 1991, I had run out of continents. Admittedly, the long flights and endless airport waiting had taken their toll on me. Knowing that I was making CNN a force for informing the planet of its news and conditions had provided me with the inspiration and motivation to keep going. Lill understood how I felt and had never asked me to find a role at Turner that would keep me in Atlanta. My very success was making this decision for me. Each of the areas I developed needed more attention and servicing. By late 1991, CNN International sales was part of the new Turner International and its future development of other TBS channels worldwide.

I flew to London and turned over my files on southern Asia and the Middle East to Ron Ciccone. He had become the company expert on

Africa and the Middle East, and was persuaded by Bill Grumbles to work full time from London.

I made my last trip to South Africa in early 1992. To say goodbye to my good friend, Fernando Carrilho in Cape Verde, I took a South African Air flight from New York that stopped to refuel on his tiny island. The large, lumbering 747 landed on the tarmac at 3:00 A.M., in front of the building where Fernando was waiting. I had already received permission from the captain to disembark during the refueling. As we embraced and said goodbye above the roaring of the turbines a few feet away, I felt a great sadness. I was saying goodbye to all the Fernandos I had met and loved during the last nine years, the most intense, dramatic, and rewarding period of my life.

After my visit to South Africa for a final CNN agreement, I continued on to Mauritius, an island south of Africa in the Indian Ocean. I pushed the Mauritius' button to put CNN on its television station. As though it had been specially arranged, a CNN anchor was the first image we all saw. He said, "This is Brian Nelson and the news." That was just the way I wanted to finish my nine-year global assignment.

CHAPTER THIRTY-FIVE

Joint Ventures and Adventures in Russia and Eastern Europe

Committees are, by nature, timid. They are based on the premise of safety in numbers; content to survive inconspicuously, rather than take risks and move independently ahead, without independence, without the freedom for new ideas to be tried, to fail, and to ultimately succeed, the world will not move ahead, but live in fear of its own potential.

—**Prof. Dr. Ferry Porsche**

At the TBS annual meeting in June 1992, Ted announced that the company's global strategies were about to intensify. Shareholders and analysts were trying to figure out what he meant by this when he added that British Sky Broadcasting's satellite network, a subsidiary of Rupert Murdoch's News Corporation, lost over a billion dollars.

"But," Ted went on, "the cost for entry is lower now than it's been." While he predicted slower growth for TBS's domestic business overall, he said, "In the rest of the world, with privatization of television, opportunities are attractive and our future does look bright."

One commentator, Janet Stilson, noted in *Multichannel News*:

To date, TBS international activities have largely been line-extensions of domestic networks, such as CNN International and Turner Network Television, with relatively small investments needed. The Cartoon Network will join that line-extension group in October when it launches in South America simultaneous with a U.S. debut.

The new expansion activity Turner alluded to, however, is likely to involve regionalized channels involving considerably more financial backing possibly supplied by outside local partners, some speculate.

This was in line with comments made by CNN President Tom Johnson in *Variety*:

CNN, facing tougher competition in the global marketplace, will focus much of its attention on CNN Intl. during the next five years, including the possible creation of country-specific CNN configurations. To shore up the company's international wing, CNN will look for new programming, bureaus, satellite distribution systems and alliances with other international broadcasters, and will spend additional dollars on marketing and promotion.

Ted had apparently decided that, since domestic growth was expected to be limited, TBS's future expansion would be related to the international marketplace.

In the nine years that I had been spearheading CNN globally, we had crossed the threshold of pay-as-you-go into an investment that included satellites, offices, and personnel worldwide for handling agreements and co-ventures. The success of my work, as well as the burgeoning success of other TBS international channels, was not lost on Ted. He was keenly aware of the potential growth in the global economy. Nor was Ted uncomfortable with developing businesses in countries with shaky economies, such as the newly emerging nations of Eastern Europe and Russia. He had always taken weak enterprises and molded them into highly successful businesses. If Ted believed he could succeed, then he spared no effort and held back no financial support. By 1992, however, there were executives in powerful positions within TBS who did not agree with this philosophy.

One day before the 1992 annual TBS meeting in Atlanta, at 8:35 A.M., when I had just arrived at my office, the phone rang. Joyce buzzed me. "It's Ted," she said, a note of warning in her voice. I picked up the phone.

"Siddddddd—How ya doin'? Got a minute?"

"Sure, Ted. I'll be right up."

Ted's office in the CNN Center was on the top floor of the 14-story office building. It was at the end of a long hall of connecting offices.

The first thing Ted usually said when I came into his office was "How's Lill?" Or "How's your tennis?" He asked, "Still playing?"

"Sure, Ted," I said, "still playing singles." I didn't want there to be a question about my physical shape. Ted smiled, and we got down to business. He was interested in joint ventures in Eastern Europe and Russia. Could I work on them? He didn't know what that entailed, didn't have a clue where to begin, except for one joint venture plan with Edward Saga-layev of Moscow Independent Broadcasting Company (MIBC) to operate his Channel 6. Ted had also met the owner of a Greek television network that was interested in partners for developing television in Eastern Europe. This man had a plan for an arrangement with Romania. That was it.

"I'll have to start with a visit to Athens and Moscow and see what I can develop," I said. Ted agreed, and that was the end of our discussion. I suspected this might be my last major project for Ted. A project of this size would take many years, and I was close to my 65th birthday. Had I known what lay ahead, I would never have embarked on this new venture. My senior years were not made easier by it.

That afternoon, Ted called a meeting in his office. Terry McGuirk, Bill Grumbles, Bob Ross and I were present. Ted outlined his joint venture concept and the assignment he had just given me. To reassure these executives that I was still physically capable of completing this obviously rigorous task despite my age, he threw in that I was still playing tennis. Ted did all the talking; no one else spoke unless Ted asked a specific question. But this was typical of meetings I'd attended in Ted's office. The real surprise came after the meeting.

I quickly became aware that all three men were upset. I couldn't understand why. As we moved slowly down the hall, they stopped occasionally and said things like, "Waste of money!" Or "We need that money for other projects." It was not the first time I'd heard people object to Ted's mandates, but McGuirk, Grumbles, and Ross were extremely resistant to Ted's solution for getting the company growing again. We had a reputation for being a highly innovative growth company, and now our stock was languishing. Why couldn't they see that?

I reminded myself that I had been out in the field for so many years that perhaps I read the executives wrong and shouldn't be concerned. In the past, even when other executives objected privately, they would still come together and do exactly what Ted wanted, giving it their all to assure the success of the new project.

I went back to my office to plan how I would go about developing one more venture with no roadmap to follow. This time, I did have experience in the international arena, good contacts with television executives all over the world, and had become sensitive to non-American methods of television management.

A few weeks later I read the Janet Stilson article I quoted earlier. She also said,

> One European country that has been a thorn in the side of most international services, Germany, has become a little less troublesome for Cable News Network. In Germany, the regulating authority that controls a large share of the cable system business, Bundesposte Telekom, requires networks to pay systems fees for carriage. CNN opted to lose its position in the 300,000 household Munich system last year when it could no longer avoid these fees after a four-month test period.

The article explained further how local cable advertising would help CNN in "relaunching in Munich, sidestepping the fees in the process." Apparently, CNN International had an agreement with a local company to sell advertising on the network, and this company would then pay the program carriage fees to Bundesposte Telekom, according to Mark Rudolph, Managing Director of CNN International Sales.

This was the first time I could recall a cable system demanding payment from program suppliers for television channel exposure rather than paying them as they did everywhere else in the world. In the United States, payment from fees charged to subscribers by cable companies to program suppliers was the foundation of the industry. Approximately 50 percent of revenue to support the cost of programming came from subscriptions and the other 50 percent from advertising. To do this special advertising, the Munich authorities were allowing CNN to break into its feed "with local advertising spots every 29 and 59 minutes in the hour."

This seemed a patchwork solution to a vexing problem. Because of the exploding potential for subscription fees all over Europe, as well as in the rest of the world, I would have agreed with the Discovery Channel that had chosen to withdraw its programming from Germany. Since I had not been privy to the reasons why CNNI had to have Germany, I assumed that all the ramifications had been weighed and the decision to give in had been made for a good reason. I did wonder what alternatives there might have been. Although the German dilemma seemed distant from the Eastern Europe project, I made a mental note to learn more about the outcome. Its complicated issues could affect the international development of cable, especially its program providers. I didn't realize then that it would ultimately affect my project.

Scott Sassa, the new head of the SuperStation, TNT, and TEN, and his assistant, Charlotte Leonard, who was in charge of programming for the Latin American TNT feed, were asked to help me in developing programming for Channel 6 in Moscow.

Since Ted had again emphasized spending as little money as possible, I tried to think of ways of financing the Channel 6 start-up. I thought of wrestling events in Moscow and in other Russian cities that we could advertise. Scott Sassa seemed to like this idea, and I made a note to bring it up in Moscow.

Bob Ross was working on a business plan for Moscow that I would take with me. Stu Loory, who had previously been CNN Bureau Chief in Moscow and had helped Ted ingratiate himself with the Russian bureaucrats locally and nationally, spoke passable Russian and was an obvious choice to introduce me to the players and the country. The two key players were Edward Sagalayev and his brother-in-law, Nugzar Popkhadze. Stu Loory sent me a report about both.

Sagalayev headed the News Department on Gostelradio, and his programming was known for bold investigative reporting and commentary. He was also President of the Russian Union of Journalists and Chairman of the Advisory Committee on Programming of Ostankino Television.

Ostankino was the state-run television network. When he was asked to choose between Ostankino and MIBC, Sagalayev chose Ostankino, but he did not actually leave MIBC, which became clear on May 20 when he joined Ted in the studio to turn on Channel 6. This came as a surprise to Yegor Yakovlev, Chairman of Ostankino, and Mikhail Poltaranin, the Russian Minister of Information.

Sagalayev and Poltaranin were political rivals. Gorbachev had nominated Sagalayev to the chairmanship of Ostankino to replace the man who had sided with the 1991 coup plotters. But Yeltsin, who had put down the coup, objected to the appointment. He wanted a voice in all major appointments since he had saved Gorbachev's neck. The man acceptable to both Gorbachev and Yeltsin was Yakovlev. Later, when Yakovlev ran into trouble at Ostankino because he had no television experience (he had been editor of the pro-Gorbachev *Moscow News*), Sagalayev was hired again as Director General.

In May 1992, Sagalayev was:

1. Director General of the largest television network in the country, with an audience of 150 million households.
2. Chairman of the Union of Journalists of Russia, a powerful organization representing all the print and broadcast journalists in the country.
3. President of the MIBC, which could become a powerful, independent voice completely outside the control of the Yeltsin government. It would draw its revenue from advertising, not from the traditional state sources.

Poltaranin, Yeltsin's information minister, and Yakovlev, responsible for a new revenue base for Ostankino, were both anxious about Sagalayev's rise to power as a television entrepreneur.

Nugzar Popkhadze was a Georgian and protégé of Eduard Shevardnadze, former Soviet Foreign Minister. Nugzar was chairman of the Georgian Gosteleradio when Shevardnadze was head of the Communist Party in Georgia. Nugzar came to Moscow in the 1980s when Gorbachev brought Shevardnadze there. Nugzar worked in the Communist Party Central Committee apparatus and was considered an important man. Henry Yushkiavitshus, former deputy chairman of Gosteleradio, in whose apartment I stayed, spoke very highly of him.

In our role as partner, we provided Channel 6 access to our MGM-RKO film library and our management experience in programming, finance, and advertising sales. In 1991, communism had fallen in the Soviet Union, and the state was ending both its financial subsidies and the television license fees the government had collected from the public and had paid to the state television channels. It was incumbent on the television networks to fund their survival through advertising revenue.

I learned that advertising was so new to both the state and independent channels in many East European countries that some pretty strange things happened. In the selling of ads, and even in the employer-employee relationships, they did not know how to sell advertising time and to define what employees could and couldn't do. Certain salespeople actually sold ads for themselves, because some camera people did their own stories or provided their services to outside sources— common business practices in Russia that did not exactly meet the ethical standards that were normal in the West.

My plan was to organize a "SWAT team" of experienced specialists to help in areas of programming and operations, finance and accounting, and advertising sales. I already had a commitment from Gene Wright to supply a technical specialist for brief periods whenever there was a need for engineering services. I also had people looking for dubbing equipment, since I assumed a large expense would be the dubbing of films into Russian. I couldn't arbitrarily take the specialists I needed away from their day-to-day work and keep them headquartered in Moscow and running around Eastern Europe to help emerging television stations.

I contacted John Barbera, head of Turner's Advertising Sales Division, and told him of our plans—there was not a lot of enthusiasm for advertising potential in Russia and Europe—the ad sales executives were preoccupied with how to meet the budgets for the current and following year. They saw no reason to plan for several years ahead.

Kay Delaney, in charge of international ad sales, had taken over from Dietz Ginzel, who had begun selling international advertising around the time I started distributing CNN internationally. Dietz found it hard to interest advertisers then, partly, I felt, because the international pioneers like Procter & Gamble and Coca-Cola had not yet made that leap to thinking of television by satellite as a new advertising medium. They needed CNN's success to show them the potential.

Kay took over in the early-1990s, just as the flower began to open, and CNN's global advertising volume had reached $40 million a year, up from only a few million in the mid-1980s. Ted and John Barbera thought that Delaney was operating at a high level, but there were others, including myself, who felt that CNN's international advertising could go much higher.

I did not convince Barbera or Delaney to participate actively in my project, even though Delaney had been with the company many years and knew of my work. They said that the expense would be too great, the opportunities in Russia too limited, the advertising market too small, and future success too far away. Between November 1992 and June 1993, I kept talking with them and their sales division, but they did nothing to help me. When I sought Ted's help, his answer was to work it through Bill Grumbles. Grumbles merely said that he could not get the commitment I sought and did not take it any further. Running in circles was new to me. So was this layer of shortsighted executives between Ted and me. I gave up talking to them. Instead I advertised and hired Mauricio Mendez as our Advertising Sales Executive to work on the start-up in Russia and to help me in Eastern Europe. Mendez had been general manager of a Telemundo Spanish-speaking station in Houston, and had a strong advertising sales background. I shouldn't have had to build my own sales operation, but I had no choice. The money had to come from TBS in any case, and this was the *specific* element we had promised in our pitch to potential joint venture partners.

The best I got from TBS in the way of cooperation was the two-month temporary assignment of an Atlanta area sales executive named John Dobson, who had been selling advertising time for the Braves television games in Atlanta. Since his sales were seasonal and concentrated during the first quarter of the year, he was available to help me in the latter part of the year.

As it turned out, Dobson was a bit of a "fire eater" himself. He was tall, thin, and quite handsome, with a taste for extravagant clothes. I remember a dinner we had at the Pizza Hut in Moscow. Since it was American-prepared, it was considered somewhat upscale, and it satisfied my occasional craving for a dish of spaghetti. We were coming out of the place after an earlier snow-storm, and as we stepped off the curb, John stepped into melted snow. I can still see his $400 alligator shoes sinking into the wet, dirty slush.

John prepared advertising studies and sales projections not only of Moscow, St. Petersburg, and the Czech Republic, but also Slovakia, Slovenia,

Romania, and Poland. He tried to get an assignment as advertising manager for Latin America, since he spoke Spanish, but had been turned down by Kay Delaney. Although he could work for me only a few months of the year, he continued to submit reports and spreadsheets on his own time for the full three years that we worked on Eastern European projects. It amazed me that the top sales executives overlooked Dobson's talents. He was smart, hard-working, energetic, and loyal. Could that have been his problem?

Joyce, who had an uncanny way of directing me to the right people within TBS, found Scott Herubin in the accounting department. He loved to do spreadsheets, was single, had a laptop computer, and wanted to travel. He also helped to find interested investors in financial institutions in New York and London. They were just waiting for us to start our projects and suggest how they could participate. One organization didn't even wait for our go-ahead. It bought a piece of the network, Kanal A in Slovenia based on our *proposed* involvement.

Gene Wright's engineering specialist was Alan Friedman, who had extensive technical experience in broadcasting and could handle engineering in a completely new facility. For program/operations, I chose Farrell Meisel, a former vice president of programming for WOR-TV in New York City.

As I assembled my team, I flew to Greece and Russia and to the dawn of a new project. I had high hopes. Or was I just being a cockeyed optimist?

Sid Pike and Scott Herubin, loyal associate on right. Young lady unidentified.

CHAPTER THIRTY-SIX

Mixed Signals and Missed Opportunities

Corporate growth is something like riding on a bicycle. If you coast too long, you fall off.

—Gordon Weil

My July 1992 trip to Athens and Moscow was my opportunity to learn firsthand about Eastern Europe. Communism had only been toppled in the Soviet bloc the year before, and I had never been to any of these countries. It felt strange not to be working for CNN. I chose, however, to keep the title President, CNN International Special Projects, since I had been known as a representative of CNN, and most government and business executives were not familiar with TBS. Many had heard of Ted, but *everyone* knew CNN.

I met Minos Kyriakou in Athens, and I was instantly pleased to hear him speak of plans to develop a television network in Greece. He was offering Turner the opportunity to invest in that network and in a project he was discussing with a group in Romania. Both projects needed Turner capital and its film library and programs. As we talked of other Eastern European opportunities, it was clear to me that TBS would have to provide most of the assets needed to make the joint ventures work. Kyriakou's Antena TV

401

was merely going to find the projects, perform minimal management, and invest enough capital to fulfill the requirements of a partnership. I said we would study his proposal, but it was apparent to me that we would be better off making partnerships directly with the local stations, since we could provide management, capital, films, and programming. Ted agreed with me.

I flew on to Moscow with a great deal of trepidation, not sure how the plans for a joint venture with Channel 6 would develop, I also didn't have a visa. This was not unusual, I was told, and a visa could be arranged at the airport. When I arrived in the evening, there was a representative of MIBC waiting for me. He escorted me to a room in the airport where I paid $110 and received a stamped visa. I was then taken to a lounge where I met Edward Sagalayev and Nugzar Popkhadze. Edward was short and stocky, with a round face and mustache. Popkhadze was also short, somewhat thinner, and had a voice that reminded me of a fog horn, but I was used to that sound by now! They drove me to the Penta Hotel, and along the way they pointed out certain landmarks, such as a monument that looked like a giant tank trap, which marked the place where the German advance on Moscow had been stopped during World War II. Stu Loory was waiting for me at the hotel and gave me an update on the meetings and plans for the coming days.

The next day's first stop was the Channel 6 offices, which were located on the 29th floor of a modern glass building and provided a magnificent panorama of Moscow. On the lower floors were city administration offices, including the mayor's. Across the street was the "White House," the white marble building where the Presidium met. In 1993 CNN would show it being blasted by tanks during a revolt organized by a group of legislators opposing Boris Yeltsin's government. The group seized the White House, then endured a military assault. A few hundred yards farther was the Moscow River and a bridge that took us to the CNN Bureau just a few blocks beyond.

The plan was for Channel 6 to rent space to operate a basic television station at the government-run Ostankino facility located in another part of the city, and eventually build or renovate its own building. Turner was expected to provide films, programs, and management expertise, but not day-to-day operations. Since May 1992, Channel 6 had been airing CNNI, translated into Russian, from 10:00 P.M. until midnight. This included a half-hour of financial news.

An English-only, 24-hour CNN signal was seen on UHF Channel 24, but it had limited distribution. It did, however, reach seven Moscow hotels.

As part of the temporary license Channel 6 received, we had to fulfill the conditions of providing seven hours each week of programs for children and teenagers. One fourth of the total programming had to be devoted to "home culture," and the winner of the long-term license had to begin all this programming no later than January 1, 1993.

One of the major problems was the Channel 6 signal. During the communist regime, a single antenna had been built on the roof of each large apartment building, and most Muscovites lived in such buildings. These antennas could receive only the state television channels. They had to be reconfigured to receive Channel 6. This was expensive and could be done only by Vyacheslav Misyulin, who was in charge of the landmark giant tower that transmitted all television signals in Moscow. Misyulin agreed to perform this task, but at one point, he stopped until the required payments had been made.

Edward Sagalayev was a well-known television personality with a reputation for outspokenness. He had a good television background and an astute business mind, but he also had a stubborn streak. Our talks were usually difficult and lengthy. Loory explained to me that Russians negotiate by giving long speeches full of references and historical examples, which often have nothing to do with the subject at hand. Then there were the dinners, vodka toasts, and more vodka toasts, in which loyalty was promised over and over. I endured many meetings and many long speeches, but I accomplished very little during my first two-and-a-half week visit.

Moscow is a dark and somber city. Although the people seemed friendly, I found it hard to develop close associations because of the language barrier. In business discussions, I always had an interpreter, even though the Russians sometimes spoke English. Edward knew a little English, but he preferred to use an interpreter, who was always available to accompany us. My earlier experiences taught me that even those who knew English were often reluctant to speak it. It was also true that the use of interpreters always helped the other side, because the time it took to interpret gave them more time to weigh their answers.

Edward showed me the locations he had chosen for the station. He wanted to maintain office space in the building we were already in and use it as a studio, which I knew would be an impossible situation because of my experience at WHDH-TV in Boston. The ceilings were too low for hanging lights and sets, and there was very little space even if the walls were taken out. When I expressed my doubts and concerns, we looked at the Atomic Building in Moscow's Exposition Park.

While Loory and I were there, some of the TBS legal staff flew in from London to be present at the negotiations and to start preliminary work on the agreement. They planned to employ a Western law firm, with an office in Moscow, that was familiar with the various Russian laws that sometimes changed while we were negotiating.

Another important player on the Turner side from London was How-ard Karshan, head of Turner Syndication in Europe, Africa, Middle East, Russia, and southern Asia. I was to coordinate with Karshan the films and programs needed in Moscow. Karshan had come to TBS as part of the MGM acquisition. Now his office was responsible for the sale of all Turner films and programs to television and cable services in those areas of the world, the best selling opportunities outside of the United States. He was a successful and experienced salesperson, and was considered essential to sell-ing the MGM library and the new productions. He knew this and enjoyed being outspoken and very independent. Offering MGM films to Channel 6 would not directly benefit his sales budget, and he might want to save the better films for future Russian sales.

In one of our business meetings, I said that I was interested in develop-ing Channel 6 into a national television network, and Edward agreed that that was one of his goals, too. This would mean great exposure for Turner's films. I needed Karshan's cooperation.

When I returned to my office in Atlanta on July 24, it seemed fortu-itous that I discovered in my mail a letter from a woman named Nadia Fino, with a company called International Television Productions. She had read in a trade magazine of our plans in Moscow. She was connected with a company in Prague called Mirofilm that provided film facilities for motion picture production and wanted to expand into television since Czechoslo-vakia was privatizing one of its television channels.

This was my first Czech source. I answered her letter, and a few weeks later I received a list of opportunities in Czechoslovakia that included applying for a private television license in competition with others in the Czech Republic, which was soon to split off from its eastern half and become the Slovak Republic (Slovakia).

In late August, I again left for Moscow and for my first visit to St. Petersburg, where I was to meet Dmitri Rozhdestvensky, Chairman of the Board of Russkoye Video.

We had the usual difficulty getting a visa. Russia desperately needed business capital and cash from tourists, and yet, as a vestige of its communist system, it still tried to prevent non-Russians from getting in, as though visitors might have some evil intent, such as spying. Sometimes you didn't know you had a visa until you arrived at the Russian airport. It was the same in Romania. A businessman couldn't go to Russia or to Romania to study business opportunities. He had to have a business relationship *before* he arrived. This was counter-productive and discouraged the very thing they were trying to encourage: investments from other countries.

Michael Mondini, chief advisor to the Chairman of Russkoye Video, faxed me an amusing itinerary:

Tuesday, 6:15 P.M. [25th]. Sidney Pike will be picked-up at St. Petersburg International airport by Michael Mondini and crew. S.P. will look for a 5'-6" beautiful blonde in a pink dress named Elena. She will have a sign that says CNN. Please identify yourself to her as soon as you see her, because only then I can send in Nikita who will walk you thru Customs.

We will proceed directly to Dacha and you may freshen up for a dinner and a little night life.

Wednesday, 26: We will have the first meeting with Dmitri Rozhdestvensky, our Chairman, from 10 A.M. till noon. We will break for lunch and do a little sightseeing.

Wednesday night is my traditional poker (for rubles) night with the General Directors of Procter and Gamble, U.S. West, etc. If you would like to meet some of the major American players here in St. Petersburg, this is a great time. If not, I will cancel the game and we can go out to dinner.

Thursday, 27: 11 A.M. visit to the Hermitage for as long as you want. There is a special showing now of Peter the Great and of course there is a world class collection of French Impressionists. If it is a nice day you will travel by speed boat and enter the Palace via the canal system.

Afternoon meeting with Dmitri.

Evening dinner at private Georgian restaurant—you will love this place!

Friday, 28: Morning visit to Pavlovsk, former residence of Paul the First, son of Catherine the Great.

Late afternoon meeting with Deputy Mayor of St. Petersburg, Director of Foreign Relations and Director General of the Committee of Economic affairs for the city of St. Petersburg (all the same guy) in his office at the City Hall.

Saturday–open with tennis option.

Sunday–open—night train to Moscow.

Please advise me of any changes you wish to make to this agenda.

My Channel 11 meetings were a pleasant surprise—everything was very cordial. I liked the players, and I detected real sincerity in wanting an alliance with TBS. I stayed in Brezhnev's former dacha, slept in the room where he hosted "lady friends," and used their unique shower—nozzles spray water at you from all sides. Clean and entertaining. The dacha was on an island in one of the many waterways of the city, completely enclosed by walls and well guarded.

We completed our meetings, and before midnight on Sunday, I was driven to the train station. The overnight train from St. Petersburg to Moscow, a 500-mile journey, proved to be an adventure. The train leaves at midnight and arrives the next morning at 8 A.M. Between departure and arrival, there are many stories of robberies. One was advised to tie the compartment doors together with ropes or a belt. The compartment I was in had two little beds and, for a small fee, tea would be served. I took this train many times both ways, and nothing ever happened during the night, but I continued to hear stories of compartment burglaries. One story had it that ether was used in certain cars to assist the thieves. I did awaken

*St. Petersburg Channel 11 consultant Michael Mondini with Sid Pike
traveling canals in that city.*

one morning to find that the people in the next compartment had been robbed. Perhaps they had not tied their doors together.

By September, I had developed a protocol with Dmitri Rozhdestvensky. Turner was to get 40 percent of Channel 11, equal to 40 percent of Russkoye, with no cash involvement. Programming and management, particularly international ad sales, were to be our contribution.

This was a very appealing arrangement for a number of reasons besides the fact of not having to make a cash investment. I did have to get the approval of the Board of Directors for all these joint venture agreements, which tied my hands considerably, and it was hard to know which way the board would go. *TBS had to grow.* That was the only way its stockholders would be satisfied. So it was incumbent on TBS's management to be tolerant of creativity and those who can make growth happen, while staying fiscally responsible and conservative overall. This balance existed within CNN, where Tom Johnson encouraged ideas, but it was absent in Turner International where Bill Grumbles' policy was so conservative that creativity was a threat frowned upon.

Grumbles once said to me when he was exasperated by my insisting that we support Ted in his desire to develop international television broadcast joint ventures. "Why don't we just buy the television companies when they succeed?" Grumbles grumbled. He missed the point entirely.

The conservative Executive Committee, particularly McGuirk, thought that Ted's decision to develop joint ventures in Eastern Europe was a waste of the company's resources because it was an investment that would take a while to yield a significant return. They believed that they had a responsibility to protect the company from wasting time and money on projects where the economies were still struggling. They didn't buy Ted's vision for the future.

But I did buy Ted's vision. We had thousands of motion pictures sitting on the shelves. We had television broadcast experience and advertising sales know-how to run the engine, plus CNN's global reputation that gave us an edge in the competition for licenses and access to established joint venture opportunities. And we had enough capital and ability to glue it all together.

The company, however, had changed from focusing on ideas to focusing on budgets. The monthly and yearly budgets had become a *bible*. There were even bi-weekly budgets. We had more budget information than we knew what to do with. I attended one weekly staff meeting run by Bill Grumbles that devoted 90 minutes of the two-hour meeting to discuss whether we would make that month's budget. What a waste of time! We should have been asked: What ideas have you got? What direction should the company take to develop? How can we work together to make it all happen? The budget is, at best, a guess about what it will take to make everything come together. It should not lead everything else, but at the newly created Turner International, it was dominant. I had to deal with the new management mindset at TI and TBS, which was time-consuming and exhausting, particularly on top of all my global travel.

Once, Ted would have called a meeting and leaned on each person who wasn't doing his part for the project, and then they would all pull together. But now, a huge joint-venture project like ours did not get enough of Ted's attention to force the division heads to work together. Grumbles, who knew Terry McGuirk was not in favor of the joint venture projects, was reluctant to insist that I receive full cooperation.

Ted himself sent mixed signals. Bob Ross was in charge of business development and was studying television joint ventures in other parts of the world. He told me that when he brought them to Ted's attention, he received no encouragement and sometimes a firm "no interest." I attributed Ted's attitude to the heavy losses elsewhere.

TBS and TimeWarner found themselves supporting competing German language news channels. TimeWarner executives suggested TBS join the TimeWarner project, called n-TV. The German news project had not been Ted's idea, but TBS had to join rather than compete with a company that owned 19 percent of TBS. I've heard figures from $30 to $60 million as the price TBS paid for its share. The 24-hour news concept did not work in Germany. After a few years, n-Net had only three percent of the audience to offer to advertisers, and the cost of operation was very high. The losses were considerable. In 1993, TBS lost $18.6 million on the project, the second year, $12 million, and in 1995, it lost $13 million. The first three years of operation resulted in over $171 million in losses, of which TBS's share was $43.6 million, plus the $30 to $60 million entry fee.

This fiasco explains why there was already, in 1992, a very negative attitude among the executives toward joint venture broadcast projects.

The timing of the German fiasco could not have been worse for me—I was trying to get cooperation from management just as they were desperately trying to contain their losses.

Ted was able to see the two ventures, television in Eastern Europe and cable in Germany, as quite different, even though they had a common broadcast denominator. The other managers could not. I also believe that McGuirk's struggle in the 1970s at WRET-TV in Charlotte negatively influenced his analyses of Ted's joint venture concepts. I could only hope that Ted would continue to trust me to get the job done. He did stick with his idea, and although I saw him infrequently, he always encouraged me. He knew something about me the others didn't know.

I almost never used money to get the job done.

* * * * *

As soon as I reached Moscow on September 1, I received an urgent phone call from home. Lill had been to her doctor and was scheduled immediately for surgery. It would take place the very next day. I turned around and came straight home on September 2. By the time I arrived, the operation was successfully completed, and she was in the recovery room. This forced me to realize how much I had separated myself from my family and had created a new "family" base through those I associated with in my work and travels. It had the effect of a "dotted line" in our relationship, and I knew I had been slipping away. Lill's phone call to me in Russia the night before her operation was indeed *my* wake up call.

Once she was out of danger, I worked as much as I could at the office, going back and forth to the hospital every day until she came home.

Early in September, I heard from Nadia Fino that the Letter of Intent for the Czech Republic had to be forwarded to the Committee for Television and Broadcast Transmission by September 30. I invited her to Atlanta to complete a contract and determine if we had time to prepare a license application or could be given a deadline extension. Fino came here and agreed to an arrangement that would give her and her partner a small percentage of the station, if we obtained the license, as well as a consultant salary. I introduced her to Bill Grumbles and later informed him of my plans. She thought she could get a deadline extension, and she did. Irene Hiemer, whose organization skills I always respected, agreed to help Nadia and me with the application.

In mid-September, Nadia wrote to me saying that there were 34 applicants, including many well-known broadcasting groups from Europe, but she felt that we would have an edge because of our international reputation and broad experience. CNN would help, I was sure.

I sent Ted, Bill Grumbles, and Bob Ross a memo recommending our participation in applying for a license and got the go-ahead. One of the urgent items to take care of, as part of the application, was obtaining a business license in Prague. I met with Andy Velcoff, one of the TBS lawyers, told him of our plans and our need for legal representation in Prague, and that we needed him to apply immediately for a business license there. I emphasized that all applicants had to comply with this requirement. Andy contacted a law firm in Prague and advised me that it would represent us and that we needed to deposit $1,000 in a Czech bank.

I always sent copies of what I was doing to Ted or went to him directly. When I had completed the application for the Czech Republic television license and had submitted it to Grumbles for approval, I learned that he was against investing our resources to operate a television network in Czechoslovakia—and he wouldn't okay it. I was shocked, and angry. That same day, I received a memo from Irene Hiemer, who had helped prepare the application for the Czech Republic, saying that she received a phone call from Andy Velcoff, who informed her that, per Terry McGuirk, Bill Grumbles had been instructed to terminate the Czech project! Letters had already been sent to Fino and her partner canceling our proposed agreement and the submission of the application for the license. We had been given an extension of the deadline, but I could not afford any further delay. I went to Ted, and he okayed it.

This was a significant moment in my career. I had chosen to become a "marked man" rather than a "team player," who would watch the company flounder. I don't think Ted was aware before I talked to him that his managers had canceled his project—a dream that I did not want to see melt like an ice cube on a hot sidewalk.

I had many balls in the air. Besides the license application and Lill's recovery, I was now working on two Russian joint ventures. I also still had CNN responsibilities in Africa, Canada, and on cruise ships. On top of it all, we had to move our office to another building. Joyce was busy coordinating and trying valiantly to keep up with all my various projects.

* * * * *

Within the TBS ranks, people were pulling in different directions on the Channel 6 project. I was trying to get Howard Karshan, who had final approval on the MGM films, to upgrade the selections he was making available to us. Meantime, Stu Loory was advising TI management by memo that because of the limited audience available to watch Channel 6, not that many antennas had yet been changed, so it would not be wise to put a lot of programs on the air that could easily be pirated. He also suggested that MIBC be responsible for half the programming.

I agreed that MIBC should produce enough programming to assure the Russian audience that Channel 6 was not an American service. But Loory's proposal ran counter to my plans. To me, pirating was not a problem at all—I saw it as extending our audience. Ted had said, "Do what you did for me when Channel 17 began," and that was exactly what I intended to do: promote Channel 6 with exciting films and projects, even though the audience was limited. This would let the word get around that if you couldn't get Channel 6, you were *missing* something. My acquisition of the Braves and the Hawks in the early 1970s for Channel 17 had this effect on the audience. Stu's memo couldn't have been sent at a worse time. Karshan's proposed film list was mostly "old dogs" from the MGM library, produced in the 1930s and 1940s—real crap. I certainly couldn't claim that we were running "new and exciting films from the Turner library." Newer Hollywood films were being shown on Moscow television, partly through piracy, but these films of the 1980s and 1990s meant that the Muscovites would definitely know the difference between the old and the new films, even though Western films were still a novelty.

Then, in the midst of the negotiations with MIBC, Sagalayev found a Russian company to provide much of the start-up capital: Luk, an oil company that was being privatized. It had already deposited $500,000 to an MIBC account in Malta, according to Sagalayev. This meant that he had money to buy films and programs if he needed to, which weakened the rationale for TBS's participation as a 50 percent partner. I was supposed to avoid providing money and to offer our assets: films, programs, and expertise. I knew that if Edward saw the list Karshan had sent, it would weaken our position in the negotiations. But I could not convince Grumbles to overrule Karshan because of Loory's memo. Grumbles mentioned it to me in his response to my memo and urged me to be more "positive" about the whole process!

I asked for a meeting with Ted so that I could get his word on the list of films that he wanted us *not* to offer in Russia. With Grumbles, McGuirk, and Herubin present, Ted said he was not concerned about using the MGM library in Russia and suggested that London cull out 100 films from more than 3,000, should we ever be interested in distributing those 100 to theaters. Despite this clear go-ahead from Ted to offer quality rerun films to Channel 6, nothing changed. Over the next year, I called two more times for a meeting with Ted and repeated my request, and he said the same thing, but still there was no change in the film list. London was never informed by Grumbles. I wondered the second and third time why Ted did not say, "Didn't we have this meeting before?"

Karshan, along with Wells in Australia, both from MGM, left a few years later. Unfortunately, Karshan's removal came too late to help us in Moscow. It was hard for me to believe that Ted's wishes were being ignored. I thought it must be because he was absent so much, but it left me in a very awkward position.

Perhaps those aligned against Ted's growth plans thought that I was going to crumble and disintegrate, but it made me madder and stronger.

CHAPTER THIRTY-SEVEN

Czechmate and Other Chess Moves

Stay true to the voice within you.
This voice is the smartest unhurt self
who knows at every juncture
what is the best to do.
And who does not ever bend to fear.

—Christopher Spence

In late 1992 I received frequent messages from Nadia Fino about our Czechoslovakia license competition, because our attorneys had not yet obtained the business license. Fino angrily claimed someone was stalling. I phoned Andy Velcoff in the Legal Department, whom I had always found very cooperative. He told me that we would have the license "soon." Fino and her partner, Miro Vostiar, were not reassured. There was great pressure on the Licensing Committee from our competitors. Fino and Vostiar felt that our not having the business license when the Committee interviewed us would be seen as a lack of interest on the part of TBS. I relayed this information to Andy.

We were given a date in January 1993 for our interview by the Committee. This was almost four months after we had authorized the application, and still we had no business license. I called Andy again. "What's going on? I'm told it should only take a few weeks." He said the Prague lawyers were doing everything possible. I said our position would be very weak if we did not have the business license at the time of the interview.

I prepared our presentation to the Committee and flew to Prague from Moscow in late January. When I met with Fino and Vostiar, we decided that, as Czech and former Czech citizens, they would appear with me. They were understandably very upset because we still had no business license. I frantically phoned Andy and was told everything was being done, that we would have it soon, and that I should tell the Committee to expect it shortly. Fino and Vostiar said that we were in a strong negotiating position and that many in the government, and possibly on the Committee, were in favor of CNN.

The next day, the three of us went to the Television License Committee meeting. We were seated at one end of a very large square table, and the seven members were seated at the other end. After the introductions, the chairman asked, "Where is the TBS business license?" I gave the answer I had been given by Atlanta, that we expected it momentarily, but I could see the disbelief on their faces. The other questions were routine, and the Committee's mood seemed aloof and skeptical. After I gave my pitch, the three of us left—we all were anxious and pessimistic about the outcome.

The Committee completed the interviews a few days later. That same night, Fino, Vostiar, and I were having dinner when Vostiar decided to phone his contact at one of the leading newspapers. He came back to the table and announced that the Committee had decided almost immediately to award the license to Central European Media Enterprises (CME), an independent company owned by Esteé Lauder's son, Ronald, a former ambassador to Hungary. This would be Lauder's first television license, and he had specifically formed CME to organize television ventures in Eastern Europe and Russia. Lauder did not own a single film or program, nor did he have any experience in television, let alone a reputation like CNN's. But he had access to financial institutions and could buy films and programs.

Fino and Vostiar were perturbed, critical of our support by Atlanta, and suggested we had been sabotaged. I had a lot to learn. My "colleagues" were specifically ignoring Ted Turner's orders to help, telling me they were trying to help, and deceiving Ted into believing they were helping. The idea of professional sabotage by my colleagues never entered my mind. The notion disgusts me.

The Czech Republic—the western half of what had been Czechoslovakia—included Prague and a network television system that covered most of the new country. CME would have only one competitor: the state television system. The market had done $40 million in advertising in 1992. CME called its network TV NOVA, and in the first year, it managed to get much of its programming through barter. They exchanged advertising for films and programs. This is the same kind of bartering that had saved many UHF independents in the United States in the early-1970s.

TBS could have grown very cheaply in these markets, given the program resources we already had. But this was not how Bill Grumbles and the executive committee saw things. He had asked me why we couldn't let the markets develop and then just buy one of the stations. You have less risk, of course, but you pay top-dollar value and you don't make money for years, I told him. The technique we had used over and over was to develop our projects from the beginning and use the resources we already had. In this case, we could have used the very expensive MGM library to help us. About this time, Andy Velcoff remarked to one of my assistants that Ted was no longer running the company. Certainly I was experiencing this, but it was still hard to believe, harder to accept…if it were true.

* * * * *

I took the rest of my team to Moscow in 1993. Mauricio Mendez and his wife, Trudy, moved into an apartment, and he organized a local sales staff. Channel 6 was already on the air, but it had no local sales experience. We didn't want to increase expenses without developing advertising revenue. I had hoped we would have an agreement before we became this involved in the station's operation and sales efforts. Oh, we would get Edward Sagalayev's signature on an agreement, but then it had to be "finalized." These agreements always had to be approved by various state institutions, and sometimes they didn't approve them. Or perhaps MIBC was just reluctant to give TBS half of the interest in Channel 6 because the future looked good and MBC was finding the capital it needed. It was sometimes difficult to know what exactly was holding up the final agreement.

Farrell Meisel also moved to Moscow to help organize the station operation and program schedule. He kept reminding me of the poor quality and age of the films London was sending, not to mention the effect it was having on Edward. I understood only too well.

Although I was now living in Henry Yushkiavitshus's apartment, I kept up with my other projects in Atlanta via the satellite phone at the CNN Moscow Bureau. Staying for as long as a month or two at a time in an environment that exacerbated my loneliness was wearing on me, particularly during the severe Moscow winter. In my free time, I often listened to Henry's stereo and read insatiably. Lill had insisted that I take the book *Truman,* by David McCullough, with me. I balked on the grounds of its weight and size, over a thousand pages. She somehow managed to put it into my suitcase without my knowing. I'm glad she did; I enjoyed it immensely. It wasn't long enough.

Scott Herubin made periodic trips to Moscow to work with us. We were all hopeful that we could overcome the nagging problems that delayed the completion of the agreement. Periodically, the lawyers from Atlanta and London would arrive, and we would have another round of meetings. Edward was not always present. He let his brother–in-law, Nugzar Popkhadze, grind away in these exasperating meetings that lasted all day, all evening, and into the early morning hours. Often, when we would finally get the Russian side to agree, and we thought the subject was closed, they would reopen it the next day. Sometimes I felt that Edward was using us—and that he seemed to vacillate between wanting TBS and not wanting it. MIBC was also having trouble obtaining an "official" and "final" license to broadcast. There were other organizations competing, some with strong ties to key government officials. One was Business University, which had a powerful justification for the license because of its name and business purpose.

A marriage was finally forced on MIBC and Turner that provided for Business University's use of Channel 6 as well. Originally, we were told that Business University would receive afternoon TV time, but, in fact, it ended up with the 5 P.M.–7 P.M. slot, some of the most valuable time for a television station. Edward often told us that Business University would leave soon and it would have its own UHF channel, but that never happened.

This arrangement, of course, affected the image of this independent news and entertainment channel. The programming Business University supplied during those crucial audience hours was dull and, while occasionally informative, would have been more appropriate on a state-run channel. Evidently, some of its funding was coming from foundations, possibly American, and frequently its programming had nothing to do with Business University. I often wondered if it were an excuse to gain partial control of the channel.

* * * * *

Channel 6 officially went on the air January 1, 1993. In order to establish an up-to-date look, I had Farrell Meisel bring in an American expert in promotion and on-air production. The station had, of course, technically already been on the air with a few hours of CNN news and Russian voiceover since the previous May, but with a very primitive television image. I didn't want the "new" television station to be associated with the old image, and I also wanted to show Edward Sagalayev the quality of on-air production.

After airing Edward's and Ted's opening remarks, and then running MGM's *Singing in the Rain* with Gene Kelly, we celebrated with Russian champagne in one of the Ostankino executive offices, as we watched the channel come to life. We were on the air but with no Founders Contract (a contract with stockholders), no Charter of the Joint Stock Society, and no Program License Agreement. One of the sticky problems for the Turner side was that the entire television channel license was under the name of MIBC, because the license could be issued only to a Russian entity. This meant MIBC controlled the license and could end the agreement after we had invested so heavily in its development. The TBS lawyers had to craft every word very carefully.

Nor were Edward and Nugzar pleased that I was also negotiating with Russkoye Video in St. Petersburg. They liked to think that they had Turner and CNN exclusively for all of Russia, even though we could not grant this because of the many agreements and arrangements already in place in the country. They also wanted to *represent* Turner in program and film sales throughout Russia, even though I had explained that was not possible.

Not long after we lost the Prague television network, I learned more about the significance of Grumbles' delaying tactics and our Legal Department's failure to get the business license. Someone at TBS had been actively working against me with the Prague network. I suspected it was members of the Executive Committee. At a time when I had expected to be winding down my career, I was working on the most difficult job I had taken on so far, with some of the top executives of the company fighting me all the way.

Grumbles took on Stu Loory as his Russian advisor. Loory had a handle on the Russian political scene and contacts in its television services, but he had no knowledge of operating, programming, or promoting a television channel. I soon realized that part of Loory's job was to report on me to Grumbles.

On the early June day that I flew to Prague to work with the attorneys in Slovakia, I sent Ted a note outlining some of my frustrations. I had been on the project for a year.

> On the subject of why it is taking so long to get the final documents signed by Edward and TV6, there are some things that I need to tell you. This has been the most painful and drawn out negotiation I have ever experienced. We have negotiated in detail every word, every phrase, and every sentence. The process involving the main document (the Founder's Contract) took four months. The additional documents, which are approval of the budget, the Program License Agreement, and the Charter, are being handled similarly for the past two months. I deal with it on a day-to-day basis, getting reports from Mauricio Mendez, our sales manager in Moscow, each day. Then, we plan our next move. I had a conference call with Edward and his associates last Friday, June 4, and we reviewed all of the points. They intend to rewrite our versions, which has to take at least another week. We have just learned that they have hired a new lawyer. This means that he will go over the Charter and the Program License agreement and make recommendations, and that involves renegotiations on some issues. The agreement with Russian Video (Channel 11) in St. Petersburg was finalized and signed in one week (subject to Turner Board approval)…

We have run into a problem regarding television facilities in Moscow. The Atomic Energy building that I showed you with the big columns is too expensive. The Exposition Park wants $600,000 U.S. per year. We are trying to find another location, but it is very difficult. Bunky Helfrich has offered to assist us. It may be necessary for us to seek out land and start building in phases. For example, Phase I would be the production studio, control room, some editing suites, and a master control. Phase II would be a newsroom, news studios and control room, and a second production studio. Phase III would consist of offices, and administration and a remote unit. Bunky has been advised that building from start may be cheaper in the long run, but he is studying all opportunities.

I also told Ted of my plans for Slovakia and St. Petersburg, expressing concern that the TBS due-diligence personnel would measure by U.S. standards rather than Russian.

By the time you receive this, I will be in Slovakia meeting with the Prime Minister and other government officials. After about a week, I will go to Moscow to press the finalization of the documents and, at the same time, try to keep our effort regarding Channel 11 in St. Petersburg alive with the extra due diligence. My concern is that our people involved in the due diligence are going to make a maximum effort similar to our acquiring or forming a joint venture with a U.S. firm, and they will find that the comparisons or substance are not equal. Some things that may not be acceptable in the United States are common practice in Russia. The question is, how severe are their problems and can we live with them? Having a Moscow/St. Petersburg dual advertising opportunity is perfect.

Stu Loory had also written to his boss, Tom Johnson, head of CNN, about the problem of Kay Delaney's unwillingness to cooperate, and had said that nothing was being done. I sent Ted a copy of that, too.

Meanwhile, Mendez wrote to me from Moscow about the people he was training as salespeople:

Leonid Sherbinin decided it was too much work and resigned last week. Although he was improving, he lacked energy and was determined to take a five-week vacation, which is too much time for a salesman! Of course, I did not object as I realize it is the law, but it did show me that he did not want to work. On the other hand, Ilya said he was not taking this long a vacation even if it is offered. That's a salesman!

His four-month sales activity totaled $645,938 net. Although we were excited that he was exceeding our advertising revenue budget, this was still very little money in 1993. It was exactly how Turner had begun in 1970-1971. The only difference was that the salaries in Moscow in 1993 averaged $60 to $100 per month, and that had to help the start-up of the television station. Our original budget for Channel 6 was less than a million dollars per year. I remember telling Mendez that it was so small ($850,000) for a television market of 10 million people that he had to raise it, at least to $1,000,000.

Procter & Gamble was the major advertising pioneer again. It had booked $275,000 for this period, close to 40 percent of the total. Proctor & Gamble and Bristol-Myers had been way ahead of other companies in their thinking toward the future when it came to buying commercial time in foreign television.

So, I returned via Slovakia to Moscow to do everything I could to complete the agreement with MIBC. In late June, Sagalayev wrote to Ted to try to get us to change our stand on the major issue of who would have the MIBC board's tie-breaking vote. Since we had 50 percent of the venture, TI did not want to give up veto power to MIBC, particularly since the venture now required a substantial cash investment, as well as programming and management. I couldn't blame TI for not wanting to give Edward a blank check. While I recognized his management talents, I was aware that his experience had been mainly with state-subsidized television with hundreds, even thousands, more personnel than were needed. Like Ted, Edward had good ideas, but he did not yet have the experience to evaluate a program's worth. I believed this would come, but I didn't want to drain our limited financial resources while he learned how to operate without state funds.

Edward wrote to Ted in late June 1993:

I suppose Sid has already informed you about the problems we are having. I have decided to write you personally about one of them. This is the tie-breaking vote of the Chairman of the Board of Directors, the representative of MIBC. This question is not of a personal nature for me but is still fundamental for the first Russian independent television Channel which has drawn a tremendous public attention…. Our foundation documents, due to the persistence of TBS's attorneys, were compiled in such a manner that the true parity is not a question for discussion…. The formal side of the business and the real situation are two different things.

In everyday practice, Sid and I have a complete mutual understanding on all the questions of our work. His highest professionalism and personal traits guarantee that there will be no conflicts in the management of the Channel. Therefore, for the term of his staying in the Board of Directors as a TBS representative and the General Director of the society, I am confident that I will never have to exercise the right of my tie-breaking vote, and we can provide for this stipulation in the Agreement. However, MIBC as well as TBS must think about the future of the Channel. The six-month experience of working together and communicating with other TBS representatives have totally convinced me that the legal or formal, side of the business is very often a deciding factor for them, and they are tough…defending TBS rights set forth in the documents. Therefore, my colleagues of MIBC and myself are convinced that the foundation documents of the Society should provide for the tie-breaking vote of the Chairman of the Board of Directors, the Russian representative.

I recognize the necessity to revise our previous arrangements and to amend the foundation documents due to the MIBC's position, but MIBC is forced to stay with it by the realities, requirements of the Russian law and the public situation.

I was pleased with Edward's confidence in me, but it was obvious that, because of my age and possible retirement, my tenure in Russia would be no longer than three or four more years, and it was clear, too, that TBS would not relent on having veto control. Ted answered Edward's letter, saying that he would be willing to reassess the situation at a future date after a substantial level of success had been achieved—when Edward had more experience and Channel 6 had become profitable. But Edward wanted written commitments, and who could blame him? I sent Edward a letter informing him that the points he wanted changed would not be changed. Since neither side would bend, the talks continued, but went nowhere.

Farrell Meisel was now living in Moscow and organizing the Channel 6 operations. Mauricio Mendez was training the sales staff, but was having problems with so-called independent sales companies that had been trying to sell Channel 6 to local advertisers. First, he had to get rid of their influence on the advertisers. I had an office and the title of Director General. Edward was Chairman and in charge of Operations. I met with him almost daily to iron out points in the agreement and to solve problems.

I did my best to keep focused on our goal, but it was too easy to become depressed in bleak, cold Moscow. What's more, I felt caught in a vise between Channel 6 and the TBS executives in Atlanta, with both sides turning their handles tighter and tighter.

CHAPTER THIRTY-EIGHT

Russian Roulette

A company needs to be constantly rejuvenated by the infusion of young blood. It needs smart young men with the imaginations and the gifts to turn everything upside down if they can. It also needs old fogies to keep them from turning upside down those things that ought to be right side up. Above all, it needs young rebels and old conservatives who can work together, challenge each other's views, yield or hold fast with equal grace, and continue after each hard-fought battle to respect each other as men and as colleagues.

—Henry Ford II

I returned to Atlanta in May 1993 to wait for the completion of the St. Petersburg Channel 11 agreement, which would be far less complicated than the one with Channel 6. However a huge hurdle still remained. Russkoye Video did not have a clear license to use Channel 11, although it had been promised one if it participated with a company called Telemax. The Russian Parliament Licensing Commission mandated this requirement. This provision illustrates how the Russian government's Commission differs from the FCC in the United States. The FCC awards a license only to one group among the competitors. The Russian Commission, in effect, forced both groups together because each had sufficient political power to keep from being eliminated. This could cause severe friction and very difficult situations, which had to be negotiated. Both our partners faced this problem in their respective cities.

In St. Petersburg, things were further complicated. Larry King told Bill Grumbles that a man named Martin Rubenstein wielded considerable influence in the St. Petersburg market and with Telemax. Rubenstein wanted TBS to invest in a television tower in the city. This resulted in Russkoye Video paying a higher price in settling its arrangements with Telemax. Again, Atlanta was making things more difficult. TBS had no interest in the tower project, and it never came to be, but Rubenstein's involvement *was* a problem.

Another fact that bothered TBS was Russkoye Video's association with a state organization, the Russian Committee for Cinematography. Since Russkoye Video had minimal funding, belonging to a state organization meant:

1. no customs duties on imported equipment or film. Such duties normally added 30 percent to the purchase price of equipment and 15 percent to film costs.

Ted Turner pointing to Sid Pike as he arrives for 25th anniversary celebration of the Turner Broadcasting System.

2. money normally used for tax purposes could be invested in future productions.
3. facilities and land required only minimum payment.
4. Russkoye Video could apply at any time for full privatization. This was not too serious a problem and was finally accepted by Atlanta.

Like Channel 6, Channel 11 was scheduled to go on the air before any agreement was completed. Dmitri Rostenkowski, Nikita Matveyev (interpreter), and Alexander Kaisarov (attorney) flew to Atlanta to complete the joint venture agreement. Both Ted and Rostenkowski would sign it. I was determined to have the document ready for his signature.

I also wanted to get the Russkoye Video principals out of St. Petersburg, since there lurked in the background other Western businesses interested in joint ventures with Channel 11. Furthermore, Rubenstein's involvement had resulted in a good deal of ill will with our potential partners, which I had worked hard to defuse.

Steve Korn, TBS's Corporate General Counsel, changed lawyers in midstream, bringing in Carolyn Dailey from London to replace Andy Velcoff in Atlanta. Carolyn had participated in a number of meetings in Moscow and St. Petersburg, yet Korn replaced Carolyn with Louise Sams. Sams was a very able lawyer based in Atlanta, but she had never participated in, or even attended, meetings in either Russian city. Korn, whom I considered unsympathetic to the Eastern Europe project, was now a member of the TBS Executive Committee. As I expected, Korn refused my request to reconsider the lawyer assignment for the final stage of the agreement, which was completed in Atlanta. TBS executives continued to place obstacles in my path.

TBS would hold a 45 percent interest and Turner would contribute $1.75 million in programs and films and $1 million in cash. Thus, TBS would be in the second largest Russian market (5.5 million people), with the possibility of SuperStation development in the future, particularly if the arrangements with Channel 6 failed.

The financial analysis of the Channel 11 project made it clear that a positive cash flow would begin in less time than was expected with Channel 6. Ted was enthusiastic about the joint venture and, after a discussion in his office, took me next door to Terry McGuirk's office to schedule the preparation for Board approval. My job was to have the business plan on Terry's desk by May 18.

The agreement was signed, and the Russians returned to St. Petersburg on May 14. TBS board approval was set for June 4. Farrell Meisel was preparing a list of 615 MGM and RKO films that could be used in St. Petersburg and eventually in Moscow, and a similar list for Moscow that could be used later in St. Petersburg.

I sensed trouble in a message from Joyce a few weeks earlier. Joyce told me Mondini had called and said, "There have been a series of tragedies at Russkoye Video." That was it. Then he talked about the plans for my visit.

When Lill and I arrived on the overnight train, Mondini met us and was his usual ebullient self. The first thing he always asked anxiously was, "Did anything happen on the train?"

"No," I said, as usual, "I strapped the door." Strapping the door had made Lill very nervous.

Mondini told us about the mysterious incidents involving people associated with Russkoye Video. He was worried that this would give credence to certain "Russian Mafia" rumors that swirled around many enterprises in Russia, particularly in the major cities of Moscow and St. Petersburg. Two Channel 11 executives had died. One was Sergei Serborsky, Chief of the International Department. He was 26 and was found stabbed to death after a robbery at his mother's apartment. Mondini explained that Sergei's wallet had been stolen about a month before the robbery and possibly the robbers had found the address. This case was still under investigation.

The other incident involved the 24-year-old Chief of Advertising, who was well educated, a professional musician, and recently divorced. He had driven back and forth from Moscow to St. Petersburg—twice in four days, with each drive taking 10 hours each way. Exhausting trips, even for a young man. On the Moscow return, he was stopped by the police, who noticed he had been drinking. He paid the policeman and drove off. In Russia, you pay your fine on the spot and go on your way. You don't know what the policeman does with the money, but most Russians believe that he keeps it to supplement his painfully small salary. It started to rain as he drove. He was stopped again by the police, whom he again paid. He soon after crashed into a wall, and the car burst into flames. When the police checked the car, they found nothing mechanically wrong that could have caused the fatal accident.

The deaths of two such young men were very unfortunate for their families and co-workers. Mondini, Nikita, Dmitri, and the others were all grief-stricken. I had no reason to believe that the Mafia was involved.

Between the time the Channel 11 agreement was signed and the June 4 board meeting, two additional incidents occurred. These worried me. Mondini told me that Alexander Bershasdsky, the Vice-Chairman, had also died in an unusual way. Bershasdsky was a workaholic, had a history of asthma, which is not uncommon in cities as polluted as St. Petersburg, and had been using inhalers. He began to feel ill and told his driver to get him to his doctor. They had driven about two blocks when Bershasdsky turned blue. The driver stopped, tried to resuscitate him, and then rushed him to a hospital, which took 10 minutes, but it was too late. Bershasdsky had died from swallowing his tongue. The death certificate stated that he had died from complications following an epileptic seizure. There was an autopsy and evidently no reason to change the cause of death.

The other incident involved a boating explosion. A Russian government official and Rostenkowski were on board. The cabin was completely demolished, and an executive from Russkoye Video was badly burned, but at least no one was killed.

What did these deaths and violent incidents within such a short time mean? I didn't know what to make of it. The explanations seemed plausible, but who knew? Was I getting TBS into something that would prove, at the very least, embarrassing? Was the Mafia behind these mysterious events? I had faith in Dmitri, Nikita, and the others. I thought these events might just have been crazy coincidences. There were many rumors of Mafia connections, which, I understood, originated among the former communists, who were displeased with the success of the new and ambitious entrepreneurs.

Needless to say, I was not sleeping well those nights leading up to the TBS Board meeting on June 4. The next day, after I'd talked to Mondini, I received an urgent message to call Mauricio Mendez in Moscow. He wanted to tell me what he had learned about Russkoye Video. He told me the name of his source, but had promised that this name would not be used. When I heard the name, I knew who he was and that he had a responsible position in one of the leading advertising agencies in St. Petersburg. He would have only benefited from our agreement with Channel 11, and said that Channel 11 had Mafia connections. Then I became very concerned. Now we definitely had a reason to worry. This agency had welcomed us to Russia and was looking forward to working with us.

I was known as a risk-taker, but there were limits. I could not risk the reputation of TBS and CNN or jeopardize careers, let alone *lives*. I called Bill Grumbles and asked that the Board approval of the TBS/Russkoye Video agreement be taken off the upcoming Board agenda until further due diligence was completed. I wanted to be able to assure the Board at a future meeting that, after a full investigation, no suspicious connections had been found to our St. Petersburg joint venture.

Terry McGuirk didn't like taking it off the agenda because the Board members had already received their copies in advance. I was also aware that some people were pleased that the approval process was slowed down. Steve Korn and the Legal Department hired Kroll Associates, which specialized in private investigations of purported criminal activities. Presumably, some of its personnel came from former intelligence services, and it used similar techniques to gather information on corporate clients.

I left on June 8 for an extended trip to Prague, then to Bratislava, Slovakia, then on to Moscow and St. Petersburg, and back to Bratislava. I would not return to Atlanta until August 1, after reports from the investigation arrived. I could only hope that there would be an honest appraisal.

On July 6 I received a copy of a memo from Louise Sams, outlining preliminary findings from Kroll Associates. She wrote:

> Kroll informant indicates that the rumors may be no worse nor more plentiful than with respect to any other Russian company. According to Kroll, companies in Russia may have been accused of criminal activities in the past on the basis of profiteering or price-fixing, which at the time conducted was not against the law but was offensive to some because it seemed capitalistic. Kroll advised that, regardless of the validity of the charge, there may be people who feel that there are old scores to settle with RVC [Russkoye Video].

By late July Sams reported that Kroll's informant would now provide information only directly and in person, not in writing or by telephone, to Kroll. The unnamed informant's reports—all based on hearsay, rumor, innuendo, and unsubstantiated claims—declared that Russkoye Video and at least five of its principals were deeply involved in organized crime ranging from murder, racketeering, and extortion to substantial black market operations in gold, jewelry, money laundering, and pornography.

In the final paragraph of this memo, Sams soberingly notes

> the informant who provided most of the foregoing information has now refused to make further inquiries about RVC and its officers and directors because he is concerned for his safety....[My contact at Kroll] indicated to me that Kroll did not ordinarily recommend to a client either to proceed with, or to withdraw from, a transaction....in this case, based upon the information obtained in the investigation and an understanding of the current climate in Russia, the individuals involved in the TBS investigation at Kroll felt that it was necessary to recommend to TBS that it not do business with RVC because of RVC's questionable activities and connections and the potential danger to TBS in being associated with such an entity.

These frighteningly serious accusations would normally be more than sufficient to cancel our contracts unhesitatingly. Yet the charges were also anonymous and uncorroborated. No self-respecting journalist would report such allegations. I didn't know whether to trust Kroll or its unnamed informant in Russia. Kroll advised that it had worked only a limited time for the funds that we had agreed to pay. However, if we paid another fee of twice that amount, then it could gather more information.

A year later, I learned that an article in the *Wall Street Journal* strongly challenged Kroll Associates' ethics and methods of collecting information.

I balanced risks against potential benefits, then decided to cancel TBS's involvement with Russkoye Video and Channel 11. I continually worried about whether I had made the right decision. For the first time in my professional life I ended a seemingly desirable agreement after the contracts were signed. I decided that we would have to wait for further developments in St. Petersburg to assure us that our partners had more acceptable associations. In my gut, I trusted Dmitri, and I was personally fond of Nikita and the other executives. We will probably never know the truth.

Three years later I knew I had made the right decision. A *USA Today* article about the "New Russians" described the situation in 1996:

> Business is conducted under the shadow of underworld hits and contract killings. Each day Moscow newspapers carry reports of the latest contract hits. There have been nearly 500 contract killings so far this year in Russia, up from 100 in 1992, according to the Interior Ministry. Among the victims at least 35 Russian bankers, three members of Russia's parliament and one prominent journalist. 'It's clear that organized crime controls large parts of the Russian economy,' says Peter Charow, executive director of the American Chamber of Commerce in Russia.

For anyone doing business in Russia during this period, criminal involvement was a way of life, but I believed that as the economy and the government stabilized, these elements would be forced out. I could not deny, however, that there were more than a few connections between Russkoye Video and organized crime. When I stayed in the dacha on the island in St. Petersburg, it was heavily guarded and surrounded by a high wall. I didn't consider this unusual—protecting one's property in an emerging capitalistic society was similar to the American West in the nineteenth century, when ranchers protected their cattle from rustlers with "hired guns" and barbed wire.

Occasionally, when one of the guards, always dressed in civilian clothes, opened a car door for me, I noticed how menacing he looked and was glad he was on "my side."

I was buried in Russian and East European projects from April to August 1993, except for the three weeks in Atlanta in May, when we signed the Channel 11 agreement, then officially terminated. There was no reason to believe that the same Mafia background lurked in our Moscow television joint venture. The Channel 6 agreement remained unsettled, and Ted was uncomfortable with the exclusivity provisions and wouldn't ask the TBS Board for additional funding. Our original investment had risen from $6 million to $12.8 million, although now MIBC was putting in $9.9 million in cash. Luk Oil informed me that it would put in $6.5 million of the MIBC share. MIBC was then paying all costs, including building

Atomic building in Moscow that Sid Pike proposed to house a new Russian/U.S. joint venture television station.

and studio rental, employees' salaries, plus $250,000 for antenna modifications. Turner's contribution so far had been staff support and access to the MGM film library, although Edward began pressing for cash.

As if my difficulties with Channel 11 weren't enough, Grumbles sent me a memo:

> Based on my recommendation that we re-involve Stu Loory in the negotiations, Ted then appointed him as chief negotiator of the team to return to Moscow to re-negotiate with MIBC. Stu will be joined by Carolyn Dailey, Harry Motro and Scott Herubin. You are welcome to join them. Your call.
>
> A letter will be sent this afternoon from me to Sagalayev informing him of the above.
>
> I will copy you.
>
> The team will plan to leave this weekend to begin work on Moscow on Monday.
>
> It was suggested in our meeting that you return to Moscow full time to oversee the day-to day at Channel 6 so that we may retain strict control. I would like for you to give that some thought.

Stu Loory, I was told, said at the meeting in Ted's office that he would have a signed agreement in two weeks since he was a good friend of Edward's. I made a painful, difficult decision: I chose *not* to be part of the team and resigned as Director General of Channel 6. I could imagine the frustration Ted was feeling about the two key Russian projects and the advice he was getting. I was not used to failing. Mauricio sent me a fax the next day with an article that recounted how Liggett & Myers had had a two-year battle with a Russian cigarette factory in order to form an agreement. The article's conclusion: "It was a long and difficult road. But if you are going to make it here, you have to stick it out."

I wasn't sure that the Channel 6 agreement would ever come to pass, and not just because I was no longer a negotiator. Edward was becoming more and more confident that he could go it alone. I sent Ted a memo to this effect.

Meantime, Edward was not pleased that I was bowing out of the negotiations. He wrote to me:

> I have become aware that your further activity will be now connected with some other projects and you are stepping aside from Channel 6 MOSCOW project.
>
> I am extremely disappointed by this, since I have connected with you the most impressive and serious plans for cooperation. And besides, all of us have come to love you as a person with not only a tremendous professional experience and wisdom, but a person with delicate and sensitive soul and a kind heart.
>
> We have the warmest recollections about meetings with you even though sometimes it was difficult and tough negotiations.
>
> We are going to miss you, your smile and your eyes.

In October 1993, I received a memo from John Agnoli, the new President of TI, telling me that Stu Loory would take over the duties of Director General of Channel 6. Grumbles would become President of Worldwide Distribution. He was also still responsible for TI. Despite his promise of an agreement in two weeks, a year later Stu Loory still had not delivered an agreement, and it was announced in late August 1994 that the proposed joint venture had come apart. Edward and MIBC now had TBS's 50 percent share to keep or dole out as they saw fit. There was a face-saving statement to the press about how Turner "will be limiting itself to the role of contract program-provider," as though this was an important arrangement. In actuality, Turner's relation to Channel 6 was now no different from that of any other relationship to supply film and programs to a station.

Edward Sagalayev and Ted Turner in Atlanta.

In my view, Turner had come up short in its contributions, and I don't mean money. It was the poor films from the MGM library that disenchanted Edward early on. And his financial resources had continued to grow. Other sources of money did not require 50 percent ownership and a major veto stipulation. I believe that Edward kept raising the TBS financial contribution, hoping to force us out. And surely he realized that he had more television experience than Stu Loory.

Ironically, one of the major reasons Edward Sagalayev was given a television license was because of his association with Turner. On my first visit to Moscow, I was invited to attend meetings with the government officials who were holding up the final awarding of the license to MIBC. I sensed that I was being used to convince these officials that, in awarding the license to MIBC, they were satisfying a desire to give something back to Ted Turner because he had lost so much money promoting the Goodwill Games, as well as on behalf of other Russian-U.S. mutual interests. His continuing "friendship" with Castro probably didn't hurt either.

Ideally, Stu Loory, who knew the ins and outs of the Russian government and was friendly with many of the officials, should have concentrated his efforts on getting government support for Turner's participation, which would have left Edward Sagalayev with no choice but to work out an agreement. But Loory, eager to fulfill both roles, TBS Russian representative and Channel 6 Director General, missed his opportunity to do what he was uniquely suited to do. And which would have contributed greatly to my work in developing the station.

In the final analysis, the question was whether TBS *wanted* an enterprise in Russia. If Ted's managers had used the same energy to help launch the Russian and Eastern European projects that they used to resist and terminate them, just imagine what we could have achieved. Yes, the Russian efforts had failed, but the opportunities in Eastern Europe were thriving.

Sid Pike in Moscow in front of TASS, 1991.

In 1995, two years after we had projected $1 million in advertising revenue for the year 1993 in Moscow, Channel 6 was grossing $4 to $6 million per *month*, which added up to $48 to $72 million per *year*. TBS's business development executives had insisted that our estimate of $2,250,000 for 1995 was much too high, and they persuaded Ted to withdraw from one of the few creative opportunities for global expansion remaining, even wasting assets already owned by the company. Both Channel 6 in Moscow and CME in the Czech Republic became successful, despite not having film libraries or management experts. They used the capital each market produced.

I believe that this myopic failure on TBS's part to understand the importance of these new projects was a contributing factor to the end of TBS as a separate company.

The management layers thrust between me and Ted now prevented us from working together and executing the impossible but successful goals we had always achieved. This reinforced my belief that I had only succeeded in developing CNN International because its earlier failure had convinced the division heads and Ted that there was no interest in U.S. television news *outside* North America. Perhaps they saw my CNN endeavors as something to keep me busy and out of their hair. The CNN project left me with the unfettered ability to get things done and reconnect with Ted. I still vividly recall how industry executives laughed and tried to boo me off the stage at a meeting of the National Association of Program Executives when I talked about the new SuperStation concept.

CHAPTER THIRTY-NINE

Executive Decisions and Other Crimes

"The global economy and labor are like water; each seeks its own level."

—Sidney Pike
At sea, aboard the *Insignia*
June, 2005

All my conflicts with Grumbles had come about because I was trying to carry out Ted's assignments. On Friday, September 17, 1993, Grumbles phoned me. I wasn't in my office, so he and Joyce set up a breakfast meeting for the following Monday. He had to catch a plane that morning, but he wanted to see me first. I couldn't wait for the weekend to be over. Why would Bill Grumbles, who always seemed so uncomfortable when I was around, want to have breakfast with me?

As soon as we ordered breakfast and the waitress walked away, Grumbles said, "The Executive Committee has decided you should leave. We're going to pay you for the rest of 1993 and through the following year." I could hardly contain myself from laughing out loud. He offered a severance of one year's pay.

Did I have any questions? No, I didn't have any questions. I got up and left. At least they hadn't asked me to vacate immediately while a security guard watched me leave. That had happened recently to another executive at TBS. I didn't have to ask; it was obvious Ted was out of town. I found out when Ted was expected in Atlanta and set up a meeting through Dee Woods.

I regret to say, with great sadness, that both loyal secretaries, Joyce Baston and Dee Woods, died of cancer. Dee passed away before I left TBS and Joyce two years after I retired.

A week later, I sat in Ted's spacious office and learned that he had no idea what had been planned for me by the Executive Committee. I told Ted I wanted to stay an additional four years, until I was 70. Ted said he would talk to Grumbles, and that was the end of it. *I never heard any more about my leaving.* Loyalty to Ted was no longer fashionable at TBS, although it saved my neck. Bill had already sent out a memo about my "retirement," complete with invitations to a retirement party.

I continued, after this abortive attempt to get rid of me, to work on the joint ventures in Eastern Europe that I had been developing while I was working in Russia. I found more financial stability and no criminal activity involving businesses. In Slovenia, Romania, and Slovakia, I competed with CME, the Ronald Lauder company that acquired the license in the Czech Republic. Its audience soared to 70 percent of the viewers in the first year. Lauder used this success to start up stations in other parts of Eastern Europe, as well as to issue stock in his new company. Even though it ran into some difficulty in a German venture, it was well on the way to developing a successful, interconnecting television network that would cover Eastern Europe and Russia, and maybe even other parts of the world. If properly managed, it could become the first global television broadcasting television station group, which I surmised was what Ted had envisioned for our Eastern European project.

I also spoke with representatives from Latvia, Estonia, and Lithuania. I had some interest in Poland, but had originally been told by Bob Ross to stay out of that country, as there was a possible joint venture with Time-Warner there. Bob, who was then head of TI, asked me to meet with John Janus, head of TimeWarner's international division so that we could coordinate our efforts in Poland. Despite many promises of cooperation, I never heard from Janus again. It seemed to me that TimeWarner's international plans lacked vision and the "know-how" that TBS had.

In the three Baltic countries, we had many contacts, including an American who had obtained a license in Lithuania. These were very small markets but could be part of a larger picture that would involve advertising opportunities in most of Eastern Europe. I intended to find a way back into Russia. Its opportunities were so vast and so important a part of the future that it had to be incorporated into our global effort.

In late 1993 and 1994, I concentrated first on Slovakia and then on Slovenia, where I found fewer difficulties and the most cooperation in developing a joint venture. Czechoslovakia split up on January 1, 1993. Slovakia had invited us to compete with other European and American television groups for a license that had belonged to the state. We were to create a business arrangement with a local individual, business, or group. When we set up an office in Slovakia in February 1993, Prime Minister Vladimir Meciar, who many believed forced the split between the Czech and Slovak governments, was still in power. Turner found itself applying for a license during a difficult political time for this small country of 5.2 million people. Some commentators thought that Meciar had forced the split to establish his own power base. He had been expelled from the Communist party and then had participated in Czechoslovakia's anti-communist Velvet Revolution of November 1989. He still had strong appeal to those on the political left.

In the Czech Republic the government became eager to find a strong competitor for CME's TV NOVA because it realized that the station was becoming too powerful. It decided to give a license to a relatively small independent station and to permit it to cover the entire Czech Republic, thereby giving TV NOVA competition. The new regional network was Premiera TV. I met Libor Prochazka, the Vice President and General Manager of the bank, which purchased 45 percent of the network from an Italian investor and now owned it all. The Italian investor had corresponded with us in Atlanta, but he wanted $7 to $8 million for his 45 percent. Since we were permitted to offer only programming and expertise for equity, with minimal investment, we had to pass on the offer.

In Slovakia, we were caught up in a national political power struggle. A group of 12 small political parties formed a coalition and defeated Meciar in March 1994. There was no consensus within the coalition, and after the election, they broke up into aimless, weak entities. The very conservative Christian Democratic Party opposed us because we represented the "sins" of Hollywood. Some viewers watching CME's TV NOVA in the Czech Republic were appalled by the sex and violence in American films, but especially by erotic films such as *Emmanuelle*, which TV NOVA introduced as late night fare. No wonder the Christian Democrats in Slovakia didn't believe me when I said we were family-oriented programmers!

We also faced considerable opposition, especially in Meciar's nationalistic party, because we were a foreign company, even though we had local participation. The fact that the two state television channels employed almost 3,000 workers, and we planned to begin our station with a staff of 50, made them look bad and added to our problems.

Nadia Fino was concerned that our telephone conversations in the Czech Republic and Slovakia were being listened to, so we devised a system of referring to our "friends" with Hollywood names. A key member of the government in Prague was Humphrey Bogart; in Bratislava, the key official was Clark Gable.

I proposed that a non-profit foundation be part of the joint venture for both the Czech and Slovak Republics. Since Turner would be providing the money to operate the stations, we could, in effect, select our partner. Since no one was stepping up with funds to buy shares in our new Slovak company, I proposed that a 20 percent share of the company be given to a foundation made up of local board members, who would use that share of the profits to assist certain non-profit enterprises. I did this with the nationalist feelings of our political opponents in mind, particularly some members of the Licensing Committee.

The President, Deputy Prime Minister, and two parties of the new coalition favored our application. These officials were aware of the importance of CNN and wanted an association with TBS. They tried to convince Prime Minister Meciar that we would be a proper choice to receive the license. But we were not acceptable to Meciar or to Ms. Baldisova, head of the Television Licensing Committee, a fervent nationalist who was against any foreign ownership, particularly by an American company. She was reported to have said as a meeting began, "Anybody but CNN." She kicked out members who were in favor of Turner and replaced them with more compliant people. She insisted that she was not required to explain her actions.

There were 22 applicants, primarily European and American companies, for the Slovakia license. The Licensing Committee members were very inexperienced about the operation of an independent commercial television station. There would be neither state subsidies nor fees from those who owned television sets. Furthermore, to make supporting the station by advertising even more difficult, there was a policy of no commercial breaks within programs, even lengthy movies. Advertising was permitted only at program breaks. Additionally, a large block of time had to be devoted to costly local productions.

Another requirement, specifically aimed at us, was that films or programs older than 10 years could be no more than one-tenth of the programming. This would limit our use of MGM films, including such popular classics as *Gone with the Wind* and *Dr. Zhivago.* The rule against older films was arbitrary and foolish, but typical of the kind of thinking we faced.

I didn't want the failure to obtain a business license to injure us in Slovakia as it already had in the Czech Republic. Ted had approved it, and on February 15, I had sent a memo to Karshan in London informing him of Ted's decision. By April we still had no business license. I personally contacted our attorneys in Slovakia, but I got only excuses. When we still had no license some months later, Nadia and I got our own lawyer.

We faced other legal and professional obstacles, too. For example, we encountered a lawyer, Milan Ganik, who liked to work both sides of the fence. Ganik, head of the Prague office of a law firm that proved unable to secure our business license in either Slovakia or the Czech Republic—the firm of Squire, Sanders & Dempsey of Cincinnati, with offices in both countries—was going to represent one of our leading competitors in Slovakia for the television license. Louise Sams and I agreed that this "switch of teams" was an unheard of breach of ethics. Apparently other officials decided no to sue Squire, Sanders & Dempsey or to take other action. I wondered why. I still wonder. Did it have something to do with the cooperation of outside organizations in the internal sabotage of my European efforts?

One reason I held on in Slovakia was because John Dobson estimated $19 million market in 1993 for Slovakia and $65 million for the Czech Republic. He estimated Russia at $8 million, but its 140 million people meant more potential advertising revenue in the future.

I fought hard for a license in Slovakia, which I wanted as a starting point for our Eastern Europe project. However, Premiera TV in the Czech Republic began to look better as a base. It was obvious to me that the ruling coalition in Slovakia was temporary. In fact, it lasted only until the fall of 1994. Meciar returned to power and returned radio and television to state control.

I did want to find out if it were true that the TBS Legal Department had deliberately kept me from obtaining a business license at the time of the first joint venture in the Czech Republic. I wanted to hear it directly from Andy Velcoff, the company attorney who had worked with me at the time. The right opportunity to ask him arose at Terry McGuirk's Christmas party in 1995. Lill, several hundred other guests, and I entered the brightly-lit house. I ended up in the kitchen, which seemed to be the center of activity. I saw Andy Velcoff and his wife enter and squeeze their way toward the champagne glasses on the kitchen table. Lill happened to be standing near them, and I thought, *Now's the time.*

I made my way to Andy through the throng of people talking, drinking, and laughing. He seemed pleased to see me. I got straight to the point. "Andy, why did the Legal Department keep me from getting a business license in the Czech Republic and Slovakia?"

Andy turned away, so that I was looking at his profile. Seconds went by, and I was saying to myself, he won't tell me. Then, after a long pause and without turning to face me, he said, "Terry was having financial trouble." I had my answer and the reason. Terry had wanted it killed. I was relieved to know this. I had no reason to stay any longer, so Lill and I left the party.

Ted had given tremendous responsibility to Terry McGuirk. It was his job to keep the Turner stock up. He had a difficult time of it because of the losses over the years. Then, when TBS began to make money, Terry wanted to use it to encourage Wall Street investments in TBS. The n-TV fiasco in Germany didn't become clear until after Ted had given me the go-ahead in Eastern Europe. Terry must have been convinced that the money for my joint ventures, minimal as it was, was needed more to increase the value of TBS stock, and he wrongly associated the German debacle with potential losses from our project. It was a short-term, short-sighted view. So, the Executive Committee, in order to prevent wasteful expenditures, simply dropped anchor. They lacked the vision and talent to sail uncharted seas, even though that was exactly what had been responsible for TBS's success.

One day, some time later, Ted and I met by accident at the entrance to the office building. He called to me with his usual "Pi-i-i-ke" bellow. Then he said, "It was good we got out of Russia and those other places, wasn't it?" His look suggested that he hoped I would agree. I smiled but didn't answer, and I walked on.

CHAPTER FORTY

Project: Meltdown

"Time sure changes things," an airline passenger told his companion. "When I was a boy, I used to sit in a flat-bottomed rowboat in the lake down there below us and fish. Every time a plane flew over I'd look up and wish I were in it. Now I look down and wish I were fishing."

—Anonymous

In 1994, I was also working with several very small countries, none very economically advanced but which had enormous potential. Romania was one of them. The Baltics were also waiting for us to form joint ventures with them. In Slovenia, a small country of two million people in northern Yugoslavia next to Italy and Austria, and well advanced in economic development, the independent station, Kanal A, headed by Vladimir Polic, wanted to reach an agreement with us. A license was already in place.

Polic wanted a joint venture, but he was having financial and personnel problems. As an engineer, he understood the technical side of television, and he had designed the system that distributed Kanal A throughout Slovenia. His only real competition was the state channel, and an infusion of Turner programs would have been just the fix Kanal A needed to become the leading television system in Slovenia. Because of Turner's interest in Kanal A, a British firm, Barings Investment, bought a 20 percent financial interest in it.

CME was dogging my heels here, too. Polic's refusal to join CME left him in a vulnerable position as CME threatened that it would build a competing network even though, initially, it would cover only 60 percent of Slovenia.

For us, Slovenia needed to be part of a bigger picture. Scott Herubin and I were preparing a business plan for Ted and TBS approval, once we completed our arrangement with Premiera TV, which had a market large enough to justify our investment in these smaller countries. We had received the okay from Bob Ross in spite of his reluctance. After the meeting with him and Scott Herubin in August 1994, I assessed the situation, reflecting on some of the new things I had learned from our meeting.

Back in 1991, Bob Ross had brought a proposal to Ted that asked for $500,000 for an application fee for U.K. television privatization. Ted had exploded and said, "I forbid you to think about broadcasting." But in mid-1992, Ted had instructed me to look at broadcast opportunities in Eastern Europe and Russia.

In January 1994, Bob Ross made another proposal to Ted to create a separate division for broadcasting opportunities worldwide. That precipitated a meeting with Terry McGuirk, Scott Sassa, and Bill Grumbles, and they pooh-poohed it before the meeting with Ted. It was killed. Ted told Bob that he was not against broadcast joint ventures, but preferred a substantial or majority stake for little cash and some programming. Unfortunately, this conversation led Bob Ross to believe that Ted was *not* interested in television broadcast systems. It was some time before Bob understood that Ted was *still* interested in my project, which had only minimal capital investment. Bob, in his role as president of TI, didn't give the Premiera project in Prague the attention it needed and deserved.

When the board memo about our joint venture with Premiera TV was completed and required his approval, Bob suddenly decided that he didn't want to discuss it. He then left immediately on a flight with John Kirtland, who had recently joined TI to help in developing projects. John promised me and Scott that he would bring it up during the trip. But John phoned us a day or two later and said Bob refused to talk about it. By the time we could get Bob to re-focus on the document, we had lost an important two weeks, even though he did, finally, approve it.

All of this extended the already drawn-out negotiations with Premiera TV. As in Moscow, each point had to be discussed in great detail and involved differing perceptions, both legally and personally. We knew that the Czech government wanted Turner to be Premiera TV's network partner, even though our cash interest was very small. A price of $17 million was set for the 45 percent that was available. A Czech insurance company was brought in to put up $8.5 million for 22.5 percent. It also put up $7 million of *our* $8.5 million as an advance on future programming and film costs. All Turner had to do was put up $1.5 million in cash. It was an incredibly good deal for us. We projected that the advertising sales market for 1995 would be $105 million, but that number jumped to $166 million, and the sales in 1996 were projected to be $180 to 200 million. TBS had blown the first opportunity in the Czech Republic, but now we had a second opportunity for a 22.5 percent share, when the first would have been 66 percent.

My first meeting with Prochazka, the banker/investor in Premiera TV, had taken place in the spring of 1994. There were interminable delays, plus the confusion about authority and the approval process at Turner. The Premiera TV joint venture took over a year and, ultimately, moved us into the "TimeWarner phase," when Gerald Levin was trying to purchase TBS. As if these problems weren't enough, we suddenly had, toward the end of this period, more and more conflicts *within* TBS.

John Barbera, who had been head of Advertising Sales, and whom I could call and talk to directly, even though I hadn't been able to convince him to help on my project, had been replaced by Steve Heyer, formerly of the Y&R International Advertising Agency in Europe and later was to become a high level executive at Coca-Cola. Steve didn't return phone calls or answer memos. Fortunately, I had friends in that division to whom I could turn for advice. I elected to work around Heyer rather than make an issue of his behavior and cause problems for the project. Meantime, Heyer had become a card-carrying member of the Executive Committee. If this committee was so effectively countermanding Ted's efforts in Eastern Europe, one wonders: What else they were doing?

This was the atmosphere in the company when I came forward with our last opportunity for a successful conclusion to Ted's proposed joint ventures in Russia and Eastern Europe. We finally reached an agreement with Premiera TV in one of the fastest growing markets in Central Europe. We would be involved in managing, and that would be our base for planned partnerships in Romania, Slovenia, Estonia, Latvia, and Lithuania. There were also expressions of interest in Poland, Hungary, and Bulgaria. All these projects required minimal cash, and each of the prospective partners understood that either they, the government, or other partners would have to finance the television network. We would primarily offer films, programs, and management, including, I hoped, the development of advertising sales.

Each division of TBS, whether CNN, Finance, or Advertising Sales, while not having offered any direct involvement in the overall planning, had to acknowledge that the agreement and the business plan were reasonable and would not harm their division. A copy went to Turner Entertainment Group (TEG), headed by Scott Sassa, who was responsible for the Entertainment Division, which comprised SuperStation TBS, TNT, Cartoon Network, TCM, TNT Pictures, Turner Pictures Worldwide (TPW), and the international channels: TNT Latin America, Cartoon Network Latin America, TNT Europe, Cartoon Network Europe, TNT Asia, and Cartoon Network Asia. Sassa had worked for TBS under Gerry Hogan, then left the company to work for *Playboy*, and had returned.

About six months before TEG received their copy of the Premiera TV proposal, Scott Sassa hired Willy Burkhardt to assist in the creative development of his division. Willy had business degrees and had worked as a consultant for Hungarian Airlines and for a management consultant company. Sassa had not been involved in my projects, nor had he interfered—he had no interest in anything I was doing. And he didn't like tying up his key people, who already had their hands full.

Willy Burkhardt saw an opportunity for TEG to take over the project and expand its division's television operations globally, since it was already operating the various 24-hour channels. That TEG, or another part of TBS, would eventually take over the Eastern Europe joint ventures was well within my line of vision. But the complicated battle for the project's survival *within* the company dictated that the transfer of the entire project to TEG would not have been timely at the stage of final approval for Premiera TV.

Willy, however, wanted it immediately. While not bright enough to create his own rising star project, he was smart enough to see the incredible opportunity our project promised. Willy convinced Scott Sassa to declare that the Premiera TV joint venture rightfully fell under TEG. This meant that Sassa's division would make the final preparation for TBS Board approval. Bob Ross, who was wondering why we continued to do a project that he thought he had been told to stay away from, agreed.

This left a very short time for Sassa's division to learn the intricacies of the joint venture and my other plans for Eastern Europe. There was no careful and orderly transition. Willy wasn't satisfied to learn the project slowly and then take charge. He wanted to be in charge instantly. He had positioned himself behind the one person no one wanted to challenge. Scott was not only in charge of all of the revenue-producing networks at TBS, except for CNN, he was the only one in the company who had motion picture management experience and could supervise the ongoing film productions for TPW.

Scott had recently managed to negotiate a very favorable employment contract based on rumors that he might leave. In the past, when I had read in gossip columns that Bob Wussler was looking at other opportunities, it was usually an indication that he was in contract negotiations with Ted. Sassa seemed to recognize the effectiveness of this tactic, as any mention of his talking to other film companies concerned Ted enough to produce the desired results. Whether MCA or another film company was seriously negotiating with Sassa, I do not know, but Sassa had all the leverage he needed to get what he wanted. Willy then chose to use Sassa to get what Willy wanted. Proof of this was when Bob Ross walked into my office, shortly after Sassa said it should be TEG's project, and announced, "I'm not going to take on Scott Sassa. He can take over the Czech/Premiera TV project if he wants it."

At this point I didn't care, as long as it got the TBS Board's approval. I had carefully rebuilt our project after the failure in Russia, and I had five small countries ready to exchange proposals with when the Czech Republic, with its $200 million potential market for 1996, became our base.

I didn't argue with Bob Ross. I contacted Sassa and asked for a meeting in his office at Techwood, which was a couple of miles from the CNN Center complex. Of course, I wasn't aware then of Willy Burkhardt's grab for power, only that Sassa wanted to take over the project. But I found that Willy had been invited to the meeting. I wasn't interested in challenging anyone when we were only weeks away from Board approval, and I told Sassa that I would cooperate. When did he want me to move my office to Techwood?

"No, no," he said. "You don't have to come over here. Stay where you are. You can just work on the joint ventures from TI."

Willy hadn't said much. I thought that he and Sassa had discussed transferring my office, and Scott, who was known for being tight with a budget, didn't want the added expense of having me there. But I was wrong. Later, I would learn that Willy wanted to get rid of me entirely.

I was surprised, but I had no objection. I ended the meeting by repeating gracefully my willingness to cooperate fully. I suggested to Willy that we arrange a trip to Prague, and I would introduce him to the principals at Premiera TV, the investment bank, and the insurance company.

Not long after the meeting with Sassa, Willy and I met in Prague. I told each of the principals at Premiera TV that TEG and Willy Burkhardt now represented Turner and that Willy was our new spokesperson. They seemed confused and not too pleased, but they, too, were eager to get the TBS Board's approval. When they asked, "Why?" I told them that TBS had decided that TEG was the proper division to run the joint venture.

I had hoped that the time in Prague would give Willy and me an opportunity to develop a working relationship, but Willy was very cold and businesslike. In spite of this, I reminded him that I would retire in two to three years and I had no company ambitions. I was trying to tell him that he could have the project and that I was only interested in seeing it to a successful conclusion. But Willy was having none of this and saw himself as taking over my responsibilities entirely. He did not even want me to be on the Premiera TV Board, as had been previously arranged with the bank and the insurance company. He wanted to do that as well.

I was offended by his treatment of me, but I was determined not to interfere and decided to fade into the background. This was hard for me to do, since normally I would have fought for continuing control of the project. By this time, I knew the company was no longer unified or operating confidently with shared goals under the leadership of Ted Turner, who had carried television broadcasting to heights unknown by the industry.

I was worried about Vladimir Polic and Kanal A in Slovenia. His network was struggling financially. I thought of it as a model for what each Yugoslavian country could become. Still, because of its communist past, it was hard to find people who knew how to sell advertising time, the only support for the network. Polic badly needed us to train and guide his sales people. Mauricio Mendez had done this for Channel 6 Moscow for two years before the joint venture fell apart, but it had learned how to do it in that time. Polic, however, could not find someone strong enough to lead his sales effort. His chief of programming, Branko Cakarmis, whom Polic relied on, "jumped ship" and crossed over to the enemy CME and its efforts to take over Kanal A. Barings, the British investment group, was impatient, since it had invested in it because of the proposed Turner involvement.

Herubin came to me, concerned because Willy was changing the estimates for 1996, the first year of the business plan. He was adding to the projected expenses and decreasing the revenue for that year so that he would look good when the actual numbers were available. This was more evidence that he knew little about operating a television system, but I was worried because of the "psychosis" that controlled so many executives at Turner. That mistake was very clear by this time because TBS had lost $18.6 million in 1993, $12 million in 1994, and it looked as if it would be losing about that much in 1995. The executives were becoming convinced that any broadcast television system would lose money.

I learned the week before the TBS Board approval was scheduled that TBS accounting had decided to review the costs of the Premiera plan, although it had previously been approved. Our cash investment was minimal, only $1.5 million, with $9 million in programs and films to be used by the network as payment for our 22.5 percent of ownership. I learned that Wayne Pace, Chief Financial Officer (CFO), and Willy had decided to treat the $9 million program commitment as cash. Why? I didn't know. Pace then declared that we would have to take the entire $10.5 million commitment as a loss in the first year (1996). For some unfathomable reason, he decided to throw in another $4 or $5 million for "unknown losses," even though we were under no obligation to cover losses for the network. Pace also didn't know, or refused to recognize, that the bank was lending the project $18 million. The Czech insurance company was putting in $8.5 million for its 22.5 percent, plus $7 million in cash as an advance for our share, for a total of $15.5 million added to the $18 million loan. That totaled $33.5 million (not counting our $9 million programming infusion) to support a network *already in operation.*

I was incredulous. What was Wayne Pace thinking? He was estimating our programming infusion as a cash *loss.* Turner had hardly sold any films or programs in the Czech Republic in years, which made it ripe territory for our MGM library. I also learned that TBS had a problem with debt covenants on its loans. It had already renegotiated its covenants with the banks in 1994, and Wayne Pace was claiming that creating a $12 million or more loss in 1996 would have an adverse effect on the covenant to the banks. Why was he doing that? We had checked with other financial investment institutions, and all of them had agreed that you do not treat a programming agreement as a cash commitment. A fundamental rule of finance is that you don't treat anything as cash other than cash. It may look like cash; it may smell like cash; it may taste like cash. But unless it's cash, it ain't cash.

Why was Pace making this strange decision after he had previously okayed the deal? Was he being pressured? His office was next to Terry McGuirk's. Was McGuirk trying to sink our second attempt at a Czech venture after his order to pull the plug three years earlier on our first effort? CME, which had gotten the venture, was valued in 1995 at $675 million. That would have been TBS's, if Ted Turner's vision had been allowed to come to fruition.

I asked for a meeting with Wayne that included Scott Herubin, our accountant. He agreed to squeeze us in. I was glad that we would see him before the Monday morning board meeting. Wayne was a friendly, affable person and made apologies for the consternation he had caused. He acknowledged that he had little experience in film syndication. After we explained how we saw the financial roadblocks that he was setting up, he agreed with most of our arguments. He then told us that he wanted to cooperate and to be given the direction the company wanted to go.

As Scott and I stood up to leave, Scott told Wayne that he had met with Bob Sauban, the head of the TBS Tax Department. Since TBS was now showing a profit, after many years of losses because of growth, we now had to pay a 40 percent tax. Thus any "perceived" losses created by the excessive figures could have been recovered in tax savings. This surprised Pace. He smiled at Scott and said, "That's really interesting."

I was sure that the executives on the fourteenth floor next to Ted's usually empty office had found another way to stop our effort in the Czech Republic. But the final decision was Scott Sassa's, since his division had taken over the project, and I learned that he and Willy were meeting the next morning. I didn't think the proposal had a chance with the phony cash deficit and extra expenses that Willy had added to protect himself. I knew that Scott Sassa's decision was a foregone conclusion, but still I hoped that he would have the guts to fight for the project he had claimed. He was a strange cat, not like the others, and willing to take reasonable risks.

Sassa *killed* the deal that he had previously *approved*. Now the proposal he had signed off on and taken away from us a month before as "rightfully his" was terminated right after the meeting with Willy. And Willy had gone from an eager supporter to a fence straddler, too scared to climb down and get in the fight. With any project there is risk, which Willy, as it turned out, had neither the character nor the stomach for.

I couldn't blame Sassa. It was as though a horse had been burdened with a 400-pound jockey in order to make sure it lost. I had to laugh. Each of those "pounds" represented cash that didn't even exist. I didn't think Sassa wanted the project. He had too many headaches already. Willy had wanted his own empire, but had panicked when the going got rough. As for Ted, he didn't have a clue about what was going on. He was fed negative information about the project, and our meetings and memos were now so rare that he probably didn't recall the positive information I had given him to offset the naysayers. He was to arrive the day before the TBS Board meeting, and I called his office for an appointment as a last ditch effort to save the project. I asked Scott Herubin and John Dobson, who had done the advertising revenue estimates, to join me in the meeting. I wanted Scott to explain the misuse of the word *cash* and John to review the Czech market's advertising potential. I knew the MGM movies were gathering dust in a vault, waiting for someone to buy them. We had never and would never get $9 million in program sales in Czechoslovakia for those films. This took a great deal of courage on Herubin's and Dobson's part to support me, knowing of Ted's mixed signals, and my status as the Executive Committee's "target."

We met in Ted's outer office and waited on the lounge chairs that are about 20 feet from Ted's double office doors. Ted led some visitors out of the office, spotted me, and for the first time since we had known each other, he let me down. He mumbled something about not needing to meet. Then he looked straight at me, and our eyes locked for a brief moment, and he changed his mind and motioned us to come in. The three of us walked in and sat down in the circle of chairs and couches near his large window. I tried to explain the potential of the Premiera TV proposal and was preparing to let John add his figures, when Ted stopped me. "Sid, I can't overrule Sassa," he said. And that was the end of it.

For years Ted, as quarterback for TBS, had thrown me touchdown passes, and we had won game after game. Then, in the last game of the season, when we had to win and were only a few points behind, I caught his pass and ran for the goal once again, with no opponents in sight, only to be tackled on the one-yard line. When I looked up, those wearing the same uniform colors I was wearing had brought me down.

This was the end of Ted's Russian and Eastern European vision, the end of TBS, too, because there were no more frontiers to explore for now. Ted had been completely boxed in by his partners and his top executives. Imagine a way-out-front leader in an Olympic marathon, everybody's favorite, who suddenly decides to fall back in the pack because he can no longer believe in his ability to win. I realized also that it was the end of our business relationship. I had worked for 25 years to make our dreams come true. *I knew at that moment in Ted's office that all that was over.* The meeting didn't last five minutes. As I walked out the door, I thought about my most recent meeting with him, when he had said in a rare, soft voice, "Sid, you can make anything happen."

This had been my last project for Ted, and I had failed to pull it off. But later, as I thought about it, I realized that the circumstances had been extraordinary. Those other small countries that were waiting would have to find another solution or accommodate themselves to CME, while the Premiera TV network and Polic in Slovenia would have great difficulty surviving.

This was the hardest part for me. For 47 years, I had built television entities, but I had never participated in demolishing them. Nor was it the way I wanted to end a career that had given me challenges and excitement that most people can only fantasize about.

I had participated in some of the most dramatic changes in television between 1950 and 1996. My development of CNN internationally was the most significant. I was sure that my contribution to global communication *would* enhance greater understanding and more concern for our planet in the coming centuries.

I thought about my career when I retired not long afterward, and decided that the chance to build TBS and work with Ted Turner was the most stimulating and creative opportunity a person could wish for as part of his working lifetime. If the United States had not been in a recession in 1973, and I had succeeded in purchasing my own television station and perhaps others later on, I would have built a mountain of wealth, but not had anywhere near the satisfaction I felt in originating CNN International and defeating the Intelsat global monopoly. This gave unrestricted free satellite signal access to every country and human being on earth.

The world would never be the same again.

Epilogue

The collapse of the Eastern European and Russian joint ventures, as well as Ted's failure to acquire a major television network, meant that he had no way to drive his company and its stock forward, as he had done time and time again. TBS's highly successful growth was the "tech" stock of the 1970s and 1980s. That all changed in the late-1990s. Despite TBS's indebtedness over the MGM purchase, I now believe that John Malone sensed that, even if Ted bit off too big a piece, he could sooner or later digest it. But Gerald Levin of TimeWarner made no secret in 1987 that he expected eventually to acquire CNN, the "jewel in the crown" of the Turner Empire. The stock purchase had stipulated that if Ted chose to sell CNN, then TimeWarner would have the right of first refusal. TimeWarner executives unabashedly admitted that CNN would belong to them. The only way to get it was to acquire the entire company since Ted would never let it be spun off.

Turner Broadcasting System was sold to TimeWarner in 1996 for over $7 billion. In 2003 CBS supposedly offered AOL-TimeWarner $5.7 billion for CNN alone. No one in the stock market, not even Ted himself, fully understood the worth of CNN and its recognition internationally. It had a 16-year lead on its global competitors, the goodwill that we had nurtured in each country, and it continued to prove its importance to the world and its leaders. I hoped that nothing would ever change the popular saying: "It was on CNN; it must be so." In 2005 CNN International was still the major global 24-hour television news service. The FOX News Service has failed as of this writing to create a separate 24-hour news service for viewers outside of the United States, as CNN did more than 15 years ago.

CNN suffers criticism from domestic viewers in the United States who resent its impartiality and presentation of global, especially European, opposition to the American political agenda and its war on terrorism worldwide. While this is relatively easy with the separation of CNN International from CNN (U.S.), the global view is predominate in its news coverage in the United States as well because CNN treasures its reputation as an impartial global news service. Remember Bernard Shaw's refusal to be debriefed by U.S. intelligence services. While this was his own decision and not a CNN policy, it showed the attitude of the news personnel and reflects the CNN editorial philosophy.

Fox television news, on the other hand, is dangerous to U.S. foreign policy. Its American viewpoint and even arrogance, as expressed on programs like Bill O'Reilly's *No Spin Zone,* geared for the consumption of domestic viewers, has a deleterious effect on global populations, particularly in the Middle East during the Iraq war and global terrorism conflict.

In yet another phase of the "food chain" syndrome of corporate America, TimeWarner itself was swallowed by America OnLine (AOL), the successful Internet provider started by Steve Case, a young entrepreneur with a "can do" personality a lot like Ted's. AOL knew that its competition was growing and that broadband, the new high-speed Internet service, would eventually erode AOL's subscriber base. It also caught TimeWarner without an understanding of this potential problem when high-tech was at its peak. AOL was desperate to find another media business and, because of Levin's lapse of foresight, took over TimeWarner, along with Turner Broadcasting.

In 2002, the bubble burst in the tech industry. Soon AOL became an enormous weight that TimeWarner and TBS carried before Case himself resigned. Levin was forced out one year earlier, in a board room revolt led by Ted Turner, for making the merger with AOL.

The Information Age in which we live, sharing our knowledge in the realms of business, economics, politics, and education, is leading to a Dangerous Age, when all of the newly educated people of the earth will add to the demand for the world's diminishing natural resources and ever diminishing usable land. My hope is that the information explosion created by satellites will offset this danger and help develop leaders who are aware of how profoundly the decisions they make during this transition period will affect the future of the human race.

* * * * *

By 2001, CNN had its competitors. In the mid-1980s Rupert Murdoch, who created the FOX Network, purchased a major Hollywood film company and skillfully embarked on developing his own major network in the United States and worldwide. His investments were so vast that he could shift large sums of money to development areas that were part of a global picture and had a promising future.

When he outbid CBS for televising NFL games, he shocked the whole industry, just as he had intended to do. In one expensive stroke, he established the FOX Network as a fourth major U.S. network. Many television entrepreneurs had attempted to create a fourth network, including Ted, at the peak of the SuperStation mania, but only Murdoch succeeded.

Turner and CBS courted each other, but never tied the knot. A marriage of TBS and CBS would have strengthened a major network for future programming competition in a cable and internet world and been a brilliant coup. CBS would have regained its dominant position because of Turner's cable success and CNN's domination of global news. That merger would have allowed Ted to continue using his imagination and vision, and given him reason to stay more closely attuned to the day-to-day operations in Atlanta. In 2003, when CBS made an offer to purchase CNN from AOL-TimeWarner, the new owners of CNN said it was not for sale, even though the parent corporation was wallowing in a $29 billion debt.

CBS's refusal to join Turner Broadcasting harmed Turner, who needed a network to continue expansion with the likes of Murdoch, but proved to be a poor decision on the part of CBS's management. Turner Broadcasting advanced TimeWarner's fortunes in the television industry. The same benefit could have belonged to CBS, since Ted's foresight and abilities were never matched at CBS by Sumner Redstone and Viacom. Indeed, CBS executives were likely quite skittish at the prospect of becoming partners with the maverick, loudmouth Ted Turner.

CBS was run by weak management until it was enveloped by one of the worst news reporting disasters in the history of television news. In the 2004 Presidential election campaign, CBS news presented a news segment on its *60 Minutes* program claiming to have documents proving that President Bush had lied about his National Guard military service during the Vietnam War. These documents proved to be a fraud. The bias to the left was pervasive at all three networks in New York City, but most particularly at CBS, where it was more interested in influencing the political outcome of that year's presidential campaign than in adequately investigating the document sources.

Ted realized that he could not compete with Murdoch in the long run. The purpose of the marriage with TimeWarner was to create so large a media entity that it could compete with, and in the case of CNN, continue to dominate, the emerging international networks. The Turner Broadcasting merger did aid TimeWarner's bottom line, and its success was growing until the AOL merger.

By the time of the 2003 Iraq war, FOX and MSNBC were competing with CNN, with FOX even beating CNN substantially in the U.S. ratings. But I doubt that any news channel competitors can even come close to reaching an audience as vast as the one we developed throughout the world.

First, CNN and CNNI are the most respected television news services on a global scale. Their roots and reputation run deep.

Second, FOX News, widely watched in the United States, has a reputation for bias to the political right. CNN, ABC, CBS, and NBC are considered to lean to the left. While this may be a U.S. domestic issue, my concern is how the networks affect present-day news seen globally. The only networks televising news by global satellite worldwide are CNN, MSNBC, and FOX. CNN and MSNBC have a separate television news channel for international service. FOX does not. FOX News shows its U.S. 24-hour news worldwide. Thus the world, including Muslim and Third World populations, see the worst of American life 24 hours a day. FOX News in prime time is the "sewer" of American humanity. Unfortunately, this depiction of the lowest form of American behavior—with interviews involving rape, murder, pornography, child molestation, racism, and such—presented to uneducated global populations overwhelms its fewer and more modest positive depictions of America. Such impressions seriously undermine the U.S. government's efforts in the Middle East and contribute ammunition and recruitment to the detractors of America worldwide.

Third, MSNBC is far superior to FOX in style and substance, but it has the smallest television audience of the three 24-hour cable news services.

Fourth, some non-American media and entertainment giants, such as NHK in Japan, the BBC in Great Britain, TV Globo in Brazil, and Canal Plus in France, had tried to develop a form of international news or entertainment, but they failed or were not truly global. Nor do any of these media giants have the two most important elements for international media success. The first is the English language. It has become either the first or the second language in most of the world. The second element is the United States itself. The majority of countries since World War II have had a love affair with all things American. Despite a particular country or group's anger at U.S. government policy in some part of the world, there still remains tremendous envy and excitement about American freedom— and its story has been sent out by satellite, particularly on CNN, to every corner of the globe.

I believe that one of the factors that ended the Cold War, tore down the Berlin Wall, and created a need among the Russians to find out more about us was this desire to emulate all things American. When I sat in a restaurant or a coffee shop in Moscow, or in a village in Romania, I could usually hear popular American music played at ear-splitting volume. While the decibels bruised my eardrums, the sounds warmed my heart. Playing American music is one way of expressing a connection to America. And volume equals enthusiasm. To me, the shattering sounds mean "I love America."

* * * * *

Despite a preponderance of unfavorable news flowing from Russia and continuing concern about "underworld" influence in a "sputtering democracy," Russia's total television advertising income went from $8 million in 1992, when we began working there, to $540 million in 1996, and it has reached billions in the new millennium. That's an indication of the huge potential for growth in a country whose vast oil, mineral, and future consumer resources have been relatively untouched. Ted Turner tried in 2001 to buy a stake in NTV, the independent Moscow television station owned by Vladimir Gusinsky, who was forced to leave Russia when the government became unhappy with NTV's editorial comments on the war in Chechnya. Bob Wussler was Ted's point man.

I have always believed in the future of Russia. I also believe that Western companies that pioneer in Russia and Eastern Europe, and have had the backbone and guts that TBS once had, would become immensely successful. Yet as I write this Epilogue about our Russian adventure, I am concerned by the autocratic governmental overtones emanating from that country. However, Russia and those countries that claimed independence after the Soviet collapse are part of the global satellite system and no longer cut off from the world. The democratic system will continue to grow globally, and that includes Mother Russia, despite those within in powerful positions that want to return to an autocracy. This will create chaos in developing its entrepreneurial business opportunities.

China is now recognized as having the largest potential market in the world, with over one billion consumers. CCTV, the China network that wanted to pay only $500 for an hour of TBS programs in 1985 and had 12 television channels at the start of the new millennium, announced in 2002 that it was planning to expand to 200 channels by 2008, the year of the Olympics in Beijing. It is building a $600 million ultra-modern skyscraper headquarters that will include studios. Let's hope it will also include the CNN news bureau that we built into the original agreement.

Speaking of China, Li Ka-shing, Asia's richest man, announced in May 2003 that he was interested in a deal with AOL-TimeWarner, which had won rights in China to build a television broadcasting system. We presume our CNN influence helped. It seems cash-hurting TimeWarner was interested in selling this opportunity to help offset its tremendous debt. Ted would never have done this, with such a great potential in a market of a billion and a quarter consumers.

* * * * *

CNN still exercises great influence on political and legal decisions worldwide. But the positive effects of CNN and satellite television are countered in many Arab countries that are unprepared for the liberal content reflected in modern, Western societies. While feature films have been shown in movie theatres globally for many years, fundamentalist religious entities were still able to shield their populations from the modern world. With the invention of the satellite, we could never have predicted the horrific effect a modern civilization would have on these closed societies.

In an opinion article in the *Wall Street Journal* of December 17, 2004, Daniel Henninger reported that in two years web [internet] logs in China had jumped from 1,000 to 600,000 and that the third heaviest used language on the internet is Farsi, after English and Chinese. Such developments began when Rene Anselmo and I succeeded in defeating the Intelsat global satellite monopoly and brought satellite signals to the worldwide population.

The 48 years I spent in television, but particularly the years between 1984 and 1996, have given me a new perspective. The people I have met and the warm friendships I've made—Fernando Carrilho in Cape Verde, Sudhir Damodaran in India, Francisco Serrador and Alvaro de Moya in Brazil, Professor Ren Yuan in China, Keiji Koyama in Japan, Shahid Ahmad in Pakistan, Paul Morton in Canada, Nikita Matveyev in Russia, Kobus Hamman in South Africa, and so many others—have helped erase any feeling of insularity left in my identity about nationality, religion, or class. I have become a citizen of the world, and I believe that my world vision will come to pass.

Because of satellite television and the Internet, in my view, there will one day be a single language, which will help erase cultural, religious, and nationalistic barriers. There will be a world without borders, and people will decide where to live and to pay taxes based on a given area's ability to absorb human populations. Law and order will be maintained on a global scale with all areas of the world participating.

Although this personal vision may seem outlandish or even naïve, remember I am projecting my view far into the future.

* * * * *

As of 2005, CNN is seen by 1.5 billion viewers in more than 212 countries and territories via 14 satellites covering six continents. It has over 900 broadcast affiliates globally with coverage from 37 CNN news bureaus and around 4,000 employees worldwide.

From a single 24-hour news channel in 1980, CNN now operates the following services: CNN, CNN Headline News, CNN International,

CNNFN (Financial News), CNN Airport Channel, CNN Interactive, and CNN *en Español,* CNN Turk, and n-TV Germany. There are separate CNN affiliations that offer region-specific news such as CNNI Asia Pacific, CNNI South Asia, CNNI Latin America, CNNI Mexico, and CNNj on Japan Cable television. There are also CNN radio services, both domestic and international, as well as web sites.

Terry McGuirk became president and CEO of TBS. In March 2001, Jamie Kellner, founder of Warner Brothers Network, whom parent company AOL-TimeWarner named as Chairman and CEO of TBS, replaced him. Kellner resigned in 2003 and returned to Los Angeles. Phil Kent was his successor. McGuirk became Vice-Chairman in charge of sports teams. Wayne Pace was named Co-Vice Chairman and later became CFO of TimeWarner. TW had given Ted the title of Vice Chairman of TW/TBS, with responsibility for his former empire, but he lost even this when AOL took over, and its owner, Steve Case, declared to the press, "Ted and I are joined at the hip." When this proved to be a farce, the public found it hard to believe that no more Ted Turner dreams would unfold.

When Ted was removed from active daily participation in the merged companies, he was left with a pile of money, estimated at $9.6 billion, although when the stock market bubble burst in 2002, and AOL stock fell precipitously, it dropped to $1.6 billion. Before the steep drop, he formed a foundation to aid the United Nations to the tune of $1 billion (paid out over 10 years) and formed another foundation to prevent the proliferation of nuclear warheads on a global scale. He retains the knack for anticipating the results of global growth and the problems that mankind faces and has worked hard on global environmental issues and humanitarian projects.

Bill Grumbles left TBS for medical reasons a few years after me. Steve Korn, who had headed the TBS Legal Department, joined CNN as Executive Vice President and Chief Operating Officer. He later resigned. Scott Sassa left, too, and became head of programming for NBC. Steve Heyer became President of a Coca-Cola division and in 2003 ran into a serious problem when he fired an executive who became a "whistle blower" regarding certain Coca-Cola business practices. He later left the company when a retired former executive was chosen over him to lead Coca-Cola. Reese Schonfeld published his book about CNN, *Me and Ted Against the World,*

*Terry McGuirk, Richard Parsons, CEO of TimeWarner, and
Gerry Levin, former TimeWarner CEO*

Tom Johnson, former President of CNN

Jane Fonda (Turner's third wife), Ted Turner, Larry King, and Burt Reinhardt at Ted Turner's 65th birthday party.

in 2001. Burt Reinhardt retired but retained an office at CNN, which meant he continued to work as a consultant for many years. Andy Velcoff left a few years later. He still has a conscience and my respect.

Scott Herubin, who assisted me loyally during the joint-venture years, got caught in the personnel downsizing when TimeWarner took over. Joyce Baston, professional secretary extraordinaire, retired when I did, on January 2, 1997. She died of cancer in 2002.

I became Chairman of the Board of the National Telecommunications Organization/Educational Satellites, and spent some years working toward its goal of utilizing satellites worldwide for educational, medical, and public service programs. As for my personal feelings and sense of accomplishment, I think I have proved what one person with limited education can do given some talent and determination. For me, the key word is *underdog*. I always searched for the weakest television station in each country because I knew the strength of CNN's impact on the market: ATV in Hong Kong, Muyleart's public broadcasting service, and TV Manchete, for example. I also championed Sudhir Damodaran in India because he ran a small company that wanted to grow, and I trusted him. In Mexico we went for Imavision and not Televisa, another giant. BOP-TV in Africa got special attention because they ran a black television service that had managed to reach all of Africa. When representatives from the Israeli government came to my office and asked why they couldn't get CNN, I made sure their request was fulfilled. In Canada, I avoided the CBC and its rampant power over the private television networks. Instead, I avidly sought Paul Morton's Global Terlevision Network and Paul Vien's French network Pathonic. Show me an underdog that my talents can help, and the creative juices flow, as Ted, and my colleagues around the world can attest. I think about how I would like to put on my rusty armor and find a new stallion with fire in its eyes because I remember some others who could have used my help, like Ed Lee and Dave Larson in Guam.

I was fortunate enough to work in an industry that suited my talents and temperament, and with a man who relentlessly demanded the most from my abilities. The best wish I can make for any young man or woman is that they are able to find a similar career path that is worthy of their natural skills.

List of Acronyms

Adling Holdings: Hong Kong company, Ronnie and Charles Ling

ABC: American Broadcasting Company, U.S. TV Network

ABC: Australian Broadcasting Company, Government TV Network

ABU: Asian Broadcasting Union, Asian broadcasters who share TV news stories.

A&E: Arts and Entertainment channel, U.S.

Africa no. 1: television station in Gabon (French speaking Africa)

AFRTS: Armed Forces Radio and Television Service (U.S.) Now known as the Global Broadcasting Service.

Alpha Lyracom Space Communications: company created by Rene Anselmo to market his PanAmSatellite; his associate was Frederick A. Landman

Antena TV: Athens, Minus Kyriakou, principal

AOL: America Online, internet company which bought TimeWarner, headed by Steve Case

ARB: American Research Bureau, rates TV programs for Television

ATV: Asian Television Ltd., TV station in Hong Kong, Chairman, Deacon Chu

Bahrain Television: Minister of Information, Tariq Al-Moayed, and Dr. Hala Al-Umran

Bandeirantes: Sao Paulo, Brazil, TV network headed by Jaoa Carlos Saad

Bermuda Broadcasting: TV station in Bermuda

BBC: British Broadcasting Corporation, government operated TV and radio network.

BOP-TV: television station in South African homeland Bophuthatswana, Director Jonathan Proctor; Dick Minton, Program Director

Cable and Wireless: British Company controlling telecommunications in Hong Kong and other British colonies and territories (see PTT)

Canal Plus: French entertainment company

Cartoon Channel: TBS cable channel (U.S.)

CATV: Community Antenna TV Association (U.S.)

CAT: Communications Authority of Thailand (see PTT)

Catvision: a cable company headed by Sudhir Damodaren, New Delhi, India

CBC: Canadian Broadcasting Corporation, a government operated TV and radio network

CBS: Columbia Broadcasting System, U.S. TV network

466

CCTV: China Central Television, government TV network (Beijing)

CDP: Civic Democratic Party, Czech Republic, headed by Vaclav Klaus

Channel 3: Thailand, Maleenont, Managing director, Andrea Cahn, his assistant

Channel 6: Moscow, Edward Sagalayev, President

Channel 7: Santiago, Chile

Channel 7: Thailand, Boontem Dhaneswongse, Mgr. Research and Development

Channel 9: Sao Paulo, Brazil, where Mr. Pike's cousin by marriage Alvaro de Moya lived

Channel 14: low power TV station, Ed Lee & Dave Larson, co-owners

Channel 36: Atlanta UHF TV station competing with Turner's Ch. 17 in 1970-71

City-TV: Toronto, Canada, independent TV station

CME: independent TV company operating in Eastern Europe formed by Ronald Lauder, TV Nova in Czech Republic

CNBC: NBC's business network

CNN: Cable News Network originated by Ted Turner

CNN2: HEADLINE NEWS: launched in 1983, half hour news format

CNN Airport Channel: available in airports

CNNFN: CNN Financial News

CNNI: CNN International, developed by author between 1984-1991

CNNSI: CNN Sports Illustrated

COMSAT: Communications Satellite Corporation of the United States. No longer exists.

CRTC: Canadian Radio-Television and Telecommunications Commission

CTS: China Television Service (network), Taiwan TV station, Y.S. Chin

CTS Enterprises: subsidiary of CTS

CTV: Canadian Television Network, (Independent) 2nd largest in Canada

CTV: TV station in Taiwan

Cubavision TV: Cuban TV

Doordarshan: state TV channel of India

DBS: Direct Broadcast Satellite

EBU: European Broadcast Union, a European association of broadcasters with affiliate members available to the world broadcasting community

Embratel: Brazilian long distance telecommunications carrier.

ESPN: U.S. sports network and cable channel

FCC: Federal Communications Commission (U.S.)

FET: Far East Telecommunications: Bangkok company

FNN: Financial News Network, purchased by NBC and became MSNBC

FOX NETWORK: U.S. domestic television network owned by Rupert Murdoch.

FOX NEWS: U.S. cable news network now seen worldwide (not an International news channel)

FTC: Federal Trade Commission (U.S.)

Fuji Television Network, Japanese

GIO: Government Information Office, controls news in Taiwan

Glieman Satellite Services: Zimbabwe antenna manufacturing at low prices

Global Television Network: based in Toronto, Canada

Gostelradio: Soviet broadcasting system

Guam Cable TV: cable system on Guam, owned by Lee Holmes

HBO: Home Box Office, movie channel on cable television

Hutchison-Whampoa: a Hong Kong company and developer of Star TV which con-
        trolled the available transponders on AsiaSat in the early 90's. Run by Li
        Ka-Shing

IBM: International Business Machines, U.S. based computer company.

ICSC: Initial Communications Satellite Committee, the original decision making
        body for Intelsat (1965-1973).

Imevision: government television network in Mexico

Information and Systems Corp.: company run by Shahid Ahmad, agent for CNN,
        Pakistan

INTELSAT: International Telecommunications Satellite Organization that was estab-
        lished as a universal membership satellite system for global services. Is now a
        private system (Intelsat LLC) held by the Zeus private equity consortium

INTERSPUTNIK: The name of the international satellite system operated by the Soviet
        Union and over a dozen other socialist countries starting in the 1970's

Iraq Television: Director, Said Al-Bazzaz

ISOG: International Satellite Operator Group of INTELSAT, of which CNN was a
        member.

ITA: International Telecommunications Administration, PTT in Taiwan, (see PTT)

ITN: Independent Television Network, Ltd., Sri Lanka

ITP: International Television Productions, Czechoslovakia, connected with Mirofilm

JBC: Jamaica Broadcasting Corporation, government TV station

JCTV: Japan Cable Television, a subsidiary of TV Asahi, Takeshi Kobayashi director

Kanal A: TV network in Slovenia, run by Vladimer Polic

KHON-TV: Honolulu TV station. Sister station of WQXI-TV, Atlanta

KBS: Korean Broadcasting System, South Korean government network

KDD: Japan, the oldest and largest telecommunications carrier

KDNL-TV, Independent station in St. Louis, formerly managed by Jack Petrik

Kroll Associates: U.S. company specializing in private investigations

KUAM-TV: Channel 11, Bankrupt TV station on Guam.

Kuwait Television: Mahmoud Al-Hennawi, a Palestinian, Head of TV News

Luk Oil: Russian oil company interested in investing in Channel 6, Moscow

MBC: Munhwa Broadcasting Corporation, independent TV network in South Korea

MMDS: multi-megabit distribution system used for wireless broadband transmission via terrestrial towers and primarily for TV signals. MMDS can be called wireless cable TV.

MIBC: Moscow Independent Broadcasting Company, Channel 6 in Moscow, Russia

MIP-TV: Marche International des Programmes de Televison, international TV programmers conference held annually in Cannes, France

Mirofilm: Czech company run by Miro Vostiar

M-Net: Cable system in South Africa

MPAA: Motion Picture Association of America

NAB: National Association of Broadcasters (Radio and TV)

NATPE: National Association of Television Program Executives

NBA: National Basketball Association, professional basketball in U.S.

NBA: National Broadcast Authority, Dhaka, Bangladesh

NBC: National Broadcasting Corporation (U.S. network)

NCTA: National Cable TV Association, (U.S.)

Nepal TV: Kathmandu, Nepal

NEC: Japanese computer and electronics company, formerly Nippon Electric Company

NETO/EDSAT: National Educational Telecommunications Organization/Educational Satellites

NFL: National Football League, U.S. professional football association

NHL: National Hockey League, U.S. professional hockey association

NTN: Nippon Television Network, Japan

NTA: Nigerian Television Authority

n-TV: German cable news channel supported by TimeWarner and TBS

NTV: Independent Moscow TV station owned by Vladimir Gusinsky

ODS: alternative acronym for political party in Czech Republic (CDC), Prime Minister Vaclav Klaus

Oman Television: Minister of PTT, Ahmed bin Suwaidan Al Balushi

OPEC: Organization of Petroleum Exporting Countries.

Optus: Australian satellite broadcasting organization.

Ostankino Television: Director General was Edward Sagalayev before joining MIBC, Moscow

OTC: The former organization known as Overseas Telecommunication Corporation of Australia. It subsequently was renamed AUSTEL.

PanAmSat: first independent (non Intelsat) global satellite system (excepting Soviet Satellites), put up by Rene Anselmo in 1988. Merged with Hughes Galaxy and acquired by Ruppert Murdoch from Boeing (2004). Resold to Hughes along with Hughes Network Systems

Pathonic: television network in Quebec, Canada, owner Paul Vien

PBS: Public Broadcasting Service, U.S. public television

Philcomsat: the Philippine PTT (see PTT)

Premiera TV: Prague, Czech Republic, TV network owned by Postovni Banka

PSTN: Public Switched Telecommunications Networks, telephone networks on satellites.

PTN: Pakistan Television Network

PTT: Postal, Telephone and Telegraph, a country's authority over its telecommunications, including satellites. Increasingly these entities are being privatized in their operation and the government only maintains regulatory oversight. In the U.S. it was Comsat.

PTV: People's Television Network, Pakistan

Rogers Cable Systems, Ltd.: Canada cable company

RVC: Russkoye Video, Ch. 11, St Petersburg, Russia

SABC: South African Broadcasting Corp.

Sevens Network: Australia. Initial user of CNN news material.

SICC: Spanish International Communications Corp.

SIN: Spanish International Network, located in NY City, managed by Rene Anselmo

SNC: Satellite News Channel. (ABC/Westinghouse's competing news channel to CNN)

Southern Satellite Systems: company Ted Turner created in order to broadcast his TV station in Atlanta by satellite over U.S., bought by Ed Taylor for one dollar.

SLRC: Sri Lanka Rupavahini Corporation, government television network,

Star-TV: company in Hong Kong owned by Hutchinson-Whampoa, bought in 1993 by Murdoch

TBS: Turner Broadcasting System. Company name: based in Atlanta.

TCI: Tele-Communications, Inc., owned by John Malone, his executive John Sie.

TCM: Turner Classic Movies, TBS cable channel.

TCNS: Turner Cable Network Sales, Terry McGuirk, President, (1987-91).

TEG: Turner Entertainment Group, President Scott Sassa.

TeleCable Nacional: Santo Domingo, associated with TCI.

Telemax: St. Petersburg, Russia. Competed with Russkoye Video for Channel 11.

Télé-Metropole: French Canadian network

Telemundo: Spanish television network in U.S.

Televisa: dominant Television network in Mexico.

TEN: Turner Entertainment Network

Tens: Television network of Australia

Thuci Associates: company in Nairobi, Kenya operated by Naomi Waiyaki.

TI: Turner International

TimeWarner: company that bought out TBS in 1996

TISA: Florida Television Americana S.A.TBS agents in Latin America.

TNT: Turner Network Television

Tohokushinsha Film Company: Tokyo, Japan, Banjiro Uemura, President.

TPS: Turner Program Services, created in 1981 to sell TBS original programs.

Tristar: Indian company headed by Siddhartha Srivastava.

TTV: Taiwan television station.

TV Asahi: Japan TV network, among first to associate with CNN

TV Cultura: public TV network in Sao Paulo, Brazil, President Roberto Muylaert

TV Globo: dominant television network in Brazil, located in Rio de Janeiro.

TV Manchete: television network in Brazil, located in Rio de Janeiro.

TV Marti: USIA television station broadcasting to Cuba.

TV New Zealand: government television network.

TVB-TV: dominant TV station in Hong Kong

TV Nova: competitor of TBS for TV license in Prague, Czech Republic

TVRO: television receive only antenna for downlinking satellite signals.

UHF: ulra-high-frequency, a band between 300MHz and 3000 MHz. This band is primarily used for television service but is also used for mobile satellite communications and other purposes.

UPI: United Press International

UPITN: United Press International Television News

URTNA: Union des Radio et Television des Afrique, organization of radio and television Stations in Africa.

USIA: U.S. Information Agency: provides global information on U.S.

Venevision: television station in Caracas, Venezuela

VHF: very high frequency band between 30MHz and 300MHz. This band was eventually saturated and thus frequencies were allocated in the UHF band for television services as well.

Visnews: British based global news service available by satellite. It was originally independent but was purchased by Reuters Ltd. in the 1980s.

WAGA: Atlanta CBS affiliated TV station.

WBZ-TV: Boston TV station owned by Westinghouse. Author worked as Producer-Director.

WCCB-TV: ABC affiliated TV station in Charlotte, North Carolina

WGN-TV: Chicago, Illinois. Early Superstation.

WGNO-TV: TV station in New Orleans, Louisiana, which author considered buying (1973).

WGST-AM & WPCH-FM: Atlanta radio stations, John Lowrer, General Manager.

Wharf Holdings: Hong Kong cable company.

WHDH-TV: Channel 5 in Boston, owned by Herald-Traveler newspaper.

WJRJ-TV: Channel 17, Atlanta. Call letters of TV station before Ted Turner acquired it. It became WTCG.

WPIX-TV: New York City early U.S. Superstation.

WQXI-TV: Channel 11, Atlanta, owned by Pacific & Southern. Brought author to city (1968).

WRET-TV Charlotte, N.C. TV station purchased by Ted Turner

WSB Radio and WSB-TV: Channel 2, Atlanta: owned by Journal Constitution.

WMEX: Boston radio station in the 1940s.

WTCG: Turner Communications Georgia, call letters of Turner's UHF Atlanta TV station.

WTBS: TBS call letters for Superstation (formerly WTCG) began in 1979.

WTN: World television News, global TV news service, formerly UPITN, Ken Coytes, President.

WWOR-TV: NY City, where Farrell Meisel was Vice President: helped author in Moscow.

Y&R International Advertising Agency: in Europe, TBS executive Steve Heyer worked there.

Zimbabwe Broadcasting Corporation: Harare, Zimbabwe.

Index

(Page numbers in italics indicate photographs.)

Sidney Pike

SIDNEY PIKE is the retired President of CNN-International Special Projects. After 22 years in television, he helped Ted Turner stabilize the Atlanta UHF TV station and led Turner to the purchase of the Atlanta Braves baseball and Hawks basketball teams. He saved the WRET-TV station in Charlotte, North Carolina, which Turner later sold for $21 million, generating the seed money for CNN. In 1984, Pike began traveling the globe selling CNN International programming on all continents and pioneering the end of the Intelsat satellite monopoly that prevented the reception of the CNN signal worldwide. In his 25 years with Turner many strange events occurred, including Saddam Hussein calling Pike to get an appearance on CNN in the Gulf War.

Pike has served on the Board of Advisors of the University of San Francisco and University of Texas at Austin, and the University of Georgia International Development Project and its European Center. He was a Board Director with the International Foundation for Global Studies, and CEO of the National Education Telecommunications Organization in Washington, D.C.